# The Other #MeToos

# OXFORD STUDIES IN GENDER AND INTERNATIONAL RELATIONS

*Series editors:*
J. Ann Tickner, American University, and Laura Sjoberg,
Royal Holloway University of London

*The Beauty Trade: Youth, Gender, and Fashion Globalization*
Angela B. V. McCracken

*Global Norms and Local Action: The Campaigns against Gender-Based Violence in Africa*
Peace A. Medie

*Rape Loot Pillage: The Political Economy of Sexual Violence in Armed Conflict*
Sara Meger

*Support the Troops: Military Obligation, Gender, and the Making of Political Community*
Katharine M. Millar

*From Global to Grassroots: The European Union, Transnational Advocacy, and Combating Violence against Women*
Celeste Montoya

*Who Is Worthy of Protection? Gender-Based Asylum and US Immigration Politics*
Meghana Nayak

*Revisiting Gendered States: Feminist Imaginings of the State in International Relations*
Swati Parashar, J. Ann Tickner, and Jacqui True

*Out of Time: The Queer Politics of Postcoloniality*
Rahul Rao

*Narrating the Women, Peace and Security Agenda: Logics of Global Governance*
Laura J. Shepherd

*Gender, UN Peacebuilding, and the Politics of Space: Locating Legitimacy*
Laura J. Shepherd

*Capitalism's Sexual History*
Nicola J. Smith

*A Feminist Voyage through International Relations*
J. Ann Tickner

*The Political Economy of Violence against Women*
Jacqui True

*Queer International Relations: Sovereignty, Sexuality and the Will to Knowledge*
Cynthia Weber

*Feminist Global Health Security*
Clare Wenham

*Bodies of Violence: Theorizing Embodied Subjects in International Relations*
Lauren B. Wilcox

# The Other #MeToos

*Edited by*

IQRA SHAGUFTA CHEEMA

*Oxford University Press*

OXFORD
UNIVERSITY PRESS

Oxford University Press is a department of the University of Oxford. It furthers the University's objective of excellence in research, scholarship, and education by publishing worldwide. Oxford is a registered trade mark of Oxford University Press in the UK and certain other countries.

Published in the United States of America by Oxford University Press
198 Madison Avenue, New York, NY 10016, United States of America.



Library of Congress Cataloging-in-Publication Data
Names: Cheema, Iqra Shagufta, editor.
Title: The other #metoos / Iqra Shagufta Cheema.
Description: First Edition. | New York : Oxford University Press, [2023] |
Series: Oxford Studies in Gender and International Relations |
Includes bibliographical references and index.
Identifiers: LCCN 2022058616 (print) | LCCN 2022058617 (ebook) |
ISBN 9780197619872 (Hardcover) | ISBN 9780197619889 (Paperback) |
ISBN 9780197619902 (epub) | ISBN 9780197619896 | ISBN 9780197619919
Subjects: LCSH: MeToo movement. | Sexual harassment of women. | Feminism.
Classification: LCC HQ1237.O84 2023 (print) | LCC HQ1237 (ebook) |
DDC 305.42—dc23/eng/20230118
LC record available at https://lccn.loc.gov/2022058616
LC ebook record available at https://lccn.loc.gov/2022058617

DOI: 10.1093/oso/9780197619872.001.0001

Paperback printed by Marquis Book Printing, Canada
Hardback printed by Bridgeport National Bindery, Inc., United States of America

*For my family.*
*And for all victims of patriarchy.*

# Contents

# Contributors

**Farinaz Basmechi** is a Ph.D. candidate in sociology at the University of North Texas. Her main areas of interests are social movements and gender. Her dissertation mainly focuses on analyzing online movements using qualitative and quantitative content analysis and text mining methods.

**Antonella Cariello** is a research assistant at TAPRI Research Centre at Tampere University. She has an MA in International Cooperation and Protection of Human Rights and currently, she is part of the EST Working Group on Gender Equality. She has attended the Leiden Summer School in Sexual Orientation and Gender Identity in International Law and also has a bachelor's degree in Intercultural Communication with studies in Arabic history and culture. She has conducted a three-month research project in Tunisia about the coping strategies and the level of the risk of the LGBT community in the country. She has recently submitted a paper to the Italian Journal *InGenere*, about the relation between the feminist movement and the LGBT activism in Tunisia.

**Amrita De** is a doctoral candidate in the Department of Comparative Literature at the State University of New York, Binghamton. Her primary research interests include Masculinity Studies, Feminist Theory, South Asian Literature, Global South Studies, and World Literature. She is also a fiction writer currently working on her first novel. Occasionally, she writes personal essays and film reviews as well.

**Ran Deng** is a Ph.D. student in the Department of Comparative Studies in Literature and Culture at the University of Southern California. Her research interests include German and East Asian literary and visual cultures, memory and trauma theory, the body, and New Materialist feminism. She is a fellow at the Korean Studies Institute and is currently working with the Shoah Foundation Visual History Archive on the narration of sexual violence during genocides.

**Zoë Antoinette Eddy** is a Lecturer on anthropology and Assistant Director of Undergraduate Studies in the Anthropology Department at Harvard University. Her research and teaching interests include Indigenous history and rights, animal studies, Ainu culture and history, Hokkaido, tourism, Indigenous methodology, contemporary Native American art and poetry, museums, gender and sexuality, and death and grief.

**Asmita Ghimire** is a graduate student in Liberal Arts, English language, Linguistics, and Literature at the University of Minnesota, Duluth. She completed her master's degree from Tribhuwan University, Nepal. She worked as faculty of English (2017–2018) at Kathmandu University, Nepal, where she taught Legal English, Technical Communication, and First Year Composition. She worked as translator and interpreter for the Red Cross Society.

She presented a paper on "Women and War: The New Historical Reading of Siba Shakib's Afghanistan Where God Only Comes to Weep," British Writing Workshop (2018), organized by the University of Birmingham, United Kingdom. She is interested in the field of rhetoric and composition, cross-cultural writing and intercultural rhetoric, feminist rhetoric, and transnational feminism.

**Maricruz Gómez** is currently completing her English doctorate at the University of North Texas. Her dissertation focuses on examining Chicana decolonial feminism in newspaper archives of the Chicana/o movement and the aftermath (1960s–1980s), twentieth- and twenty-first-century Chicana literature, and Chicana feminist theory texts.

**Fariha Jahan** is a devoted Lecturer at the Department of Women and Gender Studies, University of Dhaka. She completed her BSS (Hons) and MSS from the University of Dhaka and joined the Department of Women and Gender Studies as a lecturer. Her professional career outside of academia includes working in various projects and studying with renowned organizations such as CARE, NI, UNFPA, and BRAC as a researcher of the international organization Girl Effect. Her research interests cover gender-based violence and various issues and debates around it, sexual and reproductive health and rights of adolescents, men and masculinities, and women's representation in electronic media.

**Nicolás Juárez** is a Social Work and Native American Studies graduate student at the University of Texas, Austin. His research focuses on the libidinal economy of settler colonialism and antiblackness, with particular focus on how these structures of power shape quotidian moments of intimacy and care. His current research looks at how settler colonial genocide occurs not out of utility, but as a function of enjoyment for settlers in the Americas, deploying a combination of Black and Indigenous feminist work with Freudo-Lacanian psychoanalysis.

**Denisa Krásna** is a doctoral student at the Department of English and American Studies at Masary University, Brno, specializing in Indigenous studies. In her research, she focuses on decolonization, colonial gender violence, critical animal studies, and social and environmental justice. In her interdisciplinary dissertation she explores the emerging framework of anarcha-Indigenism, artivism, and decolonial animal ethic. Her case studies include Indigenous resistance movements in southern Mexico, Canada, and Hawaii. Besides English, she has written and translated in Spanish, Czech, and French, holds degrees in English and Spanish, and is currently pursuing a French degree at the Open University of Scotland.

**Lize-Mari Mitchell** is a Lecturer at the University of Limpopo, affiliated with the School of Law. After completing her legal candidacy, she traded the legal profession for academia, where she teaches Jurisprudence, Legal Pluralism, and Human Rights. She has a master's degree in law, within the field of international human rights, and an honors in psychology. She follows a multidisciplinary approach to research, with a focus on developmental psychology and the rights of the child. She is also actively engaged in community projects, with a focus on the empowerment of women and children.

**Atiya Murtaza** works as a special education teacher in rural Punjab, Pakistan. She has earned an M.Phil. in English Literature and two M.A.s in English Literature and Special Education.

**Ayesha Murtza** is a doctoral student in English Literature at the University of North Texas. She earned her master's in English Literature and Linguistics and then moved from Pakistan to the United States to pursue her Ph.D. Her research and teaching are in the areas of cultural criticism, ecofeminism, intersectionality, women of color feminisms, and postcolonial literature. Her research has been published or is forthcoming with *New Media and Mass Communication* and *Writers: Craft and Context.*

**Thilini Prasadika** is a graduate student following a master's degree in English Studies at the Department of English, Faculty of Arts, University of Colombo, Sri Lanka. She is also a DIY, first-generation academic who identifies as queer, struggling to navigate her way in and through the interlocking discourses of academia. Her areas of research include Queer Studies, Feminist Studies, and Cultural Studies. Currently, she is writing her master's thesis exploring how brown queer diasporic female subjectivities in memoirs subvert/resist the taxonomy of "people of color" through their various engagements with the embodied aspects of social class, ethnicity, and nationality.

**Anat Schwartz** is a doctoral candidate in the Department of East Asian Studies at the University of California, Irvine. Her current research is on contemporary South Korean feminist movements and communities. Anat is interested in the continuity of anti–sexual violence feminist activism, and the ways in which social media is both an effective tool and a platform of discord for young feminists. A recent Fulbright junior research grantee, Anat spent the past thirteen months conducting fieldwork interviews and observations in Korea. Her research interests include feminist theory, queer studies, new media, modern Korean history, and gender studies and sexuality studies.

**Umme Busra Fateha Sultana** is an Associate Professor at the Women and Gender Studies Department of University of Dhaka in Bangladesh. She earned a Commonwealth Scholarship to pursue her doctoral research at the University of Sussex, England. To mention a few among her areas of expertise: social inequalities, body and sexualities, gender and development, women's empowerment, gender-based violence, advertising and politics of representation.

**Elizabethada A. Wright** teaches in the Department of English, Linguistics, and Writing Studies and is a member of the faculty at the University of Minnesota Twin Cities' Literacy and Rhetorical Studies Program. She has published in *Rhetoric Society Quarterly, Rhetoric Review, Markers: The Annual Journal for the Association of Gravestone Studies, Studies in the Literary Imagination*, as well as in a number of other journals and books.

**Jihan Zakarriya** is Assistant Professor at Dhofar University. She completed a Ph.D. in English literature at Cardiff University (2015). She completed a Fulbright fellowship at the University of Michigan (2016–2017). Zakarriya's research interests are postcolonial studies, comparative literature, and ecocriticism and gender violence.

**Afiya Shehrbano Zia** is a feminist researcher and activist based in Karachi, Pakistan. She is the author of "Sex Crime in the Islamic Context" and several published articles on women, religion, and secularism. Her most recently published book-length work is *Faith and Feminism in Pakistan: Religious Agency or Secular Autonomy*.

# Preface

Iqra Shagufta Cheema

During one of my morning Twitter scrolls in October 2017, I noticed #MeToo trending. Intrigued, I was glued to my phone, reading tweets and responses to #MeToo for hours. I read women's experiences of gendered and sexual violence at home, at work, at schools, in markets—in all spaces, protected and neglected. Witnessing snippets of my own life in these experiences, I responded to many of the tweets with inadvertent verbal pronouncements of "#MeToo." While I was already aware of the prevalence of gendered and sexual violence, I registered its magnitude via #MeToo: women shared that they had been violated in places of rest and places of work, in places of comfort and places of commiseration, in places of recreation and places of worship—from the safest to the most dangerous to the most sacred places.

Witnessing this collective expression of trauma elicited by the hashtag, #MeToo, was simultaneously crushing and inspiring, dispiriting and empowering. Unaware of what #MeToo would eventually mean for feminist publics, praxes, and futures,[1] I evaluated tweeting about my experiences to participate in the #MeToo movement. As a Pakistani woman from a traditional Muslim family who lived most of her life in a village in Punjab, and who was now luckily a doctoral student in Texas, tweeting #MeToo was a complex decision with personal stakes for me. Like most women, I—despite mostly avoiding any presumably unsafe spaces and living a relatively sheltered life—have experienced harassment and violence more often than I would like to remember. I had learned that there were no safe spaces for women; #MeToo solidified that realization. I wanted to be a part of the movement.

I tweeted "#MeToo," sans details of my experiences. Immediately after, I became apprehensive and anxious: most of my Pakistani followers would think that I was seeking social capital by *exploiting* what are normal, everyday experiences for Pakistani women; they would think that I was defaming Pakistan, that I was bringing dishonor to my family, that I was disloyal to my roots, that I was too Westernized, that I tweeted this despite knowing that Brown and Muslim men are already demonized in the West, that I tweeted this to further malign Pakistani and Muslim men—I agonized over the questions and contentions that feminists of color have been grappling with for decades now.

I deleted my tweet.

Instantly, I felt like a coward and an enabler: I had been violated, yet I was trying to protect the communal and national patriarchal structures that enable and perpetuate gendered and sexual violence. Perpetrators of these spatial, emotional, financial, and physical acts of violence did not feel any guilt or shame, so why did I? Would I be betraying my feminist sisters if I did not raise my voice along with theirs, when millions had already done the more challenging groundwork?

I retweeted "#MeToo" *again*, only to delete it *again*.

I retweeted and deleted "#MeToo" a few more times.

However, during this absurd vacillation, I arrived at a new understanding of my own #MeToo experiences. Over the next few days, I observed #MeToo develop into a mainstream, international phenomenon. It was euphoric to witness #MeToo serve as a transnational site of feminist sharing and support, and transform into one of the most inclusive and representative global feminist movements. It felt exhilarating, like living through a revolution. My excitement, observations, and reflections, along with the international visibility of #MeToo, led me to the creation of this book.

When Alyssa Milano first tweeted the call for victims of sexual violence to respond with "me too" on October 15, 2017,[2] Twitter received more than 500,000 tweets with the hashtag, whereas Facebook saw around 12 million posts with #MeToo within one day. By November 2017, the hashtags #MeToo and #WomensMarch had been tweeted more than 2.3 million and 11.5 million times, respectively, in multiple Indigenous and national languages worldwide.[3] But these international voices that rendered the movement so diverse and impactful did not receive substantial attention in the international, particularly Western, media. "From a viral hashtag to a global organization, we are working towards eradicating sexual violence by shifting culture, policies, and institutions,"[4] reads the introduction of the official twitter account of the MeToo movement that had originated in 2006.[5] Despite reference to its global organization, media discussions and a majority of initial scholarly conversations about #MeToo—due to race and class, and their corollaries, fame and visibility—were dominated by white Hollywood cases of gendered and sexual violence.

These problematics of invisibility and exclusion of BIPOC[6] voices and communities started at the initiation of #MeToo when Milano's tweet generated the hashtag #MeToo that turned into an international movement, though the Me Too Movement had already been founded by Tarana Burke, a Black woman, who first used the term "Me Too" in 2006 on MySpace.[7] Burke's Me Too Movement had not received traction arguably because of limited social media in 2006, but the problem arose when Milano—instead of Burke—was credited with starting the Me Too Movement. Milano, upon learning of Burke's Me Too Movement, acknowledged her contribution and Burke, thereupon, accepted her role as the leader of the #MeToo movement. Burke was discredited not because of Milano's malintent, but because of cultural and political hostility against feminists—especially feminists of color. Burke's Me Too had also received traction in 2006. However, between 2006 and 2017, sociopolitical shifts—like broader cultural acceptance of feminist politics, increased international recognition of the need for feminist justice, greater awareness about intersectional feminism, increased need for safer work environments to encourage women's participation in the workforce, wider availability of feminist vocabularies, and decreased taboos around conversations about gendered and sexual violence—prepared relatively hospitable political and cultural grounds for feminist conversations. However, #MeToo highlights that white feminists[8]—as holders of privileged seats at the proverbial feminist roundtable and as a signal of solidarity—need to recognize feminists of color and acknowledge their contributions.

Burke, in an interview, commented that discrediting her for her work was perhaps unintentional, but "somehow sisters still managed to get diminished or erased in these situations."[9] While Milano's tweet received responses from celebrities like Lady Gaga, Jennifer Lawrence, Gwyneth Paltrow, Javier Muñoz, Cara Delevingne, Debra Messing, Ashley Judd, and Uma Thurman,[10] Burke only received credit for her work after Black feminists and other allies amplified her work online.[11] Burke's #MeToo supports an international sisterhood of BIPOC survivors under the assumption that all survivors are equal, but famous #MeToo cases that went viral after Milano's tweet suggest that some survivors are more equal than others.

In an interview, Burke shared that she started Me Too "as a grassroots movement" for "sexual assault survivors in underprivileged communities" where it was "us talking to us." She further insisted upon the need to reclaim #MeToo: "The No. 1 thing I hear from folks is that the #MeToo movement has forgotten us. . . . We are the movement. . . .[12] In her keynote at the *Facing Race* conference in Detroit (2018), Burke asserted that the #MeToo movement "must care as much about the original victims [presumably, ordinary people who are victims of gendered and sexual violence] as it does about actresses who wanted careers and producers who got away with career murder." Despite this initial unequal visibility and misplaced attention, the #MeToo hashtag eventually became the integrative site for Burke's and Milano's shared goals and the demonstrative tool and critical instrument for the work of Burke's Me Too Movement. From Iran, Lebanon, Egypt, Tunisia, and Morocco to India, Pakistan, Bangladesh, Nepal, and Sri Lanka, to South Korea, Japan, and China, to South Africa to Latin America—#MeToo has inspired local movements and Twitter trends like #MeinBhi and #EnaZeda, as well as transnational and collective movements and trends like #MosqueMeToo.

It is vital to examine, understand, and archive the international travel, translation, and impact of #MeToo—particularly in the Global South and BIPOC communities—to grasp the multiple ways in which #MeToo has made feminism globally mainstream and has transformed common people's quotidian understanding and praxis of feminism. This is precisely what this book aims to do—to document the revolutionary impact of #MeToo moments and movements in the Global South.

*The Other #MeToos* brings together diverse international perspectives and voices that explore the iterations, adaptations, translations, and receptions of #MeToo from non-Western countries, communities, and identities. This book not only amplifies those voices that may have been marginalized or glossed over, but also highlights what those voices have to say, what the #MeToo movement means for them, how #MeToo renders itself in a diversity of contexts, and why listening to these voices matters to the larger #MeToo movement as it continues to develop internationally. This book also elucidates the ways #MeToo affects the everyday lives of average women, advances feminist consciousness and practices, and informs the relationship between feminist theory and praxis within marginalized and minoritized communities. It further positions #MeToo within larger debates about transnational and women of color feminisms, traces the ways it interacts with and influences local and indigenous feminisms, locates it simultaneously within local and global feminist politics and discusses how it meets the challenges posed by such a positionality.[13]

*The Other #MeToos* explores #MeToo as an instantaneous and visible model of transnational feminist solidarity via a hashtag. Hashtag campaigns amplify feminist visibility and raise feminist consciousness (Griffin, 2019; Clark-Parsons, 2019; Ghadery, 2019), though issues like cisheteronormativity, patriarchy, race, location, class, and other forms of privilege continue to affect #MeToo. Through platforms like Twitter that are more instantly accessible and available than on-ground political forums, #MeToo helps identify the diverse and multidimensional constituents of gendered and sexual violence to ultimately realize global feminist solidarities unlike any other previous feminist movement. By documenting these defining feminist moments and attendant #MeToo movements in different local, indigenous, minoritized, othered, and/or postcolonial contexts, the chapters in this book acknowledge and examine the diversity and multidimensionality of feminism and its international contours. The #MeToo movement manifests a virtual, widely available model of solidarity via a hashtag which translates into mass awareness, on-the-ground activism, and alternative modes of praxis.

The instant accessibility and visibility of #MeToo conversations provide victims and survivors the emotional and linguistic tools to virtually report and document their experiences. Because of the pervasiveness of gendered and sexual violence internationally, most women grow up believing it to be the norm, an ineliminable part of their lives. #MeToo has changed that perception. #MeToo, by popularizing feminist vocabularies, has enabled victims and survivors to reckon with their experiences. The visibility of this violence via #MeToo was epiphanic to many individuals and communities, especially in locations where most of these incidents go unreported. While visibility offers an effective medium for newer, urgent political possibilities, it also creates newer constraints (Wolfson, 2014; Tufecki, 2017). This visibility of violence carries different meanings in different communities; for example, in more conservative patriarchies, women's piety, femininity, nobility, and value are often bound to their absence from public spaces. Being visible, for these women, translates into being available for gendered and sexual violence. So, when women choose to make visible their experiences with gendered and sexual violence, it is often interpreted as an indictment of their moral character, instead of an act of courage in that respective community (some of which reflects in my own initial engagement with #MeToo that I described above). I contend, borrowing Robyn Wiegman's (1995) and Sarah Banet-Weiser's (2015, 2018) terms,[14] that hashtag campaigns in the United States circle around an "economy of visibility" where individual participation and representation are the height of empowerment. On the contrary, #MeToo in non-Western locales has created a "politics of visibility" where representation is a part of the struggle to achieve larger collective, political goals.

Economy of visibility resides in "a media landscape that is many things at once: a technological and economic context devoted to the accumulation of views, clicks, 'likes,' etcetera." It is also "a set of tactics used by some feminisms and some misogynies to move into the spotlight with more ease than others" (Banet-Weiser, 2018, p. 2). Thereby, in "an era of advanced capitalism and networked media platforms," the most commodifiable and brandable feminisms become the "most visible" (Banet-Weiser, 2018, pp. 22, 13). This visibility then gets "absorbed into the economy" and "becomes the end rather than a means to an end" (Banet-Weiser, 2018, p. 23). Often, sharing one's experiences on social media platforms is also considered a cynical attempt at attracting more followers and more attention via more visibility. Hence, it becomes tricky to measure the success and ethics of #MeToo (or any other social justice movement) solely based on its visibility. Economies of visibility, then, no longer "describe a political process" (Banet-Weiser, 2018, p. 23), but rather become limited to the statistics of interactions—clicks, likes, shares, comments, tweets, and quote tweets—on various social media platforms.

Politics of visibility, on the other hand, describes "the process of making visible a political category" like gender (Banet-Weiser, 2018, p. 22). In this stance, politics of visibility combines visibility with "politics" so it adopts a "political valence" to produce social change that "exceeds the [immediate] visibility." Politics, therein, becomes a "descriptor of the *practices* [emphasis original] of visibility" (p. 22). In the United States, visibility has increasingly replaced politics—the imaginative origin of #MeToo in celebrity culture, media focus on white celebrities' #MeToo cases, push for representation without structural changes in diversity, equity, and inclusion initiatives—serve as a few examples. However, in the Global South, visibility itself constitutes politics: Iranian women taking off their hijab and cutting their hair in public, Indian Muslim women asserting their right to wear hijab, Pakistani women demanding safety from gendered and sexual violence, and Saudi women drivers on roads are only a few cases where visibility in public spaces itself constitutes politics.

Achieving visibility in public spaces has long been a fight for feminists. In the recent past, it has manifested itself in initiatives like "Girls at Dhabas" in Pakistan and "Why Loiter" in India.[15] In the contemporary social media context, visibility implies or even equates significance in a social context (see Grewal, 2005; Gross, 2012; H. Gray, 2013; Anden-Papadopoulos, 2014; Blaagaard et al., 2017). Brian Creech defines the politics of visibility as a "conflation of a seemingly natural phenomenon (what is visible, and thus perceptible and intelligible) with the dynamically shifting power relations of political representation, deliberation, and even social unrest" (2020, p. 124); he summarizes this relationship as perceptible and intelligible = visible.[16] Visibility is a prerequisite for one's recognition as a full human, a human who deserves to be treated equitably and fairly. For this reason, the politics of visibility has been and continues to be important for the marginalized and minoritized (Banet-Weiser, 2018, p. 22). While contestations of visibility, its socioeconomic imperative, and its politics are irresolvable, #MeToo has transformed their ongoing exploration and understanding in diverse communities in the Global South.

Because of the challenges that accompany visibility, women devise alternative ways to navigate the politics of visibility and "develop complex strategies to cope [with] pressures and challenges they encounter" (Mendes et al., 2019, p. 6). Many women's lack of access to public spaces and inability to leave their homes hinder their ability to join feminist protests like women's marches; internationally, #MeToo offered women a virtual space to share their experiences, without the need to leave their residential spaces. Despite the limitations of physical mobility, women's access to phones and the internet enables them to participate in these campaigns in overt or covert ways.[17] For example, many women use anonymous or fake accounts to share their #MeToo experiences and raise public feminist consciousness, especially around taboo topics like sexuality. In this way, their identities remain invisible, but the violence against them is publicly visible. #MeToo then becomes a means of participation in a global protest, a task that would have been otherwise impossible for most women. #MeToo, due to its international popularity, easy accessibility, and come-as-you-are approach, manifests a "grassroots, bottom-up approach" to digital activism that considers "social and cultural processes and their entanglement with technologies" instead of focusing merely on "digital artifacts" like social media posts (Mendes et al., 2019, p. 6). This "networked way of sharing in a visible way online" creates and contains "direct embodied impacts" (Rentschler and Thrift, 2015; Hillis, Paasonen, and Petit, 2015).

Online participation via hashtag, then, is arguably as effective as in-person gatherings and protests as a feminist political strategy. It is safer and easier for women not only because of their personal limitations, but also because of the invocation of anti-feminist propaganda and the activation of anti-feminist structures against feminists in both physical and virtual spaces. For these #MeToo participants, this virtual participation engenders a politics of visibility as it seeks to disrupt sociocultural structures and institutions that enable and support gendered and sexual violence or that obstruct women's participation in feminist politics and inhibit their access to public spaces. But the material structures and "forms of discrimination" that discourage women's participation in on-the-ground feminist politics also threaten their presence in online spaces because these structures are "built and designed into the architecture of the internet" (Mendes et al., 2019, p. 183; Harvey, 2016, p. 12). For example, algorithms amplify misogynistic or violent content and generate more traffic, further incentivizing violence and abuse.

However, social media, despite its structural and operational problems, gives relatively more urgency to tweets about gendered and sexual violence and agency to those tweeting about it. While participation in "digital feminist campaigns" serves "as a low barrier entrance for other types of (feminist) activism and political engagement" (Mendes et al., 2019, p. 5), women still encounter multiple challenges (Mendes et al., 2019, p. 6), which manifest in increased vitriol against feminists and feminisms, especially after #MeToo and women's marches. This vitriol increases in the wake of women's marches and then subsides, until there is a new women's march or a feminist hashtag trend on social media. Alternatively worded, women's visibility in public spaces inadvertently incites increased expressions of misogyny—thus a cyclical pattern of vitriol subsides and then intensifies with the decrease and increase in visibility. This mediated vitriol ranges from online abuse and threats to real-life abuse and threats of sexual violence to feminist activists, #MeToo participants, women's march organizers, and women's march participants.

Sarah Banet-Weiser terms this process "popular feminism" and "popular misogyny" (2018). Scholars have discussed various ways in which shifting media landscapes and digital technologies enable this popular misogyny, especially against more visible and popular feminists and forms of feminism (see Citron, 2014; Cole, 2015; Jane, 2014, 2016 Mendes, 2015; Penny, 2013; Poland,

2016; Powell and Henry, 2017). This trend is also termed "mediated misogyny" (Vickery and Everbach, 2018), "gendertrolling" (Mantilla, 2013; Lumsden and Morgan, 2017), "cybersexism" (Penny, 2013; Polland, 2016), and "gendered cyberhate" (Jane, 2016. Aurat March in Pakistan stands as an example of this cyclical pattern of popular feminism and popular misogyny.[18] Below, I discuss Aurat March 2021, when marchers' slogans were misinterpreted by anti-feminists as blasphemous.

Blasphemy continues to be a life-threateningly sensitive issue in Pakistan.[19] In 2021, Aurat March participants chanted a song during the march, which contained the phrase: "*mullah bhi dega aza'adi*" (we'll seize our freedom from religious leaders). Anti-feminist groups arguably advertently misconstrued and misdubbed this as "*Allah bhi dega aza'adi*" (we'll seize our freedom from Allah). Despite the organizers' and participants' repeated clarifications, the allegations of blasphemy against feminist activists and march organizers, along with a doctored video, quickly went viral. March organizers provided detailed clarifications, released statements, reported the doctored video, petitioned media reporters to circulate the original video, and requested the removal of the doctored video from social media platforms. March participants had also held up a blanket with testimonies of sexual violence; one testimony that anti-feminist factions particularly condemned was about child abuse by a religious teacher: "I was 9, he was 50. I was silenced. But his voice is still heard as he delivers the call to prayer." March organizers had to issue an explanatory statement.[20] Marchers and organizers received further backlash because some participants were holding the flag of a local feminist collective, Women Democratic Front, which vaguely resembled the French flag and further antagonized the anti-feminist nationalist factions. It is important to note here that Pakistanis have a contentious relationship with France because of *Charlie Hebdo*'s publication of Prophet Mohammad's caricatures, French president Emmanuel Macron's defense of the caricatures via appeals to the freedom of expression, and resultant controversies.[21] *Charlie Hebdo* republished the caricatures in 2021. Tehreek-e-Labbaik Pakistan (TLP), an ultra-conservative extremist religious party, organized multi-day violent protests across Pakistan on the issue of blasphemy and demanded the expulsion of the French ambassador. Tehreek Taliban Pakistan (TTP) threatened women's march organizers. A group of lawyers filed a lawsuit against the march organizers on the grounds of blasphemy,[22] with another police case filed by the police.[23] Multiple media and YouTube channels misreported the Aurat March.[24] This maliciously coordinated campaign against the Aurat March resulted in such extreme threats of violence that some participants had to deactivate their social media accounts or go into hiding. These events, both feminist and anti-feminist, occurred simultaneously online and offline. These tactics not only put these women's lives at risk but also threatened the future of these crucial feminist activities.

As a result of cultural and religious backlash from state institutions as well as religious communities, the Aurat March 2022 was much more subdued, contained fewer slogans about sexual autonomy, and focused on more palatable issues like women's labor and fair wages. These challenges further highlight the urgency for intersectional approaches that consider social, religious, and cultural processes when analyzing the affective and structural politics of digital feminist campaigns and their on-the-ground impact. Simultaneously, this intense backlash to increasing feminist visibility and feminist activism indicates that regressive and misogynist factions perceive feminism as a serious threat. Hence, they resorted to weaponizing religion, the element popularly considered the foundation of the country, against feminists in Pakistan.

However, this anti-feminist vitriol works as a double-edged visibility-accountability loop; it mandates an online, virtual expression of gendered and sexual abuse and threats of violence, while also making these abusers and aggressors visible. This visibility creates accountability: it facilitates the creation of relatively safe virtual spaces and the safeguarding of these spaces by enabling feminists to block aggressors and limit interactions with them. Contrarily, by expressing abuse or threats, aggressors also make themselves available for a public dialogue with their opponents.

The hashtag #MeToo, then, becomes the signifier or tool to access the virtual space that facilitates public dialogical engagement by enabling participants to bypass multiple physical, psychological, and/or hierarchical conversational barriers that they may encounter in their real-life dialogues about controversial subjects like feminism. This public dialogical engagement is more immediate and controllable because of the character limit on social media platforms like Twitter, inability to interrupt the opponent, and the consequences of getting reported or losing access to the social media account if anybody resorts to explicitly threatening language.[25] While these dialogues aren't always constructive or generative in an immediately discernible way, they are instrumental in popularizing feminist vocabularies and familiarizing the public with feminist debates.

#MeToo and women's marches have changed people's everyday vocabularies about women's rights and gender equality. The use of these vocabularies may not always be supportive of feminist goals, but it requires intellectual and rational engagement with feminist ideas and thereby advances feminist conversations in hostile spaces. Additionally, familiarity with and popularity of these vocabularies, regardless of their supportive or denigrative use, translates into wider normalization of feminist ideas and goals. These familiar vocabularies cognitively become less threatening, more familiar, and thereby contribute to making sociocultural spaces less hostile for feminisms, feminists, and feminist work.

But the choice of vocabularies employed in feminist politics also remains a site of contention and exclusion in non-Western countries, especially countries and communities that have histories of colonization, experiences with the War on Terror, and contentions with local religious and political factions. For example, the English word "feminism" is demonized among Muslim postcolonies that associate feminism with the Western histories of modernity, colonization, and imperialism. Instead, they prefer terms for women's rights in their local languages, for example *huqooq-e-niswan* (women's rights) in Pakistan. Though these terms carry meanings similar to feminism (which itself is an unstable term), popular feminism continues to use English words, which is an irresolvable challenge considering the international usage and localized forms of English. Furthermore, academic or transnational feminist conversations remain inherently classist because only upper-class, well-educated women are familiar with the conventional vocabularies or have access to the appropriate platforms to perform and discuss those specific feminisms.

#MeToo often surpasses communicative barriers because many social media platforms and websites include an in-built translation option. Therefore, #MeToo became the signifier and accessibility tool that didn't require *correct* feminist vocabularies or English-language fluency to take part in a global feminist movement. Instead of requiring the possession of linguistic and material tools, #MeToo feminism has a come-as-you-are approach. However, an intersectional assemblage of sociopolitical institutions like race, ethnicity, caste, class, religion, and location, among others, continues to affect women's choice and ability to participate in #MeToo.

Participation in #MeToo, then, also becomes a paradoxical feminist method, a #MeToo quandary. The success of the #MeToo movement mandates the participatory labor of sharing experiences from its participants—a labor which can be both liberating and oppressive. Sharing an experience with hundreds or thousands of others is liberating. Knowing that one has allies and supporters is reassuring. Interacting with a supportive community that fights the factors which facilitate one's traumatic experiences is encouraging. But for all this to happen, one must first share their experience, make it visible. One must tell their story to participate in the #MeToo movement. This participation is a strenuous process because of multiple sociocultural, religio-political, and juridico-legal structural barriers. It would serve us well to remember that not all individuals are afforded the same freedom to share their experiences of gendered and sexual violence. Additionally, social media platforms are inundated with content, so most #MeToo experiences shared on social media are fleeting. This is particularly true for non-famous #MeToo cases that ultimately become a part of the larger hashtag, and that make #MeToo a movement.

These experiences, however invisible or ephemeral on social media, are the inspirational acts of courage and bravery that light up the feminist world. But only the most shocking incidents and the most recognized participants become visible in this abstract accumulation of millions of participants under one hashtag,—this makes both the strengths and weaknesses of #MeToo apparent. The ubiquity of gendered and sexual violence becomes visible via tweets under the hashtag #MeToo, but victims' and survivors' struggle to provide legal evidence for these experiences, or the personal and professional consequences of sharing these experiences via #MeToo, remain invisible. Losing employment, family support, community, and friends while facing a barrage of counter-allegations are only a few among the many challenges that #MeToo participants face.

#MeToo, however, emerges as an alternative, non-punitive mode of accountability which abolition feminists have been advocating for. Reporting gendered and sexual violence to juridico-legal institutions consumes an excruciating amount of emotional, psychological, and financial energy and resources. The intersectionality of gendered and sexual violence renders the task of seeking justice via juridico-legal means difficult. For example, in countries with high corruption rates, legal fights are won by whoever among the victim or the aggressor comes from a privileged socioeconomic, religious, racial, or political background. Additionally, these complaints are often reported to men with similar histories of abuse and exploitation, who become enablers and protectors of the aggressors. For most others, reporting violence turns into a long, arduous battle against state institutions. Amidst the lack of structural and sociocultural support, #MeToo, with its outreach, immediacy, networks, and collectivity, offers an alternative way of reporting violence or seeking justice.

Multiple cases of famous men who came under fire after #MeToo allegations serve as examples. These allegations translated into punitive repercussions for some aggressors like Harvey Weinstein, but these consequences were temporary for many others, like Bill Cosby. Online networked collectives like #MeToo, then, become an alternative means of consistent communal accountability. For instance, when Bill Cosby tweeted on Father's Day after getting released from prison, Twitter users were enraged. Additionally, aggressors lose some of their social capital after their victims share their experiences. Though this does not equate legal retribution or compensation that many victims or survivors seek, aggressors pay a social price (however meager that may be). But Cosby did get out of prison, demonstrating that most privileged perpetrators can get away with gendered and sexual violence, with insignificant or zero legal and frequently even social repercussions. These intersecting structural challenges for the victims of gendered and sexual violence elucidate that lasting gender justice and equity and an end to gendered and sexual violence can only be ensured through sustained, meaningful sociopolitical and legal shifts. Meanwhile, the lasting power of the #MeToo movement (or other hashtag solidarity movements) works as a warning to potential aggressors. For example, many potential aggressors complain about the challenges of dating in a post-#MeToo world. This anticipatory caution, though an indication of the frequency and prevalence of gendered and sexual violence and its banality for most men, contributes to creating safer spaces for women.

Safe spaces are both created and strengthened by expansive feminist consciousness raising, for which #MeToo has been instrumental. Because of collective conversations, #MeToo links the deeply personal with the political, maintaining the #MeToo experiences simultaneously as private and public. Many victims and survivors reckoned with their experiences of gendered and sexual violence for the first time and consciously participated in #MeToo conversations. #MeToo and its attendant feminist consciousness raising helped women realize that their personal experiences are structural and institutional. For these reasons, the #MeToo movement is the most revolutionary international movement of the twenty-first century so far. It is revolutionary also in the way it has brought feminism to the streets and to average women, internationally, even in places and communities where such acts seemed almost impossible.

For example, after #MeToo and Aurat March, conservative religious sects in Pakistan have realized anew the need to negotiate for their version of feminism. During the Aurat March 2020, Umme Hassan, principal of Jamia Hafsa,[26] along with other religious groups, organized a parallel counter-march, called the Modesty March, centered around Islamic perspective on women's rights. Religiously conservative women of Jamia Hafsa, who consider #MeToo feminism a Western import and a threat to religio-national values, were joined by women from the Jamaat-e-Islami, Jamiat Ulema-e-Islam, and female students of different seminaries during the Modesty March.[27] While Aurat March and the Modesty March differ in their approach, slogans, and modes of self-presentation, their manifestos demanded similar rights in 2022: safety, fair wages, protections for laborers, and freedom from domestic violence. They, however, disagreed on sexual autonomy and individual agency. Eventually, Modesty Marchers, though averse to surface signifiers of Westernness, at least engaged with the #MeToo movement, an idea of feminism that they find contaminating. Historical, sociopolitical, and legal arguments and narratives are tested for their relevance for women's present and future.

Past, present, and future converge in discourse surrounding #MeToo. At the start of the #MeToo movement, participants shared their experiences, victims of violence reckoned with what had happened to them, and ultimately publicized that reckoning using the vocabularies that they learned from the #MeToo movement; it brought those aggressors, who had to that point lived without consequences, into the public spotlight. #MeToo then historicized those experiences and served as an online archive of women's experiences with gendered and sexual violence. It is largely because of the #MeToo movement that women everywhere are less willing to tolerate this violence. The #MeToo movement, inarguably, has revolutionized our quotidian understanding of feminism and women's rights; it has incited self-reflection in both victims and aggressors on an unmatched scale. It is vital to archive and analyze these conversations to commemorate them as a revolutionary cultural event in feminist histories.

For this purpose, *The Other #MeToos* has assembled chapters that address the issues discussed above from a variety of locations and communities in the Global South. I have loosely organized these chapters geographically and thematically, but have chosen not to assign section headings because of the multiple conversational intersections. Chapters by Anat Schwartz and Ran Deng explore the relationship between histories of gendered and sexual violence, historical feminist movements, and possibilities of new feminist methods and solidarities in East Asia. Schwartz assesses #MeToo as "indicative of a new method" of feminism in South Korea, while Deng highlights the erasure of comfort women to offer "#MeToo as a radical intervention that builds solidarity between survivors across time and space." Zoë Antoinette Eddy, Nicolás Juárez, and Maricruz Gómez contribute chapters about #MeToo centering on South America: Eddy highlights "how Indigenous communities have responded to not only #MeToo, but the historical and contemporary crisis Indigenous communities face"; Juárez examines settler colonial genocide of Native Americans to challenge the "normative understandings of masculinity as a protection against gendered violence" and the impact of #MeToo on these challenges; and Gómez writes about Argentinian femicides and the intersectionality of feminist fights against gendered and sexual violence.

In their focus on South Asia, Amrita De "render[s] visible the many fault lines in the #MeToo Indian landscape," "the liberal conservatism of hashtag feminism," and "material ramifications [of #MeToo] outside the digital space"; Asmita Ghimire and Elizabethada A. Wright link protest signs in Nepal to international protest signs and examine the role of "Global English" in affirming common identities of women across cultures; and Lize-Mari Mitchell analyzes #EndRapeCulture and #AmINext, respectively pre- and post-#MeToo hashtag movements in South Africa, to elaborate on how the South African movements built on the momentum of the international #MeToo movement with a decolonial and intersectional approach; Umme Busra Fateha Sultana and Fariha Jahan conduct personal interviews with #MeToo survivors to discuss #MeToo and its impact in Bangladesh; Thilini Prasadika highlights the roles of common citizens in everyday gendered and sexual violence by analyzing two movements, "16 Days, 16 Stories" and #CreateAScene, along with their campaign materials in Sri Lanka.

In chapters focusing on Muslim countries in the Middle East, South Asia, and Africa, Afiya Shehrbano Zia foregrounds paradoxes in feminist politics, contradictions in feminist activism, and tensions around religion and sexuality in the backdrop of #MeToo in Pakistan; Ayesha Murtza and Atiya Murtaza cite examples of sexual harassment in Mecca to investigate how religion is instrumentalized in Muslim societies to justify gendered and sexual violence while simultaneously being proposed as a solution to the same violence; Antonella Cariello argues that #Masaktach and #EnaZeda in Tunisia and Morocco were inspired by #MeToo but quickly evolved into movements specific to their geopolitical and cultural locations, while continuing to share similar goals of building support and seeking justice for victims. Jihan Zakarriya explores how gendered and sexual violence is used as a political tool of oppression in service of larger political incentives and goals, and that #MeToo-inspired movements in the Arab world then inform and are informed by major geopolitical and cultural developments in the region; and Farinaz Basmechi explores the connections between the global #MeToo movement and the Iranian #MeToo movement to discuss how tweets that use both hashtags create awareness as well as provide a supportive community. In the last chapter, Denisa Kraśna analyzes the reception of #MeToo in the Czech Republic to trace the historical roots of anti-feminist campaigns with a feminist-vegetarian critical lens. Due to the diverse feminist perspectives from an expansive range of locations, each chapter provides a timeline of notable feminist and women's rights events and movements in their respective contexts. These timelines increase the reach and accessibility of these chapters, especially for readers unfamiliar with the feminist histories of each location.

This book anthologizes and celebrates, but also critiques, the #MeToo movement internationally. Despite its impact, the #MeToo movement mainly remains cishet. Women, as a demographically larger number than queer populations, assume more space in #MeToo. Though LGBTQIA+ experiences of gendered and sexual violence remain marginalized in #MeToo, it is an opportunity to reflect on the ways we navigate and negotiate these movements and what a movement of this scale means for other minority communities in the Global South and elsewhere.

I hope that *The Other #MeToos* will serve as a substantial examination and archive of #MeToo, and as an invitation to evaluate the renewed role and politics of digital mediascapes for feminist goals in the Global South. While this book positions and implicates itself in the broad categories of Global South versus Global North and attempts—occasionally even claims—to be exhaustive, I want to acknowledge that exhaustiveness is an impossibility. However, to build on the feminist momentum spurred by #MeToo, we need to develop and sustain communal cultures of accountability, institutional structures of support, and personal ethos of inclusive feminism. Every wound we carry, every fight we fight, and every tear we hide are affectively personal but simultaneously inextricably communal. And this is what #MeToo has demonstrated. #MeToo, then, is a movement of solidarity and agreement, and a movement of a singular goal, despite multiple, diverse routes to that goal, which is to negotiate and carve an equitable, just, and inclusive feminist future for all.

## Notes

1. I use the term "feminist" with the understanding that it represents a diversity of feminist acts and positions; these acts and positions might be disparate, incompatible, conflicting, but this is why I don't approach "feminist" as a fixed category of subjectivity or analysis. I also employ the term "women" as a referent for all victims of sexual violence, including LGBTQIA+ individuals. Despite my acute awareness of the harms of cisheteropatriarchy, I resort to the use of "women" as an umbrella term due to the larger, international goals and audience of this book.
2. @Alyssa_Milano, "If you've been sexually harassed or assaulted write 'me too' as a reply to this tweet." Twitter, October 15, 2017, 3:21 p.m., https://twitter.com/Alyssa_Milano/status/919659438700670976.
3. Women's International League for Peace and Freedom, 2017, "#MeToo's Global Moment: The Anatomy of a Viral Campaign," http://peacewomen.org/resource/metoos-global-moment-anatomy-viral-campaign. Accessed December 4, 2022.
4. @MeTooMVMT. "From a Viral Hashtag to a Global Organization." Twitter, October 2017, https://twitter.com/MeTooMVMT.
5. A brief note on the use of terms: Broadly, any use of #MeToo refers to the general reader's understanding of the term. Specifically, #MeToo refers to the international social media movement that resulted from Alyssa Milano's tweet (2017) and then cojoined Burke's Me Too (2006). The #MeToo movement refers to the lasting international impact of #MeToo's outreach on social media and beyond. Me Too and the MeToo Movement (without the hashtag) means the movement founded by Tarana Burke in 2006 on MySpace.
6. BIPOC stands for Black, Indigenous, and people of color. I recognize that this term doesn't perfectly capture the diversity of communities I refer to here. However, I use it because it's widely recognized.
7. Though Burke's original post is no longer available, Burke's "Me Too" had also received traction on MySpace. She shares, "Adult women began responding to the MySpace page. A designer donated 1,000 "Me Too" T-shirts. Burke still wears one of them when she speaks publicly about the movement. Another supporter made them a real website." Abby Ohlheiser, "The Woman behind 'Me Too' Knew the Power of the Phrase When She Created It—10 Years Ago," *Washington Post*, October 19, 2017. https://www.washingtonpost.com/news/the-intersect/wp/2017/10/19/the-woman-behind-me-too-knew-the-power-of-the-phrase-when-she-created-it-10-years-ago/.
8. Rafia Zakaria, in her book *Against Feminism: Notes on Disruption* (2021), asserts that white feminists are not defined by their race but their refusal to "consider the role that whiteness and the racial privilege attached to it have played . . . in universalizing

white feminist concerns, agendas, and beliefs as being those of all feminists." Zakaria, 2021, *Against White Feminism: Notes on Disruption* (New York: W. W. Norton).

9. Zahara Hill, "A Black Woman Created the 'Me Too' Campaign against Sexual Assault 10 Years Ago," *Ebony*, October 18, 2017, https://www.ebony.com/news/black-woman-me-too-movement-tarana-burke-alyssamilano/#.
10. "Celebrities Share Stories of Sexual Assault for #MeToo Campaign," *Vogue*, October 16, 2017, https://www.vogue.com/article/alyssa-milano-metoo-sexual-assault-campaign.
11. @TaranaBurke, "A Year Ago Today I Thought My World Was Falling Apart," Twitter, October 15, 2018, 9:22 a.m.,https://twitter.com/TaranaBurke/status/1051840689477246978.
12. Rochelle Riley, "#MeToo Founder Tarana Burke Blasts the Movement for Ignoring Poor Women," *Detroit Free Press*, November 15, 2018, https://www.freep.com/story/news/columnists/rochelle-riley/2018/11/15/tarana-burke-metoo-movement/2010310002/.
13. I briefly summarize the history of Western and non-Western feminist conversations for the reader. Contentions between white feminism and non-white feminisms (both in feminist theory and praxis) resulted in global feminism and international feminism. Global feminism advocated for transcending national boundaries (Morgan, 1984; Bunch, 1987), whereas international feminism presupposed nation-states as "discreet and sovereign entities" (Kaplan and Grewal, 2002, p. 7; Swarr and Nagar, 2010, p. 4). But both global and international feminisms were critiqued for taking a simplistic approach to issues of race and imperialism, as well as for mischaracterizing women's oppression as a monolithic, universal, and singular phenomenon (Amos and Parmar, 1984; Lorde, 1984; Mohanty, 1991, 1995; Carby, 1997). Responding to that, Third-World feminists propose historicizing the Third World women's oppression in their locations to examine their agency and diverse forms of their activism (Jayawardena, 1986; Mohanty, 1991b; Basu, 1995, 2010), though later, transnational feminism ascended over Third World feminism. Even Mohanty leaned toward employing transnational feminism as a framework for feminism, rather than Third World feminism, to comprehend the local and national in relation to cross-cultural and international feminist processes (Alexander and Mohanty, 1997; Grewal and Kaplan, 1994; Mohanty, 2002; Alarcon et al., 1999; Moghadam, 2005; Jamal, 2005; Chowdhury, 2009; Basaruddin, 2010). These decades-old debates about intersecting and heterogeneous constituents of gender violence are visible in #MeToo as well. The indefinability and slipperiness of these feminist conceptions and terms are visible even within this brief overview. But despite their differences, all these movements agree in their criticism of reductive and hegemonic Western feminism and consideration of non-Western women's epistemic privilege, intersectionality of women's issues, deleterious effects of global capitalism, and the need for international feminist solidarity. While I do not offer #MeToo as a singular position or absolute solution, I explore the #MeToo movement as a comparative feminist studies/feminist solidarity model, proposed by Chandra Mohanty (see Mohanty, 1991) and applicable internationally. This model facilitates a "complex relational understanding of experience,

location, and history such that feminist cross-cultural work moves to the specific context to construct a real notion of universal and of democratization rather than colonization" (Mohanty, 1991, p. 238). Mohanty offers her incisive model in her discussion of hegemonic and simplistic approaches of Western feminism toward non-Western feminisms. This book builds upon and aims to further these conversations in feminist scholarship.

14. Robyn Wiegman, in *American Anatomies*, also defines economies of visibility: "the epistemology of the visual that underlies both race and gender: that process of corporeal inscription that defines each as a binary wholly visible affair" (1995, p. 8). Banet-Weiser builds on this conception of Wiegman. For this project, I'll stick to Banet-Weiser's definition and discussion of economies of visibility as it is more relevant to the topic at hand.
15. "Girls at Dhabas" and "Why Loiter" are feminist initiatives in Pakistan and India, respectively, to reclaim public spaces for women. These initiatives consider women's presence in public spaces as acts of defiance. See also Shubhra Dixit, "Gender: Hang Out with These Girls at Dhabas," *The Quint*, https://www.thequint.com/news/world/gender-hang-out-with-these-girls-at-dhabas, 2015; and Joseph Erbentraut, "Indian Women Are 'Loitering' at Night to Prove a Powerful Point," *Huffington Post*, 2015, https://www.huffpost.com/entry/why-loiter-indian-women-public-space-pri_n_560b0568e4b0af3706de6c50.
16. Brian Creech, "Exploring the Politics of Visibility: Technology, Digital Representation, and the Mediated Workings of Power," *Semiotica* 236–237 (2020): 123–139, https://doi.org/10.1515/sem-2018-0043.
17. Digital gender gap in the Global South remains an insurmountable challenge so women's access to internet and mobile phones depends upon many factors such as their socioeconomic class, location, community, education, etc. See: Digital Gender Gaps at https://www.digitalgendergaps.org.
18. Aurat March is a demonstration, gathering, or a protest against gendered and sexual violence in Pakistan. The first Aurat March was held on Women's Day on March 8, 2018. Though in solidarity with the #MeToo movement and global Women's Marches, Aurat March is a Pakistani expression of public demand of an end to gendered and sexual violence.
19. "The offences relating to religion were first codified by India's British rulers in 1860 and were expanded in 1927. Pakistan inherited these laws when it came into existence after the partition of India in 1947. . . . Data provided by National Commission for Justice and Peace (NCJP) shows a total of 776 Muslims, 505 Ahmedis, 229 Christians and 30 Hindus have been accused under various clauses of the blasphemy law from 1987 until 2018." See: "What Are Pakistan's Blasphemy Laws?" *BBC News*, May 8, 2019, https://www.bbc.com/news/world-asia-48204815.
20. Aurat March, Lahore, March 10, 2021, "Statement by Aurat March Lahore Condemning Slander against the March," https://twitter.com/AuratMarch/status/1369666866206146563?ref_src=twsrc%5Etfw%7Ctwcamp%5Etweetembed%7Ctwterm%5E1369666866206146563%7Ctwgr%5Ec0e12f63108941c9a468047cd626937d5d8bf497%7Ctwcon%5Es1_&ref_url=https%3A%2F%2Fglobalvoices.org%2F2

021%2F04%2F03%2Faurat-march-organizers-face-intimidation-and-threats-of-prosecution-in-pakistan%2F.

21. Publication of these cartoons has frequently incited protests across the Muslim world: "*Jyllands-Posten* Muhammad Cartoons Controversy," 2021, *Wikipedia*, https://en.wikipedia.org/wiki/Jyllands-Posten_Muhammad_cartoons_controversy. Accessed December 5, 2022; "France Urges Citizens to Leave Pakistan Amid Anti-French Protests," *BBC*, 2021, https://www.bbc.com/news/world-asia-56760224.
22. "Case Registered against Aurat March Organisers," *The News*; "Plea against Order to Book Aurat March Organisers Set Aside," *DAWN*, 2021.
23. Hashim, Asad. "Pakistan Police File 'Blasphemy' Case against Feminist Marchers," AlJazeera. April 16, 2021. https://www.aljazeera.com/news/2021/4/16/pakistan-police-file-blasphemy-case-against-feminist-marchers.
24. Aurat March organizers provided a list of the channels: https://docs.google.com/spreadsheets/d/1VeeABgA-TYoCPONKATQjHCWgcjznhigAOlHVBuFNxVw/edit#gid=0.
25. As I respond to the copyeditor's notes in December 2022, Elon Musk has bought Twitter and we don't know how these policies will change under his management.
26. Jamia Hafsa is a female Islamic seminary, that was established in 1992 as a sister branch of Jamia-Ul-Ulom al Islamia al Faridia.
27. Islamic perspectives on women's rights and gender equity differ according to sect, gender, and various schools of thought. The Muslim feminist politics and politicization of female religious institutes in Pakistan is another complex issue. Given the complexity of that topic, I limit myself only to their engagement in mainstream politics. See: Kalbe Ali, "Jamia Hafsa Students Claim Responsibility for Defacing Feminist Mural in Islamabad," DAWN, March 5, 2020, https://www.dawn.com/news/1538478.

## Works Cited

Alarcon, Norma, et al., eds. 1999. *Between Women and Nation*. Durham, NC: Duke University Press.

Amos, Valerie, and Pratibha Parmar. 1984. "Challenging Imperial Feminism." *Feminist Review* 17: 3–19.

Anden-Papadopoulos, Kari. 2014. "Citizen Camera-Witnessing: Embodied Political Dissent in the Age of 'Mediated Mass Self-Communication.'" *New Media & Society* 16, no. 5: 753–769.

Banet-Weiser, Sarah. 2015. "Keynote Address: Media, Markets, Gender: Economies of Visibility in a Neoliberal Moment." *The Communication Review* 18, no. 1: 53–70.

Banet-Weiser, Sarah. 2018. *Empowered: Popular Feminism and Popular Misogyny.* Durham, NC: Duke University Press.

Basarudin, Azza. 2010. "In Search of Faithful Citizens in Postcolonial Malaysia: Islamic Ethics, Muslim Activism, and Feminist Politics." In *Women and Islam*, edited by Zayn Kassam, pp. 93–128. Santa Barbara, CA: Praeger.

Basu, Amrita, ed. 1995. *The Challenges of Local Feminisms*. Boulder, CO: Westview Press.

Basu, Amrita, ed. 2010. *Women's Movements in the Global Era: The Power of Local Feminisms*. Boulder, CO: Westview Press.

Blaagaard, Bolette, Mette Mortensen, and Cristina Neumayer. 2017. "Digital Images and Globalized Conflict." *Media, Culture & Society* 39, no. 8: 1111–1121.

Bojic, Anna. 2017. "Theory in Perpetual Motion and Translation: Assemblage and Intersectionality in Feminist Studies." *Atlantis* 38, no. 1: 138–149.

Bunch, Charlotte, ed. 1987. *Passionate Politics, Feminist Theory in Action*. New York: St. Martin's Press.

Carby, Hazel. 1997. "White Woman Listen: Black Feminism and the Boundaries of Sisterhood." In *Materialist Feminism: A Reader in Class, Difference, and Women's Lives*, edited by Rosemary Hennessy and Chrys Ingraham, pp. 110–128. London: Routledge.

Chowdhury, Elora. 2009. "Locating Global Feminisms Elsewhere: Braiding US Women of Color and Transnational Feminisms." *Cultural Dynamics* 21, no. 1: 51–78.

Citron, Danielle. 2014. *Hate Crimes in Cyberspace*. Cambridge, MA: Harvard University Press.

Clark-Parsons, Rosemary. 2019. "'I See You, I Believe You, I Stand with You': #MeToo and the Performance of Networked Feminist Visibility." *Feminist Media Studies* 21, no. 03: 362–380.

Cole, Kirsti K. 2015. "'It's Like She's Eager to Be Verbally Abused': Twitter, Trolls, and (En) Gendering Disciplinary Rhetoric." *Feminist Media Studies* 15, no. 02: 356–358.

Creech, Brian. 2020. "Exploring the Politics of Visibility: Technology, Digital Representation, and the Mediated Workings of Power." *Semiotica* 236–237: 123–139. https://doi.org/10.1515/sem-2018-0043.

Ghadery, Farnush. 2019. "#MeToo—Has the 'Sisterhood' Finally Become Global or Just Another Product of Neoliberal Feminism?" *Transnational Legal Theory* 10, no. 2: 252–274. doi:10.1080/20414005.2019.1630169.

Gray, Herman. 2013. "Subject(ed) to Recognition." *American Quarterly* 65, no. 4: 771–798.

Grewal, Inderpal. 2005. *Transnational America: Feminisms, Diasporas, Neoliberalisms*. Durham, NC: Duke University Press.

Grewal, Inderpal, and Caren Kaplan. 1994. *Scattered Hegemonies: Postmodernity and Transnational Feminist Practices*. Minnesota: University of Minnesota Press.

Griffin, Penny. 2019. "#MeToo, White Feminism and Taking Everyday Politics Seriously in the Global Political Economy." *Australian Journal of Political Science* 54, no. 4: 556–572.

Gross, Larry P. 2012. *Up from Invisibility: Lesbians, Gay Men, and the Media in America*. New York: Columbia University Press.

Harvey, Alison. 2016. "Dreams, Design, and Exclusion: The Aggressive Architecture of the Utopian Internet." Paper presented at *Film, Television & Media Studies* Research Seminar Series, University of East Anglia, March 7.

Herr, Ranjoo Seodu. 2014. "Reclaiming Third World Feminisms: Or Why Transnational Feminism Needs Third World Feminism." *Meridians: Feminism, Race, Transnationalism* 12, no. 1: 1–30.

Hillis, Ken, Susannna Paasonen, and Michael Petit. 2015. *Networked Affect*. Cambridge, MA: MIT Press.

Jane, Emma J. 2014. "'Your a Ugly, Whorish Slut': Understanding E-bile." *Feminist Media Studies* 14, no. 04: 531–546.

Jane, Emma J. 2016. *Misogyny Online: A Short (and Brutish) History*. New Delhi: Sage.

Jamal, Amina. 2005. "Transnational Feminism as Critical Practice: A Reading of Feminist Discourses in Pakistan." *Meridians: Feminism, Race, Transnationalism* 5, no. 2: 57–82.

Jayawardena, Kumari. 1986. *Feminism and Transnationalism in the Third World*. London: Zed Books.

Kaplan, C., and I. Grewal. 2002. "Transnational Practice and Interdisciplinary Feminist Scholarship: Refiguring Women and Gender Studies." In *Women's Studies on Its Own*, edited by Robyn Wiegman, pp. 66–81. Durham, NC: Duke University Press.

Kellner, Douglas. 2003. "Globalization, Technopolitics, and Revolution." In *The Future of Revolutions: Rethinking Radical Change in the Age of Globalization*, edited by John Ford, pp. 180–194. London: Zed Books.

Lorde, Audre. 1984. *Sister Outsider*. Feasterville Trevose, PA: Crossing Press.

Lumsden, Karen, and Heather Morgan. 2017. "Media Framing of Trolling and Online Abuse: Silencing Strategies, Symbolic Violence, and Victim Blaming." *Feminist Media Studies* 17, no. 6: 926–940.

Mantilla, Karla. 2015. *Gendertrolling*. Westport, CT: Praeger.

Mendes, Kaitlynn. 2015. *SlutWalk: Feminism, Activism and Media*. Basingstoke, UK: Palgrave Macmillan.

Mendes, Kaitlynn, Jessica Ringrose, and Jessalynn Keller. 2019. *Digital Feminist Activism: Girls and Women Fight Back against Rape Culture*. New York: Oxford University Press.

Moghadam, Valentine. 2005. *Globalizing Women*. Baltimore, MD: John Hopkins University Press.

Mohanty, Chandra. 1995. "Feminist Encounters: Locating the Politics of Experience." In *Social Postmodernism: Beyond Identity Politics*, edited by Linda Nicholson and Steven Seidman, pp. 68–86. Cambridge: Cambridge University Press.

Mohanty, Chandra. 2002. "'Under Western Eyes' Revised: Feminist Solidarity through Anti-Capitalist Struggles." *Signs* 23, no. 2: 499–535.

Mohanty, Chandra, et al., eds. 1991. *Third World Feminism and the Politics of Feminism*. Bloomington: Indiana University Press.

Mohanty, Chandra, and M. Jacqui Alexander, eds. 1997. *Feminist Genealogies, Colonial Legacies, Democratic Futures*. London: Routledge.

Mohanty, Chandra, and Russo Lourdes Torres. 1991. *Third World Feminism and the Politics of Feminism*. Bloomington: Indiana University Press.

Morgan, Robin, ed. 1984. *Sisterhood Is Global: The International Women's Movement Anthology*. New York: Doubleday Anchor.

Penny, Laurie. 2013. *Cybersexism: Sex, Gender and Power on the Internet*. London: Bloomsbury.

Powell, Anastasia, and Nicola Henry. 2017. *Sexual Violence in a Digital Age*. Basingstoke, UK: Palgrave Macmillan.

Rentschler, Carrie, and Samantha Thrift. 2015. "Doing Feminism in the Network: Networked Laughter and the 'Binders Full of Women' Meme." *Feminist Theory* 16, no. 3: 329–359.

Rodino-Colocino, Michelle. 2014. "#YesAllWomen: Intersectional Mobilization against Sexual Assault Is Radical (Again)." *Feminist Media Studies* 14, no. 6: 1113–1115.

Swarr, Amanda L., and Richa Nagar, eds. 2010. *Critical Transnational Feminist Praxis*. Albany: State University of New York Press.

Tufecki, Zeynep. 2017. *Twitter and Teargas: The Power and Fragility of Networked Protest*. New Haven, CT: Yale University Press.

Vickery, Jacqueline Ryan, and Tracy Everbach. 2018. *Mediating Misogyny: Gender, Technology, and Harassment*. London: Palgrave.

Wiegman, Robyn. 1995. *American Anatomies: Theorizing Race and Gender*. Durham, NC: Duke University Press.

Wolfson, Todd. 2014. *Digital Rebellion: The Birth of the Cyber-Left*. Urbana: University of Illinois Press.

Young, Stacey. 1997. *Changing the Wor(l)d: Discourse, Politics, and the Feminist Movement*. London: Routledge.

# Acknowledgments

I would like to thank the contributors to this volume who made this book possible.

I am grateful to my family for their support. Thanks to Dr. Samantha Langsdale, Dr. Rebecca Bernard, Dr. Andrew Smith, and Dr. Masood Raja, all of whom have been prompt in their guidance and feedback. Thanks to countless others—the theorists, writers, scholars, thinkers who taught me word by word, thought by thought, idea by idea, and who shaped me as a human, a learner, and a writer.

Thanks to Angela Chnapko at Oxford University Press, who has been incredibly helpful and patient from my earliest communication with her.

Iqra Shagufta Cheema

# 1

# Acceptable Activism

## The History of the Anti–Sexual Violence Movement and the Contemporary #MeToo Protests in South Korea

*Anat Schwartz*

### Timeline

As South Korean[1] modern history (1900s–today) is marked by annexation, imperialism, neo-imperialism, civil war, and internal political and cultural turmoil, it is challenging to list all events that have contributed to women's rights and feminism. This timeline is an attempt to chronicle major events in the history of anti–sexual violence movements in South Korea, but it is by no means exhaustive.[2]

- 1970s–1980s: During the decades of military rule (Park Chung-hee,[3] 1963–1979; Chun Doo-hwan, 1980–1988) college students, intellectuals, and laborers formed the Minjung (the common people) movement, a national and democratic movement. Women were essential to this movement, particularly in educating students and laborers in factories.
- 1976: Founding of Ewha Womans University's Women's Studies program by professors Lee Hyo-chae and Cho Hyoung.
- 1980s: Founding of the Korean Women's Development Institute, the National Committee on Women's Policies, and the advancement of woman leadership within the Bureaus of Family Welfare.
- 1985: Founding of *Ttohanaŭi munhwa*, a major turning point in the South Korea's institution-based liberal feminist movement, by U.S.-trained feminists Cho Hae Joang (sociology, Yonsei University), Cho Oakla (sociology, Sogang University), Cho Hyoung (one of the founders of women's studies at Ewha Womans University), Cho Eun (sociology, Tongguk University), Kim Eunice Eun-Sil and Chang Pil-wha (women's studies at Ewha Womans University).
- 1986: Kwon Insook, a student who was arrested by the Bucheon police in June 1987 while working at a factory, was sexually tortured by Moon Gui-dong, a police detective notorious for using torture.

Anat Schwartz, *Acceptable Activism* In: *The Other #MeToos.* Edited by: Iqra Shagufta Cheema, Oxford University Press.
 DOI: 10.1093/oso/9780197619872.003.0001

- 1986: My Sister's Place (*durebang*) was established to bring awareness to sex workers and the *kijich'on* movement, a term used to describe the camptowns for the U.S. military.
- 1987: The Korean Women's Association United was established in 1987, creating a formalized coalition of nongovernmental and progressive women's organizations.
- 1989: The third revision of the Family Law was the most progressive change to date, following the ratification of the UN Convention on the Elimination of All Forms of Discrimination Against Women (CEDAW) in 1984 by the Korean government.
- 1991: Kim Hak-sun gave her first testimony on the Japanese Imperial Army and her experiences of being forced into sexual slavery during World War II.
- 1992: Following Kim Hak-sun's testimony in 1991, the Korean Council for the Women Drafted for Military Sexual Slavery by Japan organized a noon demonstration every Wednesday outside the Embassy of Japan in Seoul.
- 1994: The Act on the Punishment of Sexual Crimes and Protection of Victims Thereof was enacted. This was the first law passed specifically to combat sexual violence.
- 2005: The *Hoju* family register system was abolished. The family registry was a patriarchal institution under which women were added to their husband's family registration, thus eliminating their maiden familial ties.
- 2008: Candlelight Girl, a popular image of a young girl with a short bob-cut holding a single candle, became an icon for the protests against the U.S.-Korea Free Trade Agreement (FTA).
- 2015: #Nanŭnp'eminisŭt'ŭimnida (#IAmAFeminist) began on Twitter as a form of hashtag activism. Korean feminists shared personal experiences and stories about their feminist identities to oppose stigma.
- 2016: A young woman was murdered in May 2016 in a public restroom near exit 10 of the highly congested Gangnam subway station. Women's organizations and feminist activists argued that this murder was an act of femicide. Feminist film scholar Sohn Hee Jeong called post-2016 a "feminist reboot," and feminists began to self-identify as part of the "Gangnam station generation."[4]
- 2015–2016: Megalia, an anonymous radical feminist website, opened in 2015. Womad splits off from Megalia in 2016 after Megalia banned homophobic and transphobic slurs.
- 2016–2017: President Park Geun-hye (2013–2017) was impeached. During the impeachment protests, women's organizations created a "femi-zone" within the protest space: a safe space for women to gather and protest safely without fear of sexual harassment.

- 2016: #00_kye_nae_sŏngp'oklyŏk (lit. #my_sexual_abuse_in_00) began trending on Twitter, following a series of highly publicized cases of sexual abuse and assault in the literary community.
- 2017–2019: #MeToo movement (*mit'u* or *mit'u undong* for #MeToo activism) reached the height of its popularity when prosecutor Seo Ji-hyun appeared on *JTBC News Room* in January 29, 2018. Seo's interview was a catalyst for many women to come forward.
- 2018: South Chungcheong governor and president-hopeful Ahn Hee-jung was accused of sexual assault by his former secretary Kim Ji-eun in a live interview.
- 2018: The Hyehwa station protests (also known as the Uncomfortable Courage protests) began in May 19, 2018, under the title "Censuring of the crooked investigation of the illegal spy cams" (*pulbŏpch'waryŏng p'yŏnp'asusa kyut'anshiwi*). The fourth rally drew 70,000 feminists from across the nation.
- 2019: Feminist activists and organizations worked to expose and charge Korea Future Technology Corporation chairman and WebHard cartel operator Yang Jin-ho with dissemination of illegal pornography.
- 2020: Seoul mayor Park Won-soon committed suicide after his former secretary accused him of four years of sexual harassment. Park's suicide prohibited him from facing posthumous charges for sexual harassment.
- 2020: The Women's Party was established as the first-ever feminist political party.
- 2018–2020: Activists, particularly from the Korea Cyber Sexual Violence Response Center, exposed Nth Room, a network of online chat rooms operated through Telegram, an encrypted messaging application, which involved blackmail, digital sex trafficking, and the spread of violent sex crimes and sexually exploitative videos. In May 2020, the Cabinet approved the so-called Nth Room Prevention Act to strengthen penalties on sex crimes.

## Introduction

"The #MeToo [movement] online is different from [the #MeToo movement] in person. . . . We need both, but both feel different in reality."[5] I sat down with Yoon-Hee at a Starbucks in Euljiro on a slow morning in October 2018, and we wrapped up our interview by discussing the #MeToo movement in South Korea. In her mid-twenties, Yoon-Hee's primary concern for the South Korean feminist movement was changing society's attitude toward human rights. For Yoon-Hee, the #MeToo movement represents one of the ways to achieve this goal.

Throughout my ethnographic research at feminist protests and #MeToo rallies held by the *Citizens Action with #MeToo Movement* in Korea[6] it was clear that #MeToo did not have a singular identity. Rather, by using the same hashtags,[7] #MeToo became a mainstream phenomenon. However, the popularity of the #MeToo movement marked an unprecedented mainstream turn within the history of anti–sexual violence activism in Korea.

Current scholarship tends to frame contemporary civil protests within their presence on social media, or focuses on the media platforms behind the popularity of singular movements.[8] Personal narrative and sharing are integral to feminist epistemology, and that is most evident in the #MeToo movement. #MeToo highlights survivor testimonies and public expressions of solidarity. In South Korea, #MeToo posts online were frequently followed by replies or retweets with the hashtag #Withyou, a shorthand to express support and solidarity.

Although #MeToo in Korea was inspired by the movement in the United States, the Korean #MeToo movement is not a continuation or a co-optation of the American movement. #MeToo in the United States was coined by Tarana Burke in 2006 and it soared as a hashtag in 2017, while the #MeToo movement (hereafter #MeToo)[9] in South Korea has taken its own form and shape in 2017–2019. As I will discuss, #MeToo was not the first hashtag used by people to share personal experiences with sexual violence and to express solidarity with survivors. In October 2016 the hashtag #00_kye_nae_sŏngp'oklyŏk (lit. translated as *#my_sexual_abuse_in_00*) reached popularity among women and feminist activists by sharing and uncovering sexual abuse in workplaces and groups.[10] In this chapter, I demonstrate that the archival nature of hashtags and citationality connects #MeToo to previous anti–sexual violence movements. In other words, there is no "post-#MeToo" because, as a citational hashtag, #MeToo did not end. Elsewhere, Korean feminist scholars argue that #MeToo did not achieve larger societal change or concrete concessions relating to gendered violence or disparities. For Korean feminism to reach a post-#MeToo era, #MeToo needed to address social and cultural issues that intersect with harassment and gendered violence, such as the gendered wage gap, glass ceiling in the workforce, etc. (Baik, 2019).

This chapter stems from a larger project on contemporary South Korean feminist activism and communities. Using feminist epistemology and theory, in combination with sixteen months of fieldwork interviews and participation observation at feminist rallies and gatherings,[11] this chapter argues against framing activism after 2019 as "post-#MeToo." I will demonstrate that there is no "post," "revitalization," or "second wave" of #MeToo. Rather, I argue that #MeToo has become a citational tool, as it functions both as a tool for feminist archiving and as a performative utterance. More specifically, this chapter posits that feminists and women's organizations, regardless of age and class, use tools typically associated with the younger generation (i.e., social media, hashtags, slang) in rallies, protests, and in their own social media accounts and activism to refer back to societal issues that have persisted throughout the history of Korean feminism. Here, I define the #MeToo movement as a citational tool, which both creates a collective feminist memory and is used by feminist activists as a performative utterance, through which the enduring legacy of the anti–sexual violence movement is connected to the young South Korean feminist movement. As a hashtag, #MeToo is not confined to temporality. Rather, #MeToo has been widely circulated online and in person, transnationally and locally, and is a citational and archival tool for anti–sexual violence activism and solidarity.

#MeToo is not a spontaneous or stand-alone movement, but is indicative of a new method of doing feminism in South Korea. From a feminist epistemological perspective, hashtags perform citationality in two ways: (1) as a performative act of citational archiving for collective causes, and (2) as an act of feminist solidarity. I demonstrate in this chapter that feminist epistemology is embedded in citationality. #MeToo has created an archive that is collectively shared by feminist activists. As Sara Ahmed argued in *Living a Feminist Life* (2017, p. 17), "citation is a feminist memory." In this chapter, #MeToo both serves as a functional archival tool and preserves feminist activism.

## Feminist Movements and Anti–Sexual Violence Activism in South Korea

In *Feminism Is for Everybody*, bell hooks defines feminism as "a movement to end sexism, sexist exploitation, and oppression" (2000, p. viii). In this concise definition, bell hooks aptly argues that feminism is a social, ideological, and political tool for confronting and dismantling oppression, exploitation, and sexism.

Historically, feminist activists, scholars, and historians used the term "wave" to describe women's movements in the Western context. Although Black feminists have argued that the wave model obscures the centrality of race in women's protests prior to the suffrage movement in the United States in the 1960s (Springer, 2002, p. 1061), the usage of "waves" to denote mass feminist movements has stuck. In the first feminist wave in the United States, white women gained the legal right to vote through the Nineteenth Amendment to the U.S. Constitution in 1920. Second wave feminism similarly focused on women's legal and social welfare and liberation, but also drew attention to growing violence against women (Thompson 2002) and lesbian sexuality (Silver, 2002; Poirot, 2014). Third wave feminism (or post-feminism) in the West focused on intersectional feminism (Crenshaw, 1989), Black feminist scholarship (Collins, 1986; Harding, 2004, 2009), and feminist scholarship by women of color and

LGBTQIA+. While it is hard to draw a clear timeline of feminist "waves," it is especially fruitless to parse the line between the third wave and the current, fourth wave of Western feminism. Current feminist scholarship points to continued fracturing between feminist communities and identities along political and racial lines, at the same time as focusing on the intersections between social media and digital technology and the diversification of feminism.

In South Korea, feminism is less talked about in terms of "waves," although some scholars may use it as a device or for comparative analysis. Although this may read as reductionist, below is a timeline of the history of feminist movements in Korea. This timeline is not meant to be exhaustive, but is meant to establish a broad genealogy of Korean anti-sexual violence activism, in order to provide context for the #MeToo movement.

- First wave movements during Japanese colonial occupation (1919–1945): New Women and women intellectuals in the 1920s (Wells 1999);
- Second wave movements in the post-liberation period (1945–) and during authoritarian regimes (Park Chung-hee, 1963–1979, and Chun Doo-hwan, 1979–1988): *Minjung feminism* (ordinary citizens' feminism, part of a larger nationalist pro-democracy movement), and feminism in factories, the labor movement, and student movement;
- Third wave movements were more fractured in the 1990s: during this period, anti–sexual violence activism, U.S. military camptown prostitution activism, and the movement to support the former comfort women, who were victims of Japanese colonialism, emerged.[12] Feminists primarily in their teens and twenties were dubbed "young feminists."
- Fourth wave feminism stands out due to contemporary technological advances. Contemporary movements are more diverse and plentiful than previous movements, in part because of combined struggles, transnational and pan-Asian solidarity movements, and intersectional causes, but also due to the nature of digital feminism. In other words, online contemporary feminism is a nonlinear archive of past and present feminism(s) (Kim, 2019, p. 35). In addition to #MeToo and the anti–sexual violence movement, overarching feminist movements include the fight against spy cameras and illegal pornography, digital sex crimes, and surveillance, doxing, the movement to legalize abortion, and queer and lesbian feminist movements.

Prior to the mid- to late 1990s, the term "feminism" was not widely circulated. Feminist activists self-identified and used terms such as "women's liberation," "women's activism," and "women's politics." Women were integral to the democratization movement (1960–1989), from joining the garment and manufacturing labor force (Koo, 2002; Kendall, 2002) to creating women's clubs to study and educate their compatriots on politics and society, and to spearheading unionization in the garment industry (Koo, 2001).

However, the Korean social movement of the 1970s–1980s was, at heart, "a national liberation project seeking to eliminate dependence on foreign powers and to unify North and South Korea" (Jung, 2014, p. 9). While also considered part of the overarching history of the Korean feminist movement, activism in the 1970s–1980s was a class liberation movement aimed at transforming capitalist structure and overthrowing the authoritarian regime and establishing a democratic movement, and sexual violence remained a footnote in the nationalist struggle (Kim and Choi et al., 1998; Nelson, 2000; Lee, 2010). Scholars have also pointed to feminist nationalism as constructive to feminist goals, including *minjung* feminism of the 1980s (Lee, 2007; Kim, 2009). Minjung refers to the "common people" or "ordinary citizens," and was, in part, an effort by the educated class to mobilize the common people to reclaim Korea from its past as a colonial and imperial subject, and from authoritarian rule. The Minjung movement of the 1970s–1980s focused on coalition building between intellectuals, religious leaders, students, opposition parties, and the newly emerged middle class to push for democracy and representation (Lee, 2007).

In other words, the Korean women's movement rejected separation from the broader political struggle. Rather than emphasizing its autonomy and independence, the women's movement identified itself as a part of the movement for democracy and prioritized issues of democracy and nationalism. In this way, the Korean women's movement was affected by other social movements and the broader sociopolitical environment (Jung, 2014). Sexual violence was framed as a gender-specific issue and thus was overlooked within women's larger social justice movement until the late 1980s. The women's movement was confined to issues that could be framed within the nationalist democratic agenda. Thus, violence perpetrated by common men against ordinary women was sidelined, such as the case of Kwon Insook, a student who was arrested by the Bucheon police in June 1987 while working at a factory, and was sexually tortured by Moon Gui-dong, a police detective notorious for using torture. Kwon was eventually released from prison after thirteen months, Moon was sentenced to five years of imprisonment, and the state was assessed a fine in civil penalties (Cohen and Baker, 1991, p. 200).

Inspired by sexual violence cases like the above, the Korean Women Associations United (KWAU) was established in 1987. The KWAU focused on anti–sexual violence to solidify an organizational presence for women's sociopolitical engagement throughout South Korea. The KWAU saw the root cause of oppression and discrimination against Korean women not merely due to patriarchal structures, but also because of sociopolitical conditions such as the dictatorial regimes, political and economic subordination to the United States, and division of the country. While the June Democracy Movement successfully transitioned the country into a democracy in 1987 and oversaw the end to Chun Doo-hwan's authoritarian regime (1980–1987), the framing of sexual violence cases has not changed much since the 1980s. As I will argue, the anti–sexual violence movement continued since the 1980s through the 2010s, attributing to the arguable success of the #MeToo movement in Korea.

## Contemporary Protests and Feminism Post-2016

To understand the continuity between anti–sexual violence movements throughout contemporary Korean history, I begin this section with a discussion of the importance of the 2014 Sewol Ferry disaster for the contemporary sociopolitical landscape, before turning to recent events in South Korean society. The capsizing of the Sewol Ferry in 2014, along with the murder of a young woman at a Gangnam subway station, the #00_kye_nae_sŏngp'oklyŏk hashtag, and the candlelight vigils of 2016–2017, set the foundation for what is contemporarily framed as the #MeToo movement in Korea.

In the early hours of April 16, 2014, the Sewol ferry capsized on its way from Incheon to Jeju Island. The ferry held 476 people, mostly teenage students on a field trip from Ansan City's Danwon High School, and ultimately 304 passengers and crew died. The government's culpability in the Sewol's sinking and its haphazard response to it is central to the public's general perception of the tragedy. During the capsizing of the Sewol ferry, the staff told the students to "stay put," a phrase which was used during the height of the Sewol solidarity protests and candlelight vigils to push back against the Park Geun-hye government for its lack of accountability. Feminist scholars Kwon Kim Hyun-young (2018) and Yoo Ji Ahn (2018), from the young feminist community *Femidangdang*, highlight the cultural and political ramifications of the Sewol ferry as solidifying young people's distrust of the government. The aftermath of the government's mishandling of the Sewol's capsizing and delayed rescue led young people to criticize and mock Korean society by calling it "Hell Joseon" (literally, Hell Korea) and "hateful society."

It is in this sociopolitical climate that on May 17, 2016, a woman in her twenties was murdered by a man at a public restroom near exit 10 of the Gangnam subway station. The murder spurred thousands of people to place post-it notes outside exit 10 in memoriam, creating a fixed memorial in physical space, in print, and in online communities.[13] The post-it notes in the vigil noted that "she [the victim] was murdered because she was a woman" and "I only survived because I wasn't there," referring to how gender was the basis for the murder.

The vigils and the memory of the Gangnam murder had a significant impact on women, especially those in their twenties. This event was frequently brought up by many of my interview participants during my fieldwork in South Korea from August 2018 to January 2019. As a Western white feminist scholar, I acknowledge both my presence and privilege in certain spaces, and believe scholarship should proceed from one's engagement with the people and places around them (Boellstroff, 2012, p. 22). I found it important to begin interviews by asking participants to define feminism in their own words, and asking when they had begun defining themselves as feminists, both to themselves and in their communities. I met Won, a nineteen-year-old feminist working part-time jobs while contemplating attending university, at an event centered on "speaking out" for minority populations, such as youth, non-able-bodied people, sexual minorities, and others. At a small café in Hapjeong in November 2018, Won traced her awareness of feminism and her own identity as a feminist to the Gangnam murder in 2016. Won was aware that even without this incident propelling her into feminism, the Gangnam murder defined what activism looks and feels like to her. In particular, Won was moved by action, saying:

> There have been protests that surpassed [the kind of activism taken place after the Gangnam murder], but I'm not sure how they relate to me personally. . . . I loved how deep it felt to see the post-its [placed outside Gangnam subway exit 10], and how many people showed up online and in-person.

As Won points out, incidents like this murder carry heavier weight for individual feminists. For the majority of my interview participants, the 2016 Gangnam murder was significant, but not because of its violent nature. In interviews, participants were still unsure why this murder was as important as it was—not just for themselves, but for other young women. Won was also an active member of Fireworks Femi Action, an organization composed of young feminist activists, which is run by the activists collectively with no single leader and relies on detailed promises that members make to one another (such as: no discrimination based on age, sex, gender, nationality, appearance, ability, etc.).

For many feminists, the violence of the Gangnam murder was not surprising. Yeo, another interview participant and member of Fireworks Femi Action, dismissed the violent nature of the Gangnam murder as shocking, saying "you know, that [kind of violence], it's nothing new." What was new, for both Won, Yeo, and many of my interview participants, was the immediate "emergency response" of various women's organizations, feminist groups, and individual feminists to the event. Yeo had just started to work at a center providing sex education for minors, run by a nonprofit organization with financial support from the Seoul metropolitan government. In our interview, Yeo recalled that both the organization she works for and young feminist organizations got together quickly after the murder to discuss how they should respond. For many young feminists, the Gangnam murder was a call to action to organize new groups or as their own feminist awakening.[14] Young feminists galvanized by the 2016 murder have since framed themselves as part of the "Gangnam station generation" (Kim, 2020). Fireworks Femi Action formed as a response to the Gangnam murder, a response that Yeo believes set a new pattern for young activists. Yeo shares, "Emergency happens, leads to talks, [then] to action." Post-2016 feminism, however, was still pushing for a public understanding of feminism. Yeo, like several other interview participants, claimed that the Gangnam murder in 2016 "rebooted" feminism,[15] but that feminism had yet to reach mainstream society. Yeo recalled hearing incredulous reactions upon learning that people identified as feminists post-2016. In other words, for contemporary Korean feminists, there is a "pre-2016" and "post-2016."[16]

Beginning in late 2016 and early 2017, mass civil candlelight vigils were held in Gwanghwamun square in Seoul and in other central public spaces throughout Korea. The candlelight movement lasted for months, and led to the subsequent impeachment and formal removal of then-President Park Geun-hye from office, primarily due to corruption, collusion, and Park's mishandling of the Sewol ferry incident. Feminist activists read this movement as a mass desire for change. During these candlelight protests, young feminists organized a "Femizone," a physical feminist space during the candlelight vigils. Kim Young Soon, the co-chair of Korean Women's Association United and the Executive Director of the Citizens Action with #MeToo Movement, frames this movement as reflecting citizens' collective voices that "we will no longer sit still" (2018, p. 40). This slogan references the Sewol ferry staff telling students onboard the sinking ship to "stay put," as well as a growing sentiment among feminist activists that the time to put a legal end to sexual violence and discrimination has come. Specifically, as of writing this chapter, there is no comprehensive anti-discrimination law in Korea. The absence of robust anti-discrimination legal language is a point of contention not only for feminist and women's groups, but for many organizations for social justice and minority and disenfranchised groups, such as immigrants, refugees, laborers, sexual minorities, and non-able-bodied people. Activists' struggle to pass anti-discrimination legislation that is more comprehensive and inclusive of marginalized communities is reflected in the ongoing anti–sexual violence movement.

## Hashtags and Anti–Sexual Violence Protests

Prior to #MeToo entering feminist and public discourse in 2017, in October 2016, the hashtag #my_sexual_abuse_in_00 (#00_kye_nae_sŏngp'oklyŏk) began trending online. Feminist scholars and activists point to this hashtag as defining the start of a "revitalization" or "reboot" for the movement against sexual violence in Korea. Won recalls this hashtag highlighting precarity for women after the Gangnam murder, and for young feminist communities more generally. Kwon Kim (2018a, pp. 309–310) argues that the popularity of the #my_sexual_abuse_in_00 and #my_misogyny_in_00 (#00_kye_nae_yŏsŏnghyŏmo) hashtags in 2016 awakened a collective, public (occasionally anonymized) method of sharing personal experiences around sexual violence and misogyny. Without these earlier hashtags laying the foundation of women sharing their personal stories collectively online, #MeToo could not have gained the wide popularity it reached in 2018. In other words, hashtags in 2016 were not a precursor to #MeToo, but were emblematic of forming trends in activist spaces, the larger movement against sexual violence, and feminist activism post-2014. Moreover, the presence of a "femizone" during the 2016–2017 candlelight vigils left a lasting memory for many young feminists as to the image and feeling of a collective feminist mobilization. In this section, I turn to theorize that the #MeToo movement in South Korea is not defined by space and time. To do so, I put feminist organizations and activists in conversation with feminist epistemology to demonstrate how #MeToo functions as a citational tool. In other words, I argue that contemporary social campaigns take on multiple forms on social media and in protest spaces.

The popularization of #MeToo in Korea can be traced to prosecutor Seo Jihyun's interview on *JTBC News Room* on January 29, 2018. On live television, Seo shared that she was sexually harassed by a prominent male prosecutor eight years prior. In a meeting I had attended with Seo, she shared that she did not feel ready to come forward until friends supported her writing about the event on the prosecutor intranet board. After Seo shared her experiences, attendees of the meeting took turns thanking her for coming forward, as prosecutor Seo's public #MeToo moment inspired others.

From early to mid-2018, the #MeToo and #Withyou hashtags continued to trend in Korea. During this time, more women publicly, on social media and in the news, shared their experiences of sexual harassment or violence perpetuated by men. The accused men ranged from ordinary citizens to high-profile male figures, including artistic director Lee Yoon-taek, who so far has only publicly acknowledged his wrongdoings, and former presidential hopeful politician Ahn Hee-jung. #MeToo and #Withyou hashtags were at their peak in early to mid-2018.[17] While many of the English-language articles on the #MeToo movement focus on the hashtag "finally" arriving in Korea,[18] these hashtags are not part of a nascent movement. As I have argued above, hashtags in 2016 (particularly #00_kye_nae_sŏngp'oklyŏk) pre-dated the #MeToo movement in 2017–2018. The popularity and widespread reach of #MeToo in 2018 was built on earlier feminist movements and activism. The #MeToo hashtag itself circulated in Korean feminist communities after Tanara Burke first used it in the wake of the sexual assault charges against Harvey Weinstein.

During my fieldwork, many of my interlocutors working at women's organizations and centers viewed their activism within the #MeToo movement as part of a transnational feminist anti–sexual violence movement.[19] In the West, feminist epistemology has demonstrated the importance of citationality as feminist praxis (Collins, 1986; Crenshaw, 1989; Butler, 1993; Harding, 2004; Nash, 2019). Kwon Kim (2018a, 2018b) similarly urges feminist scholars to use a more feminist citational practice, such as prioritizing publications by feminist and marginalized authors. Recent publications in Korea, such as the translation of Audre Lorde's seminal *Sister Outsider* (2018) essays, including introductory remarks by Sara Ahmed and Cheryl Clarke, point to a continuation of Korean feminists citing other transnational feminist writings. Feminist transnational citational practices highlight the intersection of language, citationality, and subjectivity. That feminists share political ideology, language, methods of communication, and other forms of solidarity is not an indication that feminists are a homogenous group or that feminists have a single agenda. In response to criticism on the dissolution of body and subject into language in *Gender Trouble* (1990), Judith Butler's *Bodies That Matter* (1993) uses Michel Foucault's writing on power and subjectivity to argue that, for performativity, there is no "real" original (1993, pp. 140–156). Writing on the materiality of sex through the ritualized repetition of norms (1993, p. x), Butler illustrates the ways in which performativity functions as a "citational practice."

In other words, performativity is a reiterative and citational practice (Butler, 1993, p. xii). The repetitive nature of hashtags and the opportunity for both solidarity and conversation do not represent a single platform usage. As Butler demonstrates in *Gender Trouble*, there is an epistemological signification in a gendered, feminist *I* that is "*not a founding act, but rather a regulated process of repetition* [ . . . ] 'agency,' then, is to be located within the possibility of a variation on that repetition" (1990, p. 198, emphasis in original). Butler's focus on signification and repetition for citational practices is crucial in unpacking contemporary forms of activism. Here, feminist activism using hashtags is not bounded by its space (platform) or time, just as Butler's discussion of language is not an external medium or a simple tool. In this way, what is important about explicit performatives is their citational reflexive structures. Put differently, Butler notes that certain utterances come to carry performative force that others do not.

As we have seen, citationality is foundational in making #MeToo reach a mass audience in Korea. In my interview with Yeo, she called post-2016 feminist activism a "reboot" of the movement against sexual violence.[20] In an interview with Siwon, a recent full-time hire at the Korea Sexual Violence Relief Center (KSVRC) in her early twenties, she framed the #MeToo movement as having a "big #MeToo"—referring to the larger, social movement—and a "small #MeToo"—referring to the ongoing anti-sexual violence movement throughout the history and genealogy of Korean feminism. Siwon argued that the larger #MeToo movement was able to get traction because it was always already there, hidden in layers of previous anti-sexual violence activism and beneath the surface of every issue of sexual discrimination, harassment, or violence in society. In other words, #MeToo resonated with Korean society at its moment in time because there had been a strong foundation for it.

Hashtags and citationality are important functions of not only #MeToo specifically, but also contemporary feminist activism more generally. In an anthology titled *Humanistic Publication #Hashtag vol. 1: #hole* (2015),[21] the hashtag signs on social network services (SNS) are followed by specific keywords that appeal to a particular topic. Every hashtag invokes a collective concern which people can react to by using that shame hashtag. In other words, every new tweet, post, or comment with the same hashtag can express solidarity, interest, and support.

Returning to Butler's usage of citationality, it is important to note that Butler's turn to the physical body happens in conjunction with citationality's relation to speech acts in J. L. Austin's work. In *How to Do Things with Words* (1962), Austin demonstrates that linguistic utterances, as well as corporeal utterances, have a performative angle. These utterances are embedded in social and cultural contexts and are dependent on the environment in which they are uttered. Austin's example of "I do" in a wedding ceremony relies on performative forces: the utterance is uttered by the person designated to do so in that specific context, adheres to specific social conventions, and takes the intention of the utterer into consideration. According to Derrida, signs can be appropriated and relocated in citational grafting, or the process of quotation marks is used to refer to words in ways that may not conform to the speaker or writer's original intentions (1988, pp. 101–103). In conversation with both Austin and Derrida, Butler's use of citation and citationality highlights the potentially subversive practices of gender performativity whereby gender may cite gender in ways that reveal other contexts.[22]

Although much can be said about gender performativity and citationality in feminist activist spaces, it is important to note here that Korean feminist activists use hashtags to perform as citations, in keeping with Butler's usage and in Sara Ahmed's approach. In *The Cultural Politics of Emotion*, Sara Ahmed argues that feminist emotion encapsulates embodied aspects of thought and reason (2004, p. 170). The centrality of emotion in the feminist community connects feminists both online and offline in mediated ways that, though politicized, socially, and politically "reanimate the relation between the subject [the individual feminist] and a collective" (Ahmed, 2004, p. 171). Here, emotions work to shape and reshape the surfaces of individual and collective bodies. Ahmed argues that emotion and action are not separate realms; rather, emotions "operate to 'make' and 'shape' bodies as forms of action, which also involve orientations towards others" (2004, p. 4). In this way, emotions operate to make and shape bodies in action, through an orientation to others. For Ahmed, emotions do not function as inside out (psychological) or outside in (sociological), or as something an "I" or a "we" possess. Instead, Ahmed argues:

> It is through emotions, or how we respond to objects and others, that surfaces or boundaries are made: the "I" and "we" are shaped by, and even take the shape of, contact with others [ . . . ]. Emotions [ . . . ] produce the very surfaces and boundaries that allow the individual and the social to be delineated as if they are objects. (2004, 10)

Ahmed locates here the boundary between emotion and self, the personal and the collective, and this boundary discursively reflects the histories embedded in emotion. I felt this connection resonate during my interview with Won. According to Won, hashtags used online are able to spread further because of their accessibility and the option for anonymity. As I have argued, hashtags not only are used for protests, but also function online as an archival tool. Following my discussion on Ahmed's work on emotion and action, I argue that online tools are capable of performativity and powerful action. The physical and temporal space afforded by online tools illustrates the theoretical investments of Austin, Derrida, and Butler's work. The citational and performative nature of hashtags allows feminist activists to transition between emotionally charged archives outside of spatial and temporal constraints. I contend that #MeToo is not the only hashtag that has spread virally, but it is the first hashtag that has illustrated the potentiality for hashtags to create citational archives and to bring sociopolitical change.

What I find most compelling about Butler and Ahmed's approaches to citation is that we see this form of feminist citational practices already instituted within Korean feminists' writing.[23] In other words, feminist citationality creates a living archive, regardless of time and space. Although the #MeToo movement today might not appear as it did in January 2018, the hashtag continues the same conversation, and the act of using this hashtag is, for many feminists, an act of solidarity and, to borrow from Ahmed, that of a collective "feminist memory."

## Afterward

As is the case with writing about contemporary topics, many things have transpired in South Korea that have impacted feminist communities since I began writing this chapter in 2019. In July 2020, former mayor of Seoul, Park

Won-soon, committed suicide after being accused by a former secretary of continued sexual harassment. Park was renowned for his support of women's rights and was an advocate for the comfort women.[24] Park's death was a shock to the victim and her supporters, as his death meant the victim had no legal recourse.[25] The COVID-19 pandemic also impacted the momentum of various feminist campaigns and social justice movements. Additionally, the transition from former president Moon Jae-in's liberal government to Yoon Suk-yeol's conservative government was a blow to the feminist movement's momentum. In many ways, Yoon's successful bid was due to a persistent rise in anti-feminist backlash and pro-natalism rhetoric that placed the burden of low birthrates on women being "picky" about their partners and pressuring them to give birth. It is not only anti-feminist politicians and skewed understanding of gender discrimination that further complicate meaningful change. Biased prosecution and lack of legal resources for survivors of sexual violence continue to pose a great obstacle for young women and sexual minorities.

However, as I have demonstrated in this chapter, the citational dimensions of the #MeToo movement mean that, while the popularity of the hashtag may dwindle and other sociopolitical issues will arise, #MeToo maintains a citational reference that connects interlocking anti–sexual violence activism. The #MeToo movement in Korea affected, and continues to affect, all dimensions of feminist activism.

Discussing the "post-#MeToo era," Kwon Kim Hyun-young stresses that she views Korea's #MeToo movement in 2018 "as a historical milestone in the Korean feminist movement as it was basically women's solidarity fighting violence against women," and that the interpretation that #MeToo is an "import" from the United States is a "colonialist interpretation" (2018b, p. 104).[26] I agree with Kwon Kim's framing of Korea's #MeToo as both separate from the U.S. and other international #MeToo movements, and as an ongoing movement with considerable public presence and effect.

At "The Sixth Rally to End Gender Discrimination and Sexual Violence" held by the Citizen Action with #MeToo Movement on December 1, 2018, in Gwanghwamun square, the information pamphlet for the rally included QR codes that connected to various centers and organizations affiliated with anti–sexual violence activism. By scanning the QR codes, participants could view lists of centers available in their area, including sexual violence relief centers, sexual harassment and sexual violence hotlines, domestic abuse shelters, and hotlines with resources for sex workers. For contemporary activism, physical rally spaces are always connected to their online counterparts, through hashtags and other mediums.

One of the speakers at the start of the rally represented the School #MeToo movement. The *sŭk'ulmit'u undong* movement fought sexual harassment and violence against youth in schools, particularly in middle and high school. Youth feminist activists continue to push back against discrimination in school dress codes, sexual harassment by faculty and male students, and to advocate for feminist education and teachers (Chyuri, 2018; Nam, 2019). At the rally, the School #MeToo representative declared that they are going into 2019 confident in their efforts. The crowd shouted back in support, and the activist thanked everyone before saying, "In the end it will change! School #MeToo will prevail!"—thus echoing the slogan of the rally, "In the end it will change! #MeToo will prevail!"[27] As I have demonstrated in this chapter, there is no "post-#MeToo" or a "second wave" of #MeToo. The citationality of the #MeToo hashtag as a performative utterance online and in person allows its malleability in social time and space. In other words, the #MeToo movement is part of an ongoing citational archive for the larger movement against sexual violence.

## Notes

1. Unless indicated otherwise, Korea refers to the nation-state of South Korea.
2. For a more comprehensive timeline, see the Seoul Foundation of Women and Family's digital gender archive project in Korean: http://genderarchive.or.kr/exhibits/show/timeline/.
3. I have followed the National Institute of Korean Language's guide for the English transliteration and romanization of Korea, which was established in 2000 by the Ministry of Culture Sports and Tourism. For Korean scholars and individuals primarily known in Korea or less known to anglophone readers, I follow the Korean convention of last name, first name (e.g., Sohn Hee-jeong). For scholars or individuals who are known to anglophone readers (e.g., Namhee Lee), I follow the order and transliteration used in English publications.
4. Kim, S. H. (2020) "[Nanŭn kangnamyŏng sedaeimnida①] naega toel su issŏtta. Kŭraesŏ haengdonghanda. [[I am the Gangnam Station ①] It could have been me. So I became an activist]," *The Women's News*, [online]. Available at: http://www.womennews.co.kr/news/articleView.html?idxno=196762 (Accessed November 28, 2022).
5. The research included in this article was supported by a grant from the Academy of Korean Studies in 2018 and a Fulbright grant in 2019. All interviews were conducted in Korean and translated by the author. Unless otherwise noted, all translations from Korean to English are by the author. To maintain confidentiality, names of interview participants have been anonymized. All locations are real places.
6. The Citizens Action with #MeToo Movement [*Mit'u undonggwa hamkkehanŭn shiminhaeng-dong*] is an association representing multiple women's organizations

and feminist communities from across the nation, run by the Korean Women's Association United.

7. There are differences and common strategies employed by activists using #MeToo, #Withyou, and #Speakout. Suffice for our purposes here that these hashtags were prominent throughout the height of the #MeToo movement in South Korea during 2018–2019, but they each signify particular sentiments of speaking out and support for survivors of sexual violence.
8. Daniel Miller et al.'s *Why We Post* series, and in particular *How the World Changed Social Media* (2016), offers an interesting interruption to these tendencies; however, their project does reify other tendencies through their departure from grounded theory and attempts to standardize ethnography. In Korean studies, Jiyeon Kang's *Igniting the Internet: Youth and Activism in Postauthoritarian South Korea* (2016) adds a much welcome focus on the connections between the internet, youth, and political and social activism. However, focusing on youth's activism from the standpoint of the candlelight vigils era (2002–2017) limits the scope of Kang's project to a binary online-to-offline activist relationship.
9. Throughout this chapter, I purposefully refrain from using overtly technical terms because, in discussing communities that are driven by emotion and that are activism-based, the binaries of real/actual and online/offline do not capture the characteristics of contemporary marginalized communities.
10. *Femiwiki* is a feminist volunteer-run open wiki project aimed at providing a feminist alternative to what is seen as entrenched sexist approaches to topics related to women and sexual minority rights in the more popular *Namuwiki* and in the original Wikipedia. *Femiwiki* quotes the #my_sexual_abuse_in_00 as most popular in the literature and art worlds (#munhwagye_nae_sŏngp'ongnyŏk). For further information, see: https://femiwiki.com.
11. During my dissertation research fieldwork, I volunteered with the Korea Sexual Violence Relief Center, a leading anti–sexual violence advocacy and nongovernmental organization, and Fireworks Femi Action, a grassroots anti–sexual violence and women's reproductive rights organization. While this chapter primarily focuses on #MeToo activism in Seoul, I discuss regional feminist activism elsewhere.
12. For a more thorough discussion on the South Korean comfort women, see Zhouran Deng's Chapter 2 in this volume.
13. See: *Kangnamyŏk 10pŏn ch'ulgu, 1004kaeŭi p'osŭt'ŭit [Gangnam Subway Station Exit 10, 1004 Post-It Notes]* (Seoul: Namuyŏnp'il, 2016) and *Kangnamyŏk 10pŏn ch'ulgu ak'aibŭ* [The Gangnam Subway Exit 10 Archive] on Facebook.
14. In this chapter I follow Tom Boellstroff's approach (2012, p. 22) and do not use pluralization for the contemporary South Korean feminist movement. This chapter is invested in defining the current shape of the anti–sexual violence movement, rather than parsing out the multiplicities of South Korean feminism.
15. Although not explicitly mentioned by name in her interview, Yeo is most likely referring to a popular book among feminists written by feminist film scholar Sohn Hee-jeong, "*p'eminijŭm ribut'ŭ: hyŏmoŭi shidaerŭl ttulk'o naon moksoridŭl*"

[*Feminism Reboot: Voices That Pierce Through an Era of Hatred*] (Seoul: Namuyŏnp'il Publishing, 2017).

16. This divide is shared across organizations. For instance, the Korean Women Workers Association's reference library online separates "pre-2016" and "post-2016" references (http://kwwnet.org/).
17. There are many articles available online in English. In particular, see: Kwak, S., "South Korea Joins the #MeToo Movement," 2018, *Huffingtonpost* [online]. Available at: https://www.huffingtonpost.com/entry/south-korea-metoo_us_5a79fcfae4b06505b4e8b592 (Accessed July 18, 2021). Cho, S. H., "A Director's Apology Adds Momentum to South Korea's #MeToo Movement," 2018, *The New York Times* [online]. Available at: https://www.nytimes.com/2018/02/19/world/asia/south-korea-metoo-lee-youan-taek.html (Accessed July 18, 2021). Steger, I. "The 'Pence Rule' Is Trending in South Korea as #MeToo Takes Hold," 2018, *Quartz* [online]. Available at: https://qz.com/1223456/metoo-in-south-korea-pence-rule-trends-on-naver-as-men-try-to-avoid-sexual-harassment-accusations/ (Accessed July 18, 2021).
18. For instance: Fendos, J. "The #metoo Movement Finally Arrives in South Korea," *The Diplomat* [online], 2018. Available at: https://thediplomat.com/2018/02/the-metoo-movement-finally-arrives-in-south-korea/ (Accessed July 18, 2021).
19. #MeToo in Korea is transliterated using *mit'u* (or *mit'u undong* for #MeToo activism), thus keeping the hashtag phonetically the same, meaning the word in English is written in Korean as it is pronounced in English.
20. Although I unfold the history of modern and contemporary feminist activism in another chapter, earlier scholarly publications do fine work explaining the history and centrality of the anti–sexual violence movement. For examples, see: Chung (1997); Kim, Young-Lan (2002); and, Oh, Hye-ran (1997).
21. Originally titled "#haeshit'aegŭ #kumŏng" with the subheader "in + mun muk'ŭji [haeshit'aegŭ] vol. 1." *Inmun* can be translated as "humanities" or "liberal arts," coming from the Chinese characters for "humanity" and "literature." What the editors of this volume call "muk'ŭji" is an older term that I have translated as "publication," because these publications are neither magazines nor books, but are more similar to serial anthologies with multiple volumes and edited chapters by Moon Hyong-Jun and other collaborators. I translated the title of this publication as "*Humanistic Publication #Hashtag vol. 1: #hole*" as this is how it appears indexed in Korean on online portals, such as Naver.
22. Butler expands on this aspect of citation for gender performativity in both *Gender Trouble* (1990) and *Bodies That Matter* (1993).
23. This chapter is part of the second chapter in my doctoral dissertation, *Feminist Assemblages: Contemporary South Korean Feminist Activism and Communities*. The research for this chapter was made possible with a generous grant by the Academy of Korean Studies in 2018. An original aim of my dissertation project was to create a working list of feminist writing with the titles translated into English, but that is outside the scope of this project. At the time of writing this chapter, I was particularly thinking about publications on various mediums, whether published in scholarly edited collections (the Korea Women's Studies Institute's *Gender and*

*Society: 15 Perspectives on Women and Men* [*Chendŏwa sahoe: 15 kaeŭi shisŏnŭro ingnŭn yŏsŏnggwa namsŏng*] (2018), Kwon Kim Hyun-young's edited series (but in particular, the recent publication of *Feminism for Victims and Perpetrators* [*P'ihaewa kahaeŭi p'eminijŭm*], 2018), and numerous scholarly articles, online blog posts (such as on *Ildaro*, an online independent feminist magazine), and on social media.

24. "Comfort women" refers to women and girls forced into sexual slavery by the Japanese Imperial Army during World War II.
25. Some female National Assembly members expressed doubt in the victim and sided with Park's legacy. This form of secondary victimization, where the survivor is subjected to secondary assault or harassment, demonstrates the limitations of institutional solidarity with the anti–sexual violence movement.
26. Parts of this chapter appear in chapter 2 of my doctoral dissertation. There, I clarify the points of contact and difference between "women" and "feminism," and the ways women's organizations and grassroots feminist groups have used these, separate yet similar, terms for different purposes throughout the history of Korean feminist activism.
27. I have loosely translated here "Kyŏlgugen pakkunda! Sŭk'ul mit'u-ga haenaenda!" and "Kyŏlgugen pakkunda! Mit'u-ga haenaenda!" respectively.

## Works Cited


Ahmed, Sara. 2004. *The Cultural Politics of Emotion*. New York: Edinburgh University Press.

Ahmed, Sara. 2017. *Living a Feminist Life*. Durham, NC, and London: Duke University Press.

Austin, J. L. 1962. *How to Do Things with Words*. London: Oxford University Press.

Baik, Mi-Youn. 2019. "The Transition of Feminist Politics after the Korean #MeToo Movement: Toward 'Politics of Solidarity' [Han'guk Mit'u Undong ihu P'eminijŭm Chŏngch'iŭi Chŏnhwan: 'Yŏndaeŭi Chŏngch'i'rŭl Hyanghayŏ]." *The Korean Review of Political Thought* 25, no. 2: 68–92.

bell hooks. 2000. *Feminism Is for Everybody: Passionate Politics*. London: Pluto Press.

Berlant, Lauren. 2011. *Cruel Optimism*. Durham, NC: Duke University Press.

Boellstroff, Tom. 2012. "The Politics of Similitude: Global Sexuality Activism, Ethnography, and the Western Subject." *Trans-Scripts* 2: 22–39.

Butler, Judith. 1990. *Gender Trouble: Feminism and the Subversion of Identity*. New York and London: Routledge.

Butler, Judith. 1993. *Bodies That Matter*. New York and London: Routledge.

Chung, Hyun-back. 1997. "Together and Separately; 'The New Women's Movement' after the 1980s in South Korea." *Asian Women* 5: 19–38.

Chyuri. 2018. "The Status of School Me Too Activism and Teenagers [*Sŭk'ulmit'uundonggwa Ch'ŏngsonyŏnŭi Chiwi*]." *Journal of Feminist Theories and Practices* 38: 56–64.

Cohen, Jerome A., and Edward J. Baker. 1991. "U.S. Foreign Policy and Human Rights in South Korea." In *Human Rights in Korea Historical and Policy Perspectives*, edited by William Shaw, pp. 171–220. Cambridge, MA: Harvard University Press.

Collins, Patricia Hill. 1986. "Learning from the Outsider Within: The Sociological Significance of Black Feminist Thought." *Social Problems* 33, no. 6: S14–S32.

Crenshaw, Kimberle. 1989. "Demarginalizing the Intersection of Race and Sex: A Black Feminist Critique of Antidiscrimination Doctrine, Feminist Theory and Antiracist Politics." *University of Chicago Legal Forum* 1, no. 8: 139–167. http://chicagounbound.uchicago.edu/uclf/vol1989/iss1/8.

Derrida, Jacques. 1988. "Signature Event Context." In *Limited Inc.*, translated by Samuel Weber and Jeffrey Mehlman, pp. 1–23. Evanston, IL: Northwestern University Press.

Harding, Sandra G. 2004. "Rethinking Standpoint Epistemology: What Is 'Strong Objectivity'?" In *The Feminist Standpoint Theory Reader: Intellectual and Political Controversies*, edited by Sandra Harding, pp. 127–140. New York: Routledge.

Harding, Sandra G. 2009. "Standpoint Theories: Productively Controversial." *Hypatia* 24, no. 4: 192–200. http://www.jstor.org/stable/20618189.

Jung, Kyungja. 2014. *Practicing Feminism in South Korea: The Women's Movement against Sexual Violence*. New York: Routledge.

Kendall, Laurel. 2002. *Under Construction the Gendering of Modernity, Class, and Consumption in the Republic of Korea*. Honolulu: University of Hawaii Press.

Kim, Elaine H., and Chungmoo Choi. 1998. *Dangerous Women: Gender and Korean Nationalism*. New York: Routledge.

Kim, Eun-Joo. 2019. "Online-Feminism as Fourth Wave: Contemporary Feminism's Politic and Technology [*Che4mulgyŏllosŏ ollain-p'eminijŭm: tongshidae p'eminijŭmŭi chŏngch'iwa kisul*]." *Korean Feminism Philosophy* 31: 1–32.

Kim, Hee-Kang. 2009. "Should Feminism Transcend Nationalism? A Defense of Feminist Nationalism in South Korea." *Women's Studies International Forum* 32: 108–119.

Kim, Seo Hyun. 2020. "[Nanŭn kangnamyŏng sedaeimnida①] naega toel su issŏtta. Kŭraesŏ haengdonghanda. [[I am the Gangnam Station ①] It could have been me. So I became an activist]." *The Women's News*. http://www.womennews.co.kr/news/articleView.html?idxno=196762.

Kim, Young-Lan. 2002. "Study on the Differentiation of Women's Movement Organization of Korea in the 1980s." *Asian Women* 15: 165–196.

Kim, Young Soon. 2018. "Me Too Movement and the Feminist Movement." In *Seoul Human Rights Conference*, edited by Seoul Metropolitan, pp. 37–54. Seoul.

Koo, Hagen. 2002. *Korean Workers: The Culture and Politics of Class Formation*. Ithaca, NY: Cornell University Press.

Kwon Kim, Hyun-young. 2018a. "Me Too—The Ethical and Political Transformation of the Me Too Anti-Sexual Violence Movement [*Mit'u, Pansŏngp'ongnyŏk Undongŭi Yun-ri-Chŏngch'ijŏk Chŏnhwan*]." *Literary Community* 95: 309–310.

Kwon Kim, Hyun-young. 2018b. "For a New Society in the Post-Me Too Era." In *Seoul Human Rights Conference*, edited by Seoul Metropolitan, pp. 103–106. Seoul.

Lee, Jin-kyung. 2010. *Service Economies: Militarism, Sex Work, and Migrant Labor in South Korea*. Minneapolis: University of Minnesota Press.

Lee, Namhee. 2007. *The Making of Minjung: Democracy and the Politics of Representation in South Korea*. Ithaca, NY: Cornell University Press.

Moon, Hyong-Jun et al. 2015. *Humanistic Publication #Hashtag vol. 1: #hole*. Seoul: Booknomad Press.

Nam, Mi Ja. 2019. "Now Here, the Significance of Youth Feminist Movement." *Education Review* 43: 39–62.

Nash, Jennifer C. 2019. *Black Feminism Reimagined: After Intersectionality*. Durham, NC: Duke University Press.

Nelson, Laura C. 2000. *Measured Excess: Status, Gender, and Consumer Nationalism in South Korea*. New York: Columbia University Press.

Oh, Hye-ran. 1997. "Activities of Women's Organizations in Korea." *Asian Women* 5: 145–155.

Poirot, Kristan. 2014. *A Question of Sex: Feminism, Rhetoric, and Differences That Matter*. Amherst and Boston: University of Massachusetts Press.

Silver, Anna Krugovoy. 2002. "The Cyborg Mystique: 'The Stepford Wives' and Second Wave Feminism." *Women's Studies Quarterly* 30, no. 1–2: 60–76. http://www.jstor.org/stable/40004637.

Springer, Kimberly. 2002. "Third Wave Black Feminism?" *Signs* 27, no. 4: 1059–1082. doi:10.1086/339636.

Thompson, Becky. 2002. "Multiracial Feminism: Recasting the Chronology of Second Wave Feminism." *Feminist Studies* 28, no. 2: 337–360. doi:10.2307/3178747.

Wells, Kenneth. 1999. "The Price of Legitimacy: Women and the Kuˇnuhoe Movement, 1927–1931." In *Colonial Modernity in Korea*, edited by Gi-Wook Shin and Michael Robinson, pp. 191–220. Cambridge, MA: Harvard University Press.

Yoo, Ji Ahn. 2018. "Me Too, Speaking Out from the Position of a Survivor: On 'Exclusion' and the Possibility for Solidarity [*Mit'u, saranamŭn charieső marhagi: 'kkwŏn paejet'wa yŏndaeŭi kanŭngsŏngŭl chungshimŭ-ro*]." *Culture/Science* 9: 74–99.

Yun, Jiyŏng. 2018. "A Tidal Wave of Revolution Called Me Too: Dissecting Rape Culture through the Prism of Feminism [*Mit'uranŭn hyŏngmyŏngŭi haeil-p'eminijŭm p'ŭrijŭmŭ-ro kangganmunhwa haebuhagi*]." *The New Korean Association of English Language and Literature*: 105–122.

# 2

# The Politics of Dwelling

## Screen Memories of "Comfort Women" in the Age of #MeToo

*Ran Deng*

### Timeline

- 1900s: Instigated by the emergence of Western imperialism in East Asia in the nineteenth century, Japan adopted colonial techniques to strengthen its military and consolidate its power as a nation. By 1910, it had incorporated Korea into its empire, and by 1937, it controlled Manchuria and initiated full-scale war in China (Seybolt).
- 1932: The "comfort women" system was established in 1932 by the Japanese Imperial Army (JIA). "Comfort women" were women and girls coerced into performing sexual and physical labor for Japanese soldiers. Some were held hostage in the so-called "comfort stations", often converted from brothels or other entertainment venues, while others were repeatedly assaulted in their homes. According to the JIA, the "comfort women" system was established in an attempt to boost morale for the soldiers and avoid sexually transmitted diseases. It was also claimed that the "comfort women" system would prevent soldiers from sexually assaulting civilian women (Qiu et al., 2014).
- 1932: The first known "comfort station," *dai-ichi salon*, was established in Shanghai in 1932. It hosted "comfort women" from China, Korea, Japan, and the Philippines.
- 1945: It is estimated that, by the end of the Pacific War in 1945, approximately 200,000 women were forced to perform sexual acts by the JIA.
- 1991: On August 14, Kim Hak-Sun testified about her experience as a "comfort woman" during the war, making her the first Korean woman who publicly came forward. Kim asserted that her coming forth was encouraged by the feminist movement in South Korea. One year later, Wan Ai-Hua became the first Chinese woman who openly spoke about her experience of being sexually abused by Japanese soldiers.

Ran Deng, *The Politics of Dwelling* In: *The Other #MeToos*. Edited by: Iqra Shagufta Cheema, Oxford University Press.
 DOI: 10.1093/oso/9780197619872.003.0002

- Post-1991: Since then, there have been various forms of creative representations of the "comfort women" issue, some of which include the famous "Statue of Peace" designed by Kim Seo-Kyung and Kim Eun-Sung; the filmic trilogy documenting the lives of "comfort women" by Byun Young-Joo; and the multimedia art exhibition hosted by the House of Sharing outside Seoul, South Korea.

## Introduction

As I browsed around the archive affiliated with the Chinese "Comfort Women" History Museum in Shanghai, my attention was arrested by a wooden structure inside the windowless room. It looked like a cabin less than 30 square feet, with a small bedframe on one end and a few buckets lined up on the other, and there was almost no space in between (Figures 2.1 and 2.2). According to the description, it was a replica of the lodging occupied by a "comfort woman," one of approximately 200,000 who were coerced into performing sexual acts by the Japanese Imperial Army (JIA) and its accomplices from 1932 to 1945. Coincidentally, the screening room next door was projecting a recording of a documentary produced by China Central Television (CCTV), *Leave or Stay: On the Historical Site of a "Comfort Station."* As I watched the reporter traverse the alleyways in central Shanghai and interview residents were largely unaware that over a hundred "comfort women" from China, North Korea, and Japan used to be held hostage in their apartment building, I was overwhelmed by a strange sense of displacement. It felt as if the architecture of the "comfort station" in these multimedia facsimiles collapsed into itself and became unrecognizable. As the sole occupant of the museum space, I became acutely self-conscious of my own gaze shifting between the material and immaterial receptacles that hold on to the memories of the "comfort woman."

How do these empty spaces become sites full of meaning? Who are the imagined residents and, moreover, who are temporarily allowed into such places as visitors of "national shame?" To ponder upon these questions, one cannot but turn to the medium—the architectural, historical, and digital dwelling—that retains and rearticulates memories through its affective physicality. What is at stake when one retrospectively serves as a historical witness in a mediated state, watching a "comfort station" being converted into a parking lot on the projector screen while standing steps away from a recreation of the very site on which "comfort women" were sexually abused? Furthermore, as the documentary proceeds, one sees a video footage of Wan Ai-Hua, one of the first Chinese "comfort women" who came forward in the 1990s, faint as she testified at the Women's International War Crimes Tribunal on Japan's Military Sexual Slavery in Tokyo in 2000. As the narration carries on, however, the affective intensity of Wan's momentary loss of

**Figure 2.1.** Replica of a survivor's room in Yang Jia Zhai, "Comfort Station," 2021.

consciousness, as well as the emotive reaction it invokes in the viewer, becomes complicated by the nationalist desire to reactivate trauma as visceral evidence against Japanese atrocities during the Pacific War.

In this visual site of storytelling, the boundary between the virtual and the actual is blurred by the endeavor to recount history in a coherent narrative as stable as the structure of the "comfort station" replica. One cannot but note that the "comfort woman" lives on in the public imaginary as nothing but a body debilitated by national trauma. In addition to the affective exploitation of the sentimental capacity of the image of the "comfort woman," the filmic narrative also reveals a politics of memory that hinges upon one's relation to the present and the law. While the aging presence of survivors such as Wan serves to demand immediate action, it simultaneously reduces the women's humanity to an empty vessel for historical urgency. In other words, the survivors' willingness to come forward as witnesses of the atrocities against their own flesh becomes requisite to the efficacy of the redress movement and its transnational influence, resulting in a conception of the past only as "passing," verifiable only through a regulated and disciplined notion of the self as survivor. In this sense, the politics of memory suggests that redress relies on a form of narratology which recognizes the

**Figure 2.2.** Replica of a survivor's room (interior) in Yang Jia Zhai, "Comfort Station," 2021.

grieving self only as a component of the globalized legal homogenization. How does the figure of the "comfort woman" inhabit the contemporary geopolitical landscape in and beyond East Asia through visual documentation? Moreover, with the advent of the #MeToo movement, many East Asian filmmakers have begun to reconceptualize the redress movement for the "comfort woman" issue with the painful realization that the past is never past. Filmmakers such as Yoo Bo-Ra, Emmanuel Moonchil Park, and Cho Jung-Rae make connections between the "comfort woman," the traumatized figure whose fading memory has nonetheless been publicized, and young survivors of sexual assault who cannot yet (and sometimes are not permitted to) articulate what happened to them. How has the redress movement for "comfort women" been adapting to and learning from one of the most influential digital media movements addressing sexual violence, and vice versa? This chapter engages with the memorialization, embodiment, and "dwelling-on" of the "comfort woman," in addition to the tenuous relationships between personal and collective memory, the complexity of the state's articulation of trauma, as well as the possibility of redress and reparation through creative affiliations.

This chapter highlights the ways in which these historical figures are embodied in filmic projects and, subsequently, how they are reimagined both in the context of current geopolitical entanglements and in the context of contemporary movements against gender-based violence. Through an examination of Chinese and South Korean documentary and drama films concurrently depicting the "comfort women" issue and ongoing gender-based and sexual violence, I argue that the organization of a collective past can be harmful precisely to those who are intended to be preserved in the process. Nevertheless, even as many documentary films inadvertently run the risk of channeling extremely individualized experiences into a political rhetoric, the imagined communities that are born out of these projects can sometimes renegotiate the ways in which historically compromised subjects are co-opted and incorporated into the biopolitical construction of the nation-state. In light of the #MeToo movement, these creative projects exhibit what I term a "fragmented collectivity," or a dispersed solidarity that is predicated upon anonymity and partiality which, as a result, constitute an alternative account of clandestine yet intimate association. By centering the #MeToo movement acclimated to East Asia, I argue that the strategic adoption of the narrative of #MeToo in activist projects presenting "comfort women" not only circumvents censorship, but also reworks the dichotomies between the personal and the political, the singular and the collective, as well as the imagined and embodied truths that are at once suppressed and excavated in the process of collective memorialization. #MeToo releases the historical stasis in which the figure of the "comfort woman" is often locked and serves as a creative dwelling that animates and contemporizes the historical figure while addressing the pressing issue of sexual violence in China and South Korea.

I begin with a historical analysis of the "comfort women" issue and its entanglement with the development of feminist discourses in China and South Korea across different periods. This section aims to parse through the (post) colonial, legal, and political legacy of the issue and identify the ways in which the law, state agencies, and conventional views of female sexuality simultaneously contribute to the subjection of East Asian women. I then provide an overview of appearances of the "comfort woman" in filmic projects to illustrate how competing discourses on nationalism and feminism evolve and intersect with each other from the 1960s to the present. More specifically, I discuss two recent films whose releases coincided with the emergence of the #MeToo movement in East Asia to demonstrate the originary meanings that these projects attach to the image of the "comfort women" through forming alliances with the #MeToo survivor. In 2017, independent Chinese filmmaker Guo Ke released his full-length documentary film, *Twenty-Two*, in which he interviews remaining survivors of the "comfort women" system. Released under the supervision of the National Radio and Television Administration, the film nevertheless interlaces the formulated overtone with moments of slippage, shifting constantly between historical sites of sexual abuse and the surviving women's decaying lodgings in their twilight years. By featuring each survivor's story, *Twenty-Two* sends a coded message that the patriarchal prejudice against sexually abused women continues to haunt the survivors through a politics of respectability, and that their feeling of displacement persists due to the recognition of the redress movement only as a collective project. Similarly, the 2016 South Korean drama film, *Spirits' Homecoming*, reflects on the sense of loss of national and familial belonging. Curiously, *Spirits' Homecoming* makes a radical turn to Korean shamanism as an inventive form of reparation. The film plays with the oscillation between embodiment and displacement by repositing the consciousness of a former "comfort woman" onto a teenage girl whose father was murdered while saving her from attempted rape. Like many other recent productions, such as *Snowy Road* (2015) by Yoo Bo-Ra and *Comfort* (2020) by Emmanuel Moonchil Park, *Spirits' Homecoming* personalizes the "comfort women" issue by attending to its affiliation with ongoing events of sexual violence. It therefore unsettles the static imaginary that hems the redress movement in the national and the historical, and instead marks the presence of the "comfort woman" as an enlivened figure that perseveres through its own supernatural displacement.

Through the two films, I aim to show the affective tools that are enlisted in the collective remembering of these highly singular traumatic events, as well as the ways in which the emergence of the #MeToo movement can help us build strategies to envisage how the "comfort woman" may live beyond the public imaginary. Through a highly personal approach, these films help us make sense of the survivors' partial being, agency, and self-presence, despite the tremendous pain they carry. By remaining in solitude, participants of #MeToo, like many former "comfort women" who are not able to come forward, find avenues to commemorate singular events of trauma without making themselves fully legible. Like the films suggest, the framework of what I call "fragmented collectivity" dissolves the physical constraints posed by the surviving body of the "comfort woman" and reassembles it through translatable embodiments across generations. I argue that #MeToo and its digitalized dissimilation redefine what it means to dwell in the world, personally and anonymously, while pointing to an obscured identity that is relational and ever-expanding.

## Historical Analysis

Although the redress movement for "comfort women" was in many ways inspired by the growing feminist activities in East Asia, the trajectory of the movement did not proceed at the same pace as the development of feminist activism. While women's liberation movements were recognized in the 1970s in both nations, the figure of the "comfort woman" did not gain political currency until the early 1990s, when discussions on (post)colonial order and global capitalism reached a tidemark after the end of the Cold War. As Lisa Yoneyama (2016) summarizes, the Cold War order "[obfuscates] violence and the way it selectively addressed and redressed egregious violations during the Japanese war of aggression" (p. 30). Further, the obscurity of what Yoneyama terms "the post–Cold War redress culture" is intensified by a sense of historical urgency as the survivors pass away; the insistence on judicial closure has led to a transnational display of the surviving "comfort women" who have come forward, sometimes regardless of their health conditions and will.[1]

The status of the redress movement was further complicated when, on October 16, 2014, the Japanese government requested the United Nations to partially retract its 1996 report on the "comfort women" issue, which details the sexual abuse against women from Korea, China, Taiwan, the Philippines, and other countries during the Pacific War (Panda, 2014). Although the request was denied by the United Nations, it revealed the prevailing trend in which Japanese conservative politicians still challenged the veracity of the testimonies with regard to women's suffering during the Pacific War. More recently, in March 2021, Harvard law professor J. Mark Ramseyer published an article titled "Contracting for Sex in the Pacific War," which claims that "comfort women" were voluntary contract workers employed by the JIA, which sparked outrage in and beyond the United States (Pimentel, 2021). In the meanwhile, however, in South Korea and China, the transnational redress movement for "comfort women" has taken off and attracted much public attention as early as 1991. On August 14, 1991, Kim Hak-Sun became the first Korean woman who came forth to testify to her life as a "comfort woman" and, together with a few other survivors, filed a lawsuit against the Japanese government demanding an apology and monetary compensation in December (Soh, 1996, p. 1226). While Kim maintained that her actions were inspired by the growing feminist movements in South Korea, she was mainly assisted by the Korean Council for the Women Drafted for Military Sexual Slavery by Japan (Korean Council) (Kazue, 2016). Since then, with the help of domestic and international organizations such as the Korean Council and the Washington Coalition for Comfort Women Issues, many others have begun to speak up about wartime violence against women in South Korea.

However, although the redress movement emerged in conjunction with activities that foregrounded individuals' testimonies to some extent, many scholars notice that it was quickly co-opted by the South Korean nationalist discourse (Yang, 1998; Seo, 2008). While the women who came forward were mainly supported by non-governmental organizations, the content and presentation of their testimonies were often regulated by the state's conceptualization of the "comfort woman" as a symbol of colonial injury and postcolonial subjugation.

Further, the redress movement "deploys patriarchal norms of female sexuality," which requires the female survivors to perform a specific form of victimhood in order for their experiences to be recognized and restituted (Yang, 1998). For instance, the redress movement often portrays the "comfort stations" as concentration camps when, in reality, many "comfort women" were assaulted in their own homes (Soh, 1996). This performative narratology creates a gap between what Sarah Chunghee Soh calls "the Korean Council's master narrative," which offers a canonized story that invokes a form of "hate nationalism," and the survivors' personalized accounts of their experiences. Additionally, the implementation of a "master narrative" against Japan is partially constructed as a national strategy to draw attention away from the "collaborator issue." During the Pacific War, many Koreans, including former president Park Chung-Hee (1963–1979) and other high-profile politicians, participated in the subjugation and enslavement of civilians. Many of these "collaborators" assisted with the coercion of "comfort women," fabricating work opportunities as an attempt to lure them to Manchuria.

In "Politics of Memory in Korea and China: Remembering the Comfort Women and the Nanjing Massacre," Jungmin Seo identifies a connection between the national co-option of the "comfort women" issue and that of the first high-profile case of sexual assault in South Korea. In 1986, a twenty-three-year-old South Korean activist, Kwon In-Suk, filed charges against six police officers for sexually harassing her during interrogation in connection with public demonstration. The incident quickly became a symbol for police brutality and led to nationwide protests (*LA Times*, 1986). However, despite the social awareness that these protests raised, Seo (2008) notes that the incident itself was "interpreted, understood, and narrated as the state's brutality against the labor movement and progressive political forces, but not against women" (p. 375). Seo then compares the aftermath of the incident with the way in which Korean society publicly acknowledged the "comfort women" issue, which can only be "contextualized as part of a larger political agenda." Both events are representative of how women were narrated into the nation's remasculinization project after Japanese colonialism, becoming tropes through which Korean men regain agency by laying claim to their female counterparts.

Unlike in South Korea, the "comfort women" issue did not come to public attention concurrent with the development of feminist discourse in mainland China. As Lily Wong (2016) observes, the voices of Chinese survivors are noticeably lacking in the transnational "comfort women" redress movement. Often narrated as a part of the redress movement for the Nanjing Massacre,[2] the "comfort women" issue in China first gained public attention through the Japanese textbook controversy in 1982, during which the Chinese Foreign Ministry issued statements decrying the government-approved Japanese history textbooks' omission of atrocities such as the "comfort women" system and the 731 Unit. In the late 1980s and early 1990s, scholars who were inspired by protests and conferences in South Korea, such as Zhang Shuangbin, Su Zhiliang, and Chen Lifei, begun gathering ethnographic data about "comfort women" around China, often paying out-of-pocket for travel expenses, as their activities were not funded by the public universities. However, it was not until 1995 that Wan Ai-Hua filed the first lawsuit on the "comfort women" issue in China. Since then, the "comfort women" issue has taken off in two different directions: on the one hand, it has continued to be appropriated by the government as an ethnocentric portrayal of atrocities by Japanese imperialism; on the other hand, it has been employed by grassroots organizations as a symbolic act of redress for everyday violence against women in an attempt to bypass Internet censorship in the past decade.

As Lily Wong (2016) describes, "comfort women" "live on in the public imaginary, with a life of their own in cultural productions" in China (p. 154). Indeed, the direction of the redress movement has been largely dependent on China's political trends, especially its relationship with Japan in the past decades. During an informal interview I conducted in 2020, researchers at the Shanghai Normal University reminisced that, in the early 1990s, it was extremely difficult to secure research funding to work on the issue, since the government then had a stronger emphasis on strengthening the so-called Sino-Japanese friendship. In contrast, as Sino-Japanese relations have worsened in recent years, there has been rising interest in addressing the "comfort women" issue alongside the Nanking Massacre. The shifting discourse about the "comfort women" issue demonstrates that the survivors are "the objects of the Japanese brutality but not necessarily the subjects of suffering" in the official discourse (Seo, 2008, p. 384). In other words, the figure of the "comfort woman" is only excavated and animated at times of national need, as a spectacle of enormous pain that aims to attract public attention and encourage a form of "hate nationalism."

However, the emergence and popularization of the #MeToo movement has brought new insight to the "comfort women" issue. Although in both China and South Korea, there is still a strong sense of anti-feminist sentiment, the #MeToo movement has inspired people to address gender-based violence in a more strategic yet powerful way. In China, #MeToo as a hashtag and a slogan has been adopted by activist groups, many of which use homophones and later emojis to circumvent social media censorship. In addition, these activist movements borrow from the movement for "comfort women," portraying it not as a nationalist redress issue, but rather as a proof that sexual violence has been historically present and that change must be demanded in the here and now. From crowdfunding for films to underground publications addressing sexual violence, the "comfort women" issue has, in many ways, transformed itself and taken a new life in the feminist discourse of #MeToo.

The rest of this chapter engages with recent filmic representations of "comfort women" to showcase the creative, albeit often subtle, collaborations between the two movements. Filmic projects, unlike written texts, offer an embodiment that is visual, visceral, and affective. They can also be inventive in the associations and references that they draw upon in order to portray the subjects. The following section points to examples of feminist solidarity through filmic representations of "comfort women" and how recent films move away from framing them as fixed receptacles of national trauma. By working through the connections between the historical issue and ongoing attempts to address sexual violence against women in these films, I underscore the way #MeToo conjures up an imaginary dwelling for *all* survivors of sexual violence across time and space.

Though most people are only familiar with filmic projects addressing the "comfort women" issue in the past three decades, the first filmed proof of Korean "comfort women" dates back to 1944 (Kim, 2017). Since then, the arguably most internationally known documentary series on the issue is Byun Young-Joo's trilogy: *The Murmuring* (1995), *Habitual Sadness: Korean Comfort Women Today* (1997), and *My Own Breathing* (1999). In more recent years, docu-dramatic representations such as *Spirits' Homecoming* (Cho Jung-Rae, 2016) and *I Can Speak* (Kim Hyun-Seok, 2017) were produced and well received in South Korea.

In comparison, despite the noticeable lack of scholarship on representations of Chinese "comfort women," one of the first films about "comfort women," *The Bamboo House of Dolls* (Kuei Chih-Hung), appeared as early as 1972 (Wong, 2016). Other filmic depictions of Chinese and Taiwanese "comfort women" include *Military Comfort Women* (Ryuichi Takamori, 1974), *Gai Shanxi and Her Sisters* (Ban Zhongyi, 2007), and more recently, documentary films such as *Song of the Reed* (Wu Hsiu-Ching, 2015) and *Twenty-Two* (Guo Ke, 2017). While earlier films often "straddle the fine line between sexploitation and melodrama," films produced in mainland China in the past decade often take the form of documentary and are supervised and sometimes endorsed by the National Radio and Television Administration (Wong, 2016, p. 158). These films often take on a more serious tone, addressing the atrocities that "comfort women" had to endure, as well as condemning the JIA for its colonial expansion in East Asia during the Pacific War.

In *Unfolding the "Comfort Women" Debates: Modernity, Violence, Women's Voices* (2016), Maki Kimura asks whether representation beyond exploitation and epistemic violence is possible when approaching the "comfort women" issue. Drawing from scholarship on the representability of the Holocaust, Kimura stresses that "the attempt to probe the limit of representation reinforces its value, particularly the dichotomy of facts and interpretation" (p. 177). In the context of the Holocaust, the commercial success of comedic films such as *The Producer* (Sidney Glazier, 1967), *Look Who's Back* (David Wnendit, 2015), and *Jojo Rabbit*

(Taika Waititi, 2019) makes one question whether there can be ways to represent the Holocaust beyond the documentary approach. Similarly, the representation of "comfort women" has taken on creative forms in recent productions, which invoke an ambivalence about the truth-telling imperative and the ethics of representational accuracy.

Indeed, the demand for representational accuracy requires that only lifelike depictions of historical events should be produced in order to elicit "proper" affective responses in the audience. As a result, film directors often "attempt to create a mimetic correspondence between text and event" (Rothberg, 2009, p. 177). Although mimetic correspondence may help avoid portraying "comfort women" as sexualized figures for the male gaze, it also limits possibilities for creative presentations that cut through generational or spatial constraints. To further Michael Rothberg's observation, Kimura suggests that we consider films on "comfort women" as a communication, rather than a one-way depiction or consumption of the historical figure (2016). Kimura suggests that, much like a translation, the film is always a dialectic engagement between the filmmaker, the characters, and the audience. It is through the push and pull between encoding and decoding that the message about "comfort women" is delivered.

Unlike the representational issues related to the Holocaust, there are two unique challenges when depicting the "comfort women." First, the "comfort women" issue is inextricable from the decolonial project and how it has reconfigured the role of "Asian femininity." In anti-colonial discourses in both China and South Korea, patriarchal conceptions of women not only put them under the colonial gaze, but also subject them to the remasculinization project (Said, 1978). As colonizers adopt a vision of a feminized East to justify their possessive desires, the remasculinization project imitates the "master's tool" to reclaim sovereignty, once again by foregrounding women's compromised sexuality and reproductive possibilities (Lorde, 2007). Therefore, to reclaim the agency of "comfort women," one must move away from the narrative that "Korean women's sexuality belongs to Korean men" (Chizuko, 2001, p. 18). In addition, in South Korea, many surviving "comfort women" are in fact demanding apology and compensation from the Park Chung-Hee government due to the "collaborative issue," which explains why the redress movement was repressed while Park was in office until 1979 (Seo, 2008). In China's case, the "comfort women" issue created tension between the two oppositional parties, the Chinese Communist Party (CCP) and the Chinese Nationalist Party (KMT), as the latter has been conveniently identified as the Japanese collaborator after the former rose to power in 1949. As a result, the "comfort women" issue stands in for the division of the two Chinas as a symbolic piece of memory, which glorifies the CCP for "saving the nation's thousands of women" (People's Education Press, 2003, p. 108). In both countries, the decolonial project has complicated the redress movement as well as the conception of "Asian femininity," thus obscuring individual survivors' voices and producing a nationalist master narrative instead.

Second, representation of the "comfort women" issue also reflects ongoing problems with social and familial patriarchy in East Asian societies. Historically, Confucian ideologies rate a woman's chastity above her life. A continuation of such beliefs makes "a survivor of rape . . . impure" and "a disgrace to her family," causing a silencing effect among the "comfort women" themselves (Qiu et al., 2014, p. 23). Indeed, when I interviewed anthropologists and historians doing field work in and outside Shanghai, many recounted instances of being turned away by the families of the "comfort women." Similarly, when I completed field work in Seoul, I was told by an anonymous #MeToo activist that to call someone "feminist" is still considered derogatory in Korean society. The continuous effect of patriarchy has restricted the representation of "comfort women," as one must keep in mind that only a small number of survivors have the favorable conditions to disclose their experiences, and even those disclosures are oftentimes compromised.

Nevertheless, in films like *Twenty-Two* and *Spirits' Homecoming*, I identify a "fragmented collectivity" through the foregrounding of personhood beyond the physical body, which affords an abstract dwelling not restricted by temporality or historical accuracy. This dwelling helps construct a collective identity upon the relational intimacy between the figure of the "comfort woman" and other survivors of sexual violence. These films challenge the claim that women are no longer subjugated after colonialism has been declared as "post"; rather, they transpire a desire and a capacity for a movement beyond the legal predilection for the victim-as-witness and envisage an "infinite justice" that can only be recognized through self-translation (Rancière, 2004, p. 309). In "Who Is the Subject of the Rights of Man," Jacques Rancière (2004) proposes the possibility of an "infinite justice." It is an aspirational form of justice that would erase "all the distinctions that used to define the field of justice in general," including "the distinctions between law and fact, legal punishment and private retaliation, justice, police, and war." I follow what Rancière suggests as a possible departure from the "ontological destiny of the human animal," or a teleological project of governmentality that continuously translates the abject figure into a politically sensible subject. In other words, there shall exist an alternative present that is not mediated by structure, grid, rhythm, border, or regulated normativity. In the next section, I examine the film *Spirits' Homecoming*, which in many ways exemplifies the alternative present that Rancière proposes.

*Spirits' Homecoming* is a 2016 drama film directed by Cho Jung-Rae, who spent more than a decade producing the film and relied on crowdfunding to finance its expenses. Despite its box-office success, the film stirred unprecedented controversy at its release (Son, 2019). According to Seyon Jo, many have critiqued that the film prioritizes melodramatic effects and commercial success over historical accuracy. Other voices include the curious "popcorn argument," a popular debate among the audience over whether one should be permitted to eat popcorn while attending the film screening (Jo, 2017). This debate not only shows the Korean audience's discomfort around the "comfort women" issue, but also their contemplation on the political seriousness of film as a medium and an apparatus in the entertainment industry. In addition, one can glean from the "popcorn argument" the Korean audience's sense of ethical responsibility toward the commemoration of the "comfort women" system.

*Spirits' Homecoming* narrates the story of two girls who are drafted into sexual slavery in a "comfort station" in rural Korea during the Pacific War. The story unfolds as two plot lines, one of the past in 1934 and one of the present in 1996, intertwine with the mediation of a young shaman named Eun-Kyung. Young-Ok, a former "comfort woman" who is now in her eighties and diagnosed with cancer, meets Eun-Kyung by chance. Upon seeing the handmade charm that Young-Ok carries, Eun-Kyung immediately faints and experiences flashbacks of a young girl's traumatic story of being kidnapped and coerced into serving as a "comfort woman." At this point, the audience is made to believe that the conjured figure of the young girl is Young-Ok in her teenage years. As the film progresses, Young-Ok realizes that she is unable to come to terms with the death of her friend, Jung-Min, who was confined in the same "comfort station" but did not survive after they both fled more than fifty years ago. Thus, Young-Ok finally allows Eun-Kyung to perform *sitgimgut*, a traditional Korean ritual, to allow the spirit of her deceased friend to return home.

It is important to note that Eun-Kyung's own experience with sexual assault is depicted at the beginning of the film. A mentally disturbed prison escapee breaks into her house while she is asleep, and is attempting to assault her when Eun-Kyung's father comes to her rescue, only to be stabbed to death by the escapee. The close-ups of the escapee gently tracing Eun-Kyung's bare arm with the point of his knife and her petrified expression crystallize unwanted sexual contacts and their aftermath, which highly resemble the depicted experience of "comfort women" in *Spirits' Homecoming*. With her father now gone, Eun-Kyung loses her grounding in the present and develops a connectivity with spirits of the past. Curiously, she becomes the spiritual double for Young-Ok through her own temporal dissociation caused by sexual violence.

In *Cruel Optimism*, Lauren Berlant (2011) anticipates a present that "makes itself present to us before it becomes anything else, such as an orchestrated collective event or an epoch on which we can look back" (p. 4). If we see the growing popularity of documentaries on "comfort women" as an instance of such orchestration, the reliance on shamanism then betrays the drive to authenticate memory and proposes an alternative way to connect with the present that is grounded in a moment of hesitation. Who are the women in the film, and how do they relate to each other? How does pain unleash and actively destroy the official language of redress?

Interestingly, the desire to return home to what is familiar is mediated through the unfamiliar in the film. The uncanniness of the young shaman, who has been possessed by the spirit of a "comfort woman", renders the event both outside the homeliness (*das Heimlich*) of the present and an excavation of what has been concealed. The film's supernatural approach to narration, as well as its melodramatic horror elements, leads to a moment of hesitation in the audience. Further, the viewer of *Spirits' Homecoming* undergoes a process of disidentification and reidentification as the film progresses. When the shaman, Eun-Kyung, embodies the abused "comfort woman," it is natural for the viewer to read her as the young Young-Ok rather than as her friend, Jung-Min, who does not survive the war. It is not until the end that the viewer discovers that, in fact, the summoned young girl in Eun-Kyung's imaginary is not Young-Ok but Jung-Min, who is shot and eventually dies as Young-Ok watches in agonizing distress. Although confusing at first glance, this revelation shatters the viewer's assumption of Jung-Min's survival, with which the viewer assumes a "happy ending" for the protagonist. As Holocaust survivor Ruth Klüger (2003) points out in her memoir *Still Alive: A Holocaust Girlhood Remembered*, the "happy ending" assumption hinders the significance of the debilitating presence of past atrocities, as we tend to ascribe a futurity in the survival of a subject.

The viewer's moment of hesitation is crucial in constructing the aesthetic embodiment of "comfort women" in *Spirits' Homecoming*. It is in the opaque moment that the viewer is in contact with the elements of the poetic, which hinges on the decision to suppress one's uneasiness in order to move forward with the story with a "disbelieving belief" (Todorov, 1975). In *Spirits' Homecoming*, the mediated oscillation between the past and the present clashes with the temporality of history, which leaves the audience uncertain of what it is to be mourned. Furthermore, returning to Berlant (2011), the crisis of "comfort women," like many other crises across time and space, is "not exceptional to history or consciousness but a process embedded in the ordinary that unfolds in stories about navigating what's overwhelming" (p. 10). The repeated occurrence of sexual coercion and sexual violence that spans more than ninety years serves as a metaphorical moment of #MeToo, through which the spirit of the "comfort woman" is no longer distinguishable from every woman who must learn to reconstruct an identity after the self-shattering consequences of gender-based sexual violence.

The #MeToo movement has, in many ways, shifted the discourse on the "comfort women" issue, especially since the Korean Council's embezzlement scandal,[3] after which the public has somewhat lost trust in both the government-endorsed redress movement as well as nongovernmental reparative efforts. Young sexual assault survivors compare their experiences with the decades of silence faced by the "comfort women" to call attention to the persisting obstacles in addressing sexual violence, while many "comfort women" attend public events to stand in solidarity with the young survivors (Watanabe, 2018). As Rancière suggests, this solidarity, much like the supernatural connection between Young-Ok and Eun-Kyung, reorients the discourse of redress toward an embrace of "infinite justice," which initiates dialogues not only to achieve political goals, but also to find a vessel for the reclaimed subjecthood of these women.

If *Spirits' Homecoming* experiments with how historical temporality can be disrupted through moments of supernatural hesitation and impossible affiliation, *Twenty-Two* is rooted in the reparative act of revisiting the past through an individual survivor's own opaque subjectivity. Unlike *Spirits' Homecoming*, the director of *Twenty-Two*, Guo Ke, does not explicitly criticize the government's lack of consistency in redressing the "comfort women" and other feminist issues. Rather, Guo Ke expresses in an interview that his documentary, which consists of interviews with surviving "comfort women" in their private homes, aims to give the audience an opportunity to "gaze deeply into the eyes of the elderly one last time" (Gao, 2017). Released in 2017, the crowdfunded documentary features five out of the twenty-two interviewees, who reportedly made up all surviving "comfort women" who were alive in mainland China at the time of the film's production. The documentary was very well received in mainland China, and it broke the box-office record of Chinese documentary films in the year it was released (Han, 2017). Inspired by Korean documentaries of the same topic, Guo Ke and his team hoped to produce firsthand accounts of survivors to shed light on what Yoneyama (2016) terms "the address and redress" of the "comfort women" issue (p. 8). As shown above, the redress movement for "comfort women" has been increasingly globalized and has been taken into the narrative of the #MeToo movement in East Asia. However, while South Korean feminist activists and their actions are discouraged and sometimes even inhibited by the patriarchal social environment, the #MeToo movement in China has been subject to strict media censorship (Kuo, 2021). Not only are high-profile cases suppressed, social media discussions and the hashtag #MeToo itself have been deleted from China's monitored network. In contrast, representations of "comfort women" have been celebrated and promoted in the past decades against the backdrop of growing anti-feminist sentiment and censorship against sexual diversity.[4] Operating under such circumstances, *Twenty-Two* reflects both the nationalist hospitality surrounding redress movements for the Pacific War and the individual sense of loss that the "comfort women" themselves must grapple with.

Weaving between the first-person storytelling of surviving "comfort women" and the voices of those who know them or live in proximity, Guo Ke hopes to give voice to these women without overrepresenting their traumatic past. However, unlike the heavily censored Chinese #MeToo movement, the effort to preserve singularity seems compromised under the documentary's focus on historical preservation and collective trauma at first glance. In what follows, I will trace the development of two scenes to examine how personal sovereignty is threatened to get lost in the power of meta-narrative, and how a reading of the documentary in conjunction with #MeToo could potentially disrupt the hegemonic narration and offer an alternative temporality that allows for the self-presence of "comfort women" and their fragmented identities.

Like *Spirits' Homecoming*, *Twenty-Two* produces an interesting rendering of locality and spatiality. Private and public spaces intersect as the two lines of narration—one of individual storytelling and one of official history—intertwine. At one point in the film, for instance, the camera leaves the homes of survivors and fixes itself on a former site of "comfort station." As previously mentioned, "comfort stations" were organized by the JIA as a way to allegedly divert soldiers' sexual desire so as to reduce the number of civilian rapes. The so-called organized prostitution would also allow soldiers to "relieve themselves" without contracting sexually transmitted diseases. Therefore, the very idea of the "comfort station" is at once private and public. It is a site of the erotic in which the most personal, namely one's sexual desire, is fulfilled. It is, however, also a product of organization, a sanitized space, essentially an ironic "safe space" for both the soldiers and civilians, according to the JIA. By creating an artificial boundary between civilian women and "comfort women," the sites of sexual abuse alienate the latter with its lawful conviction that these bodies are sanitized and therefore penetrable, which, in the process of assault, become contaminated as their visceral boundaries are transgressed. The entering of "comfort stations" therefore becomes the metaphor for the entering of the female body, and while the perpetrators leave the "comfort stations" intact, the contaminated female body becomes intoxicated, the carrier of disease both literally and socially.

Therefore, the body of the "comfort woman" can be seen as a hostess, providing a hospitable *Umwelt* for both comfort and judgment. In a moment of reflection, a neighbor interviewed in the documentary reminisced about the days after the Japanese invasion, during which villagers would call female survivors of sexual abuse "Japan girls." The body of the "comfort woman" is transformed into an object of hatred for the enemy. In this interpretation, the "comfort woman" stands in for the perpetrator, and, like the "comfort station," her body furnishes a substitute, now an "unsafe space" that is foreign and under public attack in the name of patriotism.

I would like to reflect further on this metaphor of dwelling. The physicality of "comfort stations," as well as of the private homes featured in the film, animates the traumatized body. The juxtaposition of private homes and public sites of desire and torture conveys a problematic narrative, through which the physicality of the female body is displaced and refracted by the task of historical preservation, which, represented by diminishing numbers in the film, exhibits a shared anxiety about national identity. By featuring the homes, villages, and "comfort stations" with long shots, the film approaches the "comfort women" issue in a manner that privileges historical truth as concrete foundation. The camera reveals, yet it is only able to do so by animating the sites of trauma and producing a sort of collective affect that is wrapped within the historical discourse of Japanese atrocities.

We can better see this in the home repair and renovation project for survivors featured in the documentary. With the lead of the camera, the viewer enters the home of the ethnically Korean survivor, Mao Yin-Mei. In addition to helping her pay for house repairs, citizens of South Korea also sent her framed maps of the Korean peninsula and traditional ornaments. However, sitting indifferently amidst the gifted artifacts, Mao tells the camera of her love for Mao Zedong, the founding father of the People's Republic of China. Here we see not only two nationalist discourses, Chinese and Korean, competing against each other, but also a failed reparative gesture toward the survivor: the restoration project becomes a national gift, leaving the comfort women doubly indebted. Indeed, almost all women interviewed in the film showed gratitude for the production team and for the founding of the "new China," suggesting a belief in the brighter afterlife.

However, although a documentary film that attempts to record historical facts through the narrations of "comfort women" themselves, *Twenty-Two* betrays the official narrative through uncanny moments. For instance, a moment of strange embodiment was recorded during the interview with Mao. As Mao reflects on her experience, she begins to recall what she was taught to say in Japanese as a "comfort woman." In a critical moment of the documentary, Mao suddenly assumes the voice of a sweet, welcoming hostess and repeatedly says "welcome" and "please sit down" in Japanese with a coy expression on her wrinkled face. Her memory of being a "comfort woman" is revealed by her performance for the camera, under the gaze of the documentary's intended audience. And as the viewer, one sees both how this very translingual performance instantly transforms her into a colonial subject of desire during the Pacific War and how her affective performance is appropriated by the camera and, by extension, the viewer for visual fulfillment. As Mao's physical body recalls and re-experiences past trauma, her flashbacks are at once materialized into aesthetic objects under the filmic gaze.

The strange reincarnation, then, evokes the feeling of uncanniness in the audience. As a product of a different yet equally intense desire under the gaze of the camera, Mao's performative self as a "comfort woman" is not organic, but rather solicited. While this recorded moment functions as a contemporary exemplification of trauma, which gives us a glimpse of life in the "comfort station," it at the same time subjects Mao to the historical commemoration of collective trauma.

Nevertheless, rather than dismissing documentary films like *Twenty-Two* for embracing a nationalist redress movement, I see promise in the moments of slippage, in which the audience is forced to confront the dichotomy between the virtual and the actual. These moments remind the audience that gender-based violence has always been present, and that the entanglements between the personal and the collective cannot reduce the survivor to a receptacle of representational desire.

The two films suggest alternative avenues in which one can address the "comfort women" issue while keeping the "I" intact amidst nationalist adaptations. By turning to a discourse of #MeToo, this chapter suggests that the newly formed alliance can serve as a potential battleground against forgetting and homogenizing. From the analyses of the two films, we can see that such feminist elements as exist in the representations of "comfort women" are in fact not new. It appears in both Eun-Kyung's supernatural yet embodied alignment with Young-Ok, as well as the relentless negotiation with space that Chinese "comfort women" insist on despite the government's constant call of interpellation.

#MeToo works against nationalist rhetoric without minimizing the colonial violence that China and South Korea endured during and after the Pacific War. It prioritizes the "I" as both the survivor and the witness, and it is a testimony etched on one's body as a lived and ongoing experience. Having been penetrated and affected, the body becomes a carrier of excessive meaning, producing an economy in which the personal has the potential to serve as the political. Furthermore, this potential requires the audience to reimagine the grammar of redress and treat the fragmented bodies of the "comfort women" as a collectivity beyond national borders. In this way, it becomes possible to translate the experience of "comfort women" without demanding their affective performance, or even their participation or testimonial exposure, for the materiality of language always already contains its own world-making effort in which survivors of sexual violence dwell.

In sum, #MeToo offers an originary voice that re-articulates trauma across nations and generations. It disrupts the temporal and local boundaries and creates a bond beyond the surface of the scarred bodies. It echoes the pain of others without appropriating it in the name of collective unity. The #MeToo movement lives precisely in the impossibility of representation, between remembering and forgetting, and between the personal and the political. It is a transference rather than transliteration of pain, and it renders the afterlife and the post-memory no less authentic than the original. While #MeToo can be reparative, its emphasis on singularity and irreplaceability renders it a movement against discourses of organized redress and collective healing. Rather, it foregrounds singularity in a historical discourse while creating an affective network that brings visibility and solidarity to feminist movements. By borrowing the strength of #MeToo, we may be able to find new ways of addressing the "comfort women" issue in the here and now.

## Notes

1. In May 2020, activist and surviving "comfort woman" Lee Yong-Soo publicly accused Yoon Mee-Hyang, the former head of the Korean Council for the Women Drafted for Military Sexual Slavery by Japan (the Korean Council), of exploiting her and other survivors of sexual slavery for political and financial gains, including having sent another "comfort woman," Kim Bok-Dong, to tour in the United States despite her compromised health condition at the time. The scandal ignited uproar in South Korean society about the national glorification of "comfort women" as products of war atrocities (Ser, 2020).
2. The Nanking Massacre was a period of mass killing in the city of Nanking during the Japanese invasion in 1937, during which many Chinese women were raped and killed. It is estimated that more than 300,000 people were murdered between December 1937 and January 1938 (Seo, 2008).
3. See note 1.
4. In recent years, many feminist and LGBTQ social media accounts have been deleted or permanently disabled on popular platforms such at WeChat and Weibo. The government cites "public complaints" and "regulation violation" in an attempt to justify the censorship (*The Guardian*, 2021).

## Works Cited

Berlant, Lauren. 2011. *Cruel Optimism*. Durham, NC: Duke University Press.

Chizuko, U. 2001. "Narratives of the Past: Against Historical Revisionism on 'Comfort Women.'" In *Approches critiques de la pensée japonaise du xxe siècle*, edited by Livia Monnet, pp. 303–325. Montreal: Presses de l'Université de Montréal. doi:10.4000/books.pum.19872.

Freud, S. 2003. *The Uncanny*. Translated by D. McLintock. New York: Penguin Classic.

Gao, D. 2017. "Interview Guo Ke: It Is Us Who Cannot Let Go History (专访《二十二》导演郭柯：走不出历史的是我们)." *Pengpai News*, August. https://www.thepaper.cn/newsDetail_forward_1760118.

Jo, S. 2008. "Politics of Memory in Korea and China: Remembering the Comfort Women and the Nanjing Massacre." *New Political Science* 30, no. 3: 369–392.

Jo, S. 2017. "Mourning and the Movie *Spirits' Homecoming*." *International Journal of Korean Humanities and Social Sciences* 3: 105–116.

Kazue, M. 2016. "The 'Comfort Women' Issue and the Embedded Culture of Sexual Violence in Contemporary Japan." *Current Sociology* 64, no. 4: 620–636.

Kim, Bo-Eun. 2017. "First Film Proof of Korean 'Comfort Women' Discovered." *Korea Times*, July 6. https://www.koreatimes.co.kr/www/nation/2017/07/120_232456.html.

Kimura, M. 2016. *Unfolding the "Comfort Women" Debates: Modernity, Violence, Women's Voices*. London: Palgrave Macmillan.

Klüger, Ruth. 2003. *Still Alive: A Holocaust Girlhood Remembered*. New York: Feminist Press at CUNY.

Kuo, L. 2021. "Beijing Court Dismisses Landmark #MeToo Case as Authorities Censor Discussion." *Washington Post*, September 15. https://www.washingtonpost.com/world/china-metoo-censorship/2021/09/15/34390d46-15c8-11ec-a019-cb193b28aa73_story.html.

Lorde, A. 2007. *Sister Outsider: Essays and Speeches*. Berkeley: Crossing Press.

Han, J. 2017. "Box Office Success Bittersweet for Chinese 'Comfort Women' Documentary." *CGTN*, September 2. https://news.cgtn.com/news/79517a4e32557a6333566d54/index.html. Retrieved December 4, 2022.

"Outrage over Shutdown of LGBTQ WeChat Accounts in China." 2021. *The Guardian*, July 8. https://www.theguardian.com/world/2021/jul/08/outrage-over-crackdown-on-lgbtq-wechat-accounts-in-china.

Panda, Ankit. 2014. "Japan Denied Revision of UN Comfort Women Report." *The Diplomat*, October 17. https://thediplomat.com/2014/10/japan-denied-revision-of-un-comfort-women-report/.

Pimentel, Renan. 2021. "Harvard Law Professor Denies 'Comfort Women' Tragedy, Sparks Controversy." *Harvard Political Review*, March 14. https://harvardpolitics.com/hls-ramseyer-controversy/.

*Public High School Textbook Series: Chinese Modern History*, Volume I *(全日制普通高级中学教科书（必修）中国近代现代史上册)*. 2003. Beijing: People's Education Press (人民教育出版社).

Qin, A. 2015. "From Cho Junglae, a Film on Japanese Wartime Brothels." *New York Times*, March 24. https://www.nytimes.com/2015/03/25/movies/from-cho-junglae-a-film-on-japanese-wartime-brothels.html.

Qiu, P., with Z. Su and L. Chen. 2014. *Chinese Comfort Women: Testimonies from Imperial Japan's Sex Slaves*. Oxford: Oxford University Press.

Rancière, Jacques. 2004. "Who Is the Subject of the Rights of Man?" *Southern Atlantic Quarterly* 103, no. 2–3 (July): 297–310.

Rothberg, M. 2009. *Multidirectional Memory: Remembering the Holocaust in the Age of Decolonization*. Stanford, CA: Stanford University Press.

Said, S. 1978. *Orientalism*. London: Vintage.

Seo, Jungmin. 2008. "Politics of Memory in Korea and China: Remembering the Comfort Women and the Nanjing Massacre." *New Political Science* 30, no. 3: 369–392. http://dx.doi.org/10.1080/07393140802269021.

Ser, Myo-Ja. 2020. "Lawmaker at Center of 'Comfort Women' Scandal Indicted." *Korea JoongAng Daily*, September 14. https://koreajoongangdaily.joins.com/2020/09/14/national/socialAffairs/Yoon-Meehyang-Korean-Council-Lee-Yongsoo/20200914185500362.html.

Seybolt, Peter J. "China, Korea, and Japan: Forgiveness and Mourning." *Asia Society*. https://asiasociety.org/china-korea-and-japan-forgiveness-and-mourning. Retrieved October 25, 2021.

Soh, C. S. 1996. "The Korean 'Comfort Women': Movement for Redress." *Asian Survey* 36, no. 12: 1226–1240.

Son, H. 2022. "Now/Here, the Inside/Outside of the 'Comfort Women' Films, Part 1: *Spirits' Homecoming* as a Male-Oriented Movie." *KYEOL Research Institute on Japanese Military Sexual Slavery*, November 28. https://kyeol.kr/en/node/149. Retrieved December 4, 2022.

"South Korea Disperses Protest of Alleged Police Abuse." 1986. *L.A. Times* Archive, July 20. https://www.latimes.com/archives/la-xpm-1986-07-20-mn-17225-story.html.

Todorov, T. 1975. *The Fantastic: A Structural Approach to a Literary Genre*. Translated by R. Howard. Ithaca, NY: Cornell University Press.

Watanabe, N. 2018. "Young Assault Victims Using 'Comfort Women' Experience to Drive Change." *Kyodo News*, April 23. https://english.kyodonews.net/news/2018/04/1760856cd1a1-feature-young-assault-victim-using-comfort-women-experience-to-drive-change.html?phrase=Park&words=.

Wong, L. 2016. "Oscillating Histories: Representations of Comfort Women from Bamboo House of Dolls to Imperial Comfort Women." In *Divided Lenses: Screen Memories of War in East Asia*, edited by M. Berry and C. Sawada, pp. 153–174. Honolulu: University of Hawai'i Press.

Yang, H. 1998. "Re-Membering the Korean Military Comfort Women: Nationalism, Sexuality, and Silencing." In *Dangerous Women: Gender and Korean Nationalism*, edited by E. H. Kim and C. Choi, pp. 123–140. London: Routledge.

Yoneyama, Lisa, 2016. *Cold War Ruins: Transpacific Critique of American Justice and Japanese War Crimes*. Durham, NC: Duke University Press.

# 3

# Deer Women Dancing

## Indigenous Visualizations of MMIWG2S

*Zoë Antoinette Eddy*

### Timeline of Indigenous Feminism on Turtle Island

- 1876 (Canada): The *Indian Act* (An Act to amend and consolidate the laws respecting Indians/Loi sur les Indiens) is introduced.[1] In addition to other assimilation policies, this act prohibits various gender-equitable practices and limits the power of Indigenous women. In 1880 the act is amended to formally disenfranchise women from status by stating that marriage to a "non-Treaty Indian" negates their status.
- 1883: Canada formally authorizes residential schools. Indigenous children are forcibly removed from their families through re-education programs. In both the United States and Canada, residential school survivors and other witnesses will testify as to the rampant sexual and physical abuse that affected all genders of Indigenous children.
- 1887 (U.S.): The *Dawes Act* is established; similar to the Canadian *Indian Act*, this devastates cultural practices and Indigenous women's power within their communities; it also erases gender and sexuality diversity within Indigenous communities.
- 1918: Canadian women are given the right to vote; Indigenous women are not allowed to vote unless they give up treaty rights and status.
- 1924: Indigenous women are recognized as U.S. citizens by the Snyder Act; Indigenous people in their entirety are not able to vote until 1962.
- 1954: Elsie Marie Knot (Anishinaabe/Ojibwe Curve Lake First Nation) becomes, as documented by the Canadian government, the first women chief to lead a First Nation. This ushers in new visibility for Indigenous women living in Canada.
- 1960s–1970s: The Indian Health Service (IHS; U.S.) engages in sterilization of Indigenous women; IHS widely fails to gain informed consent of these women (resulting in forced sterilization). In 1976 the General Accountability Office launches an investigation.

Zoë Antoinette Eddy, *Deer Women Dancing* In: *The Other #MeToos.* Edited by: Iqra Shagufta Cheema, Oxford University Press. © Oxford University Press 2023. DOI: 10.1093/oso/9780197619872.003.0003

- 1960: Indigenous women in Canada gain the right to vote.
- 1968: The American Indian Movement is founded. A series of occupations are staged across the United States.
- 1968: Indigenous activists found the Voice of Alberta Native Women's Society (VANWS).
- 1974: (a) Women of All Red Nations (WARN) is established. (b) Native Women's Association of Canada, a development of VANWS, is founded.
- 1975: (a) Influential activist Anna Mae Aquash is murdered and her remains found in 1976; Aquash's murder launches a series of campaigns and conversations addressing violence affecting Indigenous activists and women. (b) The Gay American Indians (GAI) is founded as the first U.S.-based LGBTQ2S organization for Indigenous people. GAI will go on to hugely impact LGBTQ2S activism as it intersects with Indigenous feminism.
- 1978: The Indian Law Resource Center is established in the United States; it allies with the Strong Women, Strong Nations program to address violence against Indigenous women and girls.
- 1981: *The Bridge Called My Back: Writings from Radical Women of Color* is published. This landmark text critiques and resists white feminism. This aligns Indigenous feminists within larger intersectional movements.
- 1985: (a) Wilma Mankiller becomes the first women to be the principal chief of the Cherokee Nation. (b) The *Indian Act* is amended and allows Indian women to maintain or regain status after marrying a non-Indigenous man; it confers status to their children but not grandchildren and introduces various blood quantum policies governing status. (c) A massive contingent of Indigenous women activists establish the Indigenous Women's Network in Yelm, Washington.
- 1988: Charon Asetoyer (Comanche) establishes the Native American Women's Health Education Resource Center in Lake Andes, South Dakota.
- 1989: Winona LaDuke (Ojibwe) establishes the White Earth Land Recovery project.
- 1990: (a) At the *Empowerment Through Dialogue* conference, Indigenous women write *The Native Women's Reproductive Rights Agenda*, which addresses the sweeping inequity affecting Indigenous reproductive rights. (b) At the third Native American/First Nations Gay and Lesbian Conference, the term "two spirit" (Ojibwe: *niizh manidoowag*) is introduced. This not only replaces older racist terms, but establishes uniquely Indigenous approaches to gender and sexuality.
- 1993: Ada Bear (Menominee) becomes the first Indigenous woman to head the Bureau of Indian Affairs.

- 2007: Robert Pickton, a non-Indigenous serial killer responsible for the death of at least forty-nine Indigenous women, is jailed in Canada. This case is considered indicative of the sweeping inequities affection Indigenous women. Similar cases include the Highway of Tears murders.
- 2010: Jaime Black starts the REDress Project as a response to Missing and Murdered Indigenous Women. This launches a larger series of campaigns connected to community actions within and outside the expressive arts.
- 2011: (a) The Canadian government introduces the *Gender Equity in Indian Registration Act* enabling grandchildren of non-status Indigenous women to claim status. (b) At the *Inter-American Commission on Human Rights*, Indigenous women testify at a hearing on the violence affecting Indigenous women and girls. (c) Statistics Canada releases a report that indicates the rate of homicide for Indigenous women is nearly seven times higher when compared to other ethnic groups. d) The Bay Area American Indian Two Spirits collective (established 1999) starts the *Two Spirit Pow Wow*, which helps shape new conversations about Indigenous gender and feminism.
- 2012: (a) In response to Stephen Harper's 2011 omnibus bills, Sheelah Mclean, Jessica Gordon, Sylvia McAdam Saysewahum, and Nina Wilson found Idle No More. Idle Nor More broadly attempts to protect and reclaim Indigenous environments while also intervening into government attempts to claim and degrade Indigenous land. (b) University of North Carolina at Chapel Hill student Faith Hedgepeth (Haliwa-Saponi) is found murdered at her apartment; the homicide case becomes demonstrative of the lack of transparency in homicide cases affecting Indigenous women. (c) The activist art installation, *Walking with Our Sisters*, begins as a response to the crisis of missing and murdered Indigenous women; Christi Belcourt initially installs the exhibit.
- 2013: Mary Kathryn Nagle writes *Sliver of a Full Moon* in response to the Violence Against Women Act (U.S.) and lack of protections for Indigenous women and girls.
- 2014: The Royal Canadian Mounted Police releases a report titled *Missing and Murdered Aboriginal Women: A National Operational Overview*, stating the disproportionate rates of homicide affecting Indigenous women. Later statistics further indicate that between 1980 and 2015, while the rates of homicide decreased for non-Indigenous women, the homicide rates for Indigenous women increased.
- 2015: (a) The Truth and Reconciliation Commission publishes its final report on the residential school system; it identifies the system as "cultural genocide" and further identifies the sweeping abuses affecting Indigenous

children. (b) The REDress Project, based on Jaime Black's earlier work, achieves international visibility as it asks for community and individual donations of red dresses.

- 2016: In response to pressure from Indigenous communities and organizations, Justin Trudeau introduces the National Inquiry in Missing and Murdered Indigenous Women.
- 2019: The body of Alaskan Native woman Kathleen Jo Henry is found on Anchorage, Alaska's Seward Highway; the killer is later found to be Brian Stephen Smith, a South African man later identified as a serial killer responsible for the murder of other Indigenous women. This reinvigorates discussion of homicide rates and Indigenous women.
- 2020–2021: Movements across various social media platforms, particularly during the COVID-19 pandemic, vigorously address the need for more protection for Indigenous women, girls, and LGBTQ2S people. These movements, which are often virtual sit-ins, meaningfully incorporate discussions of LGBTQ2S people.
- 2021: Deb Haaland (Laguna Pueblo) is confirmed as secretary of the interior (U.S.). Later in 2021, Haaland introduces a Bureau of Indian Affairs unit that addresses the missing and murdered Native Americans crisis, including the violence affecting Indigenous women, girls, and two-spirit people.

## Introduction

When #MeToo swept the media, a frustrated sigh sounded across Turtle Island. This frustration echoed that of other activists: Tarana Burke started the movement for "black and brown women and girls" and yet white women dominated the mainstream narratives; indeed, Burke and others have criticized the campaign's current iteration for its focus on white survivors (Burke, 2017; Onwuachi-Willig, 2018; Tambe, 2018). To an Indigenous[2] survivor among a community of Indigenous survivors, #MeToo sometimes feels as though a bleeding wound has opened further. After all, Indigenous activists have long been seeking redress for the epidemic of missing and murdered Indigenous women, girls, and two-spirit[3] people (MMIWG2S). A conversation with a friend epitomized my own sentiments: " '#MeToo' isn't secret in Indian Country. It's *literally* the statistic: if you're looking at me and I'm Native, then it's *literally probable* that, you know, me too."

Nevertheless, the popularization of Burke's movement among white feminists and their adjacent circles has created a re-entry point for Indigenous survivors. As Abigail Echo-Hawk stated in a 2018 interview, "Movements such as #MeToo have opened up this conversation nationwide and, I believe, created a more welcoming environment for stories like these" (Pepitone, 2018). In North America, mainstream advocacy networks are literate in the language of #MeToo: Indigenous activists have seized on this moment to emphasize Indigenous approaches to ending sexual violence.

This chapter argues that Indigenous activists have, at the crossroads of the #MeToo moment, developed a viral visual language that addresses sexual and gender violence (SGV). These movements exist in solidarity with #MeToo but are uniquely Indigenous: as long neglected survivors of SGV, Indigenous survivors have created separate movements that embrace Indigenous ontologies, activism tactics, and artforms. My work is based on six years of ethnographic and archival fieldwork in North American tribal communities. Additionally, it is informed by my own experience as an Indigenous survivor-activist. I first describe the epidemic of SGV against Indigenous women. I then investigate the visual language of Indigenous SGV activism: I present three different visualizations—the Red Dress, the Jingle Dress Dancer, and the Red Handprint—in order to explore different moments in Indigenous advocacy. I position these images within the context of hashtag and viral activism. I demonstrate that Indigenous communities have developed a visual language to communicate our advocacy agendas; we have also integrated into online communities, creating both virtual awareness and global solidarity. I argue that these projects provide spaces of community reconciliation, healing, and creative expression. These efforts seize on the vibrancy of #MeToo while also challenging territories of whiteness that silence Indigenous voices.

## An Epidemic of Sexual and Gender Violence (SGV)

North American Indigenous women, girls, and two-spirit people face disproportionate amounts of SGV. A report from the National Congress of American Indians detailed that 84.3% of American Indian/Alaskan Native (AI/AN) women have experienced violence in their lifetimes, and 56.1% of AI/AN women have experienced rape; in summary, AI/AN women are 1.7 times as likely to experience violence and 2 times as likely to experience SGV as compared to non-Hispanic white women (NCAI Policy Research Center 2018). Other reports offer higher numbers that are further complicated by under-reporting and the invisibility of survivors (Woodman 2020). As a friend once said in passing, "Indian Country is Survivor Country—I just don't think anyone really cares."

The SGV crisis is not new, but instead a crisis grounded in settler-colonial histories. Rape, sexual assault, and exploitation of Indigenous women have been central to colonial policies: the sexual exploitation of Indigenous women helped to solidify colonization of Indigenous territories (Dunbar-Ortiz and Gilio-Whitaker 2016). More insidiously, racist stereotypes—such as "the squaw" and "the Indian maiden"—have depicted Indigenous women as hypersexual and submissively pliant (Mackay and Mackay 2020).

Consequently, these systems have enabled the systemic exploitation of Indigenous women, girls, and two-spirit people (Cuneen 2014; Deer 2004; Lucashenko 1996). Dunbar-Ortiz and Gilio-Whitaker summarize the current crisis:

> Indigenous women have continued to bear the brunt of colonial violence, specifically sexual violence, both within families and by settler predators, and, increasingly, sex traffickers. Incidences of rape on reservations has long been astronomical, and the majority of perpetrators are non-Indigenous men. The colonialist US restrictions on Indigenous policing authority on reservations—yet another legacy of the doctrine of discovery and the impairment of Indigenous sovereignty—opens the door to perpetrators of sexual violence who know there will be no consequences for their actions. (2016, p. 146)

Speaking to how this history has manifested on tribal reservations, White Earth Ojibwe tribal member Lisa Brunner shares:

> They [non-Indigenous men] come here [to the reservation] to hunt . . . they came here with the intent and purposes to find someone on this reservation to rape. Because they could. . . . We live in modern day cowboys v. Indians. (*Washington Post*, 2014)

Moreover, as Brunner and Theresa Pouley, Tulalip Tribal Court Chief Judge, have emphasized in interviews, justice systems deprioritize Indigenous women and contribute to the erasure of violence against them (PBS NewsHour 2015). As Pouley observes, major laws like the Violence Against Women Act (VAWA) fail to protect tribal sovereignty and, consequently, SGV survivors. Even with legal reforms that created additional protections for Indigenous women, Indigenous activists and other critics indicated that VAWA, as it stands, remains insufficient and needs further strengthening (Deer 2018; Flay 2017; Reed 2018; Whitebear 2019).

The situation in Canada is similar. The landmark volume *Keetsahnak* details the severity of SGV in Canada (Anderson et al., 2018). Michelle Good writes on the longtime exploitation of Indigenous women in Canada: nineteenth-century Indigenous women, supporting destitute families, were coerced into exchanging sexual favors for rations and goods; equally devastating, traders held Indigenous women as hostages, assaulting and raping them, in order to negotiate trade policies (2018). In summary, violence against Indigenous women served as a way to bolster the larger colonial project. The North American continent both fosters and neglects the SGV crisis that impacts Indigenous communities. Despite this, policy reform remains slow-moving. Consequently, Indigenous communities have developed their own responses to SGV.

Turtle Island Indigenous feminism—also called Native American feminism—has developed alongside Indigenous response to the SGV crisis. Situated within larger global Indigenous feminisms, which seek to destabilize colonial feminist theories, Indigenous feminism attends specifically to the Native American and First Nations context (see Suzcek et al., 2010, for a volume addressing major landmarks in Indigenous feminism). Chief among issues, within both theory and practice, is the SGV crisis. The range of work that Indigenous feminism spans is wide-ranging. Furthermore, while Indigenous feminism has broken into main feminist circles, it is grounded in much older historical cultural practices (Hall 2009). As Dina Gilio-Whitaker argues, North American feminism has roots in the cultural practices of Indigenous women who have long championed gender equity (2019). In contemporary work, activism has expanded to included not only women, but continued attention to two-spirit people and others falling under the LGBTQ umbrella.

Within this feminism, grassroots organizations have demanded action both from the U.S. and Canadian governments, as well as within Indigenous communities. Relevant to my own work, artist-activists have embraced this moment. From sweeping exhibitions to small-scale works, Indigenous agents have created arenas that challenge negligent settler-colonial narratives and practices. #MeToo has provided a complicated and virulent intersection into which Indigenous movements have entered. Within both digital and non-digital spaces, Indigenous activists have created a language of images; these images have facilitated a global community of SGV advocacy.

## Speaking in Color

I first saw Jordan Marie Brings Three White Horses Daniel's image while scrolling through Instagram. As my feed populated with pictures, the now famous photograph arrested my attention: in the photo, a woman sprints across the Boston Marathon finish line; a red handprint is painted over her mouth, and, down her leg, painted crimson letters read "MMIW." Throughout the race, the runner had also stopped at the mile markers to offer prayers for missing and murdered Indigenous women. Her image—algorithmically suggested to me because I follow the hashtag #MMIW—spoke to the thousands of words that Indigenous SGV activists have produced.

Overnight, Jordan, a Kul Wicasa Oyate citizen, was sprinting across social media platforms. Other activists and artists provided their own tributes. Professional artists created portraits of the young woman; others produced celebratory memes; more women runners emulated her work—perhaps most famously, Rosalie Fish, an enrolled member of the Cowlitz Tribe, took inspiration from and eventual camaraderie with Daniel. More people joined the advocacy work: community-mediated images of red handprints, women, braids, and strength were united by a series of both old and new hashtags: #MMIWG2S, #MMIW, #NativeRunners, #NativeWomen, and more wove the runners and their activism into mainstream media. These two athletes are now in company with the many Indigenous SGV activists whose work has built an expansive digital archive. This archive relies on an Indigenous visual language of SGV, viral hashtag activism, and community-minded engagement.

As a quick Instagram or Twitter search will show, the digital archive is seemingly boundless. In this chapter, I identify and explain three genres that represent different pulses in digital SGV activism. First, I examine the "Red Dress," a pivotal image in campaigns that created wider networks of SGV advocacy. I then present Jingle Dress Dance imagery and performance; this campaign puts contemporary cultural reclamation and gender equity in conversation with Indigenous histories. Finally, I look at the red handprint, an image that ruptures settler-colonial expectations of violence and gender in MMIWG2S movements. These images build on interrelated trajectories of Indigenous activism and cultural reclamation.

## Red Dress and Redress

The Red Dress is a ubiquitous part of Indigenous SGV activism. From people wearing Red Dresses to art representing the Red Dress and its wearers, it is a familiar part of advocacy visual language. While the use of the color red and red clothing is long established in Indigenous activism, the current use of the Red Dress owes its origin to Jamie Black's movement, the REDress Project.

Jamie Black, a multimedia Métis artist, started the REDress Project in 2010. The community-oriented and collaborative public art installation addresses the specific violence Indigenous women face. Black states on the project's website:

> The REDress Project focuses around the issue of missing or murdered Aboriginal women across Canada. It is an installation art project based on an aesthetic response to this critical national issue. The project has been installed in public spaces throughout Canada and the United States as a visual reminder of the staggering number of women who are no longer with us. Through the installation I hope to draw attention to the gendered and racialized nature of

> violent crimes against Aboriginal women and to evoke a presence through the marking of absence. (2020, n.p.)

Black's project is both stark and vibrant: the dresses, installed in both public and private spaces, are beautiful and arresting. They are also rooted in longer Indigenous aesthetic lineages. In a 2017 interview, Black explained:

> Red is a really powerful colour in Indigenous communities. . . . It's a very sacred colour, and it also represents the violence that these women are facing. When I was 17, I read a powerful book by Maria Campbell called *The Book of Jessica*. It's about a Métis woman's experience moving to an urban environment. About a year ago, I realized the book cover is a painting of an empty red dress. Obviously, the image has been in my head for a very long time. (Edwards 2017)

The exhibited dresses are not uniform, but instead a patchwork of designs redolent of different people: sparks of white trim, embroidered flowers, and marks of wear and tear individualize the dresses—every dress, like the person who might have worn it, is unique. The dresses themselves are not quite lifeless, but instead are testaments of life that once existed. Surveying the cut of waistlines, slope of sleeves, and hem of skirts, it is easy to imagine the shape of legs, bellies, and wrists that might have filled out fabric. Additionally, there is the uncomfortable ambiguity as to the dresses' former wearers: Black's community sources the garments, and the dresses' provenances are unclear. The obvious tragedy is the reality that many of the dresses may be private, quiet memorials to those still missing and/or murdered.

This near emptiness is Black's aim. In a 2015 interview, Black stated, "Seeing nothing in it is a stark reminder that someone is not there." For Black, the discomfort of emptiness, made manifest in the visual art installation, serves as an advocacy gateway, "Visual art has a kind of symbolic power that allows people to enter into a conversation . . . art has the power to allow people to feel emotionally connected to what's going on before they find out even the particulars of what happened" (ShawTV Winnipeg 2015, n.p.). The REDress Project encourages discussion, awareness, and cohesion across communities. From the donations to the installations, Black works on a collaborative level that uses the power of visual art and performance to build advocacy.

Due to this aesthetic legacy, the Red Dress has been an influential image in MMIWG2S digital activism. Those circulating images continue Black's work: they emphasize honoring the missing and lost, as well as recognizing Indigenous strength, power, and spirituality. To offer further examples of this work, Table 3.1 provides a spectrum of images taken from Instagram; I detail the image type, representative examples (including Instagram username and

Table 3.1 Red Dress and Redress

| Image Type | Examples | Related Hashtags |
|---|---|---|
| Mixed Media Art | Thealamedaartworks (https://www.instagram.com/p/B9uE89rD6Hd); tgmcclean (https://www.instagram.com/p/CB7XzmKhd8j/); candacescanvases (https://www.instagram.com/p/CE33foqgVO9/); room105sjci (https://www.instagram.com/p/BythiStgfdu/); westernuvisarts (https://www.instagram.com/p/Bqx3q_wHk_c/) | #bringthemhome #mmiw #mmiwg #justicefornativewomen #pocartists #nomorestolensisters #indigenous #indigenousrights #humanrights #nativewomen #art #native #nativesisters #nativeamerican #nativesovereignty #wewantjustice #artispolitics#redressproject #lgbtq #lgbt #blacklivesmatter #humanrightsforall #church #vancouver #canada #stopracism #peoplearepeople #human #equality #freedom #loveislove #neverforgotten #REDress #facelessdolls #stolenwomen #missingandmurderedindigenouswomen |
| Beaded Objects | Littlefeather.creations (https://www.instagram.com/p/B_SSAh5HIzR/?utm_source=ig_web_copy_link); noxs_tsay (https://www.instagram.com/p/CCt5fHynlaS/); bonitahaida (https://www.instagram.com/p/CEwo6hAnI-9/); devsdesignsbeadwork (https://www.instagram.com/p/CE1qKefsD_I/); rezchicklet (https://www.instagram.com/p/CEsV7N8hm8S/); mirsuqti (https://www.instagram.com/p/CE29ryUHaiZ/); stacinthenorth (https://www.instagram.com/p/B8k5Bqtj3-s/); bigfootmocassin (https://www.instagram.com/p/B4l75ufnPgx/); tashajami87 (https://www.instagram.com/p/CEssCHQh9xo/) | #seedbead #beading #mikmaq #mikmaqmade #indigenous #reddress #redressproject #mmiw #mmiwg #mmiwawareness #bearpaw #beadedjewelry #beadedearrings#beadedpendant #redressproject #madewithlove #beadwork #earrings #nomorestolensisters #raiseawareness #Handmade#NativeAmericanMade #PowwowBling #NativeBling #Native #InspiredNatives #Beadwork #Tassels #DangleEarrings #NativeBeadwork #WeAreStillHere #Makers #MakersofInstagram #Okanagan #OkanaganNation #Nooksack #SeedBeads #SeedBeadEarrings #BeadLife #BeadTherapy #FirstNation #Authentic #PeyoteStitch#BrickStitch #beadedearrings #beadedjewelry #edmonton #albertacanada #abbotsfordbc #abbotsford #canadianmade#downtownabbotsford #poppyfund #mmiw #abbotsfordlegion #bigfootmoccasin #shoplocal #ojibwe #auntie #artbeads #beads |

**Table 3.1** Continued

| Image Type | Examples | Related Hashtags |
|---|---|---|
| Portraits | Miikanajewels (https://www.instagram.com/p/B_4w0YKnzsR/); fdvoyageur (https://www.instagram.com/p/B7W6S2glOhC/) fauxrocious (https://www.instagram.com/p/CExwOgzJhF2/) Thedanewbreast(https://www.instagram.com/p/CE7KAZsFdTD/); aurora_artistry (https://www.instagram.com/p/CE7ZtuzAg37/); bigsistersregina (https://www.instagram.com/p/B_z5ZW7FxYh/); townofsmithsfall (https://www.instagram.com/p/CCoEjqNHyki/); heu_in_bc (https://www.instagram.com/p/BofGa-6lioB/); sharona201 (https://www.instagram.com/p/BnFrMqfg-SN/) | #redressproject #mmiwgawarenessday2020 #mmiw #missingandmurderedindigenouswomen #notinvisible #mmiwg #nomorestolensisters #sayhername #saytheirnames #mmiw #indigenousjewelry #jewelryforacause #REDressproject #nationaldayofawareness #mmiwg #FDV2020 #FestivalduVoyageur #TravelManitoba #TourismWinnipeg #OnlyInThePeg #WeOwnWinter #ExploreMB #PassionHistoire #ExploreCanada #InsideCanada #TourCanada #YWG #WpgNow #Pegcity #Winnipeg #WinnipegLife #IndigenousArt #JaimeBlack #mmiwawareness #mmiwg2s #mmip #piikani #yegphotography #ProjectChange#everywomanempowered #fundraiser #metis#wearyourstory #spiritofthedrum #powwow #ontariopowwow #reconciliation#stopviolence #endviolence #nativeartist #indigenousartist #nativeart #hospitalemployeesunion #indigenousmade #drag #dragqueen #afabqueen #fauxqueen #fauxrocious #qwerrrkout |
| Exhibit Photographs | Bandit.design.co(https://www.instagram.com/p/CCmllaknnX5/); gcindigenous (https://www.instagram.com/p/BrOevk_lsUk/); mitchellgirl13 (https://www.instagram.com/p/CBsrC_AAKl7/) shakurasaida (https://www.instagram.com/p/CCOShZFg4Fo/); nonverbalconversation (https://www.instagram.com/p/B9O3GHNnGmr/); chariscopland (https://www.instagram.com/p/B9C9TtDBpao/); | #MMIWG #MMIW #REDressProject #nomorestolensisters #livingart#remember #wecandobetter #saskatooning #treaty6 #jamieblack #haunting#winnipeg #missingandmurderedindigenouswomen #jaimeblack #metis #firstnations #inuit #indigenous #indigenouswomen #resilienceart #indigenousartists #indigenousactivism #myactionsmatter |

*(continued)*

**Table 3.1** Continued

| Image Type | Examples | Related Hashtags |
|---|---|---|
| | sunnysideexplorer (https://www.instagram.com/p/B9C_UN6JO4h/); weird.ldnont (https://www.instagram.com/p/B8pZkzdH6HR/); alovelylittleworld (https://www.instagram.com/p/B8fYciRHBdQ/); capulibrary (https://www.instagram.com/p/B8ewgkEBE7e/); miasummerson (https://www.instagram.com/p/B6_G0z7hEwq/); mikegraeme (https://www.instagram.com/p/BzaFoQtBouq/); settle_in_settlers (https://www.instagram.com/p/CEmLLYyAXCm/) | #16DaysOfActivism #canada#turtleisland #resilienceproject #endviolenceagainstwomen #endviolenceagainstindigenouswomen #artactivism #stopviolenceagainstwomen#nationalindigenouspeoplesday #reparations #reparationsnow #NativeLand #IndigenousLand #MétisContemporaryArt #IndigenousContemporaryArt #reconciliation#firstnations #humanrights #urbanart #publicart #activismbecomesart #Oneida #Cayuga #HuronWendat #Seneca #Tuscarora #Ojibwa #IndigenousArt #NativeArt#urbanart #artandactivism #publicart #StandUp #SpeakUp #SpeakOut#beaware #Canadianwomen #redressproject #indigenouswomen #capilanouniversity #capilanoU #canada #canadaday #canada152#ReconciliationIsDead #Femicide #Genocide #Ecocide #KKKanada #ShutDownCanada #Wreckconciliation |

direct link to material), and related hashtags. I have identified four major types of Red Dress imagery; these types often bleed together. First, I identify "Mixed Media Art": these are various art pieces that use the Red Dress as a visual to call attention to SGV. Second, I identify "Beaded Objects," which are objects made with Indigenous beading technique that feature the Red Dress. Third, I identify "Portraits," which are photographs, paintings, and illustrations of Indigenous people in the dresses. Finally, "Exhibition Photographs" are photos of Red Dress installations.

These images use the Red Dress to access similar themes: reclamation of cultural pride, trauma reconciliation, Indigenous womanhood, and community activism. Most importantly, Black's REDress Project broke open digital spaces and allowed for the viral circulation of Indigenous imagery and advocacy. As digital activism has advanced, the Red Dress—as both a symbol and a replicable digital artifact—has served as a launching point for SGV advocacy. Two other images, the Jingle Dress Dance/r and the Red Handprint, share similar trajectories.

## Jingle Dress Dance/rs

While I have seen Jingle Dress Dance many times, every time I watch it, I feel as though it is the first time: united by communal purpose and healing, the dance transforms the landscape. I remember one instance, at an East Coast area intertribal, specifically: I had spent the day roaming the powwow grounds and had started up conversation Jaylin, a young Abenaki woman. As we spoke, Jaylin stopped short and informed me she needed to change into her Jingle regalia. Later, I watched Jaylin and her cohort[4] dance: they moved with a quick-paced, steady grace, head held high and, in the tradition of the dance, never moving backward, high stepping, or twirling. The chorus of jingle cones made it feel as though we shared a quiet, infinite, and compassionate sacred space—a space of undeniable power.

The image of the Jingle Dress Dancer is widely circulated by digital activists within the #MeToo arena. In these images, both the dancer and the dress are indexical to Jingle Dress Dance's history and significance. The dancer, usually depicted as a woman caught mid-step, wears the iconic regalia: a cotton dress adorned with jingle cones. To those outside of Indigenous circles, the dancer's relevance to SGV activism is not immediately apparent. However, this art form and the dancer are embedded in historical and contemporary reclamations of gender.

According to members of my own tribal communities, Ojibwe groups in the Northeast and Midwest United States, Jingle Dress Dance originated in Ojibwe communities. A Mille Lacs Band of Ojibwe cultural education film explains this history (MLBO 2018). This film explains that a man dreamed of women dancing in colorful, jingling dresses. When he woke, the man explained the dream to his wife; the woman helped him translate his dream to the physical world. Following this, the woman asked for help from her tribe's women to make the dresses and perform the dance. At a subsequent healing ceremony, the group of women performed the dance for a sick girl. The girl grew healthier until she was able to join the dance circle. The film closes with tribal elder Amik Larry Smallwood stating that "many tribes have their own versions, but this is ours."

Historian Brenda Child notes that the diverse histories indicate that, during the early twentieth century, a major movement of both women's expressive arts and healing dances emerged. This coincided with not only the World War I and the influenza epidemic, but also with government restrictions on tribal religions and practices. Jingle Dance has been not only a revitalization of gender and dance, but also a resistance to colonial regimes. As Child explains, the communal power of this dance explains its popularity during the rise of powwow circuits in the 1980s and 1990s (2008, 2012).

Jingle Dress Dance has emerged as a mode of SGV advocacy and specifically one associated with #MeToo. In my New England fieldwork, a group of college students were introduced as guests at an intertribal powwow. The leader—an Anishinaabe and Abenaki woman named Megan—made a brief speech, "We run an Indigenous culture group where I teach Jingle. Today we're raising awareness for missing and murdered girls." She then indicated a tent where people could make donations. Afterward, I asked Megan how she had gotten into this activism. She explained that, in college, her peers were involved in #MeToo advocacy—Megan saw the dance as a source of camaraderie and education. She explained, since she danced with both Indigenous and non-Indigenous sexual assault survivors, she used her dance group to bring attention to SGV crises.

Megan suggested that #MeToo helped her stage this intervention: #MeToo created a foundation from which she could launch her specific advocacy. On campus social media, student activist groups used the #MeToo hashtag to advertise campaigns related to campus rape awareness and prevention. Megan thought that using #MeToo might expand her advocacy network. When she posted about events, she started tagging posts with #MeToo alongside #MMIWG2S. "#MeToo" was legible to a wider audience and helped Megan immediately position #MMIWG2S within broader networks. In response to Megan's online campaigns, both community interest and wider participation increased. Megan's experience exemplifies the power of Jingle Dress advocacy within #MeToo—it is then unsurprising that the Jingle Dress Dance/r image has exploded online.

In digital activist archives, sovereignty movements have used the Jingle Dress Dance/r image. While the Red Dress takes on an array of abstractions, Jingle Dress Dance/r visuals are often directly representative. In the majority of images, the dancer, usually coded as a woman, stands in her regalia, often holding a feather fan. The image indicates resilience, resistance, and feminine cultural power that confront colonial structures. A common theme among these images is a dancer's ability to Indigenize a space. Adam Sings in the Timber (@singsinthetimber) is a Crow photographer who has instituted the hashtag #indigenizecolonizedspaces. Sings in the Timber frequently collaborates with Jingle Dress Dancers in projects where the dancers wear full regalia in urban spaces (Sings in the Timber 2020). The images of vibrant, defiant Indigenous dancers demonstrate the Jingle Dress Dance/r genre.

Specific to SGV advocacy, the Jingle Dress Dance/r digital activism is relatively new. These digital images (a) signify the history and social movement of Jingle Dance and (b) emphasize the dancer as equal parts healer, survivor, and advocate. Some activists post portraits of themselves or others in regalia, utilizing hashtags such as #MMIW and #NoMoreStolenSisters. Others paint red handprints on their faces or, echoing the work of Indigenous athletes, paint their bodies with hashtag texts. A high-profile example of this is a portrait of Ilona Verley, a Nlaka'pamux two-spirit artist of *Canada's Drag Race* and *Vogue* fame. The portrait depicts Verley in a pink and red ribbon-skirt and Jingle Dress (Allaire 2020). Verley holds her red-stained hand over her mouth—a clear allusion to MMIWG2S advocacy. On Ilona Verley's personal Instagram, she explains not only the significance of the dress, but also her own advocacy (Verley 2020). This well-circulated portrait has become a fixture in Jingle Dress Dance digital activism.

Similarly, *Art Heals: The Jingle Dress Project* uses the dance to mobilize Indigenous healing. Activist-dancers combine MMIWG2S advocacy and COVID-19 pandemic responses (The Jingle Dress Project 2020). This has inspired dancers to share viral videos of themselves dancing; the purposes of these dances are both to help heal Indigenous communities and to promote awareness for Indigenous health risks. In particular, conversations—united around #IndigenousHealing, #MMIWG2S, and #COVID19—have emphasized that, during a pandemic, domestic and sexual violence survivors are likely at home with their abusers. In these videos, dancers translate the vibrancy of live performance to the digital archive.

These visualizations incorporate Jingle Dress's history as medicine grounded in advocacy and spirituality. They bring together the threads of Jingle Dress history with the aesthetics and themes of contemporary activism. Like Red Dress images, they emphasize the feminine and culturally profound. Comparatively, their contribution to the digital archive is more obviously situated in historical dance forms and gender movements. The final image that I will examine, the handprint, includes aspects of both Red Dress and Jingle Dress digital advocacy.

## The Red Handprint

A few weeks before Christmas, Frankie, a Wendat woman, sat at her living room table: she was tooling a handprint design into a leather ornament. Frankie made the work look effortless, but her ability to drive designs into the cowhide is practiced. The handprint would be died a blood red and the ornament would become a keychain. She was making keychains for a community fundraiser that benefited MMIWG2S projects and served as a social event grounded in public education. Frankie, a full-time graduate student, emphasized that leatherwork is a labor of love, not a job. This project gave her the opportunity to use her artistic talent to contribute material goods to an Indigenous activist project—it was an easy way, she said, to offer a little something to her community.

Frankie is one of many Indigenous activists who uses the red handprint in SGV advocacy. She is also a #MeToo activist. When I asked how #MeToo impacted her artwork and Indigenous advocacy, she responded:

> #MeToo provided a foundation for more difficult conversations. When people say "Me Too" you know they're talking about rape, power, and silencing. I use #MeToo as a way to start the conversation about Indigenous people, and then I move with my actual art into a more Indigenous space . . . but #MeToo helps communicate it to people who don't understand how bad the problem [of SGV violence affecting Indigenous communities] is.

Frankie identified that the Red Handprint was part of that Indigenous space and largely outside of the visualizations of #MeToo. As an Indigenous survivor, when I look at the Red Handprint, I have an immediate visceral response: the feel of blood on my skin, the slap of a hand over my mouth, and the jump of anxiety that comes from breathlessness. That, as Frankie has said, is exactly the point: the handprint is instinctive and immediate—it is a haptic reminder of what violence feels like.

But the handprint goes beyond violence. Both the color red and the hand itself connect to larger historical movements. Specifically, the hand evokes the fist used in both Black Liberation and Red Power movements. Relatedly, the color red has long been used in North American Indigenous sovereignty campaigns. Red speaks across tribes and invokes (variously) strength, power, and interactions with the spiritual world. Perhaps more than any other piece of digital activist media, the Red Handprint draws on a multitude of histories, cultural interpretations, and personal responses.

Returning to Frankie's work, I asked Frankie why she chose the handprint for her own art. Frankie explained that her choice was complex: foremost, she wanted to move the conversation beyond missing and murdered "women." Franke indicated that the handprint is less gendered than other images. "We started the conversation about missing women, and now we can start talking about missing girls, kids, men, and two-spirit Native people. The handprint expands the conversation to the various genders and ages impacted by SGV," Frankie affirmed. Advocates have criticized various advocacy movements, particularly MMIW, for excluding two-spirit people who do not conform to binary gender. As Alex Wilson suggests, "the issue of [MMIW] is finally gaining much needed attention . . . a narrative that essentializes women and women's 'roles,' however, has accomplished this shift. The essentializing narrative which is rooted in a binary construction of gender, risks further marginalization of two-spirit, trans, and other LGBTQ Indigenous people, and generates confusion about what constitutes tradition" (2018, p. 162). In digital activism circles, the Red Handprint is certainly used by advocacy groups that target cisgender women and girls. However, it is also used for two-spirit, trans, and LGBTQ advocacy. Additionally, groups that focus on SGV against Indigenous children, including boys, tend to favor the hand in concert with other images. For these groups, the Red Handprint helps move messaging away from tightly gendered media that excludes various communities.

The Red Handprint also encourages discomfort. Frankie noted that her keychains are "conversation starters." "It's not that they're sensationalized," Frankie offered, "but they're very simple and honest, you know? Sexual violence is violence, and I like the sort of, I don't know, discomfort they create." On Instagram, various users embrace the bloodiness of the Red Handprint: self-portraits emphasize the graphic component of what SGV entails. One user, as an example, painted a Red Handprint over her mouth, but the paint—rather than being a simple, flat red—is a gruesome and viscous blackish crimson. The mark looks as though the user has been grievously injured. Various Instagram users seize on the potential for abject imagery and remarkable visualization.

In many ways, the Red Handprint defies easy definition. Frankie noted, "It's powerful because it's so many things—ugly, beautiful, strong, dangerous. A hand is human and can communicate so much." Frankie's final point is essential. A handprint is a definitive mark of a person: it is endlessly legible and inserts the individual into conversations of statistics, massive violence, and overwhelming death. Because of this, the Red Handprint has helped unite images used in digital activism; it serves as a wellspring from which MMIWG2S advocacy can draw.

These three pieces of media can work altogether. Some of the most exciting images are those of women and two-spirit people, dressed in red Jingle Dresses, with handprints painted over their mouths (Green 2019; Verley 2020). These are visualizations, rooted in complex histories, that have worked together to create a sprawling and vocal community of digital activism. Regardless of the power of any one image, Indigenous SGV advocacy, following the path set by #MeToo and the hashtag movement, has relied on viral circulation.

## Hashtag Activism and Viral Reclamation

The hashtag (#) is one of the most important parts of contemporary SGV activism, whether that activist is within or outside #MeToo. It is a metadata tag that serves as an indexing tool and is especially prevalent on social media platforms. Social media users can create their own hashtags and tag material; this material is then put in relation to all other media, on a given platform, that is similarly tagged. Should a user want to find a given category, such as #MMIW, they can simply search for the term. Similarly, if a content producer wants to add their media to an archive, they need only hashtag it. Millions tweeted under the #MeToo hashtag to generate a global movement, and Indigenous groups embraced this momentum.

The hashtag helps unify and distribute advocacy media, which has been groundbreaking in digital activism movements (Dadas 2017; Rentschler 2017; Williams 2015; Yang 2016). The hashtag also offers a pragmatic poetry: it is equal parts virtual lyricism, techno-activism, and indelible image. In the case of popularizing images, hashtags are invaluable in creating both public awareness and group solidarity.

In this virtual space, Indigenous SGV advocacy has flourished. Importantly, and relevant to this volume, the hashtag has enabled Indigenous communities to interrupt mainstream narratives. As a Cree content creator informed me in an online chat, "I use #MeToo, but that's only so that my stuff [infographics containing SGV statistics] shows up with everything else. And so people start following #NoMoreStolenSisters and #MMIW in addition to #MeToo. It puts us in the conversation, but not just as a #MeToo afterthought." Indigenous hashtags run the spectrum: #MMIW, #MMIWG, #MMIP, #MMIWG2S, #NoMoreStolenSisters, #ProtectTheSacred, #AmINext, #WhyWeWearRed, #RedDressProject, and more. The generation of the tags is infinite and reflects the growth of the current movement.

Furthermore, the hashtag allows for a collaborative, mixed media poetry. Most hashtag users do not post an image and a single hashtag decontextualized from a larger conversation. Instead, they post a hashtag accompanied by an image, a personal story, or a video; sometimes the hashtag is put in virtual dialogue with other hashtags, resulting in a complex display of unity with various movements. The hashtag's intricacy, as well as its ability to draw together different social justice movements, has helped unify a multitude of users creating content.

Perhaps the most exciting part of the hashtag, beyond the virtual archive, is that it exists—as an image—both inside and outside the virtual world. The hashtag has become more than a social media tool; it is now a cultural artifact that has salience and meaning beyond its practical function. An example from Instagram user @sovereignbodies demonstrates how the hashtag can serve as an artistic statement in and of itself.

On April 18, 2020, @sovereignbodies posted an image to Instagram (Sovereign Bodies Institute 2020); @sovereignbodies is the Instagram handle of the Sovereign Bodies Institute (SBI), an Indigenous organization that promotes community healing and public engagement. SBI also maintains the MMIWG2 database. Their Instagram account curates media related to these initiatives. The April 18, 2020, post describes an event: "We cohosted an art therapy circle with Way of the Sacred Mountain on Land Based MMIWG2 Prayer Altars last night and it was beautiful. Definitely a healing and recentering experience that grounded us in our prayers for our stolen relatives and their families. Stay tuned for another session soon!" To commemorate the prayer altars, @sovereignbodies posted three photographs of an altar. In all of the photos, a small button-pin rests atop floral fabric; spring plants, arranged variously, garland the object. The pin itself is a button that depicts five feminine figures, dressed in ribbon skirts, on a tiered rainbow background, the figure at the top sporting a red dress; the text "#mmiwg2s" is printed across the bottom of the button-pin and serves as the images' focal point.

This post by @sovereignbodies suggests the depth of Indigenous SGV advocacy in virtual spaces. First, @sovereignbodies positions their work as art grounded in a therapeutic community moment—the image, to whom no single individual is attributed—is an image of communal creation, curation, and reflection. Moreover, the image offers nods to not only the hashtag, but also to other advocacy aesthetics: the Red Dress, the ribbon skirt, Indigenous womanhood, and LGBTQ color schemes are all integrated. Furthermore, this image successfully merges the language of the virtual space, #mmiwg2s, with the physical world: the lilacs, spring peas, and fabric, rather than seeming at odds with the hashtag, meld to create a seamless image of seasonal healing. Most importantly, there is no metadata tag in the post itself: the "#mmiwg2s" text stands outside of the virtual, though it is posted within it. Rather than being a product of Instagram, the hashtag is instead its own cultural object: an expression of a uniquely Indigenous solidarity and advocacy movement that is in conversation with the virtual world but, simultaneously, separate from it. In a settler-colonial context of Indigenous silencing and imagined absence, this image and its objects create a new presence.

There are thousands of examples of hashtag activism. As of writing, an Instagram search for "#mmiw" revealed 91,787 results, "#mmiwg" 32,411 results, and "#mmiwg2s" 7,071. Many of these results are combined with the #MeToo movement, while some exclude #MeToo entirely: this invites a range of questions about the efficacy of #MeToo as well as its limitations—while Indigenous activists perhaps initially posited themselves as "(some) Other #MeToos," dialogue has moved toward a unique Indigenous activism grounded in #MeToo's digital tactics. Indigenous SGV activists are perhaps no longer "others," but instead new voices in a rapidly expanding conversation. This speaks to the power of hashtag activism in viral Indigenous communities. The hashtag allows for an Indigenous community, united across the globe, to call for action and solidarity. It is the punctuation and coda of contemporary Indigenous advocacy language and invites an audience of billions.

## Beyond Noiseless Ghosts

The contemporary trajectory of Indigenous SGV advocacy follows a historical one: these are community-oriented projects that rely on Indigenous agency, aesthetics, and creativity. These visualizations have relied on the generative creation of projects that orbit around cultural reclamation and community legibility. Across these projects, there is a strong sense of Indigenous pride and larger community. In conversations with activists, I have been struck by the repeated assertion that "this is a community movement." Although individuals like Jamie Black are visionary, no single person owns a given image, object, or sentiment. Constant innovation and renegotiation of cultural images have allowed Indigenous activists to interrupt mainstream narratives. Indigenous activists, often relegated to spaces assumed to be offline, have seized equally both digital and non-digital spaces for advocacy work and community healing. This points to an Indigenous future grounded in community-determined gender equity and cultural reclamation.

I close this conversation with a reflection on my own experience as an Indigenous activist-survivor. In the winter of 2017, I found myself at odds with the #MeToo movement: simply, I felt left out. I had been reading, at the time, legacies connected to the compulsory sterilization of Indigenous women. As a survivor of both sexual assault and medical traumatization, my mind was cluttered with the violence of colonial systems, and I needed a different way to visualize both personal and historical pain. Jamie Black's REDress Project—the idea that we could create our own sort of haunting of the violence done to us and ours—seemed like a way to quiet the missing part of myself.

*February 17, 2017*
*Wales, Massachusetts*

*When I went down to look, this morning, I felt sick: it's the sort of worry you have when you're nursing a wild animal back to health, but you're keeping it in your basement. You wonder if it's going to be or look more dead when you next see it. But, when I got to the boundary between the field and the woods, the dress was still there, fluttering in the wind. It looked out of place: a fragile, birdlike wisp that shouldn't be among snow-laden pines and their crisscrossed fallen needles. When the wind died, the ripples of fabric quieted. The dress hung/hanged lifeless and still, an empty reminder of something once moving and maybe, in its way, breathing.*

*I retraced my footsteps through the snow. I was careful not to make any new prints—I wanted the place to stay free of everything but the hanging red dress. It was supposed to look empty and stark and almost pristine. A lonely death in an unforgiving place.*

*When I was at the base of the skinny, spiraling pine, I looked to the lowest branch. The red dress, nearly floating on a wire clothes hanger, was still there. I remembered hanging the dress up the night before—taking my gloves off, despite the icy chill, so that the shoulders of the garment fit gracefully over the hanger's divots. The dress was one of my summer dresses—a thin, cheaply made thing that had served me well through humid July nights. I mused on how the neckline was raggedy and how I knew exactly how the stretch cotton fit over my hips. I would miss it, I thought, and maybe even resent that it was gone.*

*I exhaled.*

*I ran my fingers along the fabric and tugged at it a little. I said goodbye, and I'm not sure exactly to whom. Maybe the dress. Maybe some stranger. Maybe a little bit of the fatigue, restless dreams, and nausea that were keeping me up. I imagined what it meant for the dress to stay up in those trees. A ghost to haunt these woods and the noisy ATV tracks ripping through them. A strange, wordless reminder of lives lost. A blood-red interruption to the silent snows. A piece that would, over time, decay and maybe weave itself into a birds' nest or a raccoon's hollow. The red would fade, I imagined, but would likely last—all those scraps of red fabrics, I remembered, on found corpses. "The body was badly decayed, but remains of red, heart-checked underwear were found near the corpse."*

*Red, I had been told, was the color that spirits could see. I didn't know if, in this case, that was a good thing or a bad thing.*

*I turned away and, embarrassed in the snow, staggered as I fought back tears. I was sad and angry—angry at myself for leaving her, sad that I had lost this invisible woman who had once been my dress, and then enraged that I still felt pain and hurt and loneliness after so many years.*

*The pain didn't go up and away into the dress, but it seemed like she and I now shared it. I had created my own ghost in a haunting observed by thousands. A deer woman, I mused, once more dancing.*

## Notes

1. "Feminism" in Indigenous communities is difficult to define due to the comparative gender equity found in Turtle Island Indigenous communities—indeed, while the role of women, two-spirit, and other genders varies among different groups—many Indigenous communities have been identified, by both Indigenous and non-Indigenous people, as gender equitable when compared to European norms. Colonization, girded by patriarchal settler norms, prohibited practices that enabled this equity. Furthermore, various Indigenous activists and scholars have resisted applying the term "feminism" to Indigenous movements; nevertheless, if Indigenous feminism(s) are seen as resisting conventional definitions, and moving within Indigenous ways of knowing, they demonstrate where Indigenous movements align with and resist mainstream movements. For the sake of this chapter, I have identified major movements and events since the late nineteenth century. I have identified not only the establishment of various movements, but also major landmarks in settler violence against Indigenous people. However, these should not be thought of as the entire history of Indigenous feminism on Turtle Island, let alone globally.
2. Throughout this chapter, I use the term "Indigenous." Any shift in terminology is reflective of terminology used by policymakers, individuals, and communities.
3. "Two-spirit people" refers to individuals within the Indigenous community whose genders are outside of colonial definitions of man/woman and/or are along the LGBTQ spectrum.
4. While Jingle Dress Dance is often associated with women dancers, growing numbers of collectives emphasize two-spirit dancers. While the majority of the people with whom I spoke were women, Jingle Dress Dance is not gender exclusive. Additionally, a movement of Jingle Dress Dance has embraced LGBTQ and two-spirit movement aesthetics.

## Works Cited

Allaire, C. 2020. "Indigenous Queen Ilona Verley on Bringing Two-Spirit Representation to Canada's *Drag Race*." *Vogue*. https://www.vogue.com/article/ilona-verley-canadas-drag-race-indigenous-queen. Viewed August 31, 2020.

Anderson, K., M. Campbell, and C. Belcourt, eds. 2018. *Keetsahnak/Our Missing and Murdered Indigenous Sisters*. Alberta: University of Alberta.

Black, J. 2020. *The REDDress Project*. https://www.jaimeblackartist.com/exhibitions/

Burke, T. 2017. "MeToo Was Started for Black and Brown Women and Girls: They're Still Being Ignored." *Washington Post*, 9, November 9, 2017.

Child, B. J. 2008. "Wilma's Jingle Dress: Ojibwe Women and Healing in the Early Twentieth Century: Honoring the Past. Building a Future." In *Reflections on American Indian History: Honoring the Past. Building a Future*, Albert L. Hurtado, pp. 113–136. Oklahoma: University of Oklahoma Press.

Cunneen, C. 2014. "Colonial Processes, Indigenous Peoples, and Criminal Justice Systems." In *The Oxford Handbook of Ethnicity, Crime, and Immigration*, edited by Sandra M. Bucerius and Michael Tonry, pp. 386–407. New York: Oxford University Press.

Dadas, C. 2017. "Hashtag Activism: The Promise and Risk of 'Attention.'" In *Social Writing/Social Media: Publics, Presentations, Pedagogies*, edited by Douglas M. Walls and Stephanie Vie, pp. 17–36. Colorado: WAC Clearinghouse.

Deer, S. 2004. "Toward an Indigenous Jurisprudence of Rape." *Kansas Journal of Law and Public Policy* 14: 121.1.

Deer, S. 2018. "Native People and Violent Crime: Gendered Violence and Tribal Jurisdiction." *Du Bois Review: Social Science Research on Race* 15, no. 1: 89–106.

Dunbar-Ortiz, R., and D. Gilio-Whitaker. 2016. *"All the Real Indians Died Off": And 20 Other Myths about Native Americans*. Boston: Beacon Press.

Edwards, Samantha, 2017. "Q&A: Jaime Black, the Artist Hanging Red Dresses around U of T campus." *Toronto* Life. https://torontolife.com/culture/art/qa-jaime-black-artist-hanging-red-dresses-around-u-t-campus/.

Flay, R. 2017. "A Silent Epidemic: Revisiting the 2013 Reauthorization of the Violence Against Women Act to Better Protect American Indian Native Women. *American Indian Law Journal* 5, no. 1: 5.

Gilio-Whitaker, D. 2019. *As Long as Grass Grows: The Indigenous Fight for Environmental Justice, from Colonization to Standing Rock*. Boston: Beacon Press.

Good, M. 2018. "A Tradition of Violence: Dehumanization, Stereotyping, and Indigenous Women." In *Keetsahnak/Our Missing and Murdered Indigenous Sisters*, edited by Kim Anderson, Maria Campbell, and Christi Belcourt, pp. 89–102. Alberta: University of Alberta Press.

Green, B. [@beautybybeckyo4] 2019, June 22. [Instagram post]. Retrieved from: https://www.instagram.com/p/BzCED9Fhr2b/.

Hall, L. K. 2009. "Navigating Our Own 'Sea of Islands': Remapping a Theoretical Space for Hawaiian Women and Indigenous Feminism." *Wicazo Sa Review* 24, no. 2: 15–38.

Lucashenko, M. 1996. "Violence against Indigenous Women: Public and Private Dimensions." *Violence Against Women* 2, no. 4: 378–390.

Lucchesi, A., and A. Echo-Hawk. 2018. *Missing and Murdered Indigenous Women & Girls: A Snapshot of Data from 71 Urban Cities in the United States*. Seattle: Urban Indian Health Institue.

Mackay, J., and P. Mackay. 2020. "NDNGirls and Pocahotties: Native American and First Nations Representation in Settler Colonial Pornography and Erotica." *Porn Studies* 7, no. 2: 168–186.

Mille Lacs Band of Ojibwe. 2018. *The Jingle Dress Tradition*. [Video]. YouTube. https://www.youtube.com/watch?v=gk7Cha5BVUc.

NCAI Policy Research Center. 2018. *Research Policy Update: Violence against American Indian Women and Girls*. National Congress of American Indians, February 2018. https://www.ncai.org/policy-issues/tribal-governance/public-safety-and-justice/violence-against-women.

Onwuachi-Willig, A., 2018. What about# UsToo: The invisibility of race in the# MeToo movement. *Yale LJF*, *128*, p.105.

PBS NewsHour. 2015. *Prosecuting Non-Natives for Sexual Assault on Reservations*. [Video]. YouTube. https://www.youtube.com/watch?v=1wBNKDzQvSc&t=213s.

Pepitone, J. 2018. *The Stats on Sexual Assault Rates among Native women Will Shock You. Know Your Value.* https://www.nbcnews.com/know-your-value/feature/these-stats-sexual-assault-rates-among-native-women-will-shock-ncna935661.

Reed, C. 2018. "Are We There Yet: An Analysis of Violence against Native American Women and the Implementation of Special Criminal Domestic Violence Jurisdiction." *Journal of Race, Gender & Poverty* 10: 1.

Rentschler, C. A. 2017. "Bystander Intervention, Feminist Hashtag Activism, and the Anti-Carceral Politics of Care." *Feminist Media Studies* 17, no. 4: 565–584.

ShawTV Winnipeg. 2015. *The REDress Project.* [Video]. YouTube. https://www.youtube.com/watch?v=DEWnSdJp1Do.

Sings in the Timber, Adam [@singsinthetimber]. 2020. [Instagram account]. https://www.instagram.com/singsinthetimber/.

Sovereign Bodies Institute [@sovereighbodies]. 2020. [Instagram post]. "We Cohosted an Art Therapy Circle. . . ." Retrieved from https://www.instagram.com/p/B_Ix65hFi-b/.

Suzack, C., S. M. Huhndorf, J. Perreault, and J. Barman, eds. 2010. *Indigenous Women and Feminism: Politics, Activism, Culture.* British Columbia: UBC Press.

Tambe, A. 2018. "Reckoning with the Silences of# MeToo." *Feminist Studies* 44, no. 1: 197–203.

The Jingle Dress Project [@tapahe]. 2020. [Instagram post]. "Art Heals: The Jingle Dress Project." Retrieved from: https://www.instagram.com/p/CEXySwMlT04/.

Verley, I. [@ilonaverley]. 2020, August 31. [Instagram post]. Retrieved from https://www.instagram.com/p/CEke1mEJCRn/.

*Washington Post.* 2014. "'They Come Here to Hunt': Surviving Sexual Violence on the Reservation." [Video]. YouTube, https://youtu.be/0TzguMqHkFU.

Whitebear, L. 2019. "VAWA Reauthorization of 2013 and the Continued Legacy of Violence against Indigenous Women: A Critical Outsider Jurisprudence Perspective." *University of Miami Race & Social Justice Law Review* 9: 75.

Williams, S. 2015. "Digital Defense: Black Feminists Resist Violence with Hashtag Activism." *Feminist Media Studies* 15, no. 2: 341–344.

Wilson, A. 2018. "Skirting the Issue: Indigenous Myths, Misses, and Misogyny." In *Keetsahnak/Our Missing and Murdered Indigenous Sisters*, edited by Kim Anderson, Maria Campbell, and Christi Belcourt.

Woodman, K. 2020. *Beyond# MeToo: Alternative Justice, Hashtag Movements, and Survivor-Centered Approaches to Sexual Violence* (doctoral dissertation, Arts & Social Sciences: Department of Gender, Sexuality, and Women's Studies). Simon Fraser University.

Yang, G. 2016. "Narrative Agency in Hashtag Activism: The Case of# BlackLivesMatter. *Media and Communication* 4, no. 4: 13.

# 4

# Native Men, Too

## Settler Sexual Violence, Native Genocide, and a Dream of Fire

*Nicolás Juárez*

### Timeline

Unlike other topics, Indigenous feminism, like much of Indigenous history, has difficulty fitting within the specific linear history that is common within Western academic fields. Take for example, the Haudenosaunee's creation story in which Sky Woman falls from the sky. For many, such an event would be a necessary inclusion in any timeline that considered the major events of Indigenous feminism. Such a timeline would then begin, as is commonly phrased, in time immemorial. Furthermore, given the numerous transnational and polylingual histories of Indigenous peoples that are grouped under "Indigenous feminism," any normative timeline would also require an international focus on events. This is not to mention, of course, the inevitable politics of constructing any timeline. Given the stakes and scale of such a project, in order to introduce the topic of sexual violence against Native men, this chapter begins instead with a timeline of important scholarly works, tracing the particular intellectual history which informs the chapter. It also serves, in this regard, as a form of citation and reference, naming the litany of texts which inform this project, even in the places they are not explicitly cited.

- 1977: Leslie Marmon Silko (Laguna Pueblo) publishes *Ceremony*, a novel that follows the protagonist Tayo as he recovers from his time fighting in World War II. In it, Silko examines the effects of colonialism on Native American people and the ways in which Indigenous culture can serve as a way to heal from ongoing genocide.
- 1986: Paula Gunn Allen (Laguna Pueblo) writes *The Sacred Hoop: Recovering the Feminine in American Indian Traditions*, an essential text for the emergence of Native American feminisms, which argues for the necessity of including Indigenous women and the feminine in Native American studies.

Nicolás Juárez, *Native Men, Too* In: *The Other #MeToos.* Edited by: Iqra Shagufta Cheema, Oxford University Press.
 DOI: 10.1093/oso/9780197619872.003.0004

- 1990: Leslie Marmon Silko (Laguna Pueblo) publishes *Almanac of the Dead*, a novel which explores the possibility of revolution and the end of colonialism through Indigenous storytelling.
- 1993: Haunani-Kay Trask (Kānaka Maoli) writes *From a Native Daughter: Colonialism and Sovereignty in Hawaiʻi*, explicitly connecting Native American feminism to anti-imperialist and anti-colonialist struggles.
- 1994: Haunani-Kay Trask coins the term "settler colonialism" to name the interlocking structure of colonialism, imperialism, and racism which was aimed at the extermination of Indigenous peoples, building on her work in *From a Native Daughter.*
- 1999: Linda Tuhiwai Smith (Ngāti Awa and Ngāti Porou iwi) writes *Decolonizing Methodologies: Research and Indigenous Peoples*, exploring the settler colonial influences on research methodologies and the potential for Indigenous countermethods.
- 2005: Andrea Smith writes *Conquest: Sexual Violence and American Indian Genocide*, detailing at length how sexual violence was constitutive of anti-Indian violence.
- 2011: *Queer Indigenous Studies* is published, the first collection of its kind, exploring the intersections of queer theory and Indigenous studies.
- 2013: Mishuana Goeman (Tonawanda Band of Seneca) publishes *Mark My Words: Native Women Mapping Our Nations*, demonstrating how settler colonialism endures as a specific form of gendered spatial violence and how Indigenous women play an essential role in constructing counter-geographies.
- 2013: Eve Tuck (Unangax̂) and C. Ree release "A Glossary of Haunting," exploring the ghostliness of Native life through queer Indigenous and Indigenous feminist lens.
- 2015: Sarah Deer (Muscogee Creek) writes *The Beginning and End of Rape: Confronting Sexual Violence in Native America*, exploring the historical overview of sexual violence in Native America, providing a critique of the ways such violence is naturalized.
- 2015: *Indigenous Men and Masculinities: Legacies, Identities, Regeneration* is published as the result of a conference on Indigenous men. The collection takes multiple approaches to Indigenous men, exploring the sociological, anthropological, cultural, and philosophical issues at hand.
- 2017: The collection *Critically Sovereign: Indigenous Gender, Sexuality, and Feminist Studies* is published, containing essays from a variety of Indigenous feminists who show that gender and sexuality play constitutive parts of Indigenous politics, settler colonialism, and sovereignty.

- 2020: Leanne Betasamosake Simpson (Mississauga Nishnaabeg) publishes *As We Have Always Done: Indigenous Freedom through Radical Resistance*, theorizing Indigenous resurgence through Indigenous epistemology and culture and naming it as a rejection of settler colonialism and its imbrications.

This timeline is, by necessity, incomplete given the ways in which Indigenous feminist writings, be they poetry, fiction writing, or theory, inform this text in a multitude of ways, some surely unconscious. However, what this timeline hopes to introduce is a way of understanding the following text as necessarily indebted to the struggle and theorizing of those who came before.

## Introduction

The colonization of the Americas instituted a global regime of power which initiated sexual violence as a condition of social life (Maldonado-Torres, 2007). Such a claim may seem hyperbolic, but given the public dialogue initiated by the #MeToo movement, it becomes increasingly apparent that every facet of social life—from the workplace to the university to the home to the streets to the intimacies we share with our loved ones—is either explicitly a site of sexual violence or deeply haunted by it. At the same time, such dialogue often remains hobbled by its focus on a particular archetype: a white, middle class, usually college-educated woman. Several feminists of color have lobbied critiques of this focus, attending to the ways in which sexual violence is contoured differently for different bodies, as well as to how cisheteropatriarchy itself is an insufficient frame for understanding the nature of sexual violence as it is distributed across times, places, and bodies (Adetiba and Burke, 2018; Ukoha, 2018; Ahmed, 2017, Harris, 2017). Building on these critiques, I contend that when the #MeToo movement encounters Native American men, it lacks a grammar to understand how sexual violence is constitutive of our, Native men's, experience.[1]

Focusing on how #MeToo not only fails to think, but also lacks the theoretical tools to consider Native men is not meant to detract from the claims made by women, especially women of color. I contend that taking up the position of Native men complicates and deepens discourses on sexual violence and agency, specifically as they relate to gender and race. This allows us to better understand the machinations of violence and chart alternative strategies for action in order to actualize decolonization. It is important to note that here I do not mean decolonization in its reformist connotations, especially as it relates to calls to either "decolonize" settler institutions such as the academy or fill such institutions with Native bodies. Rather, I invoke decolonization as something that ends worlds, that radically undoes, and that renders illegible in order to craft alternative ways of being for and with each other, disentangled from settler colonial genocide. In this way, I take up this project as a way of feeling toward the burning of the colony, of a way of dreaming fire.

In order to do this work, this piece begins by deploying critical Indigenous feminist theory to sketch out a framework to understand settler colonialism, while also tending to how Native men come to experience sexual violence. In the former, it does so by looking at an alternative history of settler colonial theory that begins with Indigenous women charting the specificities of settler colonial violence for Native American peoples, particularly as that violence relates to genocide. Specifically, it uses Kānaka Maoli scholar Haunani-Kay Trask's claim that "for indigenous peoples, civil society is itself a creation of settler colonies. [ . . . ] By definition, conquest is an extermination not a recognition of aboriginal peoples and their familial relationship with the earth" (1999, p. 25). Such a definition does not shy away from naming the violence of settler colonialism, nor does it excuse it as a lamentable historical incident. Rather, it names settlers for what they are—not people simply making a home, but murderers. In doing so, it offers an analysis at the level of political ontology, investigating the "powers subjects have or lack, the constituent elements of subjects' structural position with which they are imbued or lack prior to the subjects' performance" (Wilderson, 2010, p. 8). As for the latter, it explores the ways in which Native men's experiences with sexual violence tend to problematize and contradict the common theoretical assumption, both in academia and outside it, that masculinity, in all cases, serves as a protection from sexual violence. Challenging such an assumption inevitably carries risks. However, taking such risks are necessary in order to tease out how normative assumptions about agency, consent, and the body no longer provide generative means for thinking about and addressing sexual violence, especially within the settler colony. It is for both of these reasons that this piece argues that settler colonialism has rendered sexual violence constitutive of social life such that one must understand it, in the world birthed from genocide, "not as an isolated act, but as part of a spectrum of sexual coercion generated within a broader set of social, political, and economic relations regulated (but not simply controlled) by the racial state and enabling permutations of enactment" (Sexton, 2003, p. 36). Tracing out the ways in which this structure of violence impacts Native men and the #MeToo movement is the focus of this chapter.

## Settler Violence, Sexual Violence

Before tracing the structure broadly, it is necessary to examine the history of Indigenous feminist scholarship and examine the current literature on Native masculinities. Scholars in Indigenous feminism and Indigenous queer studies have been doing the work analyzing sexual violence as constitutive of settler colonialism for decades now. In 1986, Lakota scholar Paula Gunn Allen would write that rape was a constitutive element of settler colonization and, as such, a constitutive element of life within the settler colony. She'd go further to argue that this signaled the ways in which settler colonization instituted patriarchy as a mode of control, deploying it as a tactic of genocide and of breaking Indigenous relationships to land (1986). A decade later, Trask (1999) would extend this argument further, exploring the ways in which Native Hawaiian women become instruments for the sexual pleasure of settlers, speaking to a general condition by which Native women become constitutively open to sexual violence in the settler colonial order. Trask (1999) further describes the feminization of Native land bases, in which the land itself takes on gendered qualities, in order to articulate a link between the position of Native women and the land. Both of these arguments would be extended by Andrea Smith (2015), who would argue that the position of Native women made them unable to be raped since they were positioned as overwhelmingly lascivious and dirty.[2] From this point, work on settler colonialism and sexual violence would be even further extended by a litany of Indigenous scholars, including Eve Tuck, Sarah Deer, Maile Arvin, Jodi Byrd, Chris Finley, Andrew Jolivétte, Billy-Ray Belcourt, Lindsay Nixon, Kim Anderson, Lisa Tatonetti, and Daniel Heath Justice, to name just a few.[3]

Most of these writings employ Native women as the archetypal position for conceptualizing sexual violence and settler colonialism. Writings on Native American men have been comparatively scarce, especially in considering cisheterosexual Native American men's relationship to violence. Two anthologies published in the 2010s—*Indigenous Men and Masculinities: Legacies, Identities, Regeneration* (2015) and *Masculindians: Conversations about Indigenous Manhood* (2014)—contain the most prominent writing on cisheterosexual Native American men and Native American masculinity. These writings provide important scholarly work on Native men by often tracing out the ways in which Native American masculinity is understood traditionally and how it has been shaped by settler colonization. However, these works often do not discuss the ways in which sexual violence is experienced by Native American men, instead often dealing with the loss of traditionally masculine responsibilities, the vast imprisonment of Native men, or the exceptionally high rate of murder and disappearance among Native men. Even writings about queer Native men often fail to discuss at length how sexual violence is constitutive of the experiences of queer Native men.

My intervention thus addresses the gap in literature surrounding Native men's experience with sexual violence and settler colonialism, especially in cisheterosexual encounters. I argue that even though the #MeToo movement can put on the appearance of translating its terms and concerns to Native women, Native men function as an aporia in discourses around sexual violence which, if addressed, offers the possibility of extending and provoking new directions in Indigenous feminism.[4] In order to address this aporia, however, it is necessary to begin in broad strokes, laying out the theoretical scaffolding necessary to see the ways in which settler colonialism shapes the grammars of the #MeToo movement and its rhetoric. From there, we'll see how this structure of violence has not only arisen historically, but how it impacts both official government reporting on issues of sexual violence in Native America as well as the broader structure of sexual violence throughout society.

Given #MeToo's intimate connection to sexual violence, pleasure, and revulsion, it is necessary to begin by laying out a theoretical understanding of psychic life. In this instance, Lacanian psychoanalysis functions as the basis for our understanding. Broadly, psychoanalyst Jacques Lacan formulates desire as the result of a constitutive lack inherent to speaking beings. This lack arises from the fact that in order for the phenomenological subject, the ego, to come into existence, it is necessary for it to speak, to take on language so that it might say "I" or, at least, possess the "I" as a sign to which it can identify. Language imbues speaking beings with this negativity to the extent that such negativity is a prior necessity for language so that it can be an incomplete project, ever evolving and endlessly productive. This negativity is then internalized in the speaking being who, upon encountering it, tends to fantasize about some prior completion it once possessed, experiencing that negativity as a lack, assuming that it is missing an object that would quell its desire. Desire, here, marks the metonymic phenomenon of the speaking being's endless demands, constantly asking for something, only to find that, upon receiving it, it still experiences want qua desire (Zupančič, 2017). The object that would end this metonymic cycle is named by Lacan the *objet petit a*, but, rather than an object of desire, the *objet petit a* is the object-cause of desire, that which sets in motion the metonymic nature of desire by ensuring the absence or lack that allows for the phenomenological subject's existence.

Despite the impossibility of obtaining this object, given that it is a prior ontological negativity, the speaking being, seeking to quell its desires so that it might experience completion or wholeness, seeks all manner of alternative objects, imagining that they possess within them that which would end desire, the *objet petit a* (Lacan, 2015). Once some object becomes a stand-in for the *objet petit a*, it becomes the target of the drives which, following psychoanalyst Jacques-Alain Miller's thesis, take satisfaction as their object (Zupančič, 2017). This satisfaction Lacan names *jouissance*, which indicates an enjoyment that goes beyond the Freudian pleasure principle—that principle essential to the maintenance of life that seeks to keep tension at the lowest level. As such, if *jouissance* were endlessly pursued, it would culminate in our destruction (Lacan, 1991).

Yet, at the same time, Lacan remarks that the drives, despite their aim at satisfaction, have as their ultimate end, their goal, the endless circulation around the ontological negativity that is *objet petit a*, resulting in the repetition compulsion noticed by Sigmund Freud in the analytic encounter (Lacan, 1981). In this schema, the *jouissance* the phenomenological subject cares about is simply a means to an end for the drives. To quote Lacanian scholar Alenka Zupančič, "what is profoundly disturbing about the "death drive" [is] not that it wants only to enjoy, even if it kills us, but that it wants only to repeat this negativity, this gap in the order of being, *even if this means to enjoy* [emphasis in the original]" (2017, p. 104) The observation of this repetition, this *jouissance* that is endlessly and repetitively pursued despite the failure to achieve full satisfaction, should thus signal to us, just as it did to Freud, that the death drive has appeared on the scene.

Similarly, the endless repetition of acts of genocide against Native American people from contact into the present should signal to us that the death drive has appeared on the scene. Thus, settler colonialism is a *death-driven structure.* Despite different people in different places, despite different political regimes, despite different tactics, there remains a historical stillness around genocide for Native Americans. This occurs because the settler body politic narrates itself as having the capacity for infinite being, i.e., being without lack, but constantly experiences the failure to have that capacity. Recognition and identification with that failure would destroy the "well-being of our present ethnoclass (i.e., Western bourgeois) conception of the human, Man, which overrepresents itself as if it were the human itself" given that such a conception of the Human requires the narrative of its non-lack in order to justify its material and symbolic order (Wynter, 2003, p. 260; Rodriguez, 2019). In seeking to narrate itself as infinitely transcendent despite its empirical failure to be so, the Human-as-settler constructs the figure of the Indian to be an embodied lack, the psychic reservoir of all the failings of the settler. This embodied lack becomes not only a barrier to the settler's perfect body—scaled from the individual to the world qua network of settler colonies—but also the cause of any failure in the colony—shown in the anxiety surrounding "going Native." The completion of Native American genocide, then, becomes a representative of the *objet petit a*, that which, if obtained, would quell settler desire qua lack. At the first level, this would suggest that Native American genocide is the result not—*pace* Wolfe—of a movement toward utility expressed in land grabbing, but, instead, *jouissance*. To extend our analysis further, it would be to say that even when settlers do not experience pleasure from genocide, they feel compelled to repeat it since the goal of the drives is repetition.

It is the facticity of this structure of repetition's existence that allows us to extend Trask's (1999, p. 25) argument that "civil society is itself a creation of settler colonies" even further to say that the libidinal economy is the creation of settler colonies. Here, the libidinal economy names the "distribution and arrangement of desire and identification (their condensation and displacement), and the complex relationship between sexuality and the unconscious" which includes the "dispensation of energies, concerns, points of attention, anxieties, pleasures, appetites, revulsions, and phobias" (Wilderson, 2010, p. 8). Genocide thus contours the very nature of sexuality itself. As Belcourt tells us, love, anthropomorphized, "wonders if it is the possibility of being killed that partly animates his desires" (2017, p. 10). And since the settler spreads their world nihilistically like a cancer, the libidinal economy of settler colonialism has become an inescapable feature of the last several iterations of modernity (Deloria, 1969).

Both these points—the historical stillness of Native American genocide and the ways in which that genocide serves as a method of veiling the Human's lack—become clear with a cursory examination of the history of violence against Native American men. Early encounters between Indigenous populations and settler colonizers often resulted in gender-based violence given that Indigenous populations failed to (re)produce European gender organization. While some queer populations were particularly singled out in the early days of conquest, Native populations writ large were framed as failing to uphold European gender norms. In settler colonization then, as it does now, sexual violence took the form of a variety of techniques—murder, surveillance, coercion, rape, theft, torture, mutilation, and beyond.

However, as Scott Lauria Morgensen points out, coterminous with colonialism's initiation were debates over masculinity and manhood in Europe in the sixteenth and seventeenth centuries. Rather than a pregiven status associated with those assigned male at birth, masculinity was only afforded to those who achieved specific social markers. While alternative masculinities were formed in Europe at the time, they were tenuous and often failed to gain any large social traction. Yet, in encountering Native American men who were racially other, there was the possibility of European conquistadors inscribing a failure to achieve masculinity upon them, setting them up as the receptacle of their psychic fantasies, here controlled by anxiety. Then, by killing and torturing Native men as effigies of themselves, European men symbolically purged themselves of their gender anxieties while securing their own masculinity in contrast to a racial other (Morgensen, 2015). Violence, here, worked in two ways. First, it not only sought to murder Native men who were identified as openly practicing what European colonizers understood as sexual deviance; it was also a broader regime of racialized and gendered terror that sought to produce Native masculinity as definitively cisheterosexual (Morgensen, 2015). Second, it worked to stabilize a crisis in European masculinity which might be understood, drawing from Byrd, as a moment in which Native men were "rendered as an unknowable blankness that can then be used to reflect back the colonizer's desires and fantasies" (2011, p. 64).

In order to see how the historical stillness of this violence plays out in the present, it is necessary to examine current reports on violence against Native people. In their introduction to *Indigenous Men and Masculinities: Legacies, Identities, Regeneration,* Robert Alexander Innes and Kim Anderson point out that rates of murder and disappearance for Native men are not only comparable, but at times exceed the rates of Native women (2015). A shallow reading would interpret the introduction of this fact as an attempt to alleviate Native men of any responsibility for patriarchal behavior, or to say that there is nothing about Native womanhood that is noteworthy. However, as Innes and Anderson (2015, p. 7) point out, the real point of interest is that "Indigenous men and women are at much greater risk of going missing than are white men" and that "White women . . . are by far the least likely to go missing." Instead of detracting from the struggles of Native women, this points out that, despite their participation in misogyny, Native men are not rewarded with protections from violence, something that is often imagined as granted through masculinity. Though for many people, it is not simply violence, but who experiences and commits sexual violence that marks the difference between genders. In these instances, is it still true that Native men are no different? The very idea seems to contradict what is now common sense among those of us concerned with gender and its entrapments. On face, government reports suggest that our unease is justified—a preliminary review of the 2016 report on sexual and intimate partner violence faced by Native Americans suggest an easy division between Native men and women: Native men and women have comparable rates of intimate partner violence, with Native women being more likely to face physical abuse and Native men being more likely to face psychological abuse, but Native women are distinctively more likely to be sexually abused (U.S. Department of Justice, 2016). Yet, further investigation reveals a more complicated portrait of violence. The report, interestingly, partitions control over reproductive or sexual health as a "psychological violence" even though "experienced unwanted pregnancy attempts" and "experienced refusals to use condoms" are grouped there. Can we think of a violence more intimate than being forced to be made pregnant or being forced to impregnate someone? Both experiences are mired in sexual violence. Furthermore, Native men are more likely than Native women to face psychological intimate partner violence. In the particular area of control over reproductive or sexual health, Native men are over three times more likely than Native women to experience unwanted pregnancy attempts (U.S. Department of Justice, 2016). This is without mentioning either the 27.5% of Native men who face sexual violence in the form of forced or coerced penetration (including being made to penetrate, which is massively underreported), sexual coercion, or unwanted sexual contact or experiences, nor the fact that jails and prisons where Native men are disproportionately locked up face rates of sexual violence far greater than the general public (Struckman-Johnson and Struckman-Johnson, 2000; U.S. Department of Justice, 2010; U.S. Department of Justice, 2016).

This is only a government report by a settler government; like all official reports, it is inherently unreliable. But it makes us confront a disturbing truth: Despite the various differences at the level of phenomenology and different ways in which sexual violence is experienced, the rates of violence are disturbingly similar between Native men and women. This points to the fact that Native men are not afforded the protections from sexual violence that masculinity is assumed to confer. Reading all of this as part of the psychic history of settler colonialism, I argue that, in this context, cisheteropatriarchy has a similar and comparable coercive exhortation on Native men as it does on Native women. It does so because settler colonialism institutes a strategy in which regimes of terror can shore up one's position as a man, inciting in those interested in manhood their participation in an ongoing regime of terror upon all those who are non-men so that they may access a promised masculinity (that is always in crisis). The Native man, caught up as he is in the movement of the settler's libidinal economy, does not escape such a call to perform gendered violence—imagining that he, too, will reap the rewards of masculinity. However, given his ontological position as the reservoir of masculinity's failings, he fails to be protected from violence despite the performances of his violence. In spite of the rhetorical construction of his benefit, he continues to face massive violence, from imprisonment to sexual assault to murder. In contrast to the white woman who figures as the archetypal figure of the #MeToo movement, the Native man is more likely to be poor, more likely to be imprisoned, more likely to be murdered, and more likely to be used as a sexual implement. Such a claim does not excuse Native men's violence—one is not freed from ethics simply because one suffers—but it does explode the liberal, humanist grammar that sutures the #MeToo movement.

It does so because it institutes a theory of sexual violence that understands white womanhood as constitutively violent toward cisheterosexual Native men, even as they might be instituted within a libidinal economy in which Native men cannot recognize that violence as violence, since the violence they experience is not only so overwhelmingly quotidian so as to be unrecognizable from everyday life, but is also frequently regarded as enjoyable (and may even be experienced as such). Whether it be the constant compulsion to have sex with women in order to fulfill the (at times unconscious) mandate of masculinity to acquire sexual conquests, or the ways in which his choice in sexual and romantic partners is structurally controlled by genocide, he undergoes a sexual violence. If consent requires free choice outside of coercion, Native men's consent is not only illegible—something likely shared by all to the extent that the juridico-legal framework of consent frays at even a cursory examination of structural violence—but ontologically barred within and by the last several iterations of modernity. Such violence is not simply repressive, but productive—it constructs and produces the Native body and mind, paradoxically, as a result of genocide. In doing so, it simultaneously makes legible European gender, stabilizing masculinity and femininity. To be direct: the ongoing sexual violence against Native men, a violence so commonplace that it is often unrecognized as violence by Native men because it is their condition of possibility, not only secures white masculinity, but also allows for white femininity. In a contradictory logic, the same settler colonial violence that allows the white woman in #MeToo to articulate her body as violable and, therefore, worthy of redress is the same violence that institutes sexual violence as a condition of sociality.[5]

It is the condition of sociality for the very reason that the stability of the gender binary was proof of Europe and its peoples' civilization (Morgensen, 2015). Yet, such stability required the genocide of the Native before it could be achieved; even though, in the narrative of the settler, it must have always been this way, inherent to the racial-historical schema that would become inscribed on white skin. In this way, the feral life of the Native both precedes and succeeds civilization as its condition of possibility. Despite the ways in which #MeToo speaks to a general longing among white womanhood to be free from sexual violence, white women cannot achieve this without forgoing the very condition of their womanhood, defined as it is through genocidal violence. However, not only does settler colonialism institute sexual violence as a general condition of social life, but white women have a vested interested in its maintenance beyond the fact that their very condition of possibility as white women relies upon it. It is here that we must not shy away from the incendiary nature of such an analysis and go even further: Narratives of victimization have become so constitutively wedded to settler colonial theories of femininity that absent their general violation they would lose their capacity to marshal state and extrajudicial power for their settler colonial pleasure and protection. Such pleasures and protections are wide-ranging—the ontological capacity to produce and securely reside within a home, the impossibility of being marked as the violator because one is always already the violated, the capacity to marshal legal and extralegal forces to protect one's womanhood, and a libidinal ordering that positions white femininity as the pinnacle of desirability, to name only a few. In contrast, the Native man must be unable to occupy the terrain of fatherhood as a "unique disadvantage in finding a permanent and loving home," be positioned a priori as criminal and violent, and be constitutively understood as traumagenic for all involved with him, even as he is used by white women as a sexual implement to indigenize settler kinship formations (Alito, 2013, p. 14).

Applied to our discussion of #MeToo, this also means that sexual violence is performed even absent its *jouissance* because that sexual violence arises from a structure, settler colonialism, that has *jouissance* as an important, but ultimately inessential feature. While the erotics of empire are essential at the level of a subject's conscious awareness, they are not essential to the maintenance of a violence that exceeds the frame of experience. In order for sexual violence to cease to be so quotidian that it could be an organizing principle, it would be necessary for "the material and symbolic grounds of Mankind's global integrity . . . [to become] the subject of a creative disintegration" (Rodriguez, 2019, p. 126). Yet, for the archetypal subject of #MeToo, the white woman, to take on such a project, she would be forced to confront Tecumseh's call to "stain the earth red with blood" (1823, p. 48). Is this conceivable? If the white feminine imago, "the psychic formation of the body that is constructed through . . . socialization and psychic development," requires genocide in order to be coherent, then it would require not only a loss of self, the phenomenological subject, but a complete annihilation of the body as a psychic object with which the subject could identify (Henderson, 2015, p. 47). Such a project seems unlikely. In contrast, the Indian, only fantasizing about gender but not accessing it, would only have to let go of the fantasy of being part of the universality of the Human, with Native men, and here being an ontological difference between them and Native women, having to additionally forgo masculinity as a site of imagined wholeness—something that is synonymous with masculinity writ large in settler colonial economies. This is no easy project, but it requires not loss—the grammar of the Human—but only recognition and acceptance of one's position as embodied lack, albeit lack that is often rendered ontologically synonymous with wilderness. It is only here that the structural problem identified by #MeToo could be resolved—not in juridico-legal fights or in attempts to craft perfect norms in the sexual encounter, but in settler decolonization which indexes the ending of settler colonialism in both practice and metaphysics.

What does this all mean for the Native man's relationship to the Native non-men?[6] His position in relation to Native non-men is more complicated, but if he is imagined to secure some benefit distinct from them, it is because he is called upon to commit violence against them as proof of his manhood, a call he takes up willingly in hopes of securing some masculine power. His violence, here, is noteworthy, and its cessation is essential and even a prerequisite to settler decolonization, but it does not afford him power. What do we mean here? To fully flesh out the relationship(s) between Native men, Native non-men, and the respective ways they experience genocide exceeds the reach of this chapter, but it might be possible to at least illuminate the direction of this thought. To do this, it is necessary to understand power as institutional capacity. By institutional capacity, here, I mean both the capacity to marshal institutions in order to fulfil one's fantasies as well as the capacity to institutionalize, to make something normative. How can it be said that Native men lack power over Native non-men, then? Let us explore a couple of these avenues.

In one way, it is that Native men possess no more power than Native non-men over the political and libidinal economies that shape Native life. As discussed above, Native men's failure to inflict violence on and control over Native non-men is met with a disciplinary regime of terror that eradicates either the bodies or the minds of those who push against the settler colonial order such that there no longer exists a subject who possesses the will to challenge power. If such violence is less explicit in this iteration of modernity, it is only because of how assured it is that Natives will discipline and control each other. As has been shown recently at Standing Rock, state agents are more than willing to send guns, rockets, drones, and more in order to discipline Natives who break with the order instituted by the settler colony. Another way to think of this is by hypothetical example. Suppose that a Native non-man and those who know them—men, women, and otherwise—terrorized another Native non-man, we would not say that it conferred them a structural position above the other. Put another way, we would not say that simply because someone has suffered and someone has not that the one who has not suffered has power, even if they are the ones causing the other to suffer. Whether or not one Indian or another inflicts harm on another does not change the first Indian's position in the world, even if that suffering occurs over a long period of time. What must change are the relative capacities between those subjects. That subjects now discipline one another is simply an advancement in the technologies of governance, but it does not change whether or not one has power. To say that suffering confers or takes away power is to risk excusing the power of white supremacy simply because a singular white person has suffered more than a non-white person. If we find such statements objectionable, it would be equally necessary for us to reject that as a theory of the way power is distributed between subjects of the same racial position.

Exploring a final avenue, it is also necessary to point out that simply because one attains a position in an institution, that does not mean that one is structurally imbued with power. This logic of representation is at the heart of counterinsurgency (Brough, 2020). Does the fact that women graduate college more frequently than men or are more likely to win custody battles or are more likely to receive less harsh prison sentences suggest that patriarchy is over and that men are now the oppressed group? Such a claim would ignore that it is not women, ultimately, who control these issues. Women receive these things because they are imagined as more caring and less violent—features of femininity that men, over centuries, have determined. Likewise, the fact that Native men are recognized more frequently by settler institutions—and, to be clear, tribal governments often are settler institutions—does not confer on them more power, even if it might confer on them more force. It is instead emblematic of the order instituted by settler colonialism and controlled by settlers.

In naming this, I want to reify my position: None of this alleviates Native men from responsibility for the cisheteropatriarchal violence they enact, nor does it suggest that it is not of the utmost importance for Native men to be continually challenging cisheteropatriarchal actions and institutions. In fact, the point is the opposite: Native men have absolutely nothing to gain from their ongoing participation in violence against non-men, and it is only the most fallacious thinking that assumes that the power promised by masculinity will come tomorrow. Any libidinal pleasure obtained in inflicting suffering—and I will not ignore that such pleasure exists—is far outweighed by the ways in which cisheteropatriarchy maintains and supports the genocide of Native men. It is the burden of Native men to "recognize that this shit is killing you, too, however much more softly" (Harney and Moten, 2013, p. 141). The point is not that Native men and Native non-men have absolutely no difference between them, but that they are constitutively Indians, defined as such by genocide, and that their difference is purely phenomenological, not structural. This is to say that at the level of political ontology, they are not different, despite what might occur ontically, at the level of experience, between them. If such a realization is uncomfortable—that settlers will not even afford us the dignity to make differentiations in our suffering—it is because confronting the existence and extent of genocide as an ontological condition obliterates all hope for a regained humanity. The only option, then, is to dream of fire.

## On Burning the Settler Colony

To dream of fire is to dream of an otherwise, an elsewhere and elsewhen. It is to dream of *'utzil li xanavik e ta 'ach li 'osil e.*[7] There will be multiple, infinite routes to this dream, but one route to the dream of colony-burning can be found in Este Mvskokvlke poet Joy Harjo's poem "Resurrection." In it, Harjo takes the Nicaraguan mountain town Estelí as her subject, describing the way violence has been folded into multiple layers of everyday life. In one sense, the "sweet melody" of songs that "speak tender of honor and love" is "the undercurrent of gunfire" (Harjo, 1990, p. 17), signaling the ways in which normative ideals of honor or love seem to give coherence to war. Yet, Harjo interrupts this fantasy of coherence to write that

> the wounded and the dead call out in words that sting
> like bitter limes. (1990, p. 17)

Here, Harjo reveals that such sweet melodies, such conceptual instruments, cannot quell the pain of genocide. No narrative can assist us in that. She writes that

> I have no damned words to make violence fit neatly
>                                                                 like wrapped packages
> of meat to contain us safely. (1990, p. 17)

Furthermore, for Harjo, this violence is intimately connected to sex(uality) and reproduction. As soon as she invokes the dead, she adds, in parentheses that both signal the hidden and the subterranean,

> (Ask the women who have given away the clothes of their dead children.
> Ask the frozen soul of a man who was found in the hole left
> by his missing penis.) (1990, p. 17)

Dead children, a missing penis—what would it mean to reorganize the grammar of #MeToo around this? I want to read the final lines of Harjo's poem as a program for settler decolonization:

> We all watch for fire
>                                 for all the fallen dead to return
> and teach us a language so terrible
>                                                 it could resurrect us all. (1990, 17)

Where does this lead us? First, settler decolonization is a project of fire, of burning. This is inescapable. As Belcourt writes in his own poetry, it is an absolute necessity that "the Cree girl blows up the necropolis of Ottawa" wherein Ottawa is a stand-in for the necropolis of the settler colony-as-world writ large (2019, p. 17). This fire is both metaphorical and literal—settler decolonization must operate both at the level of the metaphorical and the material because Mankind is not simply the result of historical, material processes but, in fact, also a result of libidinal drives. Second, Harjo understands that the dead must rise. As Tuck and C. Ree remind us, "decolonization is not an exorcism of ghost" but rather requires an endless haunting that "lies precisely in its refusal to stop" because it "doesn't hope to change people's perceptions, nor does it hope for reconciliation" but instead "aims to wrong the wrongs" (2013, pp. 642, 648). What does it mean to wrong the wrongs of settler colonialism? It is up to us to experiment with this—but it does not seek to be incorporated into the settler colony, nor does it believe that the settler's gestures of reconciliation are anything but hallucinogenic. Most importantly, it does not forget, it remembers that one is Indian and the actions that flow from that memory are the result of sitting with the historical stillness of genocide. Third, Harjo recognizes that we lack the language to talk about this.

Part of the project of settler decolonization is the creation of language that could speak to and from the terror of genocide. As Harjo points out, this is a language we learn from the dead—it is something that comes from tarrying with those Indians who have died as a result of settler colonial genocide. To my knowledge, no Indian has ever died of anything else. Finally, it presumes, correctly, that all of us Indians are dead. Our resurrection could only result from this combination of fire, haunting, and language, but it will not be a resurrection that brings Indians into the living, but rather a decolonial resurrection into a realm beyond the living, into the elsewhere and elsewhen where sexual violence is no longer constitutive of the social. For us to both imagine what this will look like and to bring it into being will require fire, haunting, and language. However, if #MeToo is to say anything to Native people, especially to Native men, it will first have to be consumed by these flames.

## Notes

1. Throughout, I use "Native American" and "Native" to refer to the racial position of the peoples Indigenous to the Americas. I use "Indigenous" to refer to the specific ethnic or cultural belonging of an individual. I will use "settler" not only to refer to historical subjects, but to those who are structurally enabled by settler colonialism, namely all those who are non-Native and non-Black.
2. It is worth noting here that Andrea Smith's claims to Cherokee ancestry and, subsequently, her claim to Indigeneity are fraught and highly contested at best, and are completely false and examples of settler colonial elimination at worst. It is not my intention in citing her here to affirm her claim as an Indigenous woman, but, rather, to maintain an academic honesty that despite her problematic identity claims, her work has been indispensable for many Indigenous feminists.
3. For some of the prominent work by some these scholars, please refer to the Further Reading section.
4. Here I use "Indigenous feminism" to refer to Indigenous feminism, Indigenous queer theory, Indigenous masculinity studies, and their various offshoots.
5. This is not to say that this condition of violability cannot be lost. White sex workers, for example, are often considered inviolable. However, the argument here concerns less the status of a particular white woman's violability, but instead addresses the way in which the condition of violability can be gained or lost, struggled over, for white women, whereas for Native and Black persons such violability is structurally barred prior to performance by their ontological position in the world. For more on the difference between performance and ontology, see Frank B. Wilderson in Further Reading.

6. Readers may notice some slippage between "women" and "non-men" in the text. Exploring this slippage and the constitutive relationships between manhood, womanhood, and the queer space that occupies neither position exceeds the space available in this text, but, for now, it is sufficient to say that these positions are not synonymous, yet Native men are often called upon to commit violence against both in order to demonstrate their manhood.
7. The above is my translation in Tzotzil, my Native language, for decolonization. Such translation is likely imperfect and is open to comment and critique from other Tzotzil speakers. For more on sitting with imperfect words, see Eve Tuck in Further Reading.

## Works Cited


Adetiba, Elizabeth, and Tarana Burke. 2018. "Tarana Burke Says #MeToo Should Center Marginalized Communities." In *Where Freedom Starts: Sex, Power, Violence in #MeToo*, edited by Verso Books, pp. 7–11. London: Verso.

Ahmed, Sufiya. 2017. "We Must Include Women from Conflict Zones in the #MeToo Hashtag." *Huffington Post*. https://www.huffingtonpost.co.uk/sufiya-ahmed/can-we-include-women_b_18356486.html.

Alito, Samuel. 2013. *Adoptive Couple v. Baby Girl*. 398 S. C. 625.

Allen, Paula Gunn. 1986. *The Sacred Hoop: Recovering the Feminine in American Indian Traditions*. Boston, MA: Beacon Press.

Belcourt, Billy-Ray. 2017. "Love and Heartbreak Are Fuck Buddies." In *This Wound Is a World*, p. 10. Calgary: Frontenac House.

Belcourt, Billy-Ray. 2019. "Cree Girl Blows Up the Necropolis of Ottawa." In *NDN Coping Mechanisms: Notes from the Field*, p. 17. Toronto, ON: House of Anansi Press.

Brough, Taylor Jade. 2020. "Counter-Insurgency, Liberalism, & the Transmogrification of Radical Meaning," Master's thesis, Wake Forest University, Winston-Salem, NC.

Deloria, Vine, Jr. 1969. *Custer Died for Your Sins: An Indian Manifesto*. New York: Macmillan.

Harjo, Joy. 1990. "Resurrection." In Harjo, *In Mad Love and War*, pp. 17–18. Middletown, CT: Wesleyan University Press.

Harney, Stefano, and Fred Moten. 2013. *The Undercommons: Fugitive Planning and Black Study*. New York: Autonomedia.

Harris, Ida. 2017. "We Get It. It's Harvey Weinstein's News Cycle. But What about Our Black Girls?" *The Root*. https://www.theroot.com/we-get-it-it-s-harvey-weinstein-s-news-cycle-but-what-1820037770.

Henderson, Phil. 2015. "Imagoed Communities: The Psychosocial Space of Settler Colonialism." *Settler Colonial Studies* 7, no. 1: 40–56.

Innes, Robert Alexander, and Kim Anderson. 2015. "Introduction: Who's Walking with Our Brothers?" In *Indigenous Men and Masculinities: Legacies, Identities, Regeneration*, edited by Robert Alexander Innes and Kim Anderson, pp. 3–17. Winnipeg: University of Manitoba Press.

Lacan, Jacques. 1981. *Seminar XI: The Four Fundamental Concepts of Psychoanalysis*. Translated by Alan Sheridan. New York: W. W. Norton.

Lacan, Jacques. 1991. *Seminar XVII: The Other Side of Psychoanalysis*. Translated by Russell Grig. New York: W. W. Norton.

Lacan, Jacques. 2015. *Seminar VIII: Transference*. Translated by Bruce Fink. Malden, MA: Polity Press.

Maldonado-Torres, Nelson. 2007. "On the Coloniality of Being: Contributions to the Development of a Concept." *Cultural Studies* 21, no. 2–3: 240–270.

Morgensen, Scott Lauria. 2015. "Cutting to the Roots of Colonial Masculinity." In *Indigenous Men and Masculinities: Legacies, Identities, Regeneration*, edited by Robert Alexander Innes and Kim Anderson, pp. 38–61. Winnipeg: University of Manitoba Press.

Rodriguez, Dylan. 2019. "Insult/Internal Debate/Echo." *Propter Nos* 3: 125–131.

Sexton, Jared. 2003. "Race, Sexuality, and Political Struggle: Reading 'Soul on Ice.'" *Social Justice* 30, no. 2: 28–41.

Smith, Andrea. 2015. *Conquest: Sexual Violence and American Indian Genocide*. Durham, NC: Duke University Press.

Struckman-Johnson, Cindy, and David Struckman-Johnson. 2000. "Sexual Coercion Rates in Seven Midwestern Prison Facilities for Men." *The Prison Journal* 80, no. 4: 379–390.

Tecumseh. 1823. "Tecumseh's Speech to the Osages, 1812." In *Memoirs of a Captivity among the Indians of North America*, edited by John D. Hunter, pp. 45–48. London: Longman, Huerst, Rees, Orme, and Brown.

Trask, Haunani-Kay. 1999. *From a Native Daughter: Colonialism and Sovereignty in Hawai'i*. Honolulu: University of Hawai'i Press.

Tuck, Eve, and C. Ree. 2013. "A Glossary of Haunting." In *Handbook of Autoethnography*, edited by Stacey Holman Jones, Tony E. Adams, and Carolyn Elli, pp. 639–658. New York: Routledge.

Ukoha, Ezinne. 2018. "Why the #MeToo and #TimesUp Movements Are Officially the Anthem of White Feminism." *Medium*. https://nilegirl.medium.com/why-the-metoo-and-timesup-movements-are-officially-the-anthem-of-white-feminism-8fe7f3898995.

U.S. Department of Justice. 2010. *Sexual Victimization in Prisons and Jails Reported by Inmates, 2008–09*. Washington, DC: Bureau of Justice Statistics.

U.S. Department of Justice. 2016. *Violence against American Indian and Alaska Native Women and Men: 2010 Findings from the National Intimate Partner and Sexual Violence Survey*. Washington, DC: Bureau of Justice Statistics.

Wilderson, Frank B., III. 2010. *Red, White, and Black: Cinema and the Structure of US Antagonisms*. Durham, NC: Duke University Press.

Wolfe, Patrick. 2006. "Settler Colonialism and the Elimination of the Native." *Journal of Genocide Research* 8, no. 4: 387–409.

Wynter, Sylvia. 2003. "Unsettling the Coloniality of Being/Power/Truth/Freedom: Towards the Human, After Man, Its Overrepresentation—An Argument." *CR: The New Centennial Review* 3, no. 3: 257–337.

Zupančič, Alenka. 2017. *What Is Sex?* Cambridge, MA: MIT Press.

## Further Reading

Arvin, Maile, Eve Tuck, and Angie Morrill. 2013. "Decolonizing Feminism: Challenging Connections between Settler Colonialism and Heteropatriarchy." *Feminist Formations* 25, no. 1: 8–34.

Byrd, Jodi. 2017. "Loving Unbecoming." In *Critically Sovereign: Indigenous Gender, Sexuality, and Feminist Studies*, edited by Joanne Barker, pp. 207–227. Durham, NC: Duke University Press.

Deer, Sarah. 2015. *The Beginning and End of Rape: Confronting Sexual Violence in Native America*. Minneapolis: University of Minnesota Press.

Finley, Chris. 2011. "Decolonizing the Queer Native Body (and Recovering the Native Bull-Dyke): Bringing 'Sexy Back' and Out of Native Studies' Closet." In *Queer Indigenous Studies: Critical Interventions in Theory, Politics, and Literature*, edited by Qwo-Li Driskill, Chris Finley, Brian Joseph Gilley, and Scott Lauria Morgensen, pp. 31–42. Tucson: University of Arizona Press.

Nixon, Lindsay. 2020. "Visual Cultures of Indigenous Feminism." In *Otherwise Worlds: Against Settler Colonialism and Anti-Blackness*, edited by Tiffany Lethabo King, Jenell Navarro, and Andrea Smith, pp. 332–342. Durham, NC: Duke University Press.

Tuck, Eve. 2011. "Rematriating Curriculum Studies." *Journal of Curriculum and Pedagogy* 8, no. 1: 34–37.

Wilderson, Frank B. 2009. "Grammar and Ghosts: The Performance Limits of African Freedom." *Theatre Survey* 50, no. 1: 119–125.

# 5

# Ni Una Menos

## An Intersectional Movement

*Maricruz Gómez*

### Timeline

- April 30, 1977: Mothers of the Plaza De Mayo began to protest around the Argentine capital for their missing children taken by the dictatorship.
- 2009: The Argentine Congress passed *La Ley de Protección Integral de Las Mujeres*, Ley N. 26.485, a law that would protect the rights of women against violence. However, many clauses in the law were not enacted and a budget was not proposed.
- March 26, 2015: The first mass demonstration of the Ni Una Menos movement protested the horrific murder of Daiana García. Daiana García's body was found in a pile of garbage bags.
- May 2015: The body of fourteen-year-old Chiara Páez was found underneath her boyfriend's house.
- May 11, 2015: A tweet from journalist Manuela Ojeda called for collective action for Chiara Páez's murder and to address femicide in Argentina.
- June 3, 2015: Following 286 femicides in 2015 in Argentina, the Ni Una Menos movement led a mass demonstration in the Argentine capital of Buenos Aires.
- October 2016: The murder of sixteen-year-old Lucía Pérez led to further mass demonstration against femicides in Argentina. Her body exhibited horrific signs of sexual violence. The mass demonstrations expanded to other countries throughout Latin America, which included Bolivia, Chile, Peru, Mexico, Uruguay, El Salvador, Guatemala, Honduras, Paraguay, Ecuador, Costa Rica, and Brazil.
- December 2016: The brutal murder of Irma Ferreyra De Rocha, who was tortured, raped, and sexually assaulted with a tree branch that cut through her intestines, led to further protests that brought the femicides of Lucía Pérez, Chiara Páez, and others into the forefront.

Maricruz Gómez, *Ni Una Menos* In: *The Other #MeToos*. Edited by: Iqra Shagufta Cheema, Oxford University Press.
 DOI: 10.1093/oso/9780197619872.003.0005

- January 2017: The Ni Una Menos movement aligned itself with the Women's March in Washington, an alliance which continued the following years.
- March 8, 2017: Ni Una Menos took part in the International Women's strike held in the Argentine Congress and the Plaza de Mayo.
- 2017: Ni Una Menos organized a march near the Argentine Obelisk after the body of twenty-one-year-old feminist activist Micaela García was found buried under a tree in Gualeguay, Argentina. Micaela García was an active member of the Ni Una Menos movement. Marches against her femicide were held in various cities in Argentina, including Buenos Aires, Rosario, and Santa Fe.
- August 2018: An abortion legalization bill was proposed to the Argentine Congress and was passed by Congress, but the Senate rejected the bill.
- December 2018: The book that showed the theory of the Ni Una Menos movement, entitled *Amistad politica + inteligencia colectiva: Documentos y Manifestos 2015/2018,* was published in La Plata, Argentina. The book can be seen at the Ni Una Menos website: http://niunamenos.org.ar/.
- March 2020: During the pandemic lockdown, instances of domestic violence against women increased rapidly in Argentina. The Ni Una Menos movement continued throughout the pandemic, utilizing virtual tools to fight against femicides. There were over 250 cases of femicide in Argentina.
- December 2020: The Argentine Congress passed an abortion law titled *Ley de Interrupción Voluntaria del Embarazo* (Voluntary Interruption of Pregnancy Law) to allow women to obtain legal abortions up to fourteen weeks of pregnancy.
- September 2021: The Ni Una Menos movement published a letter on the Ni Una Menos website discussing how the International Money Fund (IMF) debt and income inequality have had serious repercussions for those suffering during the pandemic.

The Ni Una Menos movement addresses the critiques made by Angela Davis of the #MeToo movement: that it did not take into account "how . . . our view of gender violence change[s] if we look at it from the vantage point of Black women and indigenous women, or working class, or poor women of all racial backgrounds" (2021, p. 29). One of the things that distinguishes the Ni Una Menos movement is its intersectional approach. The movement recognized that combating violence against women is linked to other structural problems in society and institutions. As Davis, in her chapter "Struggle, Solidarity, and Social Change," states: "by adopting intersectional feminist approaches, we recognize the connection between different social problems such as gender violence in intimate and more public relationships, and state violence in institutions such as police and prisons" (2021, p. 27). In the text of the Ni Una Menos movement, *Ni Una*

*Menos Amistad Política + Inteligencia Colectiva Documentos y Manifestos 2015/2018* (referred to hereafter as *Ni Una Menos AP*), we can see the intersectional approach of the movement. The text was created by participants in the movement; the book has no individual author. The book was launched at a meeting of Latin American feminists called ELLA in December 2018 in La Plata, Argentina (2018, p. 3). In not having a specific author, the book is able to represent multiple voices of the Ni Una Menos movement. It also establishes a nonhierarchical position to the movement's platform. The introduction of the book itself states that the collective is part of a body politic that includes various perspectives. One of the important reasons to discuss this text is that it includes many of the writings and speeches that were given at marches and meetings from the start of the movement in 2015 to 2018. The Ni Una Menos movement continues to this day, so I will also be looking at current marches. It is important to look at the writings of the Ni Una Menos movement in order to understand the theory and praxis of the movement. As Giti Chandra and Irma Erlingsdóttor state in "Introduction: Rebellion, Revolution, Reformation," it is important to look at the spoken words of a movement (2021, p. 37). Examining the writings and speeches in *Ni Una Menos AP* allows us to do so. I will primarily be looking at the writings of the Ni Una Menos movement and its marches to discuss the intersectionality of the movement, which is reflected in the movement itself and in its theory.

The Ni Una Menos movement utilizes the intersectional approach of the original founder of the #MeToo movement, Tarana Burke. In an interview with Rochelle Riley for *The Detroit Free Press*, Tarana Burke explains how she hears commentary from Black, Hispanic, and Native American women about how the media's representation of the #MeToo movement has not included them. Burke explains that the #MeToo movement needs to align to its original mission of 2006, when she started the movement. Burke states, "it's in our economic justice work. It's in our mass incarceration work. It's in our community health work. It's everywhere." Angela Davis's article "Struggle, Solidarity, and Social Change" states: "Tarana Burke began using the phrase in 2006 to emphasize the pandemic dimensions of sexual violence within Black communities, but it was Alyssa Milano who was initially credited with the creation of the slogan. Unfortunately, many contemporary images associated with #MeToo are overwhelmingly white" (2021, p. 30). Burke explains in the interview that women need to take back the movement of #MeToo, and that is exactly what the Ni Una Menos movement in Argentina did. They connected it back to Burke's founding principles: "the #Metoo movement is in every single thing I said. It's in our economic justice work. It's in our mass incarceration work. It's in our community health work. It's everywhere." The Ni Una Menos movement emphasizes its intersectional approach. It is important to apply intersectionality to the analysis because gender violence and discrimination are prevalent in all facets of our life.

Gender violence is a complex issue that needs to be addressed on multiple fronts; not doing so is a disservice to the movement itself. As the movement progresses, it should be more willing to be increasingly intersectional. In the op-ed piece published in *The Guardian*, "Women of America: We're Going on Strike. Join Us so Trump Will See Our Power," Linda Martín Alcoff, Cinzia Arruzza, Tithi Bhattacharya, Nancy Fraser, Barbara Ransby, Keeanga-Yamahtta Taylor, Rasmea Yousef Odeh, and Angela Davis directly cite the Ni Una Menos movement. The Guardian op-ed piece states, "in embracing a feminism for the 99%, we take inspiration from the Argentinian coalition Ni una menos. Violence against women, as they define it, has many facets: it is domestic violence, but also the violence of the market, of debt, of capitalist property relations, and of the state; the violence of discriminatory policies against lesbian, trans and queer women; the violence of state criminalization of migratory movements; the violence of mass incarceration; and the institutional violence against women's bodies through abortion bans and lack of access to free healthcare and free abortion" (2017, p. 1). The piece directly connects the intersectional role of the Ni Una Menos movement, and demonstrates how the Ni Una Menos movement has been inclusive and representative of various women. One of the organizers of the Ni Una Menos movement said that from the January U.S. Women's March what was more impactful was hearing the voices of "African-American women, as well as the acknowledgment of the Sioux and the indigenous struggle" (Gago, 2017). This further demonstrates that the Ni Una Menos has been keen on hearing approaches from an intersectional perspective. The authors of the op-ed piece and the Ni Una Menos movement see each other as a form of shared theoretical understanding and creation of coalitions that are based on intersectionality.

The Ni Una Menos movement began as a response to a series of gruesome femicides, but understands that gender violence is a complex issue that needs to be addressed via different approaches. The recent movements that focus on women's rights in Latin America are Ni Una Menos, which began in Buenos Aires, Argentina, in 2015, and its precursor, Ni Una Más, in Mexico. Peru adopted the movement Ni Una Menos along the same path as Argentina. Ni Una Menos was formed by academics, journalists, and artists "who joined together to protest against the government's lack of response to a series of gruesome femicides" (Carlson, 2021, p. 413). The movement began with this collective and increased to a dynamic and expanding movement of over 200,000 participants in over eighty participating cities (Llorente, 2020). It became increasingly more intersectional as the movement grew and incorporated various platforms that affect various women. The movement began because of "the murder of a 14-year-old pregnant girl. The body of Chiara Páez was found buried under her boyfriend's home on 11 May 2015. She had been given medication to induce an abortion and, when she had a serious reaction to the drugs, she was beaten to death and her body hidden" (Carlson, 2021, p. 413). This led to a sense of outrage from the community itself. The people felt a sense of anger against the judicial system for the lenient sentencing of those accused of femicides and domestic violence. This case was part of a growing number of femicides in Argentina. One of the founders of the Ni Una Menos movement, Hinde Pomeraneic, explained that "a couple of months earlier, the body of Daiana Garcia, 19, was found by the roadside. Her remains were inside a rubbish bag. The body of another young girl, Melina Romero, was found a few metres away from a waste-processing plant last year. . . . In another case, the body of Angeles Rawson, 16, was found inside a rubbish-compacting machine" (2015, p. 1). These gruesome femicides, particularly that of Chiara Páez, caused a strong reaction and incited people to take to social media to protest and demand justice for the victims of these femicides. #NiUnaMenos began with a tweet by journalist Marcela Ojeda: " 'They're killing us! Aren't we going to do something?' This now historic phrase, with the support of thousands of people from all walks of life, made the #NiUnaMenos hashtag viral" (Carlson, 2021, p. 413). This tweet was a call to action to other women that they need to respond urgently to this pressing issue. Various women responded to this tweet by discussing marches that would be organized. This movement began by addressing domestic violence, gender inequality, femicides, combating patriarchy, and promoting further women's rights that were tied to social issues. As Angela Davis discusses in her chapter "Struggle, Solidarity, and Social Change," "women have been saying #metoo for a long time, so long that we should have recognised decades ago that gender violence and sexual harassment are structural, thus deeply embedded in cultures, traditions, and institutions" (2021, p. 27). The movement started by addressing these gruesome femicides, and this issue has remained at its core, but it also saw the connection that gender violence has to other societal issues. In order to address gender violence, an intersectional and multiple-front approach is needed.

The Ni Una Menos movement included in its marches a platform of intersectionality and connection to Angela Davis's theoretical approach to feminism. The text "Por qué paramos? Proclama del 8M, texto construido en asambleas y leído en Plaza de Mayo 8 de marzo de 2017," in *Ni Una Menos AP*, further demonstrates the inclusivity and intersectional aspect of the Ni Una Menos movement. The speech was read aloud to those participating in the women's strike on May 8, 2017. The text explains the points of why they are part of this international strike. One of the reasons that is listed is "por un feminismo inclusivo y de intersección que nos invite a todas, a todos, a todos a unirnos a la resistencia al racismo, a la islamofobia, al anti-semitismo, a la misoginia, a la explotación capitalista (como le escuchamos decir a Angela Davis)," which deeply connects the mission of the movement with an intersectional approach (2018, p. 53). The text explains that they are marching "for an inclusive feminism and intersectionality that invites all of us, each and every one of us to resist racism, Islamophobia, Anti Semitism, misogyny, and capitalist exploitation (as we heard Angela Davis state)" (2018, p. 53). The statement about Angela Davis is in response to the op-ed piece published in *The Guardian*, "Women of America: We're Going on Strike. Join Us so Trump Will See Our Power," described earlier.

The Ni Una Menos movement had precedents in Argentine society that led to its mobilization. In the *New York Times* article "How Support for Legal Abortion Went Mainstream," Daniel Politi and Ernesto Londoño state that "Argentina has a well-established tradition when it comes to popular organizing and mobilizations" (2021, p. 1). Argentina has a long history of protests and marches. The Madres de la Plaza de Mayo are a strong example of Argentine activism against human rights violations. The mothers protested in the Buenos Aires national square for their missing adult children taken by the dictatorship of Argentina in the 1970s to 1980s. Even after all these years, the mothers still march every Thursday to remind people of the human rights violation of their disappeared children. The main organizers of the Ni Una Menos movement, in an interview with *Jacobin*, stated that they looked to the Madres de la Plaza de Mayo as an influencing form on the tactics of their activism (Gago, 2017). The Ni Una Menos, like the Madres de la Plaza de Mayo, established a cohesive activism in the country that allied various coalitions and an increasingly supportive international community. And like the Madres de la Plaza de Mayo, Ni Una Menos has had an enduring effect on Argentine society, as well as beyond its national boundaries. In addition to the Madres de la Plaza de Mayo, the Argentine National Women's Meeting, which has been held in the country for over thirty years, was an important form of mobilization. This meeting allowed women from all over Latin America to meet and discuss the implications of neoliberalism on women (Gago, 2017). One of the founders of the Ni Una Menos movement states that the movement was able to mobilize to such a great extent because of "a lineage and feminist genealogy" (WAF Editors, 2021).

Among the hallmarks of the Ni Una Menos movement are its various demands for various groups, its ability to connect a social problem with other systemic issues, and coalition building with various organizations across the world. As the Prologue of *Ni Una Menos AP* states, "esa dimensión global del movimiento tiene que ver con su capacidad de componer un plano anti neoliberal diverso y articulado a la vez, que se masifica por radicalización e incorporación de consignas, reclamos y deseos sin perder arraigo en territorios concretos"; in translation, this means that the movement is increasingly international in its scope because it adopts a diverse anti-neoliberal approach that incorporates various perspectives without losing the distinct trait that the perspectives are part of a specific place and history (2018, p. 3). Fighting neoliberalism is key to fighting state violence against the population. The movement incorporates distinct viewpoints, but also does not want to homogenize the particular historical and spatial dimension of particular Indigenous movements. The authors further describe the reason that they are writing these texts so that theory turns into praxis. As they state, "escribimos para ocupar las calles y reinventar el espacio común, y para hacer estallar el discurso público estado céntrico, patriarcal y colonial" (2018, p. 4). The praxis and theory are a means to decenter the state, patriarchy, and coloniality. The movement's goals are also to address patriarchy and coloniality that they see tied to domestic violence and femicides. Without an intersectional approach, it is impractical to integrate praxis and theory and therefore fight against patriarchy and coloniality.

Ni Una Menos understands that in order to address gender violence, it also needs to address various inequalities among women. The essay "Nosotros paramos llamamiento al Primer Paro Nacional de Mujeres 19 de October 2016," in *Ni Una Menos AP*, discusses how social class and poverty need to be understood as part of reducing domestic violence. As the article states, "nosotras nos llevamos la peor parte: la pobreza tiene rostro femenino y nos coarta la libertad de decir no cuando estamos dentro del círculo de violencia" (2018, p. 26). The essay discusses how women are affected by poverty, which causes women to continue to stay in abusive situations because they cannot afford to leave. Poverty keeps some individuals from leaving abusive situations because they have no alternative. It is important to help the women who undergo these circumstances. This similarly echoes Kimberlé Crenshaw's "Mapping the Margins: Intersectionality, Identity Politics, and Violence against Women of Color," where she states: "many women who seek protection are unemployed or underemployed, and a good number of them are poor. Shelters serving these women cannot afford to address only the violence inflicted by the batterer; they must also confront the other multilayered and routinized forms of domination that often converge in these women's lives, hindering their ability to create alternatives to the abusive relationships that brought them to shelters in the first place" (2000, p. 1245). Ni Una Menos recognizes that the material challenges that women face are equally important in addressing any form of violence toward women. The text itself echoes many of the ideas that Crenshaw discusses in her article, demonstrating the intersectional lens of the Ni Una Menos movement.

Through the portrayal of a specific court case in the writing of the Ni Una Menos movement, we can see how it takes intersectionality into consideration. The text "Nosotros paramos llamamiento al Primer Paro Nacional de Mujeres 19 de October 2016," in *Ni Una Menos AP*, states: "contra la detención y el procedimiento judicial irregular que mantiene como rehén a Reina Maraz, migrante quechuahablante a quien los resortes de una justicia misógina y colonial han condenado injustamente a cadena perpetua. Contra las condiciones que una y otra vez hacen de las cárceles de mujeres espacios donde se amplifican las jerarquías clasistas y racistas" (2018, p. 27). The text is speaking against the juridical injustice committed against Reina Maraz, a Quechua-speaking migrant, in which a misogynistic and colonial justice condemned her to life in prison (2018, p. 27). It is poignant that in the Ni Una Menos movement, especially for rallying their cause in 2016, would use the case of Reina Maraz. She was a Bolivian Indigenous migrant who only spoke Quechua and signed documents in Spanish that she did not understand that convicted her of killing her husband (Arens, 2021). Regarding the Amicus Curiae that was submitted to Reina Maraz's case, "making use of the concept of *intersectionality*, the text sheds light on the ways in which a series of circumstances converged in Reina's life story, placing her in a very particular situation of vulnerability" (Arens, 2021).

Likewise, the text also highlights the ways in which "multiple forms of oppression—running along the lines of gender, origin, and migrant and ethnic status—ended up placing her in a particularly defenseless condition with regards to her access to justice" (Arens, 2021, p. 1). Through showing this specific case and allying the movement with providing justice for this woman, the movement aligns itself with an intersectional lens. Also in discussing this case and denouncing laws that criminalized migration, the movement is denouncing institutional racism that the state of Argentina exhibits toward Indigenous Bolivians. The text "Nosotros paramos llamamiento al Primer Paro Nacional de Mujeres 19 de October 2016," in *Ni Una Menos AP*, states: "contra la política retrógrada que inaugura un centro de detención para migrantes, en un claro retroceso respecto de la legislación vigente" (2018, p. 27). The text also declares that it is opposed to the detention center that Argentina was contemplating building. Specifically, "in August 2016, the NDI communicated through its website that it had signed an agreement with the National Ministry of Security and the Ministry of Justice and Security of the city of Buenos Aires to avail of a building destined for 'people detained for infractions of the Migration Law.' It was a statement 'against migration irregularity,' and it announced the upcoming opening of a detention center for migrants with a deportation order. This measure was in line with the punitive and police vision of migration" (Domenech, 2020, p. 9). The Ni Una Menos movement is also answering the plight of women who are migrants in the country, who do not speak the dominant language, who are of a different race, and discusses how that affects them in terms of their access to justice. By presenting the case study and a criticism of immigration laws, they demonstrate that all these interlocking factors have an effect on the access someone has within these institutions. Through portraying the case of Reina Maraz in the Ni Una Menos movement's writings and declaring it as a praxis goal, the movement aligns itself with an intersectional lens.

The Ni Una Menos movement saw it as important to create a coalition of various identities. In the text "Ni Una Menos apoya la marcha de Mujeres Contra

Trump 20 de enero 2017," in *Ni Una Menos AP*, Ni Una Menos states that it aligns itself with the Women's March in the United States in January 2017 because of its concern for marginalized communities. In the specific text, it states: "la retórica de las últimas elecciones en Estados Unidos ha insultado, demonizado y puesto en peligro a muchas de nosotras: mujeres, migrantes, aquellxs con diversas creencias religiosas y particularmente musulmanxs, personas Lgbt, personas de pueblos originarios, personas de color, discapacidadxs, personas de sectores económicamente marginalizados y sobrevivientes de violencia sexual" (2018, p. 36). The text states that "the rhetoric of the last elections in the U.S. has insulted and put in danger a lot of us: women, migrants, folx with diverse beliefs particularly Muslims, LGBT community, indigenous people, people of color, handicapped people, those in marginalized economic status and survivors of sexual violence" (2018, p. 36). Another sentiment that is echoed in this work is "reconociendo que defender a lxs más marginadxs entre nosotrxs es defendernos a nosotras mismas. Apoyamos los movimientos de defensa y resistencia que reflejan nuestras identidades múltiples y comunes" (2018, p. 36). The Ni Una Menos text is saying that it is our duty to help the most marginalized because in doing so we defend ourselves. We should align ourselves with movements that defend and resist our multiple and common identities. In this text we see that the movement is aligning itself with the Women's March on the basis of multiple identities, which is integral to an intersectional approach. The recognition of different identities and the importance of building coalitions. Even the language utilized with the "x" and lower case of categories is a way that the movement demonstrates its inclusivity through the written word. By using the "x" the movement is aligning itself with trans women who face a large number of homicides.

The alliance that the Ni Una Menos has made with Indigenous and Afro-descendent women demonstrates the intersectional lens of the movement. In the Ni Una Menos movement, the theoretical readings are denouncing racism, discrimination, and xenophobia against Indigenous, Black Indigenous, and Afro-descendent women. In the essay "¿Por qué paramos? Proclama del 8M, texto construido en asambleas y leído en Plaza de Mayo 8 de marzo de 2017," in *Ni Una Menos AP*, it states: "paramos contra el racismo, la discriminación y xenofobia hacia las mujeres indígenas, negras afrodescendientes y afroindígenas. Paramos contra el genocidio y femicidio de mujeres que tiene su origen en la trata esclavista y en la violencia colonial. Paramos por el buen vivir de nosotras y nuestras comunidades" (2018, p. 51). The movement is connecting the colonial violence done to Indigenous, Black Indigenous, and Black women. The reason they think the strike is important is to give a better life for the community which includes a wide coalition. Unlike the criticisms levied against the #MeToo movement that it was not intersectional, we can see that the Ni Una Menos is intersectional. The Ni Una Menos movement is more willing to be critical of how capital and coloniality are contributing factors to gender violence. The movement understands that "there is a whole sociopolitical and economic framework that we need to understand in order to better see how women's bodies are converted into a territory subject to conquest (hence the reference to the colonial question)" (Gago, 2017, p. 1).

The movement also recognizes how territories were taken away from Indigenous peoples, particularly the Mapuche in Argentina and Chile. The essay "La marea feminista sigue creciendo Documento del Paro internacional de Mujeres, Lesbianas, travestis y trans 8 de marzo 2018," from *Ni Una Menos AP*, states: "y porque nos reconocemos en las luchas latino americanas y afrodescendientes: remarcamos el protagonismo de las mujeres en las luchas comunitarias por la vida y los territorios y en particular de las mujeres mapuches que enfrentan la ofensiva empresarial y represiva del estado argentino" (2018, p. 115). The Ni Una Menos movement aligns itself with the Mapuche women who defend their ancestral homes and fight against the corporate state of Argentina. In aligning the Ni Una Menos movement with Indigenous people's collective right to their ancestral land, they are building an intersectional movement that encourages social justice and land sovereignty for Indigenous people. This is also bringing into focus the settler colonial state and its effects on Indigenous population. In this case the movement is centering the injustice committed against the Mapuche by the Argentine colonial state.

A march that was formed on November 25, 2018, further connected the Ni Una Menos movement with intersectionality. The last essay, "No olvidamos, no perdonamos Contra la revancha misógina de la justicia patriarcal, colonial y racista 26 de noviembre de 2018," from *Ni Una Menos AP*, states: "no es casual que esto suceda el año que millones de mujeres nos movilizamos por el aborto legal, y que nos enteremos mientras marchábamos por el 25N, día internacional contra las violencias hacia las mujeres y las disidencias desde los feminismos antiracistas, populares, comunitarias, indígenas, afro/negras, afrodescendientes, lesbianas, trans, travestis, migrantes, villeras" (2018, p. 163). The 25th of November is a significant day as it is the international day of eliminating violence against women. It was a national holiday that began in Latin America, particularly in the Dominican Republic to honor the lives of the Mirabal sisters who were killed in their activist resistance by the dictator Rafael Trujillo. Thus the significance of this day is not lost to the symbolism of the movement. The book ends with this essay, declaring the alliance of the movement that takes into account sexuality, gender, race, migration status, and geographic settings. The movement aligns itself with different forms of feminisms which include: anti-racist, popular, communitarian, Indigenous feminism, and Black feminism, and aligns itself with transpeople, lesbians, and migrants. The policy in 2018 that it sets forth is for the legalization of abortion in Argentina and anti-violence against women.

The Ni Una Menos movement incorporated the legalization of abortion in Argentina into its platform in 2018. One of the founders of Ni Una Menos movement, Maria Fernandez Alvarez, stated that "in the first Ni Una Menos rally on June 3, 2015, the leaders who read the document demanding an end to femicide had the green scarfs around their necks but in the document, there was no mention of abortion but there was talk of the right to say no to unwanted pregnancy and there was talk of comprehensive education on sex" (WFA, 2021). Although there were clear representations of a connection between legalization of abortion and the movement, this did not become a direct platform claim until 2018. It can be reflected in the ending of the text *Ni Una Menos AP.* In 2018 the Ni Una Menos movement created a series of marches, called *marea verde*, that sought to legalize abortion; women increasingly marched to the streets with green scarves to demand the legalization of abortion. The green scarves were tied to Plaza de Mayo activists who wore white scarves (Phillips, Booth, and Goñi, 2020). During the pandemic women would hold protests via social media platforms to pressure the government to legalize abortion. The article "Argentina Legalises Abortion in Landmark Moment for Women's Right" states that "it was after the 2015 #NiUnaMenos march that pro-choice campaigners realised the fight against 'femicide' could also encompass demands for access to legal abortion" (Phillips, Booth, and Goñi, 2020, p. 1). The pandemic did not impede activists from fighting for the legalization of abortion. They moved the marches to virtual platforms. In December 2020 the Argentine Congress passed the Voluntary Interruption Pregnancy Bill that made abortion legal up to fourteen weeks of pregnancy (Diaz, 2021). The legalization of abortion also stopped the decriminalization that women were facing for getting abortions up to fourteen weeks. It brought to the forefront how state violence was imposed on women for controlling the choices of their body. Many credit the Ni Una Menos movement for mobilizing women "who never stopped occupying the streets and the social networks—not even against the backdrop of the pandemic—and kept up their struggle, without haste but without rest" (Phillips, Booth, and Goñi, 2020, p. 1). María Florencia Alcaraz, one of the founders of the Ni Una Menos movement, states that "the abortion law is a starting point, not an ending point" (WFA, 2021, p. 1).

The Ni Una Menos movement continues today and still promotes marches that encompass a wide range of issues, incorporating an intersectional lens. In June 3, 2021, Ni Una Menos launched a call that took into account the current pandemic to continue its ongoing work. As Angela Davis states in "Struggle, Solidarity, and Social Change," "gender violence remains a worldwide pandemic" (2021, p. 27). The Ni Una Menos movement visibilized further the struggles of the LGBTI+ communities and LGBTI+ workers (Leszinsky, 2021). As of this year 2021 it has been six years since the start of the Ni Una Menos movement. The movement still grows and expands to encompass the needs of the community. One of the reasons that the movement still remains as strong as before is that it is intersectional and it includes various perspectives from different forms of feminisms. The femicide registry created through the work of the Ni Una Menos movement shows that femicide, along with transfemicide, is still a growing concern in Argentina. The figures released by the femicide registry in Argentina reveal that in 2020 there were 251 direct victims and 6 transfemicides. The figures revealed that every thirty-five hours someone is a victim of feminicide in Argentina (2020, p. 3). As it states in Spanish, "La Oficina de la Mujer de la Corte Suprema de Justicia de la Nación publicó la edición 2020 del Informe de Femicidios de la Justicia Argentina. Se identificaron 251 víctimas directas de femicidio en la República Argentina entre el 1 de enero y el 31 de diciembre de 2020. Esta cifra incluye 6 víctimas de travesticidio/transfemicidio. Lo anterior implica que hubo una víctima directa de femicidio cada 35 horas" (2020, p. 3). These figures reveal the need for continuous work in gender violence that the Ni Una Menos movement continues to address through an intersectional lens.

The Ni Una Menos movement continues to fight against gender violence, especially as we have seen how it has increased during the pandemic. A particularly alarming statistic is that "in the first week of the pandemic, there was a 120% spike in calls reporting domestic violence cases" in Argentina (Diaz, 2021, p. 1). Gender violence still remains an issue that needs the marches and fight to continue. In the beginning of 2021 there were two shocking femicides in Argentina. The two femicides in Argentina were "19-year-old Úrsula Bahillo filed the latest of more than a dozen complaints to authorities about her ex-boyfriend's abuse and threats. Two days later, she was murdered. Bahillo was brutally stabbed to death and her body left in a rural area near Rojas, Argentina" (Diaz, 2021, p. 1). These cases echo the femicide cases of 2015 in Argentina that started the Ni Una Menos movement. After these femicides the Ni Una Menos movement organized a march. There was a call for authorities to take domestic violence threats seriously. These cases demonstrate that Ni Una Menos movement needs to continue to work to eradicate gender violence. The intersectional connections of the movement continue during the pandemic.

A manifesto that was recently published by the Ni Una Menos organization connects its movement to intersectionality and larger social economic issues. The manifesto "Todes contra el Fondo Monetario Internacional" was published in September 15, 2021, on the Ni Una Menos movement website. The manifesto discusses how it aligns itself with those who have faced great economic inequality during the pandemic. It commits itself to those who are labeled as essential workers and are affected by inflation. The manifesto reiterates the importance of an intersectional approach that is dedicated to "fight for dignity and rights of people" (*Ni Una Menos*, 2021, n.p.). It sees the intersectional approach as key in making connections with various social issues. It acknowledges that there is not one feminism and it will not succumb to neoliberalism. The manifesto states that it will not accept economic neoliberalism, the IMF, and transphobia. The movement aligns itself with working-class individuals who have suffered greatly during the pandemic. It discusses how the government labels them essential workers, yet the government does not do enough to help its people. The document ends by stating, "La agenda de géneros es económica, social, política y popular. Por todo esto demandamos que se prioricen estas deudas antes que la deuda con el FMI" (*Ni Una Menos*, 2021, n.p.). The translation of this is that "gender agenda is economic, social, political, and popular. We demand that the state prioritize our debts instead of the debts it has with the International Monetary Fund" (*Ni Una Menos*, 2021).

Ni Una Menos is an intersectional movement because it takes into consideration various forms of feminisms and different factors that affect individuals. Ni Una Menos will continue to fight to eradicate this violence through an intersectional approach. Ni Una Menos looks at it from all these women's perspectives, and that is part of the reason why the movement has expanded and continues to fuel marches. It has been instrumental in the passage of the legalization of abortion. The movement realizes that it needs to be intersectional in order to address such complex issues as gender violence, legalization of abortion, indigenous rights, and economic equality.

## Works Cited

Alcoff, L., C. Arruzza, T. Bhattacharya, N. Fraser, N. Ransby, K. Taylor, R. Odeh, and A. Davis. 2017. "Women of America: We're Going on Strike. Join Us so Trump Can See Our Power." *The Guardian*, February 6. https://www.theguardian.com/commentisfree/2017/feb/06/women-strike-trump-resistance-power.

Arens, J. 2021. "Racist and Patriarchal Justice in Argentina: The Reina Maraz Case." *IWGIA*, April 14. https://www.iwgia.org/en/argentina/4339-racist-and-patriarchal-justice-in-argentina-the-reina-maraz-case.html.

Averis, K. 2021. "Ni Una Menos: Colombia's Crisis of Gendered Violence during the Covid-19 Pandemic." *PORTAL: Journal of Multidisciplinary Interdisciplinary Studies* 17, no. 1–2 (January): 91–96. doi: http://dx.doi.org/10.5130/pjmis.v17i1-2.7367.

Boesten, J. 2019. "Peace for Whom? Legacies of Gender Based Violence in Peru." In *Politics after Violence: Legacies of the Shining Path Conflict in Peru*, edited by H Hillel David Soifer and Alberto Vergara, pp. 157–175. Austin: University of Texas Press.

Boesten, J., and H. Scanlon. 2021. "Gender and the Arts of Transition." In *Gender, Transitional Justice, and Memorial Art*, edited by Jelke Boesten and Helen Scanlon, pp. 1–18. New York: Routledge.

Caballero, G. 2019. "Usos de las redes sociales digitales para la acción colectiva: el caso de Ni Una Menos." *Antropológica* 37, no. 42 (January): 105–128. doi: http://dx.doi.org/10.18800/anthropologica.201901.005.

Carlson, M. 2021. "#METOO Argentina: A Protest Movement in Progress." In *Routledge Handbook of the #MeToo Movement*, edited by Giti Chandra and Irma Erlingsdóttir, pp. 410–422. New York: Routledge.

Chandra, G., and Irma Erlingsdóttir. 2021. "Introduction: Rebellion, Revolution, Reformation." In *Routledge Handbook of the #MeToo Movement*, edited by Giti Chandra and Irma Erlingsdóttir, 1–22. New York: Routledge.

Crenshaw, K. 1991. "Mapping the Margins: Intersectionality, Identity Politics, and Violence against Women of Color." *Stanford Law Review* 43, no. 6 (July): 1241–1299. https://doi.org/10.2307/1229039.

Davis, A. 2021. "Struggle, Solidarity, and Social Change." In *Routledge Handbook of the #MeToo Movement*, edited by Giti Chandra and Irma Erlingsdóttir, 27–33. New York: Routledge.

Diaz, Jaclyn. 2021. "How #NiUnaMenos Grew from the Streets of Argentina into a Regional Women's Movement." *NPR*, October 15. https://www.npr.org/2021/10/15/1043908435/how-niunamenos-grew-from-the-streets-of-argentina-into-a-regional-womens-movemen#:~:text=Press-,Six%20years%20on%2C%20the%20work%20of%20%23NiUnaMenos%20activists%20in%20Latin,rights%20movement%20across%20Latin%20America.

Domenech, E. 2020. "The 'Politics of Hostility' in Argentina: Detention, Expulsion and Border Rejection." *Estudios Fronterizos* 21: 1–25. doi:https://doi.org/10.21670/ref.2015057.

"Feminist 'Green Tide' Delivers Legal Abortion in Argentina." 2021. *Buenos Aires Times*, January 2.

Fregon, R. 2003. *MeXicana Encounters: The Making of Social Identities on the Borderlands*. Berkeley: University of California Press.

Friedman, E., and C. Tabbush. 2016. "#NiUnaMenos: Not One Woman Less, Not One More Death!" *NACLA*, November. https://nacla.org/news/2016/11/01/niunamenos-not-one-woman-less-not-one-more-death.

Gago, V. 2017. "Argentina's Life-or-Death Women's Movement: An Interview with Luci Cavallero and Veronica Gago." *Jacobin*, March 7. https://jacobin.com/2017/03/argentina-ni-una-menos-femicides-women-strike/.

Hola, C. 2016. "Lucia Perez Murder: Mother's Plea to End Argentina Gender Violence." *BBC News*, October 21. https://www.bbc.com/news/world-latin-america-37731501.

Leszinsky, L. 2021. "#NiUnaMenos Six Years On: Triumphs and New Demands of Argentina's Feminist Movement: What Progress Has Argentina's Feminist Movement Made So Far?" Translated by Emma Dewick. *Global News*, June 22. https://globalvoices.org/2021/06/22/niunamenos-six-years-on-triumphs-and-new-demands-of-argentinas-feminist-movement/.

Llorente, A. 2020. "Ni una menos: Chiara Páez, la adolescente embarazada de 14 años cuyo brutal asesinato dio origen al movimiento contra la violencia machista." *BBC News Mundo*, June 3. https://www.bbc.com/mundo/noticias-52900596.

Morris, L. 2019. "Fighting Machismo: Women on the Frontline." In *Voices of Latin America: Social Movements and New Activism*, edited by Tom Gatehouse, pp. 25–46. Rugby: Practical Action Publishing.

*Ni una menos Amistad Política + Inteligencia Colectiva Documentos 2015–2018*. 2018.

Ojeda, M. 2015. *Twitter* post, May 11, 2015, at 9:24 a.m. "Actrices, políticas, artistas, empresarias, referentes sociales . . . mujeres, todas, bah . . . no vamos a levantar la voz?

NOS ESTAN MATANDO." https://twitter.com/marcelitaojeda/status/597799471368564736.

Phillips, T., A. Booth, and U. Goni. 2020. "Argentina Legalises Abortion in Landmark Moment for Women's Rights." *The Guardian*, December 30, 2020. https://www.theguardian.com/world/2020/dec/30/argentina-legalises-abortion-in-landmark-moment-for-womens-rights#:~:text=The%20landmark%20decision%20means%20Argentina,has%20been%20legal%20since%201995.

Politi, D., and E. Londo. 2020. "Argentina Legalizes Abortion in Milestone for Conservative Region." *New York Times*, December 31. https://www.nytimes.com/2020/12/30/world/americas/argentina-legalizes-abortion.html#:~:text=BUENOS%20AIRES%20%E2%80%94%20Argentina%20on%20Wednesday,of%20rallies%20into%20political%20power.

Pomeraneic, H. 2015. "How Argentina Rose Up against the Murder of Women." June 8. https://www.theguardian.com/lifeandstyle/2015/jun/08/argentina-murder-women-gender-violence-protest.

"Registro Nacional de Femicidios de la la Justicia Argentina Resumen de la Edición 2020." 2020. Corte Suprema de La Nación República Argentina Oficina de la Mujer. https://www.csjn.gov.ar/omrecopilacion/docs/resumenfemicidios2020.pdf.

Riley, R. 2018. "#MeToo Founder Tarana Burke Blasts the Movement for Ignoring Poor Women." *Detroit Free Press*, November 15. https://www.freep.com/story/news/columnists/rochelle-riley/2018/11/15/tarana-burke-metoo-movement/2010310002/.

"Todes contra el fondo Monetario Internacional." 2021. *Ni Una Menos*, September 19. http://niunamenos.org.ar/manifiestos/todes-fondo-monetario-internacional/.

WAF Editors. 2021. "The Contribution of #NIUNAMENOS Was to Massify Feminism, Says Florencia Alcaraz, Ni Una Menos Founding Member." *Women Across Frontiers*, March 4. https://wafmag.org/2021/03/the-contribution-of-ni-una-menos-was-to-massify-feminism-says-florencia-alcaraz-ni-una-menos-founding-member/.

# 6

# From the Confessional to the Ground

## Understanding Indian #MeToo Feminism

*Amrita De*

### Timeline

- 1829: Sati, or the practice of burning widows alive on their husband's funeral pyre, was declared punishable by the criminal court under then governor-general of India Lord William Bentinck.
- 1848: Savitribai Phule started the first school for girls in India.
- 1920–: National organizations such as the All India Women's Conference (AIWC) and the National Federation of Indian Women (NFIW) emphasized women's education issues and the struggles of working-class women.
- 1930–: Women's rights were integral to the anticolonial resistance and the nationalist movement.
- 1973: Section 53A of the Code of the Criminal Procedure of the Indian Law lays down the provision for the medical examination of the accused in a sexual harassment case, while Section 164A deals with the medical examination of the victim.
- 1987: The Parliament of India passed the enactment of the Commission of Sati (Prevention) Act with the government of Rajasthan.
- 2006: The Indian Parliament passed the Protection of Women from Domestic Violence Act.
- 2013: Sexual Harassment of Women at Workplace Act is a legislative act that seeks to protect women from harassment in their workplace.
- 2013: The Criminal Law Amendment Act introduced new changes in sexual harassment laws to the Indian Penal Code. The definition of rape was extended. Sexual harassment was now punishable for at least three years of imprisonment and/or with a fine. Section 376 also mandates minimum punishment in certain cases. The death penalty for most extreme cases is also specified. The age of consent is also raised from sixteen to eighteen years, with any sexual activity with someone less than eighteen years now regarded as statutory rape.

Amrita De, *From the Confessional to the Ground* In: *The Other #MeToos*. Edited by: Iqra Shagufta Cheema, Oxford University Press. © Oxford University Press 2023. DOI: 10.1093/oso/9780197619872.003.0006

- 2019: The practice of triple *talaq* or instant divorce was declared unconstitutional and punishable by law.

## Introduction

On October 24, 2017[1], Raya Sarkar, a student at the University of California–Davis, circulated through social media a list of over seventy names of alleged sex offenders in twenty-five elite liberal arts programs from the United States, India, and the United Kingdom. The list slipped into oblivion within a year. In her clarifications regarding the list, Raya Sarkar identified herself as a Dalit Bahujan feminist activist, while insisting on the pervasive caste blindness in the multigenerational feminist movement in India (Roy, 2018; Mani, 2019; Phillipose and Kesavan, 2019; Anitha, 2020). LoSHA (list of sexual harassers in academia) started as a whisper network but soon gained enough prominence to command national attention. The prominence was in part due to social media's stealth power in amassing public opinion and in part due to the opaqueness of the list. The controversy revolved around the authenticity of mostly unillustrated claims, bringing to the fore a divide between contemporary feminist activists and the generational elders who laid the foundations of the Indian feminist movement at the epicenter of the social media maelstrom. Many prominent Indian feminists responded to the naming and shaming of their colleagues in a series of articles condemning the absolute dismissal of due process and reliance on hashtag activism by contemporary gender activists. While the #MeToo movement triggered by LoSHA became a beacon for students to protest entrenched toxicity, sexism, and violence in Indian academia (Dey, 2020), the nature of the list raises urgent questions about the widespread culture of naming and shaming popularized by hashtag feminism.

In the second case, on May 1, 2019, a viral ten-minute video clip of a middle-aged woman slut-shaming a group of girls for wearing short dresses started trending on Indian social media platforms (*The New Indian Express*, 2019). The woman alleged that these girls deserve to be raped for their clothing, which incited conversations on the patriarchal logic that women's choice of clothing extends an implicit invitation for sexual harassment. In the long ten-minute clip, the woman endorsed this view even as she was confronted by a group of angry women who demanded that she apologize for her sexist comments. She refused to do so, repeating her words, and even challenging them to post the video. Shivani Gupta (presumably one of the affronted girls) posted the long clip on her Facebook account in the next few hours, inviting other people to share the video. Gupta's video went viral, alongside posts circulating the middle-aged woman's picture with her phone number and address. Soon, the backlash was directed at the woman's appearance, broken English, and her own choice of clothing, rather than her regressive ideas. The #MeToo hashtag started trending again as droves of Indian women participated in her social media trial while simultaneously denouncing and calling out the women in their own families who have participated in similar accounts of shaming over the years. The woman apologized for her comments in a written statement on social media, despite unequivocally insisting that she would not apologize in the viral video. A spirit of retributive justice prevailed through a digitally mediated collective. This incident underlines a critical quandary about the ethical ramifications of naming and shaming, begging the question of whether an apology coerced through a social media trial engenders the beginning of feminist consciousness.

In the third incident, in May 2020, screenshots of Instagram chats of high school boys from elite schools in Delhi went viral (*The Indian Express*, 2020). The contents ranged from sexual objectification of their female peers, comments on their physical appearances, and planning of physical assault, alongside circulation of morphed photos. Even as social media conversations surrounding toxic masculinity and rape culture trended, high school Delhi girls were tormented by the threat that their nude photos would be leaked online. This incident, alongside highlighting issues of digital slut-shaming, reignited debates about the pervasive cultures of toxic masculinity in high school systems: that "boys will be boys," and the onus is on young women to preserve their bodily autonomy under structural patriarchy. There had been similar previous instances of bullying, starting from the infamous Delhi Multimedia Messaging Service scandal[2] (Padte, 2018) to the controversy at another elite school in Mumbai. Still, for the first time, as screenshots went viral, the explicit sexualization of young women's bodies and direct access to an exclusive homosocial male space unleashed a veritable digital storm in middle-class consciousness. Generations of urban upper-middle-class parents, content with neoliberal channels of elite English education for their offspring, now contended with their failure to reckon with the internalized toxicity of these spaces. An extraordinary denouement followed as a girl confessed to posing as a boy to elicit truthful confessions from her male peers (Bharadwaj, 2020). Then, in a horrific turn of events, a young boy implicated in this controversy committed suicide, bringing the whole discourse surrounding internalized toxic masculinity in boys to a standstill (Dayal, 2020). Soon after, the boy's father registered a formal complaint with the high court, seeking justice for the death of his son. Despite their specific contexts, all three incidents engaged in different variations of naming and shaming, pointing to the ethical limitations of the #MeToo movement. I will now underline the main conflicts that directly emerge from naming and shaming to understand its fraught politics better.

## The Violence of Naming and Shaming

The function of violence, seeming or otherwise, is often deemed the common register between different iterations of sexual abuse, insofar, violence has become the most important metric in ascertaining the authenticity of an incident. Such an a priori view complicates matters when violence appears various or continuous—impossible to restrict or categorize. Mary E. John (2020), in an incisive commentary on the Indian #MeToo movement, notes that violence has "become a kind of touchstone for the recognition of an issue as a 'women's issue,'" and the presence of coercive violence in different kinds of acts, ranging from rape to sexual harassment, putatively mobilizes feminist issues, granting recognition as such, and thereby enabling them to "acquire resonance within a larger, otherwise unsympathetic public" (John, 2020, p. 138). If violence is the bedrock of hashtag confessions, it is necessary to also attend to the registers that violence visibilizes and simultaneously obscures. What is then the nature of the violence committed in each of the above cases?

Raya Sarkar's list presents a comprehensive curated account of various forms of harassment, ranging from physical to emotional, with little to no details of said acts of harassment. In the case of the middle-aged Delhi woman, she becomes a victim of the violence of online naming and shaming even as she perpetuates patriarchal violence against a group of women for their choice of clothing. In the third case pertaining to screenshots shared from the boys' locker room conversations—the violence stems from the language in circulation within the digital homosocial space. However, in this case, the tragic outcome of the social media trial points to a more complex dimension of violence and its constantly mutating politics in different contexts. Instant reactionary responses, such as collective naming and shaming—strengthened by an accessible digitally mediated language—generate a feeling of occasioned justice while often obscuring a sustained dynamic engagement with the material structures that make violence possible in the first place. It becomes necessary then to think of the associated violence of naming and shaming as a problem of language and interpretation, where the interpretive schema must not be seen as fixed but constantly variable.

The language necessary for articulating different dimensions of sexual violence is available through the circulation of free-floating signifiers, like consciousness-raising slogans such as #MeToo; however, the transmission of such a shared language depends on a sociocultural exchange that invariably flows from the Global North to the Global South. This language is generative, multifaceted, and easily adaptable to local contexts,[3] but the interpretation—affectively generated through a prior disposition—remains similar. #MeToo, after first originating in America, soon mutated into different variations of the same—sometimes referring to specific problems in the Indian community, such as caste, especially that of Brahmanical patriarchy. However, all these variations of #MeToo invoked the same language of collective belonging and consciousness-raising, building on affective affinities that had originated in the West and then actively circulated through neoliberal social media channels. The issue here is not one of direct import from the West or dependency on confessional feminist consciousness-raising hashtags, but on the mode of redress emphasized here—trial by social media. Due to the specific nature of its articulation, trial by social media remains embedded within an exclusive space of digital accessibility, even when it aspires for local resonances.

In a different context, Sara Ahmed (2017), extending Spivak's (1988) diagnosis of the imperial mission as "white men saving brown women from brown men," says that "imperial feminism can take the form of white women saving brown women from brown men." Ahmed's condemnation of imperial feminism speaks to the contemporary condition of neoliberal feminism, and its emphasis on identity politics—a manifestation of which is directly visible in the vocabulary and attendant modes of redressal considered the touchstone of the hashtag Indian #MeToo movement. The #MeToo movement in the United States resulted in the incarceration of people such as Harvey Weinstein and Jeffrey Epstein. But in the Indian #MeToo iteration, while some accused actors and journalists faced professional loss, there were no sustained redressal modes producing a material change in circumstances. When the *HuffPost* (2018) team reached out to the universities cataloged in Raya Sarkar's list of sexual harassers, they were met with radio silence. The report confirmed that the universities did not take any *suo moto* action. Only in a few cases, following official complaints and only after the accused had gone through due process, was there evidence of actions taken against the accused.[4]

In the case of the middle-aged woman and the boys implicated in the locker room controversy, except for one, due legal process was not followed. This not only problematizes the redressal being sought, but also raises further questions: Is it just about naming and shaming, loss of economic capital, or loss of sociocultural capital after being exiled from communities the accused previously had access to? The implicit ambivalence of curated anonymous accounts, as in the case of LoSHA, further complicates the nature of redressal being sought—are we supposed to single out named individuals from the list, or merely read it as an overwhelming confirmation of the toxicity within public university spaces. In the third case, the due process remains the only possible legible register for a father to seek justice for the trauma inflicted on his teenage son.[5]

All three cases in their denouement allude to the specter, often simultaneously reviled and hailed—the complicated discourse on rights and due process and the slippery slope between the two. Research in the Indian context (Menon, 2004; Geetha, 2016) demonstrates that the underpinnings of due process are predicated on the very internalized classist caste-ist patriarchal structures that reify and naturalize sexual harassment in the first place. Often, preconceived notions inflected by caste-ist registers impel the idea of justice received through due process. In the case of Dalit, Bahujan, and Adivasi (DBA) communities, the burden of perpetration is always placed on the lower caste body until proven otherwise (Geetha, 2016). So, any iteration of carceral justice, especially in the case of accused individuals hailing from DBA communities, slips into the double bind of first calibrating the accused according to historical class-caste markers. Even in digitally mediated accusations, class-caste markers remain valid. A statement released by the Twitter account "Dalit Women Fight" with the accompanying hashtag #DALITWOMENFIGHT stated that "we have been wondering about the 'me' in #MeTooIndia, but we have not been able to locate ourselves in this current framework." They further highlighted that all the perpetrators outed in the list came from dominant caste power, urging everyone to be aware that the perpetrators amassed enormous institutional power through their caste power. While discourses around the list of sexual harassers reanimated conversations about the need for institutional accountability and structural reform, caste as a category remained muted or tokenistically acknowledged as compilation done by a Dalit student (Rao, 2018). A multipronged analysis understanding the violence of caste patriarchy and the need for an intersectional critique largely remained obscure, even as more women came forward with their stories.

Moreover, the case of the middle-aged woman presented an ugly side of the social media trial, invoking a similar degree of vituperative carceral imperative, as deployed regularly by the patriarchal state. As countless women shared personal testimonials of similar accounts of shaming done to them by other women, the online ecosystem quickly devolved into an act of confessional mudslinging—unfortunately, mimicking an iteration of toxic masculinity's fantasy playbook: that of women fighting other women. Many feminist social media responses condemned hate speech directed at the middle-aged woman because of her looks and broken English. Some questioned the coercive act of filming the woman and egging her for a response, pointing to the fact that her privacy was explicitly violated. In the third case, after news of the young boy's suicide broke out, social media responses questioned the ethical register of collective naming and shaming, again highlighting its dissonance from restorative justice.

The broader Indian feminist community was particularly divided on the nature of retribution justice afforded by naming and shaming in the list, which incidentally marked the beginning of the #MeToo movement in India. By virtue of its enumerative quality, the list reinforced a totalizing impulse, flattening distinct discourses into a binary of survivor and the alleged harasser. The list brought to the fore fraught debates that are necessary for the progressive future of the Indian feminist movement and its key ancillaries.

The critical fissures in the reception of LoSHA are best visible in the generational divide within the context of the Indian #MeToo movement. One of the major criticisms of LoSHA was that it conflated different types of acts, such as an exploitative but consensual relationship, unwanted sexually explicit messages, and groping with physical assault and rape (Anitha 2020). Following the list's release, a joint statement was released in Kafila, a prominent liberal progressive outlet, by prominent feminist activists who have pioneered the feminist movement in India from its inception. Their ambivalence toward the list underscored their concerns about the active dismissal of due process and unequal conflation of different kinds of acts. A statement by prominent feminist academic and activist Nivedita Menon (2019, n.p.) was released after the blanket statement that further clarified her stance, saying that she was worried about "merging different degrees of harassment." She, however, clarified in a comment under her piece that she was mindful of the fraught optics of naming patriarchal power within the academy but intended to underscore the importance of naming the problem and putting it through the corrective channels in place. Menon further emphasized the need to differentiate between sexual harassment and inappropriate consensual relationships. In a separate piece, she called the recent spate of consciousness-raising feminist activism "fingertip activism." This was followed by a separate piece authored by another prominent Indian feminist activist, Brinda Bose and Rahul Sen (2018), who underscored the need to problematize the location of desire, warning against the blunt moralizing imperative taken up by snap judgments which focused the conversation more on the binary of aggressor and victim, rather than teasing out the complex relational modes between these categories.

The new generation of feminist activists (primarily students and early career researchers) responded to these criticisms by railing against the obvious blind spots in the older generation of feminist activism, which they identified as synonymous with *savarna* upper caste, urban, metropolitan activism (Anitha, 2020; Bargi, 2017).[6] Obviously, there was a clear divide between the two generations of feminist activism: the older generation accused the newer generation of being rash without participating in previous hard-won struggles, and the younger generation simply accused them of being "out of touch."

While the list of sexual harassers reframes the vulnerability of the woman's body in male-dominated spaces in the language of sexual harassment and violence, the attendant discourses (both online and offline) do not sufficiently address the gender disparity in modes of employment.[7] It also does not dwell on the complexity and implicit violence structurally embedded in the relationship between teachers and students on Indian campuses and the conditions of this relationality. John (2020) points to the gendered dynamics within higher education spaces, noting that even as gender sensitization drives increase women's enrollment, most of the faculty members are still men. In this case, it was particularly striking that all the accused men putatively belonged to liberal university spaces with demonstrated scholarship on matters of social justice.

I am not suggesting that there is implicit danger in thinking about sexual injustices through the language of sexual harassment or violence, but rather that it is necessary to be wary of shorthands serving as an interpretive frame of reference in the identification of symptoms rather than conditions. The conditions that led to harassment in each of these cases: employment stability and impunity borne out of patriarchal privilege, in the case of the accused male professors; patriarchal conditioning, which delineates the morally acceptable length of clothing women should wear in public, in the case of the middle-aged woman; the substratum of toxic hypermasculinity within male homosocial spaces, in case of the "bois locker room." As individual confessions of sexual harassment exist as distinct iterations on social media platforms, trending hashtags mobilize a concerted effort to address hitherto invisibilized acts of violence against generations of women. It, however, does not emphasize violence as a continuous social phenomenon—one that has seen enduring participation from a diverse set of actors. Lata Mani (2019) makes a case for a priori identification of sexual violence as a social phenomenon rooted in history or culture, which might explain some of the affective intensity around the issue. In viewing sexual violence as a continuous social phenomenon, it would be further possible to reconcile the generational divide and emphasize the complex history of patriarchy in every societal sector.

The main problems signposted here dial back to different aspects of neoliberal feminism:[8] obscuring specific voices (across caste and classed registers), an unequal conflation of different acts, and finally, the generational divide acting in opposition to building enduring solidarity networks. These elements can be critiqued by unpacking the neoliberal imperative dominant within these articulations and identifying its main trappings. Such interrogation is crucial to any concerted effort to genuinely forge solidarity networks among diverse groups of people.

## Hashtag Feminism: The Specter of Neoliberal Politics

The transnational spread of the #MeToo movement gestures to a rhizomatic[9] transmission of affective intensities, allowing for multiple non-hierarchical entries and exit points depending on the context. While it is necessary to draw attention to its neoliberal framework, failure to accommodate its concomitant affective intensities would do a great disservice to the cause of feminist activism in the present moment. In this section, I first consider the affective potential of hashtag activism, then proceed to delineate its many elisions in the context of the Indian #MeToo movement. Kaisu Hynna, Mari Lehto, and Susanna Paasonen's (2019) theorization of "affective body politics" is a handy methodological tool to examine the embodied ways by which "bodies experience practices of governance, how they affect and are affected by other bodies."[10] Social media platforms like Twitter and Facebook amplify specific hashtags, generating feelings situated in a broader trajectory, while simultaneously providing a putative democratic space for individual expression and activism to thrive. Generated affect is then transmuted into a collective voice that can reconfigure and recalibrate modes of being and belonging in the world. In such contexts, the conceptualization of affective body politics is instructive in examining the public intimacies produced through the transmission of rhizomatic affect, and its effect on transnational feminist movements.

The affective turn in cultural theory since the late 1990s (Clough, 2008; Gregg and Seigworth, 2010) draws attention to the idea of affect as something existing outside the bounds of the pre-subjective. Affect is qualitatively defined as an evidentiary potentiality, so affective body politics is attuned to the capacity to impress and be impressed, to affect, and then to create dynamic connections between human and non-human objects, giving shape to social movements, as in the case of the #MeToo movement. Lauren Berlant (2008, p. 4) further notes that "the structure of an affect has no inevitable relation to the penumbra of emotions that may cluster in the wake of its activity, nor should it" (4). So, the public intimacies formed from an affective discharge do not necessarily engender the same set of responses everywhere, but it is important to mark out the specific elisions in large-scale transmissions.

The #MeToo movement in the United States first originated in 2006, over a decade before it was popularized by a tweet from a white actress Alyssa Milano, as discussed elsewhere in this volume. In 2006, Black feminist thinker Tarana Burke created an organization named MeToo, to help rehabilitate young victims of sexual harassment through healing (Burke 2018). Eleven years later, this phrase was appropriated by white feminists, largely obscuring the Black feminist thinker who started it (Mendes, Ringrose, and Keller, 2018; Phipps, 2019).[11] White feminism then stands in contrast to Black feminism, but whiteness is centered and amplified in its public articulations (Phipps 2019). Similarly, in India, the #MeToo movement is not the first iteration of mass-scale public engagement. In December 2012, mass-scale citywide protests broke out after the brutal gang rape of a Delhi student, Jyoti Singh (John 2020).[12] The following year, 2013, saw several public feminist protests, especially from young students in urban university campuses, including campaigns such as "Take Back the Night in Kolkata," and an online forum "Hyderabad for Feminism" for combating violence and harassment in the city (Madabhushi, Grace, and Joshua, 2015); the "Why Loiter?"

groups, following Shilpa Phadke's 2012 book of the same name, demanded access to public spaces and performative participation in "risky behavior," such as loitering in spaces deemed unsafe for women; the "Pinjra Tod" (break the cage) movement also emerged in Delhi's colleges and universities, calling for an end to discrimination in women's hostels. These groups also took up conversations surrounding women's menstruation and sexual desire. LGBTQ groups in cities like Hyderabad, Bengaluru, and Chennai also came together to talk about everyday sexual violence and humiliation they were subjected to by the police (Banerjie, 2016; John, 2020). Limited to English-speaking urban spaces, these movements gained prominence through social media, where social media engagement helped to facilitate and coordinate shared information. These protests imitated popular Western feminist movements, such as the Slutwalk movement that originated in Toronto.

The Indian #MeToo movement also showed similar transmission of affect, inspired by the American wave of the #MeToo movement. While the movement did inspire several women to come forward with their documentation of sexual harassment, it did not effectively include voices of women who have been historically marginalized, like Dalit women (see Roy, 2018; Bansode, 2020; Pain, 2020). Notably, Rupali Bansode draws attention to the erasure of Dalit women's testimonies by focusing on the case of Satyabhama, a victim/survivor of a caste-based incident of sexual violence in Maharashtra. Paromita Pain's comprehensive analysis of over 35,000 tweets similarly reflects the exclusion of vernacular language–speaking suburban voices. Pain's incisive article is particularly instructive in rendering visible the digital labor undertaken by feminist activists who played a major role in popularizing the hashtag on social media.

The affective body public generated from the viral hashtag also had material ramifications beyond a cathartic show of solidarity with other women on social media. Women actively refused to be part of professional spaces with the accused men (Moraes and Sahasranaman, 2018). However, Pain's article reveals that even though lower-class working women and members of LGBTQ communities did participate in the online movement, the majority of the participation was limited to English-speaking urban crowds, demonstrating the hegemony of upper-middle-class professional tech-savvy working-class populations in the digital space (Belaoir Gagnon et al., 2014). The tweets and participant interviews showed that categories such as race, class, and gender acted as key negotiators when ceding space to marginalized narratives. The muted participation of poor suburban women from the unorganized working-class sector reveals the neoliberal character of #MeToo as a consciousness-raising movement and its limitations in reaching populations who do not enjoy the digital literacy of the urban English-speaking population. Above all, this highlights the consumerist nature of digital literacy, with its main purveyors being metropolitan middle-class women who readily imbibe the language of neoliberal feminist consciousness.

The cases outlined at the beginning also demonstrate this. Raya Sarkar's List again raises questions of material access to digital channels; the crowdsourced list was limited to liberal universities in urban spaces. The social media trial of the middle-aged woman reveals a deeper engagement of a prevailing consciousness that allows for instant behavioral responses accompanying a specific iteration of digital literacy—such as pulling out your phone and recording a perceived affront in real time. This sets a dangerous precedent for women who do not have access to this kind of digital literacy and its affordances, like a phone with a video recorder and internet access; they are at a disadvantage because they cannot collect or record evidence. In the case of the "bois locker room" incident, a moral ethical-political imperative overwhelmingly pervaded critical interpretations of the incident without making any allowance for reparative modes of engagement; most of the attendant discourses around this case attributed blame to young boys and girls for being overtly sexualized. Without doing the work required to generate restorative/reparative modes of communication that would entail a transparent therapeutic transference of why young boys in India turn to such overtly sexualized discourses in the first place, media conversations were more invested in assigning moral value claims. Such interpretations relegate conversations around sexual desire to a liberal, conservative position, where erotic desire ends up becoming pathologized rather than normalized.

## The Nature of the Event

If we think of the Indian #MeToo movement as an ongoing event, feminist critique must find a way to understand its ambivalences without operating from a paranoid position or even legitimizing a carceral imperative.[13] Such an inquiry necessitates deeper interrogation of the genre of naming and shaming and its accompanying affects rooted in structural violence, while remaining attentive to the history of patriarchal collaboration with the police state. Perhaps the controversy surrounding the list and its aftereffects best exemplifies the danger of a paranoid position. Brinda Bose and Rahul Sen (2017) contend that despite the rhetorical rallying around a need for structural critique, the Indian #MeToo movement (based on the list) did not follow through in critical rigor. The momentum of the hashtag devolved into a collective cathartic outpouring without adequately accounting for the fundamental ambivalence surrounding unverified claims. Bose and Sen highlight an a priori moralizing impulse embedded within the list, which casts non-normative intensities and relationalities in the vocabulary of shame. The very idea of a list depends on a taxonomic organization of discrete entities with shared commonalities; therefore, the structure of a list does not leave room for ambiguities that do not fit within its organizing schema. From its inception to circulation, the list in question demands of its interlocutors a shared understanding of the vocabulary of sexual violence, and conversely, a prior understanding of the constitution of sexual desire—for desire and violence often operate in the same continuum. The crisis of the list stems from its prevarication around the location of sexual desire in each of the unverified claims as if the desire is the unnamable unconscious (not named)—meant to be interpreted from its anonymous contents as absent or violated. But the politics of desire, like sexual violence, is often messy, impossible to categorize. Paromita Vohra (2018), an important activist for sex-positivity in India, underlines that the idea of consent goes beyond fixed boundaries of a "yes" or a "no," veering often into the territory of a "maybe." Moreover, the idea of consent too extends in the same spectrum as shifting sexual desire and cannot always be categorized. The list aspires to collective unambiguous politics, which brings to mind Berlant's (2011) "crisis ordinariness"—which is essentially a crisis of desire for the political where the political is seen as a means to an end, but the desire for the political isn't capacious enough to contain the plurality of the politics of desire.

As feminists, if we believe in cenetring the politics of desire, we must find a way to parse through the unsaid unconscious of the Indian #MeToo movement while remaining conscious of its sustained "liveness" and important work in centering collective emotions. Despite the ambivalence surrounding the list, hundreds of survivors came forward on social media with their stories of personal abuse. For many survivors disillusioned with the workings of capitalist patriarchy and caste-ist underpinnings of Indian academia, social media afforded an alternate space for their stories,[14] subverting some of the formal trappings of due process. However, feminists need to think deeper about the nature of social justice affectively metabolized through the politics of naming and shaming. In each of the three outlined cases, a feeling of justice sought and occasioned is imbricated with an understanding of unquestioned authenticity—the "believe all victims" paradigm. This ethico-political imperative stems from histories of victim shaming and is undeniably a needed protocol. Still, it enters a slippery transaction when it becomes the source and object of a political movement. The collateral damage from such a precondition can push back decades of social justice movements highlighting class and caste atrocities alongside gender. At best, it participates in cathartic exchange; at worst, it embeds discomfort and distrust at the heart of the movement, as is evident from the three cases discussed above.

All three cases presuppose a dynamic of perceived aggressor and clear victim; in fact, naming and shaming become an effective tool to harness the power of social media. That such a mediated mechanism can become a deterrent for progressive feminist change is not an overdetermination but a heuristic failing that must be accounted for in the near future. All three cases outlined here, in the aftermath of the respective events, calibrate varying levels of anxiety with the process of naming and shaming—from the generational divide provoked by the list to the affective discomfort connected with public shaming of women by other women, and finally, the disturbing death of a high schoolboy. The inherently fraught dynamics of the movement then demand a critical assessment of the scope and temporal reach of the event in its ongoing attachment to its subjects and emergent relationalities. Such an assessment must first ask hard questions about the nature of desire and the possibility of restorative justice from its subjects: the people directly involved in the event; and attachments: the social, the political, and the collective.

## Toward Reparative Networked Solidarities

My intention here is not to discredit a movement that has demonstrated tremendous reach, but rather to complicate our reception by foregrounding some of the faultlines embedded within. If we take the beginning of these three incidents as different nodes in the same continuum, where patriarchal violence emerges as naturalized and continuously replicated—we must be careful not to replicate violence or substitute one form of violence with another. Such a critical exploration must necessarily think about future possibilities of the feminist movement, especially taking care not to reinforce histories of exclusion.

In a separate but related article, underscoring the racial dynamics of the #MeToo movement, Ashwini Tambe (2018) points to the history of Black men being lynched based on unfounded allegations that they sexually violated white women. Tambe reflects on how Black men are unjustly incarcerated, noting that the dynamics of #MeToo, in which due process has been reversed—with accusers' words taken more seriously than those of the accused—is a familiar problem in Black communities. In the context of the three incidents outlined in this chapter, feminists must similarly attend to historical precedents while critically assessing the ambiguities of the present moment. Such an assessment must begin with the absence of historically disenfranchised communities such as the Dalit, Bahujan, and Adivasi communities from within the purview of the greater feminist movement.

Tambe also points to the divide between populist iterations of the #MeToo movement and current trends in academic feminist movements, noting that while populist iterations focus more on pain, trauma, and consciousness-raising, recent academic trends, particularly by Lauren Berlant and Judith Butler, have focused more on the idea of play, pleasure, and healing. Similarly, other prominent academic feminist theorists have elaborated on the transformational register of a sex-positive sociality, distinguishing between being fixated on trauma and "wounded attachments" (Brown, 1995) as the source of agentive subjectivity in one, and arriving at agency through sex positivism in the other. To elaborate on this further, I turn to Berlant's (2017) writing on the #MeToo movement titled "The Predator and the Jokester." Here, Berlant notes that while everyone has sexual appetites, of whatever order or scale one might choose to calibrate that appetite, many people in the wake of the #MeToo movement seem to think that "their aversion to sex or ways of managing desire are evidence of moral virtue" (n.p.). This aligns with Tambe's analysis, where she considers a distinction between predatorial sex and transactional sex, noting that they have come to occupy interchangeable imaginaries. Both Tambe and Berlant believe that to build a truly equitable workplace, one must first address the notion of privilege and what a privileged position can putatively get away with. By privilege, Berlant (2017) emphasizes "control over time and space and the framing of consequences in domains of capital, labour, institutional belonging, and speech situations where the structurally vulnerable are forced to 'choose their battles' or just act like a good sport."

In a similar vein, Tambe makes a strong case for sex positivism by warning against categorizing all transactional sex as coercive sex and placing utmost importance on sex as a means of ontological subjectivity. Specific to this exploration is the idea that transactional sex should not always be viewed in the moral register because it can be consensual, with willing participants who participate in sexual transactions to arrive at a personal goal. The idea of consent should then adopt a critical vocabulary beyond liberal viewings of it only through the binary frame of assent or dissent. It is more important to emphasize why people end up saying "yes" when they would have preferred to say "no" in certain situations. Suppose transactional sex occurs in a situation where there is a fear of negative consequences or direct threat of loss. In that case, it is coercive sex: even in the absence of a direct "no," it should be treated as a violation. Therefore, the valence of fear or threat that manifests in a situation is directly linked to a material assessment of concomitant privilege. If cis males are found to be repeated offenders, as clearly demonstrated in Raya Sarkar's list, one must first ask what gives cis males greater immunity and visibility in the workplace. Conversely, as some of the anonymous allegations on the list demonstrated—under what circumstances were survivors coerced into entering a transactional relationship with the aggressor? The goal of the feminist movement is to loosen an object world structured around the unmarked stability of the patriarchal register, which ratifies gender-based violence in the first place.

Any effort to build transformational solidarity networks must first discard the paranoid position born out of anxiety, and instead, adopt a reparative position (Sedgwick, 1997) geared toward building collective affinities and intensities that do not stem from the idea of victimhood that but reimagine newer ways of building community. Eve Sedgwick (1997) warned against a paranoid inquiry which comes to interchangeably assume the place of critical theoretical inquiry, rather than being regarded as one kind of cognitive/affective theoretical practice among other, alternative kinds. The controversy surrounding the list demonstrates the workings of paranoid inquiry, where the translation of an important political document occurs through opposing forces. On the other hand, a reparative position would be more engaged with the idea of repair and restorative justice, instead of merely foregrounding conflicting interpretations. The generational feminist divide that emerged in the wake of the list has cost the Indian feminist movement a huge setback, which, will take a long time to be repaired (Chadha, 2017).

Additionally, the Indian #MeToo movement must grapple with the neoliberal trend in identity politics where hashtags with full-bodied affective potentiality are transmuted into a literalizing, mimetic, and sometimes performative articulation of wounded attachments. This chapter shows that the language of such performative praxis is predicated on classed caste-ist modes of being, which make digital visibility possible. Reparative networked solidarities can emerge from a space of sex-positivity which identifies repressive Brahmanical patriarchal structures and then locates spaces where they can be potentially destabilized. The anger turned outward through the literal use of a hashtag can also be used to look inward—to recognize modes of being and attachments beyond hurt politics so that the anger can be collectively invested in "feminist futures" (Ahmed, 2004) beyond the neoliberal appropriation of gendered oppression. Such feminist futures, as the complexities around the opening incidents demonstrate, must also navigate the complexity of building worlds that go beyond naming and shaming and carceral retributive politics. Instead, they must focus on restorative justice and community building.

## Notes

1. This was one of the first instances of the #MeToo movement in India as it unfolded in America. The movement was limited to calling out elite liberal arts professors in academia. The #MeToo movement officially picked up later in 2018 when a Bollywood female actor Tanushree Dutta accused a famous male actor Nana Patekar of sexual harassment. Soon similar accusations were directed at other members of the Bollywood film industry and prominent journalists. This signaled the official emergence of the #MeToo movement in India, but this chapter highlights the critical currents around accusations that aren't associated with famous celebrity figures. For more information on the list of famous people accused in the Indian #MeToo movement, see Abhery Roy (2018) reporting for *The Economic Times*.

2. The 2004 Delhi Public School scandal is the first instance where the danger of viral digital technological affordances comes to a head. The "MMS scandal," as it came to be referred, featured a teenage couple engaged in oral sex. The boy, who shot the video, focused only on the girl and then circulated the two minute thirty-seven second clip through multimedia messaging. While there were no video clips circulated in the May 2020 case, screenshots of conversations between boys discussing their female peers immediately brought to mind the 2004 event.
3. Even when the hashtag mutates to speak to local contexts, like in the case of India, when #MeToo was used by Dalit women to articulate their struggles—the interpretive schema relied on the collective affect generated by the broader movement.
4. The *HuffPost* report found that some of the men mentioned in Sarkar's list were later found guilty following official complaints against them. Some of these names are Gopal Balakrishnan from University of California, Santa Cruz; Lawrence Liang from Ambedkar University, Delhi; and Sadaanand Menon from Asian College of Journalism.
5. The teenage boy's father maintained that his deceased son had been unfairly accused. In March 2021, the police filed a chargesheet for abetment to suicide against the girl and her friend who had accused the seventeen-year-old boy (Mirror Now Digital, 2021).
6. Several Dalit feminists (Bargi, 2017; Mondal, 2018) pointed to the implicit upper class *savarna* bias in the Indian #MeToo movement.
7. Notably, recent surveys of Indian income data reveal that "women's education has a U-shaped relationship with [their] labour force participation" (Chatterjee, Desai, and Vanneman, 2018, n.p.), which, further, underscores the pervasive patriarchal character of Indian higher education systems.
8. While the idea of neoliberal feminism can take on different definitions, I am focused more on how a particular feminist iteration emphasizes individualism while taking on a collective character. Solutions to historical conditions of inequality under such a rubric often get reduced to a matter of attitude or surface-level representation without any transformative engagement with the material forces that enable permanent change. For more on neoliberal feminism, look at Rottenberg (2014), "The Rise of Neolliberal Feminism."
9. I am aligning here with Deleuze and Guattari's (1987) concept of the rhizome from "A Thousand Plateaus" to highlight multiple non-hierarchical data entry and exit points.
10. Hynna, Lehto, and Paasonen's (2019, p. 1) incisive article makes a key distinction between body politics from the Foucauldian theoretical apparatus, which focuses more on how power operates through discourses maintained by the state and its various institutions; and the focus on affective politics invested in how power is experienced intimately in and through the body (Abel, 2007).
11. Phipps's (2019) article demonstrates how whiteness shapes public feminism around sexual violence.
12. The Delhi rape case is a landmark event in the case of the feminist movement in India. It stood out in the national consciousness for its extraordinary brutality; and partly due to the upper-caste modest middle-class positioning of the victim, who

was merely trying to survive in a big city. As a country somewhat densensitized to regular acts of violence against lower-caste Dalit, Bahujan, and Adivasi bodies, Jyoti Singh's brutalized body stood out as an undeniable marker that no woman was safe in India.

13. The term, following Bernstein (2010), is now generally used to level critique against mainstream feminist movements. This label critiques decades of anti-violence feminist collaboration with the caceral state or that part of the society associated with the police state or channels of incarceration (Kim, 2018).
14. Adrija Dey and Kaitlyn Mendes (2021), based on interviews with seven sexual violence survivors who had come forward with their stories on social media, provide insight into reasons why survivors sometimes choose to avoid formal due process and instead rely on digital spaces for their search for justice and healing.

## Works Cited

Abel, Marco. 2007. *Violent Affect: Literature, Cinema, and Critique after Representation*. Lincoln: University of Nebraska Press.

Adkins, Brent, 2015. *Deleuze and Guattari's A Thousand Plateaus*. Edinburgh: Edinburgh University Press.

Ahmed, Sara. 2004. *The Cultural Politics of Emotion*. Edinburgh: Edinburgh University Press.

Ahmed, Sara. 2017. *Living a Feminist Life*. Durham: Duke University Press.

Anitha, Sundari. 2020. "From #MeToo to #HimToo in the Academia: New Forms of Feminist Activism to Challenge Sexual Violence." In *Collaborating for Change: Transforming Cultures to End Gender-Based Violence in Higher Education*, edited by Susan Marine and Ruth Lewis, pp. 47–71. Oxford: Oxford University Press.

Banerji, Annie. 2012. "Public Fury over New Delhi Gang-Rape Sparks Protest across India." *Reuters*, December 22. doi:https://www.reuters.com/article/india-delhi-gang-rape-protests/public-fury-over-new-delhi-gang-rape-sparks-protest-across-india-idINDEE8BK09N20121221.

Bansode, Rupali. 2020. "The Missing Dalit Women in Testimonies of #MeToo Sexual Violence: Learnings for Social Movements." *Contributions to Indian Sociology* 54, no. 1: 76–82.

Bargi, Drishadvati. 2017. "On Misreading the Dalit Critique of University Spaces." *Economic and Political Weekly* 52, no. 50: 7–8.

Belair-Gagnon, V., S. Mishra, and C. Agur. 2014. "Reconstructing the Indian Public Sphere: Network and Social Media in the Delhi Gang-Rape Case." *Journalism* 15, no. 8: 1059–1075.

Berlant, Lauren. 2008. "Thinking about Feeling Historical." *Emotion, Space and Society* 1, no. 1: 4–9.

Berlant, Lauren. 2011. *Cruel Optimism*. Durham, NC: Duke University Press.

Berlant, Lauren. 2017. "The Predator and the Jokester." *Supervalent Thought*. https://supervalentthought.com/2017/12/12/the-predator-and-the-jokester/.

Bernstein, Elizabeth. 2010. "Militarized Humanitarianism Meets Carceral Feminism: The Politics of Sex, Rights, and Freedom in Contemporary Antitrafficking Campaigns." *Signs: Journal of Women in Culture and Society* 36, no. 1: 45–71.

Bharadwaj, Ananya. 2020. "A 'Girl' Started Rape Talk on Snapchat. Bois Locker Room on Insta Had No Link: Police." *The Print*, May 10. doi: https://theprint.in/india/twist-in-bois-locker-room-case-a-girl-started-it-all-posing-as-a-boy-police-says/418577/.

"Bois Locker Room Case: Girl to Face Trial for Abetment to Suicide over 17-year-old Boy's Death." 2021. *Mirror Now Digital*, March. https://www.timesnownews.com/delhi/article/bois-locker-room-case-girl-to-face-trial-for-abetment-to-suicide-over-17-year-old-boys-death/736906.

Bose, Brinda, and Rahul Sen. 2017. "Liberal Vertigo, Eros, and the University." *Café Dissensus Every Day*, August 17. https://cafedissensusblog.com/2018/08/17/liberal-vertigo-eros-and-the-university/.

Bose, Rakhi. 2020. "Bois Locker Room: Instagram Page by Delhi Teens Misuses Photos of Minor Girls to Spread Rape Culture." *News18.com*, May 5. https://www.news18.com/news/buzz/bois-locker-room-this-instagram-page-is-misusing-minor-girls-photos-to-spread-rape-culture-2604659.html.

Brown, Wendy. 1995. *States of Injury: Power and Freedom in Late Modernity*. Princeton, NJ: Princeton University Press.

Burke, Tarana. 2018. "Me Too Is a Movement, Not a Moment." Opening talk at TedWomen, November 28, Palm Springs. https://www.ted.com/talks/tarana_burke_me_too_is_a_movement_not_a_moment?language=en.

Chadha, Gita. 2017. "Towards Complex Feminist Solidarities after the List-Statement." *Economic and Political Weekly* 52, no. 50.

Chatterjee, Esha, Sonalde Desai, and Reeve Vanneman. 2018. "Indian Paradox: Rising Education, Declining Womens' Employment." *Demographic Research* 38: 855.

Clough, Patricia T. 2008. "The Affective Turn: Political Economy, Biomedia and Bodies." *Theory, Culture & Society* 25, no. 1: 1–22.

Dabrowski, Vicki. 2021. "'Neoliberal Feminism': Legitimising the Gendered Moral Project of Austerity." *The Sociological Review* 69, no. 1: 90–106.

Dalit Women Fight. 2018. "Anti-Caste Feminist Statement on #MeTooIndia." #DALITWOMENFIGHT, October 10. https://twitter.com/dalitwomenfight/status/1049914884417355776.

Dasgupta, Piyashree. 2018. "#MeToo In India: 75 Professors, 30 Institutes, What Happened to Raya Sarkar's List of Sexual Harassers?" *HuffPost*, October 27. www.huffingtonpost.in/2018/10/25/metoo-in-india-75-professors-30-institutes-what-happened-to-raya-sarkar-s-list-of-sexual-harassers_a_23571422/.

Dayal, Sakshi. 2020. "Don't Want Repeat of Incident: Kin of Gurgaon Teen Who Killed Self." *The Indian Express*, May 9. https://indianexpress.com/article/cities/delhi/dont-want-repeat-of-incident-kin-of-gurgaon-teen-who-killed-himself-6400948/.

Deleuze, Giles, and Felix Guattari. 1987. *A Thousand Plateaus: Capitalism and Schizophrenia*. Translated by B. Massumi. Minneapolis: University of Minnesota.

"Delhi Woman Slut-Shames Girls for Wearing Short Dress, Asks Men to Rape Them." 2019. *New Indian Express*, May 1. https://www.newindianexpress.com/nation/2019/may/01/watch—delhi-woman-slut-shames-girls-for-wearing-short-dress-asks-men-to-rape-them-1971394.html.

Dey, Adrija. 2020. "'Me Too' and the 'List': Power Dynamics, Shame, and Accountability in Indian Academia." *IDS Bulletin* 51, no. 2: 63–80.

Dey, Adrija, and Kaitlyn Mendes. 2021. "'It Started with This One Post':# MeToo, India and Higher Education." *Journal of Gender Studies* 31, no. 2: 204–215.

Geetha, Varadarajan. 2016. *Undoing Impunity: Speech after Sexual Violence*. Delhi: Zubaan.

Gregg, Melissa, Gregory J. Seigworth, and Sara Ahmed, eds. 2010. *The Affect Theory Reader*. Durham, NC: Duke University Press.

Hynnä, Kaisu, Mari Lehto, and Susanna Paasonen. 2019. "Affective Body Politics of Social Media." *Social Media + Society* 5: 1–5.

John, Mary E. 2020. "Feminism, Sexual Violence and the Times of #MeToo in India." *Asian Journal of Women's Studies* 26, no. 2: 137–158.

Kim, Mimi, E. 2018. "From Carceral Feminism to Transformative Justice: Women-of-Color Feminism and Alternatives to Incarceration." *Journal of Ethnic & Cultural Diversity in Social Work* 27, no. 3: 219–233.

Madabhushi, Tejaswini, Grace Marantha, T. Wahalang, and Joshua Gitanjali. 2015. "Locating 'Hyderabad for Feminism' in the Present Struggle against Violence." *Economic and Political Weekly* 50, no. 44: 38–46.

Mani, Lata, 2019. "We Inter Are: Identity Politics &# MeToo." *Feminist Review* 122, no. 1: 198–204.

Manral, Mahendra Singh and Somya Lakhani. 2020. "Bois Locker Room Case: 15-Year-old Held in South Delhi, Police Probe Online Chats." *The Indian Express*, May 5. https://indianexpress.com/article/cities/delhi/bois-locker-room-scandal-fir-against-south-delhi-teens-for-obscene-instagram-chatter-6393840/.

Mehra, Nishta J. 2017. "Sara Ahmed: Notes from a Feminist Killjoy." Interviewed in *Guernica*, July 17. https://www.guernicamag.com/sara-ahmed-the-personal-is-institutional/.

Mendes, Kaitlynn, Ringrose, Jessica and Jessalynn Keller. 2018. "#MeToo and the Promise and Pitfalls of Challenging Rape Culture through Digital Feminist Activism." *European Journal of Women's Studies* 25 (2): 236–246.

Menon, Nivedita. 2004. *Recovering Subversion: Feminist Politics beyond the Law*. Champaign: University of Illinois Press.

Menon, Nivedita, 2017. "Statement by Feminists on Facebook Campaign to 'Name and shame.'" *Kafila*, October 24. https://indianexpress.com/article/opinion/a-dalit-womans-thoughts-on-metooindia-5402538/.

Mondal, Mimi. 2018. "A Dalit Woman's Thoughts on #MeTooIndia." *The Indian Express*, October 15. https://indianexpress.com/article/opinion/a-dalit-womans-thoughts-on-metooindia-5402538/.

Moraes, Esther, and Vinita Sahasranaman. 2018. "Reclaim, Resist, Reframe: Re-imagining Feminist Movements in the 2010s." *Gender & Development* 26, no. 3: 403–421.

Padte, Richa Kaul. 2018. "What the DPS MMS Tells Us about Consent in the Digital Age." *Times of India*, May 20. https://timesofindia.indiatimes.com/home/sunday-times/what-the-dps-mms-tells-us-about-consent-in-the-digital-age/articleshow/64238647.cms.

Pain, Paromita. 2020. "'It Took Me Quite a Long Time to Develop a Voice': Examining Feminist Digital Activism in the Indian# MeToo Movement." *New Media & Society* 23, no. 11: 3139–3155.

Phadke, Shilpa, Sameera Khan, and Shilpa Ranade. 2011. *Why Loiter? Women and Risk on Mumbai Streets*. Delhi: Penguin Books India.

Philipose, Pamela, and Mukul Kesavan. 2019. "The# Metoo Movement." *Indian Journal of Gender Studies* 26, no. 1–2: 207–214.

Phipps, Alison, 2019. "'Every Woman Knows a Weinstein': Political Whiteness and White Woundedness in# MeToo and Public Feminisms around Sexual Violence." *Feminist Formations* 31, no. 2: 1–25.

Rao, Pallavi. 2018. "Caste and the LoSHA Discourse." *Communication Culture & Critique* 11, no. 3: 494–497.

Rottenberg, Catherine. 2014. "The Rise of Neoliberal Feminism." *Cultural Studies* 28, no. 3: 418–437.

Roy, Abheri. 2018. "The Year When #MeToo Shook India." *The Economic Times*, June 1. https://economictimes.indiatimes.com/magazines/panache/2018-the-year-when-metoo-shook-india/2018-the-year-of-metoo-in-india/slideshow/66346583.cms.

Roy, Srila. 2020. "#MeToo Is a Crucial Moment to Revisit the History of Indian Feminism—Centre Tricontinental." *CETRI: Southern Social Movements Newswire*, November 9. https://www.cetri.be/MeToo-Is-A-Crucial-Moment-to?lang=fr.

Sedgwick, Eve Kosofsky. 1997. "Paranoid Reading and Reparative Reading, or, You're So Paranoid, You Probably Think This Introduction Is about You." In Sedgwick, *Novel Gazing: Queer Readings in Fiction*, pp. 1–37. Durham, NC: Duke University Press.

Spivak, Gayatri Chakravorty. 2003. "Can the Subaltern Speak?" *Die Philosophin* 14, no. 27: 42–58.

Tambe, Ashwini. 2018. "Reckoning with the Silences of# MeToo." *Feminist Studies* 44, no. 1: 197–203.

Vohra, Paromita. 2018. "Why We Don't Get Consent." *The Economic Times*, October 14. https://economictimes.indiatimes.com/news/politics-and-nation/thoughts-on-metoo-why-cant-men-understand-the-concept-of-consent-a-flimmaker-explains/articleshow/66198444.cms.

# 7

# #RageAgainstRape

## World Englishes, Protest Signs, and Transnational Identity

*Asmita Ghimire and Elizabethada A. Wright*

### Timeline

- 1920–1940: Nepal began its first feminist movement, initiated by a campaign led by Yogmaya Neaupane against the sati system, caste system, and other systemic injustices.
- 1947: Nepali laws permitted women's right to vote.
- 1947: Right to education for girls was legally granted.
- 1948: Padma Kanya School, Nepal's first school for girls, was established.
- 1953: Nepali women were voted into office for the first time.
- 1958: Nepali women were voted into Parliament for the first time.
- 1990: The Constitution of Nepal prohibited rape. However, rape was defined as "forced penetration" only, which resulted in not attempting to address, for example, men's rape, child's rape, and others. Additionally, it was not well enforced.
- 1990: The Constitution of Nepal guaranteed women's right to property.
- 1996–2007: In the Maoist Revolution, a large number of women, most of them Dalit (low caste), served in the armed forces, mostly from the Maoist side, marking the first time in history when a large number of Nepalese women served in the military.
- 2015: The Constitution of Nepal expanded the definition of rape and strengthened enforcement.
- 2015: Bidhya Devi Bhandari was elected as president of Nepal, becoming Nepal's first woman president.
- 2016: Sushila Karki was appointed as a chief justice in the Supreme Court, becoming the first woman to be elected as a chief justice in the Supreme Court in the history of Nepal.

Asmita Ghimire and Elizabethada A. Wright, *#RageAgainstRape* In: *The Other #MeToos*. Edited by: Iqra Shagufta Cheema, Oxford University Press. © Oxford University Press 2023. DOI: 10.1093/oso/9780197619872.003.0007

## Introduction

Chandra Mohanty argues in "Under Western Eyes: Feminist Scholarship and Colonial Discourses" that "third world" women should not be seen as part of a "homogeneous 'powerless' group often located as implicit victims of particular socioeconomic systems" (Mohanty, 2003, loc. 396), as Western feminists tend to perceive them. This conjecture is affirmed by a comparison of Nepal's responses to the #MeToo movement with that of other countries in South Asia. When the global #MeToo movement began to gain traction and South Asian women joined #MeToo to recount their stories of sexual violence, women across Nepal also joined the chorus and shared their experiences of harassment.

However, the #MeToo movement has not been as successful in Nepal as it has been in other countries. For example, panelists at a February 2020 conference organized by Nepal's Kantipur Media Group pointed out in their session नेपालको "मी टू" किन अगाडि बढ्न सकेन? (Why #Me Too in Nepal Failed?) that the environment in Nepal discourages women to speak out regarding their sexual and gender exploitation. One of the panelists, political activist Manushi Yami Bhattarai, commented that part of the reason for the failure of Nepal's #MeToo movement is that in Nepal women have few legal means to address their claims of sexual harassment, and when women do make claims, there is extensive victim-blaming (Shrestha 2020). Another panelist, theater activist Akanchha Karki, added that the lack of communal solidarity for these women exacerbated the failure of the #MeToo movement in Nepal. Instead of action against the perpetrators of violence, #MeToo in Nepal resulted in more harassment and trolling against the victims. On the other hand, while Nepali women have been unsuccessful with their accusations of harassment, they have made more progress by focusing on crimes like rape and using that focus to challenge their country's legal and judicial systems.

One reason the #MeToo movement has not succeeded in Nepal may be the diversity of the women within the country; this diversity that Mohanty illustrates must be examined for its particularities (Mohanty, 2003, loc. 385). One example of this diversity in Nepal is the practice of *chhaupadi,* a Nepali tradition based on superstition that isolates menstruating women from society for four days (Kadariya and Aro, 2015, p. 54). This ritual has caused the deaths of many women for various reasons, most notably that the "menstrual huts" that women are sent to are frequently inhabited by poisonous snakes or can cause suffocation (Nirola 2017). While only a few women die via this practice, many more suffer mentally and physically. However, Nepali women do not uniformly participate in this tradition. While this practice is common in the far and midwest regions of Nepal, most of the women in Kathmandu, the capital of Nepal, do not engage in this practice. Additionally, just as most women of the Global North have not heard of the practice, most women in Kathmandu know little of it (Kadariya and Aro, 2015, p. 59).

Besides that, the numerous differences between women in Nepal and women in India influence the citizens' responses to the #MeToo movement, just as the differences add credence to transnational feminists' assertions that women in the Global South differentiate themselves not only from women in the Global North, but also from each other (e.g., Anzaldúa, 2012; Cooke, 2007; Naples, 2013). While these examples illustrate the diversity of experiences and epistemologies of women across the globe, this chapter takes a different tack. Going beyond the concept of intersectional differences and using theories of Kenneth Burke, Suresh Canagarajah, and Alastair Pennycook, this chapter proposes that feminists across cultures rethink their paradigm of intersectional differences. Considering Mohanty's " 'Under Western Eyes' Revisited," this chapter also goes beyond interpretations of Mohanty's earlier essay as defining "Western" and "Third World" feminism in such oppositional ways that there would be no possibility of solidarity between "Western" and "Third World" feminists (Mohanty, 2003, loc. 3998). Instead, this chapter uses as a springboard the failure of the #MeToo movement with Nepali feminists and the success of Nepal's own #RageAgainstRape movement to show how transnational women, even with their myriad differences, relate with each other. In particular, this chapter examines how women of Nepal have borrowed rhetorical strategies from the #MeToo protestors across cultures to make their own movement, #RageAgainstRape, successful and partake in a condemnation of global patriarchy.

An examination of these shared strategies illustrates that women across the globe who engage in protest rhetoric share in identification, as they recognize that patriarchal forces limit the rights of women. The incidents of rape in South Asia as well as in North, South, and Latin America are not autonomous incidents and are linked to their specific cultural contexts; however, they symbolically share commonality. The incidents of rape in Nepal in 2019 brought women to the streets in protest, just as incidents of rape in other countries worldwide brought women from those countries to the streets (Barbara, 2020; Shrestha, 2020). What stands out is that these protestors across the globe, from differing contexts and cultures, came to the streets with very similar placards and other protest signs articulating their resentments and demands. For example, the chant "The Rapist Is You," which originated in Chile ("A Rapist," 2019), became part of the Nepali #RageAgainstRape movement. Likewise, the feminist protest signs "We Want Justice," "Justice Delayed Is Justice Denied," "No Mercy Against Rapist," "Rage Against Rape," and "Police Uncle Am I Safe? (Shrestha 2018) were used both in Nepal and India. The shared factor in all of these protest signs was also their use of World English. This travel and exchange of protest literature across cultures blurs the national divisions and magnifies the similarities in the conditions of women in various cultures.

By reading the protest signs written in World Englishes, this chapter claims that "semiotic resources" (Canagarajah, 2019, p. 6) in placards exemplify a common identification of women across cultures: the patriarchal justice system routinely rapes women across the world. While cultures vary, patriarchal oppression is remarkably consistent. The travel of protest signs to Nepal suggests that women in these various locations identify their common oppression in patriarchal structures and therefore build on each other's protest rhetoric as they engage in similar outcries against rape. By sharing the unifying consciousness against systemic and systematic oppressions which unite them, women protesters across differing cultures and positionalities evoke shared identities. In order to formulate this point, this chapter first overviews the history of the women's movement in Nepal, illustrating its only modest success. The chapter then outlines the incidents that launched a new wave of Nepali feminism with the #RageAgainstRape movement. Analyzing the placards used in Nepal, this chapter shows their similarities to placards used in similar protests across the globe. Then, using the theories of Burke, Canagarajah, and Pennycook, this chapter argues that despite their myriad differences, feminist protestors identify with others, sharing a common identification as global citizens by using World English.

## History of the Women's Movement in Nepal

To understand why the #MeToo movement has not taken off in Nepal while the #RageAgainstRape movement has, one must consider the history of Nepal's women's movement, a movement that has been slow to evolve. Just as Malcolm O. Sillars states that social movements are shaped by political movements (2001, p. 118), Nepal's feminist movement has been largely defined by the country's past century of politics, a century that began with a religion-based monarchical government, experienced the Maoist Revolution and Nepali Civil War, and felt the repercussions of a postbellum society (Sellars-Shrestha and Tamang, 2015; Tamang, 2009). From the mid-nineteenth century, Nepal was governed by the Rana dynasty, which had a Hindu legal system that excluded Nepali women from political and legal rights, subjecting them to polygamous marriage, widow discriminations, and child marriages, and rendering Nepali women as the country's second-class citizens. Though this environment might not seem to provide fertile ground for any kind of women's movement, somehow, at the beginning of the twentieth century, poet and ascetic Yogmaya Neupane (Aziz, 2001; Ghimire, 2022) took action that gave her the title of Nepal's first feminist.

As a Hindu religious figure herself, Yogmaya fought for "alms for righteous governance"—a system of government based on justice and truth. Her primary contribution to the women of Nepal was that she led a campaign to eradicate the *sati* system, a religious practice of burning to death the widow in the funeral pyre of her husband after he died. While a campaign to end the killing of widows may seem a nominal feminist movement in comparison with other women's movements elsewhere, Yogmaya's actions empowered Nepali women.

After Yogmaya's death in 1941 in Nepal's largest mass suicide, a suicide protest against Nepal's brutal government policies, several other Nepali women began to fight for democracy, as well as other social and political causes. In 1947, Nepali women achieved the right to vote and the right for girls' education because of their continuous collective effort. In 1953, one of these women, Sahana Mangaladevi, became the first elected woman representative in Nepal, and another, Dwarika Devi, was the first parliamentarian and minister of the country in 1958. Additionally, women's political organizations were established, and it was through these formal organizations that Nepali women were able to influence policy and acquire some legal rights (Pandey, 2016; Tamang, 2009; Shrestha and Tamang, 2015).

However, these feminist efforts had been limited because they advocated for only one segment of Nepali women: high-caste women. Inevitably, then, Nepal's women's movement was very partial, excluding women from marginalized and rural areas, those from the lower class, and other ethnic minorities. The Maoist Revolution, which lasted from 1996 to 2006, changed that focus, making Nepal's civil war against the government a landmark movement in the campaign for women's rights and social justice. During this revolution, one of the fundamental changes was that women were given primary positions in combat, a change which altered many Nepali men's perception of women. Additionally, since most of the women who participated in combat were marginalized women from rural villages, perspectives regarding women shifted in these rural areas. After the Maoists come to power in 2006, 17% of the interim parliament was female, the highest percentage of women participating in politics in Nepali history. Additionally, the subsequent government guaranteed that women possess 33% of parliamentary seats in the constituent assembly. The Maoist Revolution, in this sense, brought a huge change in terms of women's participation and contributions in politics and political life which had never been seen before in the history of Nepal.

However, the post-Maoist period was not ideal for women. Without a doubt, the 2015 constitution of Nepal that guarantees seats for women in Parliament, as well as in other central roles in Nepali government, was an achievement. This new government enabled the appointment of women prime ministers, Bidhya Devi Bhandari, in 2015; the first female unopposed elected speaker, Onsari Gharti

Magar, in 2015; and the first female chief justice of the Supreme Court, Sushila Karki, in 2016. But these were exclusive leadership roles that did not guarantee social justice and equal treatment of Nepali women. The status of women became worse because of the feeble governmental system, patriarchal institutional structures, and a weak legal system. The post-Maoist period exposed the lack of justice for horrific sexual crimes against women that were committed on both the Maoist and government sides during the time of insurgency. Additionally, as Seira Tamang writes, the feminist movement in Nepal has had a high degree of tokenism as well as class hierarchy, as it "has been and continues to be dominated and led by high-caste Hindu women" (2009, p. 63). As a result, it has continually relegated the participation and contributions of women to those from largely marginalized castes, classes, and spheres. In sum, Tamang states that the feminist movement in Nepal has always been a liminal movement, affecting some but not all Nepali women.

## #RageAgainstRape

In this precarious situation, sexual autonomy and safety from sexual harassment and violence seemed impossible for some women. As the February 2020 conference session, नेपालको "मी टू" किन अगाडि बढ्न सकेन (Why the Nepali #Metoo Movement can't move forward?), pointed out, with the slow progress of Nepal's women's movement, much of Nepali culture has been wary of women's accusations of sexual harassment, and many Nepali blame women for the accusations more than they blame men for harassment and violence. In other words, women who stated "#MeToo" found little support (Shrestha 2020).

However, this marginalization of Nepal's feminist movement started to shift in July 2018, when a twelve-year-old girl, Nirmala Pant, was found raped and murdered in a sugarcane field near her family home in Kanchanpur, Nepal. Though the police did go to the crime scene to investigate, and though her autopsy examination determined that Pant died by asphyxia (Udwin 2015), the investigation was severely compromised by the police's mishandling of the crime scene. For example, in a video captured and later released by a member of the public, the police officer can be seen washing the dirt and blood from the legs of the victim and cleaning up the trouser that the victim was wearing during her murder. Either because of police ineptitude or malintent, the rapist/murderer was not identified. Outraged, the parents of the victim—with support from the public—constantly protested for #JusticeForNirmala. As a result, the police department presented a false perpetrator to curb the ongoing public protest. However, these attempts to mislead the public sparked further public protests and demonstrations in the streets, as well as increased media demands for justice. It was not until this mass protest against Nirmala's rape and murder that anything resembling the #MeToo Movement gained any traction in Nepal, as people came to the streets carrying signs, written in English, that condemned the acts of the patriarchal government. With the protests signaling a clear mass awareness of structural and systemic violence and injustices against women, powerful women began to come forward with their tales of harassment at the hands of powerful men. As journalist Bhrikuti Rai wrote, "there was a flicker of hope that Nepal's MeToo movement was finally taking off" (2019, n.p.).

However, even within this movement, most were afraid to name their attackers. For example, in October 2018, theater artist Akanchha Karki bravely tweeted: "A middle-aged pervert feels he is entitled to the 'love' of someone half his age, just because he cast her in a play. Has the audacity to harass her, kiss her in the name of exercise, and say she gave him 'signals.' Tells her to #gotohell after she calls him old and sick." Yet Karki was not brave enough to say who this man was. The reasons for her hesitancy became apparent when two more women from the governmental sector and one from the Nepali arts sector came forward with accusations of sexual assault and harassment against powerful men whom they named. However, these women received little public support; instead, there were attempts to deny the allegations, contain the protests, and make these women appear unreliable. Eventually, two harassers who worked in the government sector issued their brief apologies and then it was back to business as usual for them. Another named harasser, theater founder Sunil Pokharel, never apologized and continued his life as if nothing had ever happened. Dejected by the lack of accountability, Anbika Giri, a Nepali writer, tweeted: "It is infuriating and also disappointing to see how institutions are complicit in enabling these men to get away with their abuse of power, without stern repercussions" (Rai, 2019, n.p.).

However, the #RageAgainstRape movement continued in Nepal, just as the #MeToo movement did elsewhere. This movement became stronger in Nepal when 1,482 women and girls reported rape in 2017 and 2018 alone (Shrestha, 2018). With sexual violence against women growing in Nepal, the number of women from all castes, classes, and ethnicities who have joined these protests has grown so much that the movement, #RageAgainstRape, in Nepal can no longer be considered liminal. Additionally, the protests have been covered by most print and broadcast media, showing the demonstrators' protest signs and placards, which carried slogans such as "Justice for Nirmala," "Justice for Nirbhaya," "Police Uncle Am I Safe" (Shrestha 2018), "Justice Delayed Is Justice Denied," and "The Rapist Is You!" (Thapa 2020), all of which were written in World English, English that is appropriate for the context in which it is used and does not necessarily abide by England's or the United States' rules of grammar. These World English signs and placards were not unique to Nepal, however. Those incensed by sexual violence in Nepal borrowed protest slogans from campaigns in other countries, and via their use of World English, what was written could be shared across the globe.

## Identification via Placards

One reason for the success, then, of this new Nepali movement may have been the transference of protest rhetoric across national borders. If Nepali women could not find sufficient support for their protests within their nation, they could benefit from symbolic support from women with similar causes in other nations. They could share their protests and find support and solidarity.

In particular, Nepali protestors learned from Indian feminists. Six years earlier in India, many women joined forces to condemn women's rapes and murders. The Indian movement began when a twenty-three-year-old female physiotherapy intern, known with the pseudonym Nirbhaya, was gang-raped and tortured. Nirbhaya had been traveling on a private bus with her male friend when the men driving and controlling the bus attacked her and her friend. Thirteen days after the assault, she died, and the incident received widespread national and international coverage. Subsequently, public protests "Justice for Nirbhaya" were organized in New Delhi and across the country, where thousands of protesters clashed with security forces as the protesters revolted against the ineffective policies of state and central governments (Sinha, 2017). Although the factual details of these two incidents were different, most of these placards used for "Justice for Nirbhaya" in 2012 in India were reproduced in 2018 for the "Justice for Nirmala" protests. In other words, despite the demographic, ethnographic, and structural differences, the protestors in both of these cases used similar slogans against the issue of rape.

In the case of Nepal and India, protestors used placards written in the national languages Nepali and Hindi: *Nirmala le Naya Kahiye Pauchin Sarkar* (When Will Nirmala Get Justice), *Sarkar Betiyo Naya Bhetiyena* (Justice Failed and the Government Succeed), respectively (Shrestha, 2018). Additionally, Indian protests frequently used local dialects in addition to local adaptations of English. In both countries, the placards included phrases such as "We Want Justice," "*Sarkar Betiyo Naya Bhetiyena*," "Stop Rape Now," "No Means No," "Rapists Should Be Hanged till Death," "No Mercy to Rapists," "Zero Tolerance to Rape," "#Justice Delayed Is Justice Denied," and "Police Uncle! Am I Safe?" (Shrestha, 2018). What is particularly notable is that all these phrases had traveled around the globe.

Another placard used in #RageAgainstRape protests in Nepal had histories in other countries. "The Rapist Is You," used more recently in Nepal (Thapa, 2020), is a phrase from a well-traveled protest anthem created in Chile, "Un violador en tu camino," or "A rapist in your path":

> Patriarchy is our judge
> That imprisons us at birth
> And our punishment
> Is the violence you don't see.
> . . .
> It's femicide.
> Impunity to my killer.
> It's our disappearances.
> It's rape.
> And it's not my fault, not where I was, not how I dressed.
> . . .
> And the rapist was you.
> And the rapist is you.
> Its [*sic*] the cops,
> It's the judges,
> It's the system,
> . . .
> The oppressive system is the macho rapist. (Colectivo, n.d., n.p.)

Originally created in November 2019 by the feminist collective Las Tesis during a flash mob in Chile's northwestern city of Valparaíso (Larsson, 2019), this anthem has been performed all over the world via its translation into World English. For example, in December 2019, groups of women joined in Mexico City to point at the Palacio Nacional, the home of the Mexican president, to chant the song condemning the patriarchy (Pierson, 2019). Additionally, the song was translated into English in the same rhythm and music as it also traveled to Mexico, Kenya, France, Germany, Italy, the United States, Nepal, and India. In January 2020, in the United States during the jury selection for infamous Hollywood film producer Harvey Weinstein's criminal trial, dozens of women gathered outside a Manhattan courthouse to perform a version of the chant. Singing first in Spanish, then in English, these New York protestors sang: "Patriarchy is our judge that imprisons us at birth/And our punishment is the violence you don't see" (Barbara, 2020, n.p.). Not only this, but the lyrics have even been translated into sign language to enhance the inclusiveness of the song and to push its message even further. If an individual wants to learn the song, or the dance that accompanies it (designed specifically for flash mobs), they have only to check a website such as Yahoo's Finance's "Learn the lyrics and dance steps for the Chilean feminist anthem spreading around the world" (Merelli, 2019). Factual details of these incidents in the countries in South Asia, Latin America, and North America are different, but the linguistic and extralinguistic elements of the protests in each of the incidents demonstrate similarities in regard to these women and their movements. And their expression in World English makes the similarities easier for protesters to recognize.

## The Rapist Is You

Numerous journals and scholars have pondered the reasons for the Las Tesis feminist anthem's worldwide popularity. For example, Paula Serafini argues that the anthem "displays an ethos of collective ownership and horizontality" (Serafini, 2020, p. 293); this means that though the song did have an original performance, the original performers make no claim to what the "correct" interpretation of the song should be, allowing each group that performs it to take ownership. Additionally, the dance steps readily available on YouTube are easy to learn and just as easily adapted.

However, one of Serafini's other explanations of the anthem's success discusses not only the song's popularity, but also its movement to placards and protest signs across the globe:

> The song puts into words that which has been silent for too long: it is the system that is killing us. It is the government officials and police officers. It is the judges. It is you. Participants in the performance are speaking truth to power in a collective act of denunciation that marks a point of no return: we are no longer silenced, and you are no longer shielded. The result of this approach is a performance that allows participants to feel empowered as political subjects through an instance of political and artistic participation. Their bodies in the street are simultaneously demarcating a feminist space of political action and of collective creative expression. Through their song and their movements, they are protesting, but they are also enacting a series of values such as sorority and (transnational) solidarity, horizontality, collectivity and the accessibility of both political and artistic participation. (2020, p. 294)

The phrases from the anthem, particularly, "the rapist is you," allows women to direct their anger at the patriarchy. Addressing not individual circumstances but the patriarchal structures, the placards tell representatives of the systems that enable rape: "You are the problem," "you allow the rape." Not only were the phrases on the protest placards identical in Nepal, Chile, the United States, as well as in Mexico, India, and many other countries, but the protesters also shared similar resentments and demands. All of these protests target the patriarchal systems of government and justice. No longer are these women allowing themselves to be vilified for wearing the wrong clothes, staying out too late, or being where they aren't allowed to be. Within these protests, the wrongdoer is the patriarchy, not women of any culture. Women can wear what they want, stay out as late as they want, and be everywhere. In fact, by "enacting" a transnational group, the protesters are everywhere.

While the Chilean sexual violence that prompted the phrase was localized and unique to Chilean culture, the Nepali public also recognized that the larger patriarchal structures are to be blamed for its violence. The blame is upon law enforcement and government for allowing the crime scene to be compromised, for evidence to be destroyed, for the police to let the offenders get away, and for arresting poor, innocent individuals as scapegoats. Nepali protestors blame the government for cover-ups as well as for legal malpractices, and they blame the government for laws and court rulings that enable rape. Similarly, the women in Mexico City shout at their president to announce he has allowed rapists to go unpunished; he collaborates on laws that do not protect women; he turns a blind eye to the sexual violence prevalent in the country. In New York City, women condemn the legal system, the Hollywood industry, and all that support them for allowing Harvey Weinstein to abuse so many women.

Additionally, as Serafini observes, the protesters, in using this phrase, gain power. By echoing their sisters across borders, the protesters not only condemn the system, but they also gain the strength of unification for judicial responsibility and stronger legislation against sexual assault and rape from the worldwide collective. While their situations are different and their oppression is intersectional, they all gain influence via their solidarity. In condemning the patriarchy, they are not merely trying to "struggle for a just society . . . in terms of the move from powerless to power for women as a group" (2003, loc. 693) as Mohanty criticizes some Western feminist movements as doing. The protesters, via their protests against patriarchy, are looking for a change in system, for a system that "is sufficient to dismantle the existing organization of relations" (Mohanty 2003, loc. 693).

"The Rapist Is You" is not the only placard written in World English that has crossed borders. Found on many protest signs, especially in Nepal, are the words "Justice Delayed Is Justice Denied," a maxim of the Western judicial system (Melcarne et al., 2021) and almost identical to the phrasing from Martin Luther King Jr.'s "Justice too long delayed is justice denied" from his "Letter from a Birmingham Jail." With this phrase, protesters of non-Western countries are not necessarily pledging allegiance to Western judicial systems, but they are simultaneously observing the justice system's apathy and condemning it for its hypocrisy. It not only denies women justice, but also enables violence against women.

## Identification: Marginalized Females across Cultures

The travel and exchange of these protest slogans show that all these protesters identify themselves as the victims of systemic violence, as they all portray the governments of their respective countries as the perpetrators of the crimes. With this identification, feminist protesters demonstrate that they share similar interests and principles, that they all want the patriarchy to end and to be replaced with a more equitable system. Such a sharing of similar interests and principles is what Kenneth Burke describes when he illustrates that identification is a matter of being "substantially one" with another person. As Burke writes:

> A is not identical with his colleague, B. But insofar as their interests are joined, A is *identified* with B. . . . In being identified with B, A is "substantially one" with a person other than himself. Yet at the same time he remains unique, an individual locus of motives. (1969, pp. 20–21)

When we apply Burke's theories of identification to feminist protesters across the globe, we can see that the principles and interests that the two groups share do not deny the protestors' uniquenesses, nor does Burke's theory deny the power differentials between women in various countries across the world. In fact, for Burke, divisions are fundamental qualities of interlocutors. While the feminists in the protest movements in Nepal, India, Chile, Mexico, and the United States have differences of all kinds, they are conjoined by their resentments against rape. Though this transference of rhetoric might not be purposeful, the demonstrations show that, indeed, it has occurred, which shows the protestors' similarities in principles and ideas.

This way of developing identities through the sharing of common substances is a sharing of commonality. Defining all rhetoric as a form of symbolic action, Burke says:

> a speaker persuades an audience by the use of stylistic identification; the act of persuasion may be for the purpose of causing the audience to identify itself with the speaker's interests; and the speaker draws on the identification of interests to establish rapport between himself and his audience. (1969, p. 46)

Of course, the manner of identifying one's interests and principles to others is symbolic, meaning that it is not necessary for the individuals to clearly identify themselves with each other. The women in Nepal do not know the women in Chile, Mexico, or the United States. They do not know of each other's unique circumstances, privileges, or obstacles. However, as Burke notes, interlocutors are united in some interests and depart from each other on others. This means that while there are enormous differences among the women of the world, their engagement in this rhetoric of identification creates commonality. As Burke states, "Belonging, in this sense, is rhetorical" (1969, pp. 27–28).

## Uses of World Englishes

The work of Canagarajah (2006) and Pennycook (2003) is also very useful in understanding how protest signs can enable this identification. Canagarajah focuses on how transcultural writing and rhetoric expand the concept of language. Considering not only the linguistic repertoires of dominant social spaces, but also those of non-dominant social spaces, Canagarajah explains how language can be used across transnational social spaces. According to Canagarajah as well as Pennycook, World English involves creative adaptations of standard English by the postcolonial countries and cultures in the world (Canagarajah, 2006, p. 587; Pennycook, 2003, p. 519). These adaptions are not limited by colonialist rules. Instead, the adaptations are creative expansions that tend to defy colonialist norms. In other words, the creative expansion becomes a means of resistance to Standard English.

To illustrate this resistance, Pennycook and Canagarajah explore the application of World English in popular culture, arguing that it can depict the act of "semiotic reconstruction," an act that is less about whether one is born in a particular type of community than it is about what one does with language (Pennycook, 2003, p. 526). Taking World English's ahistorical approach to language, Pennycook studies a form of Japanese rap culture, Rip Slyme. The use of World English in the genre of the rap song illustrates how language can be an expressive resource within interconnected societies. "Englishes" do not belong to Western countries; "Englishes" are standard means of communication (Pennycook, 2003, p. 517; Canagarajah, 2019, p. 610). World English, in this sense, is a globalizing trend in both verbal and written communication, and it provides a means for protesters across the world to perform their identities as global citizens.

Thus, while still using local languages, these protesters adopt varieties of English which undermine dominant Standard English–language norms. Just as the protesters' signs do not adhere to dominant English norms, the signs similarly do not adhere to their local and national language norms. As these protest signs enter what Pennycook terms *linguascapes*, "language signs are no longer tied to locality or community but rather [they] operate globally" (Pennycook, 2003, pp. 523–524) as they creatively adopt punctuation to express feminist ideas. With random spelling, unusual punctuation, or visual additions, the signs misplace English syntaxial and grammatical norms, exemplifying the protester's creative adaptation of World English. For example, the question mark after "Police Uncle Am I Safe?" is often marked in red on the posters, representing the horror and shock of these rapes; the frequent use of exclamation marks creates emotion and surprise. Additionally, the hashtag, an octothorpe symbol which became popular with Twitter statuses, helps the readers to easily find the messages within specific contents and themes. By using varying punctuation and nonverbal signs creatively, the protestors make their placards easier to disseminate through the media in and across cultures. For example, #JusticeForNirmala and #JusticeForNirbhaya are the popular Twitter hashtags used in Nepal and India for female rights.

People come from different positionalities, but they have commonalities that they themselves define. Our argument regarding the usages of World English in protest literature across cultures builds on the idea of World English creating affiliations outside the hegemonic First World English. We argue that Global English is also the language of political resistance, protest, and social movements. Specifically, we argue that protest movements against rape across cultures demonstrate that World English can be recognized as the language of protest events and/or resistance, not of the patriarchy.

In this sense, the usage of World English in protest placards has two core functions. First, this usage makes protest signs relevant to multiple cultures, allowing them to travel from one national border to another. Second, through this travel, this usage of World English affirms the common identities of women across cultures, thus marking the protestors as global citizens who are together fighting for a better world. Language itself does not assert identity. The context in which a language is used matters far more. The manner in which the semiotic resources are used by protestors narrates the identification of protestors across cultures as world citizens, not merely as representatives of each of their cultures and countries.

The usages of the World English, thus, have a discursive and performative function in the protest events across cultures. Pennycook notes that World English within the transcultural global flow helps people to "partake in multilayer modes of identity at global, regional, national, and local levels" (Pennycook, 2003, p. 529). Pennycook further claims that by using World English, no matter what their national language is, people discursively construct a global identity. This identity, too, is not the "historical, universal unity between women based on a generalized notion of their subordination" that Mohanty condemns (2003, loc. 541). Instead, it is a form of refashioned identity that locates the protesters in transnational spaces. Since World English is "used to perform, invest, and refashion identities across the border" (Pennycook, 2003, p. 529), feminist rhetors enter the community of global audiences. Thus, their protest signs do not belong to a single community, but address global communities, and the protesters' entrances into global spaces create their new and common identities. Simultaneously, this entrance into global communities invites their global audiences to join them. In other words, this performance of identity is not unilateral. Once people perform their identities by understanding "local contingencies" (Pennycook, 2003, p. 529), they expect their addressees to join them.

## Limitations to Identification

However, there are limitations to seeing World English as enabling the transnational identification. Unfortunately, the identification does not always transfer in all directions. For example, one placard phrase, "Police Uncle Am I Safe?," used commonly in Nepal and India, has not made a transcontinental jump. Often used in conjunction with "Justice Delayed Is Justice Denied," "Police Uncle Am I Safe?" uses irony to comment on law enforcement's inadequacies. As an idiom not found outside of Asia, "Police Uncle" has a variety of meanings. It can refer to the benevolent police officer who is a friend to all (Menezes 2019), as the character of a Police Uncle is part of some tutorials for teens and children in India (Ranjan, 2021). It can also be a derogatory term used to reference a lazy police officer ("Dad," 2015), or a lying law enforcement officer ("Arora," 2011). When the protesters, via their sign, then, call on this quasi-benevolent/lazy/lying officer to see if they are safe, the answer is already known: the Police Uncle is a puppet of the patriarchy. Police Uncles look out for themselves, as does the patriarchy.

As a form of World English, the phrase "Police Uncle Am I Safe" could certainly be used in any nation. The irony it invokes (by calling on the often-ineffective law enforcement that should be—but is not—guaranteeing safety) would be familiar in Western nations. However, the placard has not traveled outside of Asia. Some of the reason for that might well be that the idiom is not used outside Asia, but World English and the transnationally shared experiences of the ineptitude, corruption, violence, and failure of the police potentially could make the idiom universal. This lack of travel from Asia to Europe or the West suggests that while the identification with women across the globe is something women in countries like Nepal long for, Western women do not have such desires. Although Nepali women identify with those protesting Harvey Weinstein, most of those protesting Weinstein see themselves as far removed from Nepali women who are still fighting for basic rights. As scholar H. G. Widdowson noted almost twenty years ago (1994), while World Englishes are more common in the world than are British or American Englishes, Western countries still are reluctant or refuse to join in the use of World English.

Such reluctance and refusal may be what prevents women from so many different situations from joining together to change the status quo. Western women may find it impossible to identify with women whose grandmothers were burned alive when the grandfathers died. Western women may find it impossible to identify with women who perceive the ability to combat in a Maoist Revolution as liberation. Western women may find it impossible to identify with women who cannot say #MeToo, but instead say #RageAgainstRape. Such reluctance and refusal are an affirmation of the patriarchy that most of these placards condemn. We, like Mohanty (2003, loc. 649) and the women with the protest signs, are not opposed to unity; however, we acknowledge that there is a hesitation to recognize and accept particularities of difference while joining together in identification.

## Conclusion

Certainly, much of this argument appears to contradict many of Chandra Mohanty's well-established claims. The main thesis, that these shared placard mottos reveal protesters' identifications with one another, appears much too similar to Mohanty's condemned characterization of women as a "singular group on the basis of a shared oppression" (Mohanty 2003, loc. 385). However, we think the two arguments are compatible: the difference between Mohanty's criticism of this universalization and identification of women by feminist scholars and this chapter's discussion of protesters' shared identification is that the protesters appear to recognize their discrete materiality while discursively identifying with others across the globe.

This brings us to the conclusion that this decade's trend in feminist protest movements may be a configuration of global resistance to the sexual abuse and assault against women across cultures. The uses of World English in most of the protest signs show that while women's resistance to sexual abuse and rape is often culturally specific, the resistance can also be unified. Women in one culture can identify with the sexual abuse in another culture, and the women together may attempt to unify to end the abuse. However, Western feminists' refusal to look across cultures or consider other possibilities may be hindering this unification. This chapter's identification of commonality and women's common voice does not aim to blur the differences of women across cultures in other disciplines. Rather, it aims to suggest that women's movements against abuse and rape across cultures allow women to develop their identities as global citizens who protest the sexual violence against women on international levels.

In a similar vein, a deeper understanding of linguistic and thematic resources in the feminist protest signs across cultures asks us to rethink the theoretical underpinnings of the intersectional differences of women, at least when examining the abuse of women across cultures. This understanding also implies that women in the Global North and South share experiences in terms of their disenfranchisement from their judicial rights and political justices. Simultaneously, this new understanding also suggests that in some instances the transnational feminist idea of different forms of representation needs to incorporate more in-depth studies of intersectional identities of women in both the Global South and North.

## Works Cited


Anzaldúa, Gloria. 2012. *Borderlands/La Frontera: the New Mestiza*. 4th ed. San Francisco: Aunt Lute Books.

"Arora vs. State." 2010. September 29, 2011. https://bit.ly/3C40ETx.

Aziz, Barbara Nimri. 2001. *Heir to a Silent Song: Two Rebel Women of Nepal*. Nepal: Tribhuvan University Press.

Barbara, Vanessa. 2020 "Latin America's Radical Feminism Is Spreading." *New York Times*, January 28. https://www.nytimes.com/2020/01/28/opinion/latin-america-feminism.html.

Bunyan, Rachael, and Sanya Mansoor. 2019. "'Nothing Has Changed.' 7 Years after a Gang Rape That Shocked a Nation, Brutal Attacks against Women Continue."| *Time*, December 23. https://time.com/5754565/india-rape-new-delhi-bus-attack/.

Burke, Kenneth. 1969. *A Rhetoric of Motives*. Berkeley: University of California Press.

Canagarajah, Suresh. 2006. "The Place of World Englishes in Composition: Pluralization Continued." *College Composition and Communication* 57, no. 4: 586–619. https://www.jstor.org/stable/20456910.

Canagarajah, Suresh. 2019. *Transnational Literacy Autobiographies as Translingual Writing*. New York: Routledge.

Colectivo Lastersis. n.d. "A Rapist in Your Path." Zürcher Theater Spektakel. n.p. https://www.theaterspektakel.ch/en/article/colectivo-lastesis-a-rapist-in-your-path.

Cooke, Miriam. 2007. "The Muslimwoman." *Contemporary Islam* 1: 139–154. doi: 10.1007/s11562-007-0013-z.

"Dad Abroad, Step-mom Elopes, Kids Left to Their Fate." 2015. Center for the Study of Labour and Mobility, August 2. https://www.ceslam.org/news/6626.

Garcia, Lorena. 2015. *Respect Yourself, Protect Yourself: Latina Girls and Sexual Identity*. New York: New York University Press.

Ghimire, Asmita. 2022. "Yogmaya Neupane: The Unknown Rhetorician and the Known Rebel." *Peitho* 24: 17–28. https://cfshrc.org/journal/peitho-volume-24-issue-3-spring-2022/.

Gottipati, Sruthi, Anjani Trivedi, and S. Rai. 2012. "Protests across India over Death of Gang Rape Victim." *New York Times*, December 29. https://india.blogs.nytimes.com/2012/12/29/protests-organized-across-india-over-death-of-gang-rape-victim/.

Kadariya, S., and A. R. Aro. 2015." Chhaupadi Practice in Nepal: Analysis of Ethical Aspects." *Medicolegal and Bioethics* 5: 53–58. https://doi.org/10.2147/MB.S83825.

Larsson, Naomi. 2019. "'The Rapist Is You': Inside the Women-Led Protests against Sexual Assault in Chile." *The Independent*, December 8. https://www.independent.co.uk/news/world/americas/chile-protest-rape-sexual-assault-women-violence-santiago-a9235656.html.

McCall, Leslie. 2005. "The Complexity of Intersectionality." *Signs: Journal of Women in Culture and Society* 30, no. 3: 1771–1800.

Melcarne, Alessandro, Giovanni B. Ramello, and Rok Spruk. 2021."Is Justice Delayed Justice Denied? An Empirical Approach." *International Review of Law and Economics* 65. https://doi.org/10.1016/j.irle.2020.105953.

Menezes, Sharon. 2019. "Experiencing Justice Delivery: Women Exploited for Commercial Sex Speak." *Journal of Victimology and Victim Justice* 2, no. 1: 11–25.

Merelli, Annalisa. 2019. "Learn the Lyrics and Dance Steps for the Chilean Feminist Anthem Spreading Around the World." *Yahoo! Finance*, December 2. https://finance.yahoo.com/news/learn-lyrics-dance-steps-chilean-212411525.html.

Mohanty, Chandra T. 2003. *Feminism Without Borders: Decolonizing Theory, Practicing Solidarity*. Durham, NC: Duke University Press. Kindle.

Naples, Nancy A. 2013. "'It's Not Fair!' Discursive Politics, Social Justice and Feminist Praxis SWS Feminist Lecture." *Gender & Society* 27, no. 2: 133–157. https://journals.sagepub.com/doi/10.1177/0891243212472390.

Narayan, Uma. 1998. "Essence of Culture and a Sense of History: A Feminist Critique of Cultural Essentialism." *Hypatia* 13, no. 2: 86–106. https://doi.org/10.1111/j.1527-2001.1998.tb01227.x.

"Nepal's Parliament Speaker Resigns after Woman Alleges Rape." 2019. *Al Jazeera*, October 1. https://www.aljazeera.com/news/2019/10/1/nepals-parliament-speaker-resigns-after-woman-alleges-rape.

Nirola, Isha. 2017. "Chaupadi, a Tradition in Nepal, Turns Menstruating Women into Untouchables." *STAT*, February 17. https://www.statnews.com/2017/02/17/nepal-tradition-chaupadi-menstruation/.

Panchal, J. M. 2010. " on 13 January, 2010." *Casemine*. https://indiankanoon.org/doc/880070/?__cf_chl_jschl_tk__=c859727aea8711eb6447b73350347d550b14207f-1626043574-0-AeWGFBSN0p4jYMH6naTxP3LmsdsOfRkS_lF.

Pandey, Binda. 2016. "Feminist Movement in Nepal: Historical Foot-steps toward Gender Equality." In *Population and Development in Nepal*, pp. 1–22. Nepal: Ministry of Population and Environment. https://www.linkedin.com/pulse/feminist-movement-nepal-historical-foot-steps-toward-gender-pandey.

Pennycook, Alastair. 2003. "Global Englishes, Rip Slyme, and Performativity." *Journal of Sociolinguistics* 7, no. 4: 513–533. https://doi.org/10.1111/j.1467-9841.2003.00240.x.

Pierson, Carli. 2019. "'The Rapist Is You' Is the New Feminist Battle Hymn Emanating from Central and South America." *The Independent*, December 2. https://www.independent.co.uk/voices/rapist-you-dance-metoo-flashmob-feminism-south-america-a9230156.html.

Ranjan, Mukesh. 2021. "'Police Uncle Tutorial': Mission to Help Dropouts Reclaim Their Future in Maoist Hotbed." *The Indian Express*, April 25. https://www.newindianexpress.com/good-news/2021/apr/25/police-uncle-tutorial-mission-to-help-dropouts-reclaim-their-future-in-maoist-hotbed-2294405.html.

"'A Rapist in Your Path': Chilean Protest Song Becomes Feminist Anthem." 2019. *Guardian News*. YouTube. https://www.youtube.com/watch?v=s5AAscy7qbI&ab_channel=GuardianNews. Accessed July 11, 2021.

Rai, Bhrikuti. 2019. "Less than a Year Later, Nepal's Men of #MeToo Are Back to Work." *Kathmandu Post*, September 21. https://kathmandupost.com/art-culture/2019/09/20/less-than-a-year-later-nepal-s-men-of-metoo-are-back-to-work.

Ruptly. 2020. "USA: Feminist Flash Mob Sings 'The Rapist Is You' Outside Weinstein Trial." YouTube, January 11. https://www.youtube.com/watch?v=-35JYJvMBa8&ab_channel=Ruptly.

Serafini, Paula. 2020. "'A Rapist in Your Path': Transnational Feminist Protest and Why (and How) Performance Matters." *European Journal of Cultural Studies* 23, no. 2: pp.290–295. https://journals.sagepub.com/doi/10.1177/1367549420912748.

Sellars-Shrestha, S., and L. R. Tamang. 2015. "Revolving Revolutions: The Inclusion of Women in Peace Building in Nepal after the War." In *Women's Leadership in Peace*

*Building: Conflict, Community and Care*, edited by Mirjam van Reisen, pp. 113–129. Trenton, NJ: Africa World Press.

Shrestha, Elisha. 2020. "Why #MeToo Movement Failed to Take Off in Nepal." *Kathmandu Post*, February 8. https://kathmandupost.com/national/2020/02/08/why-metoo-movement-failed-to-take-off-in-nepal.

Shrestha, Subina. 2018 "#justicefornirmala: Anger Spreads in Nepal over Police 'Cover-Up.'" *Al Jazeera*, August 28. https://www.aljazeera.com/videos/2018/8/28/justicefornirmala-anger-spreads-in-nepal-over-police-cover-up.

Shrestha, Sujan. 2018. "In Pictures: Protest in Maitighar Mandala Demanding Justice for Nirmala Pant." *myRepublica*, July 13. https://myrepublica.nagariknetwork.com/news/in-pictures-protest-in-maitighar-mandala-demanding-justice-for-nirmala-pant/.

Sijapati, Alisha. 2018. "Why #MeToo Never Really Took Off in Nepal." *Kathmandu Post*, December 31. https://kathmandupost.com/special-supplement/2018/12/30/speaking-out-and-aloud-20181230125754.

Sillars, Malcomb O. 2001. "Defining Social Movements Rhetorically: Casting the Widest Net." In *Readings on the Rhetoric of Social Protest*, edited by Charles E. Morris and Stephen H. Browne, pp. 115–124. State College, Pennsylvania: Strata.

Sinha, Jyoti. 2017. "India's Daughter Directed by Leslee Udwin." *Visual Studies* 32, no. 2: 183–185. https://doi.org/10.1080/1472586X.2017.1321246.

Tamang, Seira. 2009. "The Politics of Conflict and Difference or the Difference of Conflict in Politics: The Women's Movement in Nepal." *Feminist Review* 91, no. 1: 61–80. https://journals.sagepub.com/doi/10.1057/fr.2008.50.

Thapa, Kakaj. 2020. "'The Rapist Is You'—Nepali Youth Resort to Creativity to Raise Awareness about Sexual Violence." *The Nepalese Voice*, November 8. https://nepalesevoice.com/banner-first/the-rapist-is-you-nepali-youth-resort-to-creativity-to-raise-awareness-about-sexual-violence/.

Udwin, Leslee. 2015. *India's Daughter*. BBC Storyville documentary. https://www.imdb.com/title/tt4058426/.

*Washington Post*. 2018. "Facing #MeToo Accusations, Indian Men Retaliate with Lawsuits, Claiming They Are the Ones under Attack." *South China Morning Post*, October 16. https://www.scmp.com/news/asia/south-asia/article/2168764/facing-metoo-accusations-indian-men-retaliate-lawsuits-claiming.

Wright, M. W. 2011. "Necropolitics, Narcopolitics, and Femicide: Gendered Violence on the Mexico-US Border." *Signs: Journal of Women in Culture and Society* 36, no. 3: 707–731.

# 8

# Hashtag Activism and #MeToo in South Africa

## Mobilization, Impact, and Intersectional Feminism

*Lize-Mari Mitchell*

### Timeline

- 1889: Women's Suffrage Movement began, mainly driven by the Women's Enfranchisement Association of the Union.
- 1913: Black and colored women in the Orange Free State protested against the carrying of pass books (a form of internal passport system designed to segregate the population, manage urbanization, and allocate migrant labor).
- 1914: Pass laws for women were relaxed.
- 1918: The Bantu Women's League was established by Dr. Charlotte Maxeke.
- 1930: White women were given the right to vote after a twenty-year campaign.
- 1933: White women voted at the general election.
- 1933: Leila Wright was elected as the first female Member of Parliament.
- 1948: The African National Congress Women's League was established.
- 1950: The Women's Defence of the Constitution League (known as the Black Sash) was founded; this group was active from 1950 to 1994 against the Apartheid regime, injustice, and inequality.
- 1954: The Federation of South African Women (FEDSAW) was established.
- 1954: The Women's Charter was adopted.
- 1956 (August 9): 20,000 women held a protest march at the Union Buildings in Pretoria to protest against pass books for women.
- 1956: Members of FEDSAW were arrested for treason.
- 1957: "The Bail Fund" was set up by the Black Sash to assist African women who were being arrested and imprisoned for contravening the pass laws.
- 1983: Asian women and women of color were given the right to vote.

Lize-Mari Mitchell, *Hashtag Activism and #MeToo in South Africa* In: *The Other #MeToos*. Edited by: Iqra Shagufta Cheema, Oxford University Press. © Oxford University Press 2023. DOI: 10.1093/oso/9780197619872.003.0008

- 1984: The Matrimonial Property Act 88 was passed, which changed married Whie, Indian, and colored women's legal status from that of a legal minor to an adult who could enjoy social liberties and own economic assets.
- 1988: The Matrimonial Property Act 88 was extended to African women.
- 1990: The African National Congress released a statement titled "The Statement of the National Executive Committee of the African National Congress on the Emancipation of Women in South Africa," which was the first national acknowledgment of the need for gender equity in order to advance a truly democratic nation.
- 1993: The Prevention of Family Violence Act criminalized marital rape and other domestic violence.
- 1994: The 1954 Women's charter was reviewed and the Women's Charter for Effective Equality was adopted.
- 1995: August 9 was declared as National Women's Day to commemorate the 1956 march and all South African women.
- 1996: The first Commission on Gender Equality was established.
- 1998: The Rural Women's movement was established.
- 2002: The National Policy Framework for Women's Empowerment and Gender Equality was adopted.
- 2005: Phumzile Mlambo-Ngcuka was elected as the first female deputy president of South Africa.
- 2016: Mass student protests against gender-based violence took place on university campuses under the hashtags #RhodesMustFall, #OpenStellenbosch, #FeesMustFall, and #EndRapeCulture.
- 2019: A mass protest to Parliament was held, protesting gender-based violence under the hashtag #AmINext.

## Introduction

In South Africa, the #MeToo campaign influenced social justice activism by demonstrating the potential of social media to mobilize and affect change. However, it did not manage to mobilize womxn to the same extent as it did in the global North because any gender-based violence (GBV) campaign in South Africa must consider the legacy of Apartheid/colonialism and womxn's intersectional oppression and identities.[1] In this chapter, I analyze these intersections to argue that the #MeToo movement could not adequately speak to these intersections because these aspects can only be addressed by rejecting a traditional, Western (first and second wave) approach and by using a decolonial, intersectional feminist framework. I use intersectionality as the analytical framework for this discussion. This chapter explores intersectional feminism within the South African context and uses this to unpack both the lack of mobilization under #MeToo as well as the similarities, differences, and influence that #MeToo had on later South African feminist campaigns. This is followed by an examination and comparison of two South African hashtag campaigns, namely #EndRapeCulture and #AmINext, that followed a more decolonial, intersectional approach.

Kimberle Crenshaw (1989, p. 140) argues that a single-axis framework advantages a "distorted analysis of racism and sexism because the operative conceptions of race and sex become grounded in experiences that actually represent only a subset of a much more complex phenomenon." Instead she offers intersectionality as an alternative feminist analytical approach. Intersectional feminism (IF) is consequently a response to the dominant logic and whiteness of classic feminism and is a system of analyses and praxis that acknowledges the existence of various forms of female oppression due to intersections of systems of power (Ciurria, 2019, p. 2; Bruwer and Dundes, 2018, p. 50). It is an approach that works from the understanding that "the synthesis of these oppressions (like race, class, gender) creates the conditions of [Black women's] lives" (The Combahee River Collective 2014, p. 272). Although intersectionality started as a comment on the experience of Black Americans, women of color (WoC) in South Africa and their lived realities are also prime examples of intersectional oppression.

The relationship between classic feminism and South African womxn is "uncomfortable" because of classic feminism being a "white, Western import" (Gouws, 2017, p. 19) that is based on privilege (Shefer, 2019, p. 421).[2] For many womxn in South Africa, there exists an intersection between blackness and womxnhood which extends beyond the single categorical analytical axis of classic feminism that is based only on the categories of sex and gender. Therefore, a feminist approach that emphasizes white struggles is inappropriate and silencing in a country where the white identity reflects less than 8% of the population (Statistics SA, 2020, p.,9).

However, since 1994, the South African feminist movement has started moving away from the largely white upper-class intellectual profile of the Apartheid era toward a new feminism that is steered by younger womxn, WoC, and the LGBTQIA+ community (Shefer, 2019, p. 421; Kahn, 2017, p. 113). Younger feminists find intersectional feminism particularly more relatable and effective. For example, the slogan "my feminism will be intersectional or it will be bullshit" (Dzodan, 2011) was one of the main slogans of the 2016 #EndRapeCulture student protests (Gouws, 2017, p. 21). Amanda Gouws (2017) describes the intersectionality of female oppression in South Africa as a matrix of domination, which consists of white supremacy/Apartheid, heteropatriarchy, colonialism, and poverty (p. 23). This chapter discusses colonialism, Apartheid, and cultural oppression as examples of intersecting elements of gendered violence in South African feminism, with the acknowledgment that this list is not exhaustive.

## Women's Rights in South Africa and #MeToo

For purpose of this chapter, I emphasize two consequences of colonialism in South Africa: the removal of the African womxn from her position in society, and the sexualization of WoC. I also give selected examples of oppressive Apartheid legislation as a limited illustration of the extent to which these systems oppressed womxn both in their own tribes as well as in the wider political system. Precolonial tribal systems were by no means systems of gender equality; however, African womxn as the agricultural producers still enjoyed a position of social prestige within their tribes (Ochonu, 2018, p. 28). However, in the seventeenth and eighteenth centuries, colonial authorities and missionaries ignorantly viewed this as female slave labor and inappropriate female behavior. Both church and school were consequently used to indoctrinate young African girls with Western norms and gender definitions (Walker, 1990, p. 9). Womxn were to be domesticated and were no longer perceived as productive, economic members of society. This approach "undermined a precolonial ideology that emphasis female initiative, activity, and self-reliance" (Walker, 1990, p. 9). The colonial ideology of gender was refracted through the prism of race by incorporating African womxn within the settler households as domestic workers (Jansen, 2019, pp. 19–23). Even today, this power dynamic of WoC being domestic workers is the norm, while a white womxn in the same position is practically unheard of in South Africa. Colonial authorities, in their arrogance and ignorance, failed to comprehend the social significance of many precolonial practices (Lues, 2005, p. 105). As a result, the enforcement of individual rights and European settler norms within a society based on communal responsibility and kin "tore holes in the tightly woven fabric" of indigenous societies (Walker, 1990, p. 9) and removed African womxn from their rightful and significant place within their own societies.

Another major source of oppression was the double standard of sexual morality. The virgin/whore dichotomy was racialized: white womxn were perceived as the symbol of European bourgeois civiliaation and were protected from all illegitimate male advances, while female slaves were raped by their white masters (Arnfred, 2004, pp. 16–19). Sexuality was defined via racialized narratives wherein Black men were labeled dangerous and animalistic, and Black womxn were fetishized and labeled as hypersexual (Gqola, 2015, p. 43) and "unrapeable" (Gqola, 2015, p. 55; Phipps, 2019, p. 9) for the sexual gratification of the white man (Gouws, 2019, p. 5; Phipps, 2019, p. 9). These racialized notions continued into Apartheid, and these historical dynamics still prevail (Arnfred, 2004, p. 18). Examples of colonial oppression can also be found in the indentured Indian womxn in colonial Natal and the Khoi and San of the Western Cape.[2]

Following colonialism, Apartheid was implemented in 1948. Apartheid was designed to enforce racial segregation and to institutionalize white supremacy (Ndimande, 2013, p. 22). For example, the African family unit was broken down through the Bantu Authority Act 68 of 1951, the Promotion of Bantu Self-Government Act, Act 46 of 1959, and the Bantu Homelands Citizenship Act of 1970: these acts introduced homelands and enforced racial segregation by grouping ethnic tribes into allocated areas, away from white areas. This arrangement stripped non-white South Africans of any rights within "white" South Africa. African men were forced to search for work outside the homelands, closer to the white cities. Husbands, living away from home, engaged in new relationships, which normalized polygamy and extramarital affairs—practices that disadvantaged women. Examples of the consequences of this system include increased risk for sexually transmitted infections (STIs) (Lues, 2005, p. 105), men ceasing to providing financially for their families, the breakup of marriages, female- and/or child-headed households, increased poverty, and girls being unable to stay in school (Johnson, 1992, p. 90).

Second, the Apartheid government introduced the Bantu Education Act 44 of 1953, which was a discriminatory educational policy that ensured Black students were only taught the necessary skills to become low-skilled workers and that guided girls to only be prepared for marriage and motherhood (Flood et al., 1997; Johnson, 1992). Math, science, and critical thinking were not included in the curriculum, and there existed a profound shortage of qualified teachers (Ndimande, 2013, pp. 22–24). The education system created a stereotype that Black womxn were only skilled for domestic chores. Another example is the Black Administration Act 38 of 1927, which determined that a Black womxn shall be deemed to be a minor under her husband's guardianship (Robinson, 1995, p. 461; Abrahams, 1997, p. 4; Budlender, 1998, p. 11). The Apartheid regime policies continue to affect womxn in South Africa even now, three decades later. Below, I discuss the intersection of GBV and cultural oppression in an attempt to describe the nuanced reality of WoC in South Africa.

During a presidential address, President Cyril Ramaphosa (2020, n.p.) described the rampant GBV:

> Violence is being unleashed on womxn and children with a brutality that defies comprehension. These rapists and killers walk among us. They are in our

> communities. They are our fathers, our brothers, our sons and our friends; violent men with utterly no regard for the sanctity of human life.

Female homicide in South Africa is five times higher than the global average (Statistics South Africa, 2018, p. 9), with one of the highest rates of rape (138/100,000). One in three womxn experience intimate partner violence (NSPGF, 2020, p. 26). However, sexual violence is severely underreported due to a culture of silence and shame; approximately only one in twenty-three instances of sexual violence is reported (NSPGF, 2020, p. 27). Freedom of movement and access to public space are quite simply a luxury not afforded to most womxn in the country (NSPGF, 2020, p. 27). Additionally, a large majority of Africans identify with some tribal heritage (Baloyi, 2018, p. 6). Many of the tribal traditions are based on the primacy of male authority, and tribes are still fiercely patriarchal (Khan, 2017, p. 113). For example, South African men are the highest percentage of South Africans who think it acceptable for a man to hit a womxn (Statistics SA, 2018, p. 3). Within the African value system, womxn are seen as a supplement to society, whose presence should only revolve around her family and home (Lues, 2005, p. 104).

There are various cultural and religious practices that directly infringe on the dignity, equality, and physical integrity of females, some of which are still widely practiced (Turley, 2012). Once such example, found among the Zulu tribe, is the annual Reed dance, which includes virginity testing of young girls as an integral part of the celebrations (Rafudeen and Mkasi, 2016, p. 119). Despite rejection from the courts and the Commission for Gender Equality and the Human Rights Commission, it is a prevailing practice as it is held under the patronage of the Zulu king. *Lobola* is another practice that commodifies a woman. *Lobola* determines that a male, when expressing the wish to marry, must negotiate a payment of cash and cattle to the womxn's family. This practice reduces a womxn to an exchangeable commodity. Zulu custom also determine that in the event of a man's death, his brother takes over his household and becomes husband to his sister-in-law; her consent, even sexually, is irrelevant to the matter (Cele, 2009, p. 169).

In addition, it is also rare to find female chieftains in these tribes or female leaders for the tribal courts. These courts are the only accessible courts for many womxn, but many womxn do not approach these courts because the courts are biased toward men (Dolweni, 2009, pp. 171–172). This is especially true in rape cases, where rapists are often only fined, or sometimes the rapist marries the victim if she is pregnant (Cele, 2009, p. 170). This brief background establishes that #MeToo is not relatable for most South African womxn. #MeToo and the womxn associated with the movement were not representative of the intersectional oppression of South African womxn, which is why #MeToo failed to mobilize them.

## Mobilization of South African Womxn under #MeToo

A primary reason for the lack of uptake among South African womxn is related to the racial and Western nature of the campaign (Gouws, 2019). South African womxn could possibly relate to Burke's version of MeToo. However, #MeToo was initiated by a white, privileged actress and initially gained attention due to the support of a similar demographic, with most initial key figures being Western, white, and privileged (Fileborn and Phillips, 2019, p. 2). Despite positioning itself as neutral and universal (Thapar-Björkert and Tlostanova, 2018, p. 1027), it did not attract the attention of South African womxn. In early coverage, despite focus on the global nature of the campaign, no major network cited a single African-based #MeToo campaign (Gouws, 2019; Ajayi, 2018). One of the few South African stories that is referenced in international media was that of white singer and political activist Jennifer Ferguson (Burke, 2018a). Although her trauma is acknowledged, it remains a white woman in a privileged position with a prominent white male perpetrator. It is not relatable to the majority of the population of South African survivors.

The demographics of disclosure under #MeToo in South Africa also bear witness to the whiteness of the campaign. Globally, 29% of the #MeToo tweets were written in a language other than English; 7% (the largest non-English group) of these tweets were in Afrikaans (Anderson and Toor, 2018), a language primarily spoken by white South Africans, and spoken only by 8% of WoC. One can therefore argue that the #MeToo movement was only partially adopted by a minority of Afrikaans-speaking, mostly white womxn in South Africa because they could relate more to #MeToo. Another barrier in the access of #MeToo was the different nature of GBV in South Africa. Wilhelmsen and Kristiansen (2018) interviewed young, Black South African females about #MeToo, and these womxn noted that the number of cases of sexual violence and the gravity of sexual crimes in South Africa far exceeds those of the cases highlighted in #MeToo. The interviewed womxn also shared that they relate more with Tarana Burke's original movement than #MeToo due to the intersectional elements discussed above (Wilhelmsen and Kristiansen, 2018).

Although #MeToo did not instantly mobilize South African womxn, the movement inspired other feminist movements in South Africa which were specific to South African context. These other, more relatable South African campaigns were spearheaded through hashtags. The following section will discuss two intersectional, South African social media campaigns: #EnRapeCulture, prior to #MeToo, and #AmINext, after #MeToo.

## #EndRapeCulture

This chapter discusses #EndRapeCulture for two reasons: first, as an illustration of the reach that social media hashtags can have in the mobilization and creation of social awareness in South Africa, and second as an attestation of the initiatives that existed before #MeToo. This shows that #MeToo was not a new phenomenon to South African womxn. However, prior to #MeToo, South African campaigns were more often than not focused on a single group of very specific womxn, whereas #MeToo saw the rise of larger scale, inclusive movements and mass-scale mobilization.

#EndRapeCulture started in 2015 when university students demanded the decolonization of tertiary institutions after dissatisfaction at the slow rate of institutional transformation. Students demands included racial and gender diversity of staff, decolonization of the curriculum, access to education for financially disadvantaged students, and redressal of racial and gender inequality (Paphitis and Kelland, 2016, p. 186). It started with the successful hashtag movement #RhodesMustFall, when students demanded demolition of colonial symbols like the statue of a colonial prime minister Cecil John Rhodes at the University of Cape Town. Moving from colonialism to socioeconomic equality, students changed #RhodesMustFall to the #FeesMustFall campaign. As a result of the campaign, tertiary education costs were significantly reduced in 2016.

As with #MeToo, social media was pivotal to the mobilization of students and the wide reach of these movements (Orth, 2018; Gouws, 2018). WoC were central to the success of these campaigns. However, even at this time of solidarity between male and female students, female students frequently experienced on-campus GBV. In 2016, these reports of sexual violence culminated in the RU Reference list, a list of alleged rapist at Rhodes University campus. Female students demanded institutional transformation of rape policies and that the men on the RU Reference list be brought to justice. The institution, however, refused to take immediate action against unproven allegations. Protesters perceived this as the institution's unwillingness to reform and as their support for perpetrators of sexual violence (Orth, van Wyk, Andipatin, 2020a, p. 193). The womxn students started a mass protest, most reclaiming their sexuality and bodily autonomy by protesting bare breasted or only in their bras, with many brandishing sjamboks (whips). The movement rapidly gained momentum through social media (Orth, van Wyk, Andipatin, 2020a, p. 194), and soon students all over the country expressed their solidarity via hashtags such as #nakedprotests, #endpartriarchy, #RUReferencelist, and the most prominent, #EndRapeCulture.

However, #EndRapeCulture mobilized primarily young female university students. Although intersectional, it did not manage to mobilize womxn outside this demographic. It was only after #MeToo that a campaign uniting various womxn would be seen in South Africa; however, both #EndRapeCulture and #MeToo campaigns had pivotal roles in the eventual success of later hashtag campaigns. In her analysis of these protests, Gouws (2017a) argues that these protests started a larger movement that expressed that young WoC will no longer be silent in their oppression or be subdued in their culturally, racially, socially, and gender-dictated positions. She asserts that their uprising caused "moral panic." The truth of this is visible in the amount of backlash they received, from both the older generation of feminists and other men and womxn, who felt offended by the nakedness and loudness of these "dangerous womxn" and told them to cover up and get back in line (Msimang, 2016). They were accused of being "un-African" and of overtly sexualizing and objectifying themselves (Gouws, 2019, p. 4).

The danger of these young womxn seemed to lie in the perceived threat of their persistent questioning of deeply engrained patriarchal cultural norms (Miller, 2016, p. 272; Msimang, 2016). They were taking back their own power, but their nakedness, their vulnerability, and the desperation of the situation threatened others. Their sexualized bodies were changed to fighting, defiant instruments. They also paid homage to generations of African womxn who have used their naked bodies as a form of protest against social ills (Mathebula, 2018). The movement has been described as a "new wave of activism" (Msimang, 2016), where the protesters follow a feminism that is rooted in Black consciousness and Black pain within a post-Apartheid society (Gouws, 2019, p. 3). This wave is not only against the white oppressor, but it extended to a deeply intimate confrontation with their own tribal cultures and African males. They, therefore, protested against both white and Black, past and present oppression.

South Africans are deeply attached to their past and their cultural heritage; that is why student protestors invoked past iconography to mobilize people. This invocation of past symbols is a strategy that roots the South African feminist movement in its cultural context, despite its similarities with #MeToo. Two of the most prominent symbols that the students used were the brandishing of sjamboks and the wearing of headwraps. Such iconography served to strengthen the intersectionality of the #EndRapeCulture movement.

Sjamboks were traditionally cattle-herding whips used by indigenous tribes (Bowley et al., 2002, p. 300). Today they have various uses, including punishment and disciplining, especially by vigilantes (Buur, 2008, p. 576; Bowley et al., 2002, p. 300; Traynor et al., 2020, p. 1793). It is unfortunately also a tool used in rural areas to beat womxn and children (Cordelia, 2020, p. 3; Kruger, 2019, p. 65). Historically, sjamboks were a popular tool used to "discipline" Africans, both men and womxn, during the colonial and Apartheid eras (Super, 2017, pp. 520, 523). However, in a unique show of power, womxn used it during the Apartheid era to punish transgressors. For example, in the 1980s, sjamboks was used to punish men accused of rape throughout the large township (area allocated to Africans during Apartheid) of Soweto. In many cases, the rapists were lashed by local womxn (Mathebula, 2022, p. 21)). The sjambok is therefore symbolic of a tool used to oppress, but also empower womxn. Including this item in the protests gave recognition to various levels of racial and gender identity, power, and sexual relations, both past and present. Furthermore, it showed womxn reclaiming their autonomy.

Wearing of a headwrap or *doek/dhuku* also holds significant position within many of the religious and ethnic groups in South Africa. Siamonga (2017) described the various connotations of the *dhuku* as "a helmet of courage," "a uniform of communal identity," and rebellion against the "loss of self-definition." What distinguishes the *doek* from other headwraps is that the knot of the material is always placed near the crown of the head, resembling a regal coronet. It is therefore more than a mere accessory; it is symbol of African femininity, heritage, and status (Katsande, 2015). Within the #FeesMustFall movement and #EndRapeCulture, the *doek* became an unmistakeable symbol of African womanhood and the power that they can harness when they come together (Koole, 2017, p. 39). The protesters adopted the *doek* as a statement of womanhood, African tradition, and African feminine and feminist identity. The symbolism of taking both the tools of past oppression and reminders of women's status, combined with the display of their own sexuality by appearing bare breasted, created a strong intersectional narrative of identity and power. The campaign was successful in raising awareness of rape culture and sociocultural mechanisms which allow and enable rape, according to a study (Orth, Andiaptin, and van Wyk, 2020). The study analyzed the comment section of Facebook posts related to #EndRapeCulture and found that the campaign increased public conversations about sexual violence, impacted public discourse, and highlighted the lack of male mobilization in this struggle.

Most importantly, broad nationwide student engagement brought actual change at an institutional level. University management appointed task teams to investigate policies and claims of rape culture (Gouws, 2019). Universities have improved their security measures, have established stronger support systems for victims, have introduced better disciplinary procedures, and have adopted a zero tolerance approach toward sexual violence at various campuses (Naidu, 2018). Though #EndRapeCulture had a profound impact on a specific section of womxn in universities, it failed to reach those outside higher institutions. The following section analyzes #AmINext, a social movement that started after #MeToo and mobilized womxn on a much larger scale. The movement was strongly influenced by #MeToo, while still being uniquely South African.

## #AmINext

On August 24, 2019, a nineteen-year-old university student, Uyinene (Nene) Mrtwetyana, visited a post office in broad daylight. She was raped and bludgeoned to death by a post office worker. Despite South Africa's previously high levels of violence and casual acceptance of GBV, Uyinene's death shook the nation and ignited a movement. Inspired by #MeToo, South Africa's own version #AmINext and #IamNene started trending all over the country. Uyinene's death became grotesquely emblematic of the government's complete failure to protect womxn. The hashtag quickly culminated in a mass protest consisting of South African womxn (and men) of all walks of life, from the whole country. They marched to Parliament to demand that the government give a stronger response to GBV.

In a country where femicide is a daily occurrence, Nene's death surprisingly stirred public rage and engagement. This happened while the conversations about sexual violence were taking place globally. This public reaction also resulted from a range of factors, including the age, appearance, and background of the victim, the nature of the crime, as well as the location and time of its occurrence. The reason the campaign had such a reach and mobilized so many South African womxn is perhaps best described by one of the popular slogans during the protest: "She is all of us. We are her. I am Nene" (Johnson, 2019).

The connected nature of the #AmINext and #MeToo campaigns and the consistent recognition of the #MeToo movement during #AmINext protests is best illustrated in the simultaneous use of both these hashtags on social media posts. The very womxn that posted under #AmINext recognized the influence of #MeToo. I contend that #MeToo paved the way for a large-scale social media campaign and protests against sexual violence, which would not have been possible if womxn had not witnessed the power of a joined, strong movement in #MeToo. #MeToo made womxn aware of the power of social media to bring institutional change and the ease of offering solidarity with a hashtag and still having an impact. One can also contend that the symbolic meanings of the hashtags relate to each other. Asking "Am I next?" can be seen as the anxious prelude to the recognition of "#MeToo." Although the womxn in South Africa could have simply used #MeToo, they opted to start their own movement. These campaigns are related, but different because of the monolithic identity of #MeToo in comparison with the intersectional nature of #AmINext.

During the initial stages of the hashtag, women used intersectional consciousness and social media activism not only to raise awareness of the prevalence of GBV, but also to create a platform for womxn to express their anger and solidarity. Nene's death became representative of the struggle that many womxn face. As the campaign progressed, it emphasized many intersectional issues, for example, the exploitation and mistreatment of womxn in the criminal justice system, the bias of the courts in bail hearings, the danger womxn face in social spaces, and the extreme poverty many womxn have to live in. The phrasing of the hashtag also encapsulates the deeply realistic fear that all womxn in South Africa carry within them, the fear of intersections of various factors in violence against them.

Like #MeToo, many influential South African WoC (influencers, entertainers, and activists) shared and supported the movement on Twitter. This campaign united womxn of various ages, races, sexual identity, and social class. #AmINext therefore does not represent a new, uniquely intersectional movement in South Africa, but rather a more inclusive strategy and mobilization that previous campaigns may have overlooked. This also explains the wider reach and greater impact of #AmINext.

Informal analyses of #AmINext, both during the protests and on social media, highlight its intersectional consciousness. For example, messages on protest posters included:

> "#enough #kwanele #genoeg" (enough in three official South African languages). (News24, 2019)
> "I am a woman with many wounds that this country has scarred me with." (Mamacos, 2019)
> "I don't want to die with my legs open." (Mamacos, 2019)
> "All the women in me are tired." (Pretorius, 2019)
> "We are tired of walking around hungry and scared!" (Pretorius, 2019)
> "We have traded apartheid shackles for shackles of GBV." (Bargales, 2019)
> "When will we finally be free?" (Pretorius, 2019)
> "If our lives do not outrage you, you are not paying attention." (Pretorius, 2019)
> "We are a rainbow country with only rain and it is running red, warm and bruised between her thighs." (Varsity News, 2019)
> "We mourn generations of oppressed Black women." (Eybers, 2019)
> "Being a woman in Africa is to already have one foot in the grave." (Norton, 2019)
> "The only thing more challenging than being disabled is being a woman in South Africa" (said by a disability activist with cerebral palsy). (Mycroft, 2019)
> "In my country it is easier to get raped than to get a job." (Mogoatlhe, 2019)

These selected examples of protest posters illustrate and confirm the intersections of race, historical oppression, GBV, poverty, education, and cultural oppression. In order to compare these posters and those of the #MeToo movement, I did a Google image search with the search terms "#MeToo" "United States" "protest posters."

From an informal comparison of 450 image results, the following main themes emerged: workplace harassment, accountability, ending the patriarchy, consent, solidarity, believing victims, and female empowerment. Many of these messages could also be found in the #AmINext protests. However, I found limited images addressing specific intersectional issues as described both in the discussion and in the South African slogans above, and none that included cultural issues or poverty. This is a simplistic illustration of the narrative similarities and difference in the protests.

#AmINext had a strong impact in the country as it mobilized and united a diversity of womxn and men. I, however, argue that the greatest outcome of #AmINext was its impact on legislative and policy level (Hasan, 2020). #AmINext made conversations around GBV a national priority. At the initial protests at the Parliament, President Cyril Ramaphosa met with protesters in an attempt to address demands. In this meeting, he promised a joint sitting of the National Assembly and National Council of Provinces to focus on the GBV crisis and the establishment of a commission of inquiry. He also announced a special fund to combat femicide.

Less than three weeks after the protests, a joint parliamentary sitting, only reserved for serious issues affecting the nation (Kiewit, 2019), took place. During the sitting a five-point emergency plan was announced, and measures were debated to combat gender-based and sexual violence. The president also instructed the reopening of unresolved sexual offenses, training of more female officers at police station level to interact with GBV victims, and post-rape training for healthcare providers (Kiewit, 2019). Following the sitting, the minister of Justice and Constitutional Development announced approval for legislation surrounding the (re)establishment of Sexual Offences Courts (Elliot, 2019). Finally, in 2020, the government announced three amendment bills to target GBV. In an official news letter from the president (Ramaphosa, 2020a), he acknowledged the pivotal role of the #AmINext movement in "the most far-reaching legislative overhaul" in the fight against GBV:

> From all social backgrounds, young and old, students and working womxn, the peaceful protesters held aloft placards that read "Enough is Enough" and "Am I next?" The anguish and the anger was [*sic*] palpable that day. As I received their clearly articulated demands, it was clear to me that we needed to act urgently and with determination. . . . Through the introduction of these Bills, we are honouring the promise we made to the protestors last year and to all the women of this country. (Ramaphosa, 2020a, n.p.)

## Conclusion

This discussion of #MeToo and its impact in South Africa highlight the ways in which #MeToo impacted the conversations on sexual violence in South Africa and influenced social justice movements by illustrating the power of social media to mobilize and effect change. It also unpacks the reasons why the campaign in its original syntax did not manage to mobilize South African womxn. They needed to conceptualize their own African version of #MeToo, that speaks to the larger South African project of gender and social justice and that recognizes that womxen's intersectional identities are central to the complexity of the violence and oppression they face.

This need resulted in two South African hashtags campaigns, #EndRapeCulture and #AmINext. In 2016, the #EndRapeCulture campaign emphasized the normalization of sexual violence on university campuses and on a symbolic level expressed an African feminist identity and articulated how the intersectionality of race, gender, and sexuality positions Black African women as sexual subjects. This pre-#MeToo campaign, although powerful, was limited in its relevance and reach. Post-#MeToo, in 2019, the more inclusive #AmINext campaign followed the #MeToo example and used social media to create solidarity and mobilize womxn of various identities and backgrounds. The campaign culminated in protesters handing over a memorandum to the president. #AmINext eventually surpassed the reach of #MeToo, as it included intersectional mobilization and constant affirmations of the many nuances and causes of sexual violence in South Africa. Along with raising awareness, these campaigns led to actual change in legislations and policies, as well as changes on sociocultural levels. These campaigns have been pivotal in the struggle to make GBV a national priority. The success of localized South African protests and campaigns would not have been possible if people had not witnessed the global impact and strength of #MeToo.

## Notes

1. This chapter uses the spelling "womxn" as opposed to the traditional spelling to emphasize the intersectional inclusion of trans, non-binary, womxn of color, womxn with disabilities, and marginalized womxn. This spelling also breaks free from the patriarchal norms by removing the suffixes "-man" and "-men."
2. For further reading on South African feminism: R. Frenkel, 2008, "Feminism and Contemporary Culture in South Africa," *African Studies* 67, no. 1: 1–10; A. Kemp, N. Madlala, A. Moodley, and E. Salo, 2018, "The Dawn of a New Day: Redefining South African Feminism," in *The Challenge of Local Feminisms*, edited by Amrita Basu, pp. 131–162 (London: Routledge).

## Works Cited

Abrahams, Annie. 1997. *Challenges Facing Women in Management, the Nature of These Challenges and How They Cope with It*. Master's thesis, Business Administration, submitted to the University of Cape Town.

Anderson, Monica, and Skye Toor. 2018. "How Social Media Users Have Discussed Sexual Harassment since #MeToo Went Viral." *Pew Research.* //www.pewresearch.org/fact-tank/2018/10/11/how-social-media-users-have-discussed-sexual-harassment-since-metoo-went-viral/. Accessed July 11, 2020.

Ajayi, Titilope. 2018. "#MeToo, Africa and the Politics of Transnational Activism." https://africasacountry.com/2018/07/metoo-africa-and-the-politics-of-transnational-activism. Accessed August 16, 2020.

ANCWL. 2012. "Homepage." http://womensleague.anc.org.za/. Accessed July 16, 2020.

Arnfred, Signe. 2004. *Re-Thinking Sexualities in Africa.* Uppsala: Nordic Africa Institute.

Baloyi, Elijah. 2018. "Tribalism: Thorny Issue towards Reconciliation in South Africa—A Practical Theological Appraisal." *HTS Theological Studies* 74, no. 2: 1–7.

Bell, Katherine. 2018. "Critical Race Theory." *Feminist Media Histories* 4, no. 2: 57–60.

Bergales, C. 2019. "South Africa: #AmINext, a hashtag against violence against women – RFI." *Teller report.* September 16. https://www.tellerreport.com/news/2019-09-16---south-africa---aminext--a-hashtag-against-violence-against-women---rfi-.SkMHAT1aLS.html.

Bowley, Douglas, Craig Buchan, Laurence Khulu, and Kenneth Boffard. 2002. "Acute Renal Failure after Punishment Beating." *Journal of the Royal Society of Medicine* 95, no. 6: 300–307.

Brajanac, Amina. 2018. *Addressing Intersectionality in the #MeToo Movement.* Master's thesis, submitted to Goteborgs University.

Brewer, Sierra, and Laura Dundes. 2018. "Concerned, Meet Terrified: Intersectional Feminism and the Women's March." *Women's Studies International Forum* 69: 49–55.

Budlender, Debbie. 1998. *Country Gender Profile: South Africa.* Pretoria: Sida and Bridge.

Burke, Tarana. 2018. "Me Too Is a Movement, Not a Moment." Opening talk at TedWomen 2018, November 28, Palm Springs.

Burke, Louise. 2018a. "The #MeToo Shockwave: How the Movement Has Reverberated around the World." *The Telegraph.* March 9. https://www.telegraph.co.uk/news/world/metoo-shockwave/. Accessed May 2, 2020.

Buur, Lars. 2008. "Democracy & Its Discontents: Vigilantism, Sovereignty & Human Rights in South Africa." *Review of African Political Economy* 35, no. 118: 571–584.

Cele, Mpho. 2009. "Report of Cedara Workshop with Rural Women's Movement." In *The Traditional Courts Bill of 2008: Documents to Broaden Discussion to Rural Areas*, pp. 42–91. Cape Town: LRC and LRG.

Ciurria, Michelle. 2019. *An Intersectional Feminist Theory of Moral Responsibility.* London: Routledge.

Combahee River Collective. 2014. "A Black Feminist Statement." *Women's Studies Quarterly* 42: 271–280.

Cordelia, Khoza. 2020. "The Hidden Gendered Anger in Marriages: The Case of Xitsonga Culture." *Aggression and Violent Behavior* 55: 1–7.

Crenshew, Kimberle. 1989. "Demarginalizing the Intersection of Race and Sex: A Black Feminist Critique of Antidiscrimination Doctrine, Feminist Theory and Antiracist Politics." *University of Chicago Legal Forum* 140: 139–167.

Daniels, Jessica. 2015. "The Trouble with White Feminism: Whiteness, Digital Feminism and the Intersectional Internet." In *Intersectional Internet: Race, Sex and Culture Online Brock*, edited by Safiya Noble and Brendesha Tynes. Frankfurt: Peter Lang Digital Edition series.

Dolweni, Sandile. 2009. "Report of the Meeting in Qunu Eastern Cape with TRALSO." In *The Traditional Courts Bill of 2008: Documents to Broaden Discussion to Rural Areas*, pp. 8–32. Cape Town: LRC and LRG.

Dzodan, Flavia. 2011. "My Feminism Will Be Intersectional or It Will Be Bullshit!" http://tigerbeatdown.com/2011/10/10/my-feminism-will-be-intersectional-or-it-will-be-bullshit/. Accessed September 15, 2020.

Elliot, Jo. 2019. "South Africa in the Wake of Gender-Based Violence Protests." February 3. https://joelliott-49955.medium.com/south-africa-in-the-wake-of-gender-based-violence-protests-whatcomesnext-c36c86e6db0c. Accessed September 14, 2020.

Eybers, Christa. 2019. *Eyewitness News*. September 4. https://ewn.co.za/2019/09/04/cele-booed-by-gender-based-violence-protesters-in-ct.

Fileborn, Bianca, and Nickie Phillips. 2019. "From 'Me Too' to 'Too Far'? Contesting the Boundaries of Sexual Violence in Contemporary Activism." In *# MeToo and the Politics of Social Change*, edited by Bianca Fileborn and Rached Loney-Howes, pp. 99–115. Cham: Palgrave Macmillan.

Flood, Terry, Madima Hoosain, and Nathan Primo. 1997. *Beyond Inequalities: Women in South Africa*. Cape Town: Southern African Research and Documentation Centre.

Gouws, Amanda. 2017. "Feminist Intersectionality and the Matrix of Domination in South Africa." *Agenda* 31, no. 1: 19–27.

Gouws, Amanda. 2017a. "Dangerous Naked Women." *Dangerous Women Project*. http://dangerouswomenproject.org/2017/02/24/4663/. Accessed September 22, 2020.

Gouws, Amanda. 2018. "#EndRapeCulture Campaign in South Africa: Resisting Sexual Violence through Protest and the Politics of Experience." *Politikon* 45, no. 1: 3–15.

Gouws, Amanda. 2019. "#InternationalWomensDay: MeToo Isn't Big in Africa, But It Has Made a Difference." *Independent Online*, March 8. https://www.iol.co.za/lifestyle/love-sex/relationships/internationalwomensday-metoo-isnt-big-in-africa-but-it-has-made-a-difference-19697305. Accessed August 22, 2020.

Gqola, Pumla. 2015. *Rape: A South African Nightmare*. Johannesburg: MFBooks Johannesburg.

Griffin, Penny. 2019. "# MeToo, White Feminism and Taking Everyday Politics Seriously in the Global Political Economy." *Australian Journal of Political Science* 54, no. 4: 556–572.

Hasan, Sarah. 2020. "The# MeToo Movement and Its Effect on Proposed Federal Policy." *ONU Student Research Colloquium*. https://digitalcommons.onu.edu/student_research_colloquium/2020/posters/23. Accessed April 24, 2021.

Jansen, Ena. 2019. *Like Family*. Johannesburg: Wits University Press.

Johnson, Chris. 1992. *Women on the Frontline*. London: Macmillan.

Johnson, Simone. 2019. "#AmINext: Protesters Rally for 19-Year-Old South African Girl Raped & Murdered in Post Office." *Madam menoire*. September 19. https://madamenoire.com/1101076/aminext-protesters-rally-for-19-year-old-south-african-girl-raped-murdered-in-post-office/. Accessed September 3, 2020.

Katsande, Rukariro. 2015. "The Significance of Head Ties in Africa." *Wilderness safaris*. January 26. https://wilderness-safaris.com/blog/posts/the-significance-of-head-ties-in-africa#:~:text=In%20Africa%20in%20general%2C%20and,woman%20to%20show%20her%20hair. Accessed August 11, 2020.

Khan, Khadija. 2017. "Intersectionality in Student Movements: Black Queer Womxn and Nonbinary Activists in South Africa's 2015–2016 Protests." *Agenda* 31, no. 3-4: 110–121.

Kiewit, Lester. 2019. "Ramaphosa Moves to Allay Fears of Government Inaction on Gender-Based Violence." *Mail and Guardian*. September 18. https://mg.co.za/article/2019-09-18-ramaphosa-moves-to-allay-fears-of-government-inaction-on-gender-based-violence/. Accessed October 5, 2020.

Koole, Gregory. 2017. *Doek and Dagger, Smoke and Mirrors: How Has the Print Media Represented Women of# FeesMustFall 2015?* Doctoral dissertation submitted to University of Witwatersrand.

Kruger, Lou-Marie. 2019. "Of Violence and Intimacy: The Shame of Loving and Being Loved." *Philosophical Journal of Conflict and Violence* 3, no. 1: 56–82.

Lues, Liezel. 2005. "The History of Professional African Women: A South African Perspective." *Interim: Interdisciplinary Journal* 4, no. 1: 103–123.

Mamacos, E. 2019. "#AmINext Protests: South African Women and Students Have Had Enough." *News24*. September 4. https://www.news24.com/parent/Family/Parenting/in-pictures-south-african-women-and-children-have-had-enough-20190904.

Mathebula, Mpho. 2022. "Nakedness as Decolonial Praxis." *Body & Society* 28: 3–29.

Miller, Darlene. 2016. "Excavating the Vernacular: 'Ugly Feminists,' Generational Blues and Matriarchal Leadership." In *Fees Must Fall*, edited by Susan Booysen, pp. 272–273. Johannesburg: Wits University Press.

Mogoatlhe, Lerato. 2019. "#SandtonShutdown: Hundreds of Protesters March in Johannesburg to End Gender-Based Violence." *Global Citizen*. September 13. https://www.globalcitizen.org/en/content/sandton-shutdown-gender-violence-south-africa/.

Mpho, Mathebula. 2018. "Naked Body Protest Is Here to Stay." *News24*. January 28. https://www.news24.com/news24/columnists/guestcolumn/naked-body-protest-is-here-to-stay-20180128-2. Accessed April 15, 2021.

Msimang, Sisonke. 2016. "South African Topless Protesters Are Fighting Shame on Their Own Terms." *The Guardian*, May 5. https://www.theguardian.com/world/2016/may/05/south-africas-topless-protesters-are-fighting-shame-on-their-own-terms. Accessed August 1, 2020.

Mycroft, Chaeli. 2019. *Between 10 and 5*. October 7. https://10and5.com/2019/10/07/the-only-thing-more-challenging-than-being-disabled-is-being-a-woman-in-south-africa-says-chaeli/.

Naidu, Edwin. 2018. "Universities Making Campuses Safer after 47 Rapes in 2017." *University World News*. October 9. https://www.universityworldnews.com/post.php?story=20181009130251203. Accessed August 20, 2020.

*News24*. 2019. https://twitter.com/hashtag/iamnene.

Ndimande, Bekisizwe. 2013. "From Bantu education to the fight for socially just education." *Equity & Excellence in Education*, *46*(1), pp.20–35.

Norton, Clifferdene. 2019. "#AmINext-optog: 'n perspektief." *Litnet*. September 6. https://www.litnet.co.za/aminext-optog-n-perspektief/.

NSGBF, Department of Women, Youth and Persons with Disabilities. 2020. *National Strategic Plan on Gender-Based Violence & Femicide Human Dignity and Healing, Safety, Freedom and Equality in Our Lifetime*. file:///C:/Users/lizemari.mitchell/Downloads/NSP%20GBVF%202020-2030P-FINAL.pdf. Accessed September 25, 2020.

Ochonu, Moses. 2018. "Africans and the Colonial Economy." In *The Palgrave Handbook of African Colonial and Postcolonial History*, edited by Martin Shanguhyia and Toyin Falola, pp. 123–143. New York: Palgrave Macmillan.

Ortega, Mariana. 2006. "Being Lovingly, Knowingly Ignorant: White Feminism and Women of Color." *Hypatia* 21, no. 3: 56–74.

Orth, Zaida. 2018. *Rape Culture and Social Media: Exploring How Social Media Influences Students' Opinions and Perceptions of Rape Culture.* Master's dissertation submitted to the University of Western Cape.

Orth, Zaida, Michelle Andipatin, and Brian van Wyk. 2020. "Exploring Rape Culture on Facebook in South Africa." *Gender Issues* 38, no. 1: 1–17.

Orth, Zaida, B. van Wyk, and M. Andipatin. 2020a. "'What Does the University Have to Do with It?': Perceptions of Rape Culture on Campus and the Role of University Authorities." *South African Journal of Higher Education* 34, no. 2: 191–209.

Paphitis, Sharli Anne, and Lindsay Kelland. 2016. "The University as a Site for Transformation: Developing Civic-Minded Graduates at South African Institutions through an Epistemic Shift in Institutional Culture." *Education as Change* 20, no. 2: 184–203.

Phipps, Alison. 2019. "'Every Woman Knows a Weinstein': Political Whiteness and White Woundedness in# MeToo and Public Feminisms around Sexual Violence." *Feminist Formations* 31, no. 2: 1–25.

Pretorius, A. 2019. "At #SandtonShutdown, South African Women Disrupt Business as Usual as Fury Over Gender-Based Violence Boils Over." *Common dreams.* September 13. https://www.commondreams.org/news/2019/09/13/sandtonshutdown-south-african-women-disrupt-business-usual-fury-over-gender-based.

Rafudeen, Auwais, and Lindiwe Mkasi. 2016. "Debating Virginity-Testing Cultural Practices in South Africa." *Journal for the Study of Religion* 29, no. 2: 118–133.

Ramaphosa, Cyril. 2020. "Full Speech." *News24.* June 17. https://www.news24.com/citypress/news/full-speech-these-rapists-and-killers-walk-among-us-ramaphosa-20200617. Accessed August 15, 2020.

Ramaphosa, Cyril. 2020a. "From the Desk of the President." September 7. https://us20.campaign-archive.com/?u=dcd34ec94620d939a2de5e60c&id=35cf2f83cf. Accessed 21 August 21, 2020.

Robinson, Kim. 1995. "The Minority and Subordinate Status of African Women under Customary Law." *South African Journal on Human Rights* 11, no. 3: 457–476.

Shefer, Tamara. 2019. "Activist Performance and Performative Activism towards Intersection Gender and Sexual Justice in Contemporary South Africa." *International Society* 34, no. 4: 418–434.

Siamonga, Evelyn. 2015. "African Women and the Significance of a Head-wrap (Dhuku)." *The Patriot.* March 12. https://www.thepatriot.co.zw/old_posts/african-women-and-the-significance-of-a-head-wrap-dhuku/. Accessed September 2, 2020.

Statistics South Africa. 2018. *Crime against Women in South Africa.* http://www.statssa.gov.za/publications/Report-03-40-05/Report-03-40-05June2018.pdf. Accessed July 28, 2020.

Statistics South Africa. 2020. *Mid-Year Population Estimates.* Isabalo House: Pretoria.

Super, Gail. 2017. "What's in a Name and Why It Matters: A Historical Analysis of the Relationship between State Authority, Vigilantism and Penal Power in South Africa." *Theoretical Criminology* 21, no. 4: 512–531.

Thapar-Björkert, Surichi, and Madina Tlostanova. 2018. "Identifying to Dis-identify: Occidentalist Feminism, the Delhi Gang Rape Case and Its Internal Others." *Gender, Place & Culture* 25, no. 7: 1025–1040.

Traynor, Micheal, Grant Laing, John Bruce, Matthew Hernandez, Victor Kong, Mariela Rivera, Martin Zielinski, and Damina Clarke. 2020. "Mob Justice in South

Africa: A Comparison of Blunt Trauma Secondary to Community and Non-community Assaults." *Injury* 51, no. 8: 1791–1797.

Tswane, Tebogo, and Nozipho Mpanza. 2016. "Wits FMF Feminists Stand in Solidarity with #RUReferencelist Protestors." *Wits Vuvuzela*. April 26. https://witsvuvuzela.com/2016/04/26/wits-fmf-feminists-stand-in-solidarity-with-rureferencelist-protestors/. Accessed July 25, 2020.

Turley, Melissa. 2012. "South Africa: Law of the Land." *Pulitzer center*. September 26. https://pulitzercenter.org/reporting/south-africa-law-land. Accessed July 25, 2020.

Varisty News. 2019. September 4. https://twitter.com/varsitynews/status/1169160714201817088.

Walker, Cheryl. 1990. *Women and Gender in Southern Africa to 1945*. Claremont: New Africa Books.

Weeks, Sindiso. 2011. "The Traditional Courts Bill: Controversy around Process, Substance and Implications." *South African Crime Quarterly* 35: 3–10.

Wilhelmson, Martine, and Heidi Kristiansen. 2018. "How Is the #MeToo Campaign Reflected in South Africa?" *Studentenes og Akademikernes Internasjonale Hjelpefonds*. February 7. https://saih.no/artikkel/2018/2/the-metoo-campaign-from-a-south-african-point-of-view. Accessed July 8, 2020.

# 9
# #MeToo and Everyday Sexism in Bangladesh

*Umme Busra Fateha Sultana and Fariha Jahan*

## Timeline

- 1971: Women participated, directly and indirectly, in the liberation war of 1971.[1]
- 1970s: The war heroines (Begum, 2002; Banu, 2015), later named freedom fighters (bdnews24.com, 2014; Dhaka Tribune, 2015), were rehabilitated; women were involved in the nation-building process through organizations such as Bangladesh Mahila Parishad (BMP), Naripokkho (NP), and Women for Women (WFW).
- 1972: Constitutional equality was declared, with reserved seats for women in the national Parliament in the first constitution of Bangladesh.
- 1974: Marriage and Divorce Registration Act 1974 was passed (especially needed for the rehabilitation of women in the war-torn country).
- 1980s: Under military dictatorship, Bangladesh saw the degradation of women's personal and political rights (Begum, 2002).
- 1980s: The Dowry Prohibition Act, demand of Uniform Family Code (UFC), emergence of women as political leaders of two leading political parties, activism against violence against women, introduction of "radical" concepts and theories such as patriarchy, "my body, my rights," women's empowerment, and debates regarding social, cultural, and religious prejudices against sex workers signified the decade (Begum, 2002).
- 1984: Bangladesh ratified the Convention on Elimination of all forms of Discrimination Against Women (CEDAW) with reservation on four articles.
- 1990s: Women emerged as political leaders of two leading political parties of Bangladesh. Affiliation between academia and feminist activism, "NGO-ization" of women's issues, and increase in women's participation in the educational, developmental, political, and economic sector occurred.

Umme Busra Fateha Sultana and Fariha Jahan, *#MeToo and Everyday Sexism in Bangladesh* In: *The Other #MeToos.* Edited by: Iqra Shagufta Cheema, Oxford University Press. © Oxford University Press 2023.
DOI: 10.1093/oso/9780197619872.003.0009

- 2020: Following mass public protests, legislation was passed that imposed the death penalty as the supreme punishment for rape.
- 2020s: Women's participation increased in development, politics, and academia. As a result of affiliation with different national and international donor agencies, the "NGO-ization" of the women's movement became stronger, since the beginning of the 2000 (Begum, 2002; Nazneen and Sultan, 2009).

## Introduction

Bangladesh has made significant development in reducing the infant mortality rate and gaining access to education and health (Statistical Year Book Bangladesh, 2020). Between 1990 and 2019, Bangladesh's Human Development Index (HDI) value increased from 0.394 to 0.632, life expectancy at birth increased by 14.4 years (Human Development Report, 2020, p. 2) and more girls than boys are attending primary and secondary schools. Studies have further observed massive inclusion of women in the formal as well as informal economy, larger than any time before (Human Development Report, 2020, p. 2; Kabeer, 2004, p. 6; Sen, 2015, pp. 305–307). Despite such progress, the rate of violence against women (VAW) in Bangladesh remains alarming (Khan et al., 2017; Wahed and Bhuiya, 2007).

Among the different types of VAW, domestic violence, acid throwing, rape, trafficking, and forced prostitution gain more attention due to their frequency, visibility, and better reporting (Ahmed et al., 2014; Wahed and Bhuiya, 2007). According to a study by Bangladesh Rural Advancement Committee (BRAC), 94% women in Bangladesh experienced sexual violence in different forms in public transport. Sexual violence and gender-based violence leave a deeper and damaging impact on women's physical and mental health, though it is often taken lightly and mostly remains underreported (Ahmed et al., 2014). One woman in a study by Ahmed et al. (2014, p. 2697) shares:

> You will hardly find any Bangladeshi girl who traveled on the streets and has not experienced sexual harassment. Some women are brave enough to talk about it, while others remain silent [ . . . ].

Despite widespread sexual violence, women in Bangladesh usually do not report it, or usually do not protest against it, because instead of punishment for the perpetrator, it could bring shame and danger to the victim's family. Her access to public spaces may become more restricted, or more people may harass or blame the victim (Ahmed et al., 2014). Consequently, when # MeToo spread all over the world, many asked how #MeToo has been received in Bangladesh and whether it has changed the feminist landscape here. Although only a few shared their experiences of sexual violence allegedly committed by some renowned personalities, patriarchy pressed still hard on them. The survivors wiped out their revelations and tried to erase the trace of the disclosure of their experiences from social media (Iftakhar, 2020). Focusing on the experiences of the women who participated in the #MeToo movement in Bangladesh, this chapter offers a sociocultural and feminist analysis of #MeToo in Bangladesh. We had conversations with six women who had shared their experiences following #MeToo and one journalist. This chapter, then, presents and archives the experiences of the victims and survivors of sexual violence, the ways in which participating in the #MeToo movement affected their personal and professional lives, and the lack of support for the survivors and lack of accountability of the perpetrators. In doing so, this chapter highlights what remains invisible in most other #MeToo stories, i.e., how sharing these stories affects the lives of the survivors after the initial support and popularity of #MeToo has dissipated.

## Flashback #MeToo

Sexual violence against women remains globally rampant, as the chapters in this book demonstrate. Most of the time, survivors do not reveal their experiences of sexual abuse due to stigmatization and further harassment by the society and legal institutions. Steadily, this sad reality is changing, where survivors no longer want to carry the burden of the secret of the crimes committed against them. The term "#MeToo" did justice to that thought and transformed that idea into actions (Chicago Tribune, 2020). Despite continuing debate over "movement or moment," "he said she said," the actual impact of #MeToo, Eurocentricity, and efficacy, #MeToo has inspired many survivors to come forward (Chicago Tribune, 2020).

In Bangladesh many were in doubt whether such a movement is possible here at all, given its religious and cultural values. Nevertheless, on October 29, 2018, the first #MeToo case was posted in a simultaneous video on YouTube and Facebook by an Irish-Bangladeshi pilot and renowned model, Maksuda Akhter Prioty, against a business tycoon and an influential political figure, Rafiqul Islam, owner of Rongdhonu Group, one of the largest multinational companies of Bangladesh (bdnews24.com, 2018; Iftakhar, 2020, p. 128).[2] Prioty went to his office to collect her payment, where he forcefully kissed her and groped her body (Iftakhar, 2020, p. 128). Prioty described the incident as "an attempt to rape." However, Rafiqul Islam denied all the allegations, labeling them as false and politically motivated (Iftakhar, 2020, p. 130). On November 7, 2018, Asmaul Husna accused a media personality, Jamil Ahmed, of attempted rape. According to Husna, Jamil Ahmed groped her, forcefully kissed her, and touched her body against her will while she was walking back from Shilpa Kala Academy (Iftakhar, 2020, p. 129; Dey, 2018). On November 14, 2018, Mushfika Laiju posted on Facebook that she was forcefully kissed and sexually assaulted by renowned dramatist and professor Salim Al Din, thirty-one years ago (Iftakhar, 2020, p. 129). She described it as an attempted rape (Iftakhar, 2020, p. 129). After Prioty, eight other women – Shuchismita Simonti, Mushfika Laiju, Asmaul Husna, Dipanita Sen Roy, Tasnuva Anan Shishir, Shabonti Kanta, Nadira Dilruba, and Alpha Arzu – shared their #MeToo posts (Iftakhar, 2020). Some of them posted on Facebook, some wrote in newspapers, and a few shared their experience in human chains which were arranged to unite the #MeToo survivors. There was a tenth #MeToo disclosure on Facebook by Samiha Tutli against Ali Riaz, a distinguished professor at Illinois State University in the United States, which turned out to be a false accusation (TDC Report, 2018). Anecdotal evidence suggests that this incident caused a negative impact on the #MeToo movement, and the validity of the #MeToo accusations were brought under question.

After some initial engagement with the #MeToo posts on social media, the initial focus on #MeToo subsided and its survivors lost their earlier visibility (Interviews with Haque, 2021; Huq, 2021; Shopsburry Talks, 2020). Besides, although #MeToo's first cases of allegation between celebrities gained attention, the eventual lack of legal actions and a complicit silence rendered #MeToo ineffective in Bangladesh (Shopsburry Talks, 2020). All those accused of sexual violence (with one or two exceptions) still have their jobs, as there was no investigation of accusation of sexual violence against them (Shopsburry Talks, 2020).[3] In this connection, renowned feminist activist Khushi Kabeer comments:

> While there were collective attempts to hide the #MeToo allegations and survivors were pressed hard to withdraw their complaints, this same system stood for the perpetrators and tried to protect them. We talked to the HR of one of the TV channels against whom a #MeToo case was raised and requested them to make a formal enquiry, to which they agreed first, but actually they did nothing. Patriarchy is everywhere, it is not necessarily male, but our mindset. (Shopsburry Talks, 2020, n.p.)

Khushi Kabeer's statement here coincides with MacKinnon's (1979) argument that men use sexual harassment as a strategy to achieve and sustain the structure where women are subordinate, and men are dominant. As a result, it is unlikely that the victims/survivors of sexual violence will get any justice; sexual harassment then becomes a tool to sustain the system. But still, we cannot conclude that #MeToo has been a complete failure in Bangladesh. Rather, on the basis of our interviews, this chapter contends that the reception of #MeToo in Bangladesh is not a replication of the Western movement. Although ignited by the same hashtag tweet, it has been transformed into a language of protest – speaking up against sexual violence, instead of suffering in silence.

Most of the initial survivors belonged to media, who later inspired students, nongovernmental organization (NGO) workers, garment factory workers, and other women to speak against sexual violence. For our narratives, we also interviewed three women from this latter category of survivors. There is no comprehensive study that encapsulates the lives of #MeToo survivors, their reasons behind disclosing their #MeToo incidents, and the ways family and wider society responded to the survivors' stories. Therefore, this chapter attempts to highlight survivors' perspectives on #MeToo and what happened in their lives after they shared their stories. Through a snowball sampling approach, we tried to connect with as many survivors as possible. However, due to the Covid-19 outbreak and the sensitivity of the issue, we were only able to interview six survivors and a journalist who was closely involved with the survivors. Among the six survivors, four (Maksuda Akhter Priyoti, Mushfika Laiju, Zakia Sultana, and Asmaul Husna) are from the initial nine #MeToo survivors. The other two survivors (Navia Novelly and *Laboni Huq*)[4] shared their experiences of being inspired by the initial nine. Our seventh interview was with journalist Shajeda Haque, who was heavily involved in providing different kinds of support to the #MeToo survivors.

Along with the challenges posed by Covid-19, some survivors' unavailability to take part in the interview further revealed some structural tensions which cannot be overlooked. After #MeToo disclosure, some of the survivors had to leave the country because of threats; some removed all traces of the information they had shared online and never responded to our request for interviews. A couple of them declined to be interviewed due to the suffering they had gone through after disclosing their experience of sexual harassment. Due to frustration and an arduous journey that they had to make alone, they did not wish to talk to us, as this might cause them to relive the whole experience. One of the initial nine #MeToo survivors refused to be interviewed and mentioned to us that interviews by some other people in the past did not bring any good to her, except emotional breakdown. Our interviewees shared this sentiment with us, too, when they expressed how talking about their experiences did not do any good for them.

Another survivor, who works in a well-known TV channel, wanted to talk about her experience with sexual violence that she had shared under #MeToo. Later, she told us that she had to seek permission from the authorities at work to take part in a conversation with us. The administration at her workplace did not permit her to talk to us. They told her, "It is not necessary now, people have almost forgotten, revitalizing it might affect your career and the place where you work." She confirmed with us that we will not disclose her name or professional identity. She had to convey that information to her work administration, too. These interviews reveal the structural barriers and sociocultural hindrances that enable gender and sexual violence in Bangladesh. #MeToo survivors, who initially shared their experiences online when the movement was strong globally, were later silenced and coerced into removing those posts.

## #MeToo and the Changing Landscape of the Women's Movement in Bangladesh

Throughout the first three decades since its independence in 1971, the women's movement was exceedingly associated with the unstable political circumstances of Bangladesh (Begum, 2002; Banu, 2015). In the 1970s, the main challenge for women's movement and organizations was to rehabilitate the war heroines, who were later called freedom fighters (Basher, 2015). Under the period of military dictatorship (1983–1990), the 1980s saw the degradation of women's personal and political rights (Begum, 2002). However, the Dowry Prohibition Act of 1980, the ratification of the Convention on Elimination of all forms of Discrimination Against Women (CEDAW) with four reservations, the demand for a Uniform Family Code (UFC), the emergence of women as leaders of two leading political parties, and activism protesting violence against women mark the decade (Begum, 2002). The democratic government and female leadership in the 1990s showed the promise of a better future for women. But unfortunately, religious fundamentalism became worse in Bangladesh, which affected both legislation and culture. Women's increasing rate of involvement in international feminist platforms such as Beijing conferences, the withdrawal of two reservations from CEDAW, and the establishment of Women's Studies as an academic discipline (Begum, 2002) made this decade a significant one.

Women's movement took a turn in the first two decades of the twenty-first century. As a result of affiliation with different national and international donor agencies, the "NGO-ization" of the women's movement began (Begum, 2002; Nazneen and Sultan, 2009). Technological advancement and the availability of social media also allowed individuals to raise voices against injustices. It turned out that social media protests were successful in affecting both the people and the law enforcement agencies–sometimes more than offline platforms. For instance, some students and female visitors were sexually assaulted at the Dhaka University campus on April 14, 2015, at the occasion of the first day of the Bangla year. A public protest, *Houk Protibad* (Let us Protest), was organized at the Dhaka University campus on April 18, 2015. The protesters included students, artists, academics, feminist activists, and various cultural and civil society organizations.

Along with the protests on the ground, protestors organized protests online on social media platforms like Facebook. Some of these protests turned into protests against terrorism and other injustices. The rise of #MeToo strengthened these ongoing protests against the alarming increase in sexual violence and murders after rape.

## Drawing Inspiration from #MeToo: From Individual to a Collective Movement

Some key studies (Hassan et al., 2019; Islam, 2018; Moitra et al., 2020) on #MeToo in Bangladesh have concluded that the #MeToo movement did not have much impact in Bangladesh. But in our conversations with the survivors, all of them mentioned being inspired by the global #MeToo movement. The wave of awakening in the Global North certainly reached South Asia; this global platform provided a huge opportunity to all, and the survivors of Bangladesh entered the "evocation stage of inspiration" (Thrash and Elliot, 2003) by remembering the similar offenses that happened to them. The Twitter hashtag assured them that they had supporters out there, and they were not alone in experiencing this violence and harassment. Thus, this online impact extended to the real world. Nevertheless, many Bangladeshis consider #MeToo as a Western discourse that is not culturally appropriate in Bangladesh (Hassan et al., 2019; Moitra et al., 2020). For many, the inspirational moment was when Bollywood actress Tanushree Dutt brought #MeToo allegations against a senior famous actor, Nana Patekar. Even though Dutt is a celebrity, Zakia Sultana, one survivor and our interviewee, shared in her interview:

> I was in awe of Tanushree Dutt's revelation, but not courageous enough to do so myself then. Then I was moved by Prioty and Sucheesmita's posts, but they do not live inside the country. Then Asmaul Husna wrote. I also wanted to write at the same time, and I did!

Survivors had in mind that their revelations will obviously inspire others to come forward with their incidents and at a large scale that will make people more aware, more empathetic. But others, like Zakia, also looked for inspiration in other people's posts. Revealing the identity of the perpetrators, who are usually well-respected individuals, was a cause of stress but also of assurance. Maksuda Akter Prioty in her interview with us shared:

> Who will speak against them if I hesitate? Consider my position and fame [ . . . ] my strength and dignity. [ . . . ] At least one person's courageous step

> would encourage others to break the silence. Perpetrators will be afraid of being publicized; they take the advantage when we do not speak.

Prioty was successful, as other survivors were inspired by her revelation. Survivor Asmaul Husna echoed:

> I think this is the right time to talk about it. [ . . . ] I revealed it because I do not want my next generation to suffer like me. It is an individual movement with a conscious effort to create a safe future for the next generation. My nieces are dearest ones to me and due to the unavailability of my sister, I have been raising them. During the hype, I just felt an emotion of doing something for them, for me, for others out there.

During our conversations, other survivors also shared that though patriarchal and conservative attitudes of society and close family members had restricted survivors for some time, they were motivated by acquaintances and survivors with more vulnerable and precarious conditions to eventually share their stories. Furthermore, as most of the perpetrators worked in print or electronic media or creative sectors, survivors knew their accusations would not get any attention in conventional mediums of reporting.

Besides, although the relationship between real-life social change and "hashtag feminism" is quite complicated, as Keller (2018) argues, social media platforms such as Twitter were considered the safest and easiest places to raise a voice for women or talk about their issues and rights, rather than offline platforms, even with friends or family members. Moreover, lack of survivor-friendly legal options was also part of the reasons that motivated the survivors to come forward. Survivors also pointed out that the definition of sexual harassment in the legal framework of Bangladesh is not victim friendly. Iftakhar (2020) too notes that the Prevention of Women and Children Repression Act (2000) vaguely addresses the diverse nature and extent of sexual assault or sexual harassment, and the onus of collecting proof of harassment or assault is completely on the survivor. One survivor, Navia Novelly, who revealed her sexual harassment experience on Facebook, told us:

> When I wanted to file a police complaint, I realized it would be a long, extremely hard, time and money consuming process which will not only hamper my education, my normal life, but also my mental health. [ . . . ] realized that my case could be thrown out with the excuse of circumstantial evidence even though it was extremely clear to any sane human being that my abuser was wrong. Laws of my country as well as the system were not fair enough, so I chose to lean on the most accessible platform.

Some of the survivors mentioned cathartic treatment (Deal et al., 2020) to work as an inspiration behind the disclosure. The years, even decades of silence affected the survivors' ability to fully grow as emotionally healthy human beings in many different ways. Besides, viewing the perpetrators living normal lives and moving forward in their lives was also agonizing for the survivors when survivors' lives were deeply affected. It was tormenting for some to see the perpetrators of violence against them being celebrated by the nation, being invited to several national ceremonies, and being applauded for their creative work and performances. With #MeToo, survivors had a platform to express their pain and be believed by others. A sense of relief, even for a short span of time, was experienced by the survivors when they shared their experiences. This sense of relief and power worked as a source of inspiration for many others too. Novelly shared:

> A senior acquaintance of mine had posted about her experience of sexual harassment and I could relate with her. When I talked to her, she told me how liberated and better she felt after speaking about her traumatic experience with the world. When I was struggling with my trauma, slipping into depression for the lack of justice, her courage truly inspired me, made me feel like I can do the same and shame the person who committed violence against me.

Such feeling resonated among other survivors as well. Although the disclosure did not come with many expectations, the least they had in mind was to name the perpetrator, take away some of their social respect, and to make other people aware so that the perpetrator or any other man thinks twice before making an abusive move again. Laboni told us:

> I do not know whether I will win the lawsuit, what matters the most is the power, his money can change everything. But I am glad that I unmasked him, I posted on Facebook, shared audio-visual recording, and everyone knows the criminal. Even if I lose the legal battle, at least people know the truth.

In different professions, survivors received support and appreciation from various people. They were especially moved by empathy and solidarity, extended to them by younger generations. Zakia, a teacher, told us:

> I did not want to go to my workplace the next day after I shared my story. But the students insisted that I come because it was their last day. When I reached, I realized it had reached to them. Their tone, body language, gaze was saying something different. Just the question "Are you okay? Are you alright?" in a compassionate manner – that made all the difference.

This sense of solidarity was prolonged. Many other groups also extended solidarity and support to the survivors. The survivors mentioned the feminist talk shows and conversation in print and electronic media. Based on anecdotal evidence, they further suggest that there is a rise in online movements against sexual abuse, on Facebook and other online platforms, to continue conversations and to hold the state accountable to come up with preventive measures. "Ga Gheshe Daraben Na" (Do not stand too close to my body)[5] (Islam, 2019; Khyum, 2019), "Me too Bangla," and "@MeTooBangladesh" are among the online signs that emerged after the rise of the #MeToo movement. The spirit of #MeToo also united textile workers to protest sexual harassment in the workplace in a covert way, even though structurally it is impossible for them to report it. "If garment workers didn't face retaliation for exposing sexual harassment, many of them would be screaming #MeToo at the top of their lungs" (cited in Chowdhury, 2019, n.p.). Another "unconventional" incident of protest happened after almost a year and a half of #MeToo in the United States. Nusrat Jahan Rafi, a student at a madrassa (an institution for religious education), filed a complaint against sexual assault by the madrassa principal (Dhaka Tribune, 2019). Later, she was brutally set on fire and killed for protesting. Nusrat's funeral saw the biggest turnout of people in the Feni district, from across the country – united, to demand justice (Dhaka Tribune, 2019). Protests against sexual violence after reports of abuse and violence were not common in Bangladesh before, which suggests that these protests were a result of the influence of the #MeToo movement. But the violence against Nusrat for sharing her experience was not a singular event after #MeToo. It is hard to say that #MeToo was a non-aggressive movement in Bangladesh.

## Chaos, Shame and Insecurity: The Aftermath of #MeToo

While the world saw the stories that the survivors shared; they did not see what consequences the stories had for those who shared them. Conversations with the survivors indicates that they faced unexpressed repercussions that affected the survivors, their family members, relatives, and all of their personal, social, and professional lives. These effects range from life threats to emotional taxation to being ostracized by friends or colleagues to being treated as a menace to any professional team or organization. #MeToo survivors were commonly accused of seeking attention, possessing questionable moral character, maligning others out of vindictiveness, and so on. Some of the survivors refuse to talk about their #MeToo stories any longer, as continuous threats have made them reticent about discussing their experiences.

The majority of the survivors faced life threats, either from the perpetrators directly or from friends or colleagues of the perpetrators. Prioty shared:

> I was under pressure. I got some calls just after posting and they threatened me and told me to remove the post. [ . . . ] I got worried about my children. Although I am in another country, one phone call from his end is enough for contract killing.

Another survivor, Laboni Huq, who filed for a legal battle, was stalked by suspicious people and received threatening phone calls. She told us:

> I was under threat and there were suspicious cars and people around my house, following me. I received security service from police force for two nights at my place. After that, there was no service though the threat remained.

The threats and scathing attacks also affected their psychological health. A few of the survivors even had to leave Bangladesh after such hostile reactions. A few cases also showed that these attacks from families and relatives devastated them in many ways. For instance, Prioty recalls:

> They think I brought shame to my family by revealing this, as my parents are no more, they believed I had misused my freedom, just threw away my parents' honor in the society.

Likewise, Novelly shares her upsetting experience:

> In my family, the aftermath was disastrous as well. My extended family members (aunt, cousins) decided to pay my parents a visit to express their views on "how shameful it was to write such obscene (!) things online." My sister tried to reason with them, saying if I did not speak up, more innocent girls would have become victims of sexual abuse and I did a noble thing. But her words of rationality and support were muffled by angry, bitter words of disapproval.

However, one thing that became clear from the interviews is that husbands, friends, and family members who were comparatively young were more supportive of the survivors. In addition, after one showed the courage to keep talking about the harassment that took place, they gradually gained some support. Survivor Zakia mentioned:

> When I decided to disclose the incident, my husband did not agree with me. [ . . . ] But he gradually understood the issue and then he commented on one

> of my Facebook posts and primarily revealed the incident, and then I posted details with all proofs.

Apart from the personal level, survivors also mentioned struggle in their professional lives. After revealing incidents, some survivors lost their jobs, some lost other professional opportunities. Some did not get any promotions or were not able to move to other jobs even if their previous work record established them as suitable and competitive for these positions. Prioty shared:

> I was in good connection with all print and electronic news media of Bangladesh. After the post, they stopped communicating with me. They did not offer a slight hint, let alone publishing news on it. I did not get any support or help from any media of Bangladesh. My contracts, dealings went downward which was following an upward trend previously before the post.

Furthermore, Laiju adds:

> After the disclosure, I feel organizations see us as feminists, protestors who would protest whenever there is such a thing. So, they are afraid of hiring us and think we will create a chaos even for slightest things. It is risky for their reputation.

These threats and abuse were not even hidden. Organized groups were trying to defame the survivors in various ways, such as questioning their character, asking/teasing them for nudes, vilifying their work and behavior, etc. They saw the worst form of hatred just after disclosing the harassment. Mushfika Laiju's Facebook account got reported and then closed for posting #MeToo against renowned dramatist and professor Salim Al Din; actors and theater performers jointly reported her account. Famous media personalities came together to save him and started campaigns and posted publicly against the survivor. As most of the #MeToo perpetrators were from the media sector, it was easy for them to manipulate the coverage in different platforms and to deny or distort the incidents in various ways on media. The initial support and solidarity extended to the survivor after their #MeToo posts did not last long, especially when it came to taking actual action. Journalist Shajeda Haque revealed:

> If we could get the majority of Press Institute of Bangladesh (PIB) at least by our side, this movement would last longer and have had more impact. Initially there were human chains, round table discussions and talk shows, but eventually the numbers reduced. We sent letters to every organization to join us. We demanded boycott of the perpetrators; to put them under mental stress as

> a punishment. But there was no result. Feminists and women's organizations were also divided on this issue.

Whenever survivors tried to pursue their #MeToo post further, they faced resistance and restrictions from workplace, family, friends, and relatives. Most survivors shared the belief that eventually they were all alone in the battle against sexual harassment. Survivor Laboni realized that posting a statement on social media and fighting a legal battle are two completely different things when it comes to getting actual support. In her words:

> You will have to fight alone. No one will be by your side when you are going to fight. [ . . . ] I come to the court alone, handle everything and hear the verdicts alone. Witnesses were there at the beginning, but now they have lost interest; even though they also suffered same harassments caused by the same perpetrators.

The survivors further reflect that the media platforms did not even ask these women to talk about their experiences. On the contrary, they were pushed in the background and were replaced with more malleable feminists. Different media platforms were either completely silent or took a very strategic neutral position. Laiju told us:

> No news channel called us, no one. They called others who were not directly involved. News did not show the video footage of the rally or human chains, they just created still image from the video and maintained a minimum coverage. During different seminars and workshops, distinguished guests talked about #MeToo incidentally. But when later as an attendee, I revealed my identity as survivor, they quickly changed the topic or avoided the conversation.

Such a "cynically neutral" position by the media did not dampen the survivors' efforts, but reinforced the culture of injustice and silence in cases of violence against women.

## Conclusion

Almost five years after the #MeToo allegation against Harvey Weinstein, in this chapter we have looked back at the impact of #MeToo in Bangladesh. Based on seven conversations with #Me Too survivors and a journalist, this chapter has revealed some unique positions of #MeToo survivors in Bangladesh.

#MeToo in Bangladesh inspired the survivors and victims of sexual violence to speak up, but the culture remained the same. Because of the class and professional interests of the perpetrators, people unhesitatingly supported the perpetrators and rejected the survivors. #MeToo revelations of the survivors were considered socio-culturally inappropriate. So instead of the perpetrators facing legal accusations, the survivors faced social humiliation, defamation cases, and some even lost their jobs. The applause and the human chains of the initial responses to those who shared their experiences under #MeToo were soon replaced by a culture of silence, shame, and misogyny. Soon after, the survivors found themselves in a battle ground – fighting against both misogyny and incredulity both on social and legal levels, mostly alone. Our conversations further reveal that although civil society (some journalists, academicians, and a few NGOs) and some women's organizations, as well as a few human rights and feminist activists, extended their support to victims/survivors, their support was mostly limited to taking part in discussions and talk shows. Such discussions exhibited an unexpected exclusion of the survivors, who were hardly invited to take part in the discussions happening around their experiences. Finally, drawing on our conversations with survivors and a journalist, this chapter suggests that the #MeToo movement remains internal, with no specific and/or united demand (except for social ostracization of the perpetrators claimed by a few) and hence, an organized effort hitherto has not been seen.

Even then, it cannot be argued that the spark of resistance that emerged with #MeToo did not last long. After #MeToo, many young girls came to know that victim blaming for sexual harassment should not be "normal"; rather, protest and solidarity against sexual abuse and violence should be the norm. Despite not including the #MeToo survivors in conversations, some feminists on TV and talk shows have highlighted that the survivors have created exemplary cases against sexual harassment, and now people know that sexual harassment and violence against women should not be taken lightly and the preparators can be brought under legal charges. Though survivors felt a sense of relief after sharing these stories under #MeToo, it was challenging for them to deal with the waves of judgments, abuse, and threats that were unleashed on them afterward.

It is too early to decide whether #MeToo was a success or a failure in Bangladesh. Our conversations and secondary research suggest that although not many of the offenders were punished or socially ostracized, the first success of #MeToo is that conversations about gender and sexual violence took place, and that people know the crimes of the perpetrators of this violence even when law does not punish them. Although initially #MeToo in Bangladesh could not encourage many women to protest publicly, it has been successful in leaving a strong message against gender and sexual violence. Keeping #MeToo alive requires a more organized effort. This effort will build enough pressure on the legal authorities to also punish the perpetrators for the violence they commit against others.

## Notes

1. This timeline of women's movement is based on the work of Banu (2015), Huq and Azad (2013), Nazneen and Sultan (2010), and Begum (2002).
2. Available at https://www.youtube.com/watch?v=bBzdhuEUQN0, last accessed on July 25, 2021.
3. Among the nine initial survivors, we interviewed three. None of their offenders has been punished yet. Informal talks with some feminist activists and journalists who were involved in the #MeToo movement suggest that they have not heard of any of the accused who got punished – suggesting that most of the investigations never reached a final verdict. Moreover, it was impossible to present the kind of proofs that the court required in some cases.
4. Some survivors chose to speak to us with their original names, whereas other preferred pseudonyms.
5. This is an online-based movement against sexual harassment in public transport.

## References

"94% Women Victims of Sexual Harassment in Public Transport." 2018. *BRAC.* https://www.brac.net/latest-news/item/1142-94-women-victims-of-sexual-harassment-in-public-transport. Accessed August 29, 2020.

Ahmed, Syed, et al. 2014. "Protibadi: A Platform for Fighting Sexual Harassment in Urban Bangladesh." *CHI for Social Development*, no. April 26–May 1, 2014: 2695–2704.

"Bangladesh Redefines Freedom Fighters, Recognizes Biranganas as FFs." 2014. *bdnews24.com*, October 13. https://bdnews24.com/bangladesh/2014/10/13/bangladesh-redefines-freedom-fighters-recognises-biranganas-as-ffs. Accessed July 22, 2021.

"Bangladeshi-Irish Model Prioty Alleges Sexual Harassment by Businessman-Politician Rafiqul." 2018. *bdnews24.com*, November 1. https://bdnews24.com/entertainment/2018/11/01/bangladeshi-irish-model-prioty-alleges-sexual-harassment-by-businessman-politician-rafiqul. Accessed July 29, 2020.

Banu, Ayesha. 2015. "Global-Local Interaction: First Three Decades of the Women's Movement in Bangladesh." *Journal of the Asiatic Society of Bangladesh* 60, no. 2: 203–230.

Basher, Syed Samiul. 2015. "41 Birangonas Get Freedom Fighter Status." *Dhaka Tribune*, October 13. https://web.archive.org/web/20170422132434/http://archive.dhakatribune.com/banglabang/2015/oct/13/41-birangonas-get-freedom-fighter-status. Accessed July 23, 2021.

*Statistical Year Book Bangladesh*. 2020. 40th edition. Dhaka: Bangladesh Bureau of Statistics.

Begum, Maleka. 2002. *Nari Andoloner Paacnh Dashak* (Five Decades of Women's Movement). Dhaka: Annyaprakash.

Chowdhry, Jennifer. 2019. "#MeToo Bangladesh: The Textile Workers Uniting against Harassment." *The Guardian*, September 10. https://www.theguardian.com/global-development/2019/sep/10/metoo-bangladesh-the-textile-workers-uniting-against-harassment. Accessed June 7, 2021.

Deal, Bonnie-Elene, et al. 2020. "I Definitely Did Not Report It When I Was Raped . . . #WeBelieveChristine#MeToo: A Content Analysis of Disclosures of Sexual Assault on Twitter." *Social Media + Society*. https://journals.sagepub.com/doi/full/10.1177/2056305120974610. Accessed July 26, 2021.

Dey, Sameer. 2018. "Bangladesh e Berei Choleche jouno nipironer ovijog" ("The Sexual Harassment Complaints Are Rising in Bangladesh"). https://www.dw.com/bn/ Bangladesh e Berei Choleche jouno nipironer ovijog/a-46370176. Accessed July 26, 2021.

Gibson, Emily. 2020. "Violence against Women in Bangladesh Reaches Breaking Point." The Organization for World Peace, December 10. https://theowp.org/violence-against-women-in-bangladesh-reaches-breaking-point/. Accessed July 24, 2021.

Haque, Shajeda. 2021. "#MeToo Interview with Journalist Shejeda Haque by the Authors." Unpublished.

Hassan, Naeemul, et al. 2019. "Nonparticipation of Bangladeshi Women in #MeToo Movement." *ICTD 2019, Ahmedabad, India*. http://bbs.portal.gov.bd/sites/default/files/files/bbs.portal.gov.bd/page/b2db8758_8497_412c_a9ec_6bb299f8b3ab/S_Y_B2017.pdf. Accessed March 8, 2021.

Human Development Report. 2020. UNDP. http://hdr.undp.org/sites/all/themes/hdr_theme/country-notes/BGD.pdf. Accessed June 2, 2021.

Huq, A. Moshreka, and Ashraful Azad. 2013. "Four Decades of Women in Bangladesh: Changes and Challenges in Empowerment and Development." *Gender Studies* 1, no. 3: 23–34.

Huq, Laboni. 2021. "#MeToo Interview with Laboni Huq by the Authors." Unpublished.

Iftakhar, Shampa. 2020. "#Me Too in Bangladesh: Can You Change." *Journal of International Women's Studies* 21, no. 2: 126–142.

Islam, Maisha. 2019. "Ga Gheshe Daraben Na: The Power of a Young Entrepreneur." *The Daily Star*, April 15. https://www.thedailystar.net/star-youth/news/ga-gheshe-daraben-na-the-power-young-entrepreneur-1729897. Accessed July 23, 2021.

Islam, Zyma. 2018. "Why #MeToo Is Not Happening in Bangladesh." *The Daily Star*. October 19. https://www.thedailystar.net/star-weekend/opinion/news/why-metoo-not-happening-bangladesh-1648678. Accessed July 16, 2021.

Kabeer, Naila. 2004. "Snakes, Ladders and Traps: Changing Lives and Livelihoods in Rural Bangladesh (1994–2001)." *CPRC* Working Paper 50, *IDS*.

Keller, J., et al. 2018. "#MeToo and the Promise and Pitfalls of Challenging Rape Culture through Digital Feminist Activism." *European Journal of Women's Studies* 25, no. 2: 236–246. ///D:/Dhaka%20University/Article/MeToo_and_the_promise_and_pitfalls_of_challenging_.pdf and https://journals.sagepub.com/doi/abs/10.1177/1350506818765318?journalCode=ejw. Accessed September 3, 2020.

Khan, Tabassum, et al. 2017. "Violence against Women in Bangladesh." *Delta Medical College Journal* 5, no. 1: 25–29.

Khyum, Kohinur. 2019. "How a T-shirt Turned into a Campaign." *Dhaka Tribune*, April 11. https://www.dhakatribune.com/bangladesh/nation/2019/04/11/how-a-t-shirt-turned-into-a-campaign. Accessed July 23, 2021.

"Leaving the LDCs Category: Booming Bangladesh Prepares to Graduate." 2018. *United Nations: Department of Economic and Social Affairs*, March 13. https://www.un.org/development/desa/en/news/policy/leaving-the-ldcs-category-booming-bangladesh-prepares-to-graduate.html.

Lorde, Audre. 1984. "Age, Race, Class and Sex: Women Redefining Difference." In Lorde, *Sister Outsider. Essays and Speeches*, pp. 114–123. California: Crossing Press.

MacKinnon, Catherine. 1979. *The Sexual Harassment of Working Women: A Case of Sex Discrimination*. London and New Haven, CT: Yale University Press.

"#MeToo: A Timeline of Events." 2020. *Chicago Tribune*, August 10. https://www.chicagotribune.com/lifestyles/ct-me-too-timeline-20171208-htmlstory.html. Accessed August 30, 2020.

"#MeToo Brought Down 201 Powerful Men: Nearly Half of Their Replacements Are Women." 2018. *New York Times*, October 23. https://www.nytimes.com/interactive/2018/10/23/us/metoo-replacements.html. Accessed August 29, 2020.

Moitra, Aparna, et al. 2020. "Understanding the Challenges for Bangladeshi Women to Participate in #MeToo Movement." *Proceedings of the ACM on Human-Computer Interaction* 4. GROUP: 1–25. Accessed August 29, 2020.

"More than 12M 'MeToo' Facebook Posts, Comments, Reactions in 24 Hours." 2017. *CBS News*, October 17. https://www.cbsnews.com/news/metoo-more-than-12-million-facebook-posts-comments-reactions-24-hours/. Accessed August 30, 2020.

"Nationwide Protests Spark Demanding Justice for Nusrat." 2019. *Dhaka Tribune*, April 11. https://www.dhakatribune.com/bangladesh/nation/2019/04/12/nationwide-protests-spark-demanding-justice-for-nusrat. Accessed July 26, 2021.

Nazneen, Sohela, and Maheen Sultan. 2009. "Struggling for Survival and Autonomy: Impact of NGO-ization on Women's Organizations in Bangladesh." *Society for International Development* 52, no. 2: 193–199.

Nazneen, Sohela, and Maheen Sultan. 2010. "Reciprocity, Distancing, and Opportunistic Overtures: Women's Organisations Negotiating Legitimacy and Space in Bangladesh." *IDS Bulletin* 41, no. 2: 70–78.

Rai, Dipu. 2019. "Sexual Violence Pandemic in India: Rape Cases Doubled in Last 17 Years." *India Today*. https://www.indiatoday.in/diu/story/sexual-violence-pandemic-india-rape-cases-doubled-seventeen-years-1628143-2019-12-13. Accessed August 28, 2020.

"SDGs and Country Process in Bangladesh: EquityBD Campaign Paper." 2017. *EquityBD Campaign Brief*, March, pp. 1–2. http://www.equitybd.net/wp-content/uploads/2017/03/SDG-and-Country-Process-in-Bangladesh_EquityBD-Campaign-Paper.pdf.

Sen, B. 2015. "Growth, Poverty and Human Development." In *Bangladesh: Promise and Performance*, edited by R. Jahan, pp. 293–307. Dhaka, Bangladesh: The University Press Limited.

Shopsburry Talks. 2020. "Me Too Movement in Bangladesh." 2020. *Shopsburry Talks*. Live on July 23, 2020. https://www.youtube.com/watch?v=6WMtlmD5BzY. Accessed September 3, 2020.

TDC Report. 2018. *The Daily Campus*. https://thedailycampus.com/crime-and-discipline/16542/. Accessed July 20, 2021.

Thrash, Todd, and Andrew Elliot. 2003. "Inspiration as a Psychological Construct." *Journal of Personality and Social Psychology* 84, no. 4: 871–889.

Wahed, Tania, and Abbas Bhuiya. 2007. "Battered Bodies & Shattered Minds: Violence against Women in Bangladesh." *Indian Journal of Medical Research* 126: 341–354.

# 10

# "Smashing Spatial Patriarchy?"

## #MeToo, #CreateAScene, and Feminist Resistance in Sri Lanka

*Thilini Prasadika*

## Timeline

- 1960: Sri Lanka became the first nation in the world to elect a female head of government, Sirimavo Bandaranaike.
- 1970s onward: Loan and microfinance options were set up for women.
- 1975–1985: Multiple policies and acts were introduced for women's rights.
- 1981: The Convention on the Elimination of All Forms of Discrimination against Women was held.
- 1981: The Constitution on Fundamental Rights was also adopted into the Constitution.
- 1996: The National Plan of Action for Women and Women's Charter was introduced.

## Introduction

> *The doors to alternative feminist utopias don't open up when the light bulb of resistance comes aglow above one's head. . . . [N]ow that we have done a lot to mark the ubiquitous presence of moments of resistance, what do we make of these gestures? Do they lead us to a liberatory feminist politics, or merely to a celebration of small lost moments of nay-saying?*
>
> (Basu, 2000, p. 186)

Since August 2017, the #MeToo movement has been adapted, appropriated, transformed, and reinvented in many ways to suit particular geo-cultural contexts of many countries, spanning all the way from the Global North to South[1]. However, such movements seem to be monopolized by tight-knit, metropolitan feminist groups, who gear the feminist rhetoric to "raise awareness"

Thilini Prasadika, *"Smashing Spatial Patriarchy?"* In: *The Other #MeToos.* Edited by: Iqra Shagufta Cheema, Oxford University Press. © Oxford University Press 2023. DOI: 10.1093/oso/9780197619872.003.0010 of day-to-day sexual harassment and play the role of custodians/gatekeepers of such campaigns. In this chapter, I argue that the Sri Lankan response to the global #MeToo movement is marked by politics of social class and (digital) literacy and that interventions (in the form of a local response to a global movement) predominantly cut across a certain urban politic of knowledge, informed consent, acknowledgment, and agency.

The objective of this chapter is to foreground how, despite its timely intervention, such initiatives have particular nuances (albeit unspoken) of sociocultural and economic privilege (especially in terms of conceptualization, sustenance, and mediation of such initiatives), which the initiators, such as the Oxford Committee for Famine Relief, Sri Lanka, its partners (hereafter referred to as OXFAM Sri Lanka) and the United Nations Population Fund, Sri Lanka (hereafter referred to as UNFPA Sri Lanka), seem to have conveniently ignored. The purpose of this study is to trace the contours of how middle-class feminism has co-opted and appropriated the radical imperative of the feminist project—mainly, the ways in which the revolutionary potential of feminism has been channeled into what Marcuse (1964) calls "repressive desublimation" or appropriation of radicality by institutionalization. This does not intend to romanticize a preferred version of feminism over the other, since, as recorded history informs, the Sri Lankan (mainstream) feminist movement has been largely written and maneuvered by a handful of privileged circles of women in the past. This, however, attempts to bring to the fore a certain feminist politic based on marginal and everyday forms of resistance which produce a counter-narrative to mainstream, hegemonic forms of feminism that have taken hold in society, hand in hand with the neoliberal corporate projects. This study, therefore, opens up new avenues for scholarship based on personal responses from the margins and women's everyday forms of resistance which do not fall under the radar of such mainstream versions of feminism.

## Beginnings: Sri Lanka in Context

In 2018 and 2019, Sri Lanka responded to the global #MeToo movement through initiatives such as #CreateAScene and "16 Days, 16 Stories," launched by OXFAM and UNFPA Sri Lanka, respectively, to address the glaring concern of women being harassed in public transport systems such as buses and trains. This initiative calls for not only victims but also witnesses to break silence and reach out to women who are being harassed. Public initiatives launched in Sri Lanka range from large-scale nongovernmental organization (NGO)–assisted projects to small-scale projects featured on social media. Personal responses, particularly of the urban-educated middle class, were in the form of Twitter/Facebook status, and videos of harassments on public transport.

In a study conducted by UNFPA Sri Lanka in 2017, it was discovered that 90% of the women who use public transport have been in some way subjected to harassment. It further revealed that 74% of such forms of harassment are physical in nature and that only as little as 8% of victims reported it to law enforcement. The study also reveals that 92% of the bystanders do not come to assist/get involved in such situations. This has then been the basis for an initiative by the OXFAM Sri Lanka, under its global project "enough," where hashtags #NotInMyBus and #CreateAScene (#සද්දයක්දාන්න, #குரலெழுப்புவோம் in Sinhala and Tamil vernacular) were used as a form of affiliation toward the global #MeToo movement.

The #MeToo movement first caught fire when two Sri Lankan cricketers were accused of sexual misconduct in India in 2018. Arjuna Ranatunga and Lasith Malinga were thus the center of the formative stages of the movement. Mainstream media were quick to follow up on this, and many opinion pieces were produced in response to how Sri Lanka has been responding to the wave. NDTV Sports reported the incident, stating that,

> [t]he MeToo movement has taken the social media platforms by storm, with women coming out and disclosing the incidents of sexual harassment they have faced. Now a woman alleges that a Sri Lankan cricketer once harassed her during one of the Indian Premier League (IPL) tournaments. Singer Chinmayi Sripaada uploaded an image of a note written by the woman, which described her ordeal during the incident. Chinmayi further updated that the "said girl will speak on anonymity to a journalist." (Tirkey, 2018, n.p.)

Interestingly, in 2017, Groundviews, a web-based news platform, conducted a keyword search in which they have discovered that this movement is *not only* about sexual harassment. From a sample of 40,000 tweets obtained from October 15 to 18, 2017, the writer states:

> In our sample, the word "assault" appeared 5,681 times. Groundviews also searched for other assault-related keywords such as rape (1,344 occurrences), slap (19), grab (204), punch (27) and attack (101). In comparison, harassment appeared 1,240 times. Words like whistle appeared 11 times, while words such as catcall (28) leer (20) and remark (9) also appeared in the sample. This debunks the idea, put forward in many opinion pieces including [the] piece from the *Telegraph*, that the hashtag was solely related to sexual harassment broadly and street harassment in particular. However, even this doesn't truly give a sense of what the interactions around the hashtag were. Of the 5,681 tweets tagged

> using the word "assault" approximately 250 were of people sharing their personal experiences of assault, including rape, marital rape, childhood molestation, sexual assault and intimate partner violence. (Wickrematunge, October 26, 2017, n.p.)

The movement slowly began to gain momentum on the internet when women started to proclaim that their "inboxes are open" if anyone wants an outlet to talk about their experiences. This was particularly taking place on Twitter, where users affirm (in English, Sinhala, and Tamil) that:

> I believe you. I'm here for you. Are you a woman who has faced or is facing sexual harassment and/or violence? You're not alone. *My inbox is open and safe. I can listen and if you like, help document your story on a public list* (you can be anonymous). #MeToo #MeTooSriLanka #lka. (@Amethystinia, 2019, emphasis added)
>
> මං ඔයාව විශ්වාස කරනව. ඔයා තනි වී නෑ. ඔයා ලිංගික අතවරයකට පත් වෙලා තියෙනවනම් හෝ පත් වෙමින් ඉන්නව නම් මට *inbox* කරන්න. මම ඔයාගේ කතාව අහන්නම්. ඊට පස්සෙ අපයෝජකයාගේ විස්තර පොදු දත්තගබඩාවකට දාන්න ඔයා කැමති නම් ඒක ආරක්ෂිතව සහ නිර්නාමිකව කරන්න උදව් කරන්නම්. #MeToo #MeTooSriLanka #lka. (@Amethystinia, 2019, emphasis added)
>
> நீங்கள் ஒரு பெண்ணாக பாலியல் துஷ்பிரயோகத்துக்கு முகம் கொடுத்தவரா?நீங்கள் தனியாக இல்லை.உட்பெட்டி மூலம் உங்களது கதைகளை என்னுடன் பாதுகாப்பாக பகிரலாம். கதைகளை கேட்கவும் விரும்பினால் பெயரை வெளிப்படுத்தாது பாதுகாப்பாக பொதுத்தளத்தில் ஆவணப்படுத்தவும் உதவுவோம். #metoo #MeTooSriLanka #lka. (@EnHui, 2019)

While such individually driven initiatives were rampant on social media, public initiatives such as that of OXFAM Sri Lanka were being launched to urge victims to speak up, and bystanders were urged to create a scene in the case of any sexual harassment. Thus, in order to publicize the project, the initiative staged such scenes on buses to train and urge the public to respond. They also formulated a seven-step method for bystanders in instances where they encounter such situations. This method urges the bystanders to be seen, distract, engage, speak up, notice details, report, and support. A special short film festival was organized to get the word out and to encourage the public to participate in the initiative.

UNFPA Sri Lanka launched a project titled "Don't Look Away: 16 Stories of Sexual Harassment on Public Transport" (hereafter referred to as "16 Stories") in 2018. This project has worked in collaboration with Eliza Hatch, the Founder of

Cheer Up Luv, a photojournalism series. As such, this project is a visualization of the victims and their stories in photographic, video, and narrative mode. Women who are featured in the project use either Sinhala, Tamil, or English languages in their narratives, with a translation or subtitles in English. According to Hatcher, the aim of the UNFPA project "has always been to empower women who don't have a public voice" (Hanoun, 2019, n.p.). While further expanding on her collaboration with UNFPA Sri Lanka, she states, "It was one thing finding women who would speak to you openly, but another finding those willing to have their faces as part of a global campaign, and on bus stops around SL. It was a lot to ask" (Hanoun, 2019, n.p.). She further responded saying that their aim has been to "shift the conversation [of the #Metoo movement] from a Western Perspective" (Hanoun, 2019, n.p.). The two projects by OXFAM and UNFPA thus mark Sri Lanka's response to the global movement of #MeToo in attempting to address issues of sexual harassment of a particular group or "community" of women—namely, those who use public transport as their day-to-day mode of travel.

## "16 Stories": Personal Narratives and Politics

What is problematic, however, is "the privilege of digital and linguistic access" (Shenoy, GEST Podcast, 2020, 1:53) that the two initiatives hinge on. As Kinita Shenoy too observes, "[a]s far as I could see and other researchers could see as well, it was limited to English-speaking women, affluent communities—women who use the internet and women, who, to some extent, have franchise" (Shenoy, GEST Podcast, 2020, 1:53). Exploring the "16 Stories" project further, those who were featured in the project are photographed inside buses, a common mode of public transport in Sri Lanka. Participants of the project seem to represent ethnically and sexually diverse groups. However, their narratives inform that social class seems to cut across the form of storytelling and speaking out; for instance, "who gets to tell the story and whose story counts as 'truth' determine the definition of what [harassment] is" (Higgins and Silver 1991, p. 1). Politics of access, narrative style, and modes of resistance are indicative of how the participants cement an urban middle/upper-middle class rhetoric of agency and occupying space. As Srila Roy observes, "[u]rban middle-class women are in this manner not merely asserting women's right to public space but are also testing the limits of what counts as feminist agency and activism" (2012, n.p.). What is significant in the project is the urgency of "speaking out"—narrating their experience as victims of sexual harassment. It is, therefore, important to analyze how the politics of "speaking out" has defined the parameters of feminist intervention and thus becoming gatekeepers of these movements and knowledge production—which means, through these initiatives, knowledge about consent, agency, and resistance of women is produced as the standard. Dissemination of such knowledge always already presupposes a particular subject position that embodies the particular standard. As such, the performative aspect of these stories is highly mediated to fit the agenda of the project and its respective audience.

A useful framework to explore the above would be Serisier's (2018) contemplation on narrative politics and feminism. She observes that "[t]he political model of speaking out offers political benefits to survivors but it also asks and even demands a lot from them. Feminist politics both supports survivor stories and requires survivors to tell these stories and to tell them in specific ways" (p. 11). It is in this context of "speaking out" as resistance that greatly bespeaks sociocultural privilege "as a form of discursive activism "directed at promoting new grammars, new social paradigms through which individuals, collectivities, and institutions interpret social circumstances and devise responses to them" (p. 11). Placing a strong emphasis on the belief that "producing and disseminating a genre of personal experiential narratives" (2018, p. 4) and "breaking the silence" through telling personal stories," in fact, will end violence has noticeably marked mainstream feminist interventionist politics. Serisier notes that "[t]he production of this genre of stories is one of the key legacies of second-wave feminist politics, as is the widespread cultural acceptance of the political and ethical necessity of speaking out as a response to rape. Speaking Out is concerned with the consequences, both intended and unintended, of this commitment to the transformative political potential of experiential storytelling" (p. 4). Thus, what counts as a story and its narrator presumes (accumulated) social, economic, and cultural capital—a certain security/strong foothold in their respective communities. A close analysis of the language used in the "16 Stories" project shows that the project fails in achieving its described agenda.

> I was brought up in a strict, conservative household where I was always chaperoned and driven to wherever I needed to go. I used to crave independence and think it was the "coolest" thing that my classmates could travel alone on buses. [ . . . ] It took me years before I was brave enough to get on public transport on my own again. (16 Stories, 2018, n.p.)

Experience narrated by the above participant/survivor particularly demonstrates how the "right to occupy public space" goes hand in hand with independence and breaking away from the clutches of a conservative family. Traveling by public transport, in this singular instance, is conceived of as something "cool" and "brave"—something that her family has imposed restrictions on, and which demarcates sociocultural exposure and upbringing. Here, the narrator attempts to articulate what freedom means to her, subjectively. But the narrative excludes and renders absent the everyday forms of resistance that women employ when they use public transport on a daily basis. Silence, in this context, is marked as an act of claiming independence from an otherwise conservative background. Srila Roy's research on Indian women reverberates, to a certain extent, the ways in which the privileged narrative of resistance occupies and excludes those that have been defined otherwise:

> Unlike middle-class feminists of a previous generation, young Indian women are articulating a feminist politics that is neither defensive about its borrowing from Western feminist repertoires or, indeed, about its middle-class and urban location. Mitra-Kahn points, however, to their reflexivity with respect to "multiple markers of privilege," and activist efforts to transgress a caste/class-infused digital divide. (2012, n.p.)

Roy's scholarship speaks to highlight privilege-driven responses to feminist politics in Sri Lanka that is manifest in the "16 Stories" project. Such responses underpin that activism based on "personal stories/narratives" are "marked by multiple markers of privilege" such as social class, geographical location, access to education and ideas, and thoughts that form their subjectivity and social consciousness.

Similar to the previous participant, the following accounts also relate a similar feminist politics:

> I normally wore cute frilly dresses and went for classes after school, but that day I was wearing Khaki cargo pants and a T-shirt. [ . . . ] I was too afraid to tell my mum or anyone about the incident because I thought they would stop me from traveling alone or tell me that I shouldn't have worn pants.
>
> I didn't tell my parents—thinking they would never allow me to travel in a bus again. (16 Stories, 2018, n.p.)

The narrators' view of the public space as a "liberatory" and "adventurous" one, or of maintaining silence, speaks to a particular power dynamic which an average member of the lower/working-class or the gendered subaltern does not have. However, as one participant suggests, "[w]e are reluctant to speak up in fear of being judged by society. But by being silent we are encouraging harassment. I think we should speak up about these problems. Our voices should be heard" (16 Stories, 2018, n.p.). Here, the participant's view on silence implies that it encourages the perpetrator. Therefore, speaking out is framed as a preferred, albeit the only way of confronting the harasser. This renders absent "silence" as a mode of resistance employed by the less privileged or socially uneconomically marginalized women. To put it simply, speaking out is a luxury a few can possess.

> They told me it was normal and I should never travel alone. I decided to never use public transport ever again after that. (16 Stories, 2018, n.p.)

In other words, what is predominant here is what is rendered absent from the narrative—namely, the harassment faced by women who do not occupy privileged positions to claim that "I decided to never use public transport ever again after that"—rather than what is being articulated.

The survivors also complain how they have been ignored by bystanders when they were being harassed. For example, one participant reflects:

> The other passengers did nothing except glower at me, assuming I was flirting with the boys. Most Sri Lankans believe that a victimized girl is often "asking for it," or that it is none of their business to get involved. Even the bus conductor ignored me. (16 Stories, 2018, n.p.)

This is perhaps why Jordan Fairbairn (2020) acknowledges that "[b]ystander intervention programs aim to move beyond the victim–perpetrator relationship to engage third-party individuals and the community at large in violence prevention" (p. 2). The initiative primarily took wings on the digital space, while the message has been delivered in the form of stickers, short films, and drawings in order to "raise awareness" about sexual harassment. As such, social class seems to play a crucial role in defining the parameters of resistance and feminist intervention, at least in ways that Sri Lanka has responded to the global #MeToo movement.

## #CreateAScene: Bystanders and Civic Surveillance

#CreateAScene and #NotOnMyBus were two hashtags trending during the #MeToo movement in Sri Lanka. Carrie Rentschler notes that "[t]he bystander is increasingly being touted as a key agent of change for addressing racialised and gendered violence and street harassment" (2017, p. 565). Thus, in the wake of the spirit of the #MeToo movement in Sri Lanka, people who use public transport have been given a choice: "to ignore or intervene."

> It is time we fortified a culture of zero tolerance for violence against women and acknowledge standing against harassment as a civic duty. This is why bystander intervention is going to be a pivotal point in countering high levels of sexual harassment in public transportation in Sri Lanka. The Not On My Bus campaign seeks to instill a sense of responsibility through a series of simple steps to

> prompt people to not ignore sexual harassment in public transport. (Create a Scene, 2019, n.p.)

What the above passage highlights is an interesting framing of one's civic duty. The emphasis on values and virtues and their relationship caters to, perhaps, conceptualizing effective citizenship through which the agenda of the state and neoliberal, corporatized bodies mutually inform each other. "Bystander" then becomes an embodiment of this expected citizen—one who is responsible and civic-conscious. The initiative attempts to instill in the public consciousness that they can be agents and provocateurs; above all, it attempts to instill in the mind of the perpetrator a sense of being watched over or surveilled. The mechanism is the public becoming their own policing agents—a means of exerting discipline and control through gaze. Mostly, it is about making such attempts visible on the digital space. The initiative specifies that

> [b]ystander intervention can be as simple as being seen. Make your presence known. Move close to the victim and the harasser.
>
> If you see something, do something. Everyone has a role to play in ending sexual harassment in public transport.
>
> This is not a spectacle. If you witness sexual harassment in public transport, do something. (Create a Scene, 2019, n.p.)

The imperative "do something" seems to make it part of their civic responsibility, which is also indicative of the monopoly of NGOs in controlling the means of knowledge production about how such situations need to be acknowledged and responded to. Mostly, bystanders exert different means of resistance other than getting involved in the scene. The following narrative exemplifies this.

> On the bus today: The conductor kept touching my shoulder while moving up and down the aisle. An older lady noticed I was uncomfortable, she told me to move towards the window and sat in my place. There are good people. The world can be a better place. Be a good person. (Create a Scene, 2019, n.p.)

"Be a good person" is what the "victim" seems to advocate—in other words, bystander intervention is presumed as a demarcation of "being good"—an embodiment of a value or virtue. Allocation of meaning to what is considered "good" in this narrative is highly political, despite being coated in socially acceptable ways of behavior, alias, "being good." The call for intervention/resistance as "doing something," "speaking out," or "breaking silence" has thus been conceptualized as the "normal" and "morally right" thing to do by its organizers.

## "NGO-ization" of Resistance

Lukose articulates the #MeToo movement as the "galvanizing moment where the universalizing horizon of feminism has newly arisen" (2018, p. 35). It is under this universalizing umbrella—the Western, Eurocentric, dominant paradigm of feminism imposed on particular experience—that Sri Lanka has "appropriated" and responded to the #MeToo movement. This kind of paradigm, as discussed previously, is permeated through the discourse of "NGO-ization" and neoliberal, hegemonic politics. The impact of policies, development frameworks, and toolkits that have so far guided gender mainstreaming have led to a form of "gender technocracy." As such, these spaces, sometimes liaising with the academy, have become hubs of production and dissemination of knowledge about gender. Murdock (2008) questions whether "the professionalized feminist NGO [is] the most appropriate form of feminist political practice" (p. 5). In a similar vein, many scholars, including Gayatri Chakravorty Spivak and Arundhati Roy, have questioned the role played by NGOs in the Global South. For example, Arundhati Roy responds that "[t]he ngoization of politics threatens to turn resistance into a well-mannered, reasonable, salaried, 9-to-5 job. With a few perks thrown in" (2004, p. 45). Spivak maintains that:

> Today, with the highly gendered and self-styled International Civil Society—the positive name for that which is not the state (nongovernmental)—it can perhaps be advanced that inserting women into the question of institutionalized friendship ("democracy"—as the code name for the political restructuring entailed by the transformation of [efficient through inefficient to wild] state capitalisms and their colonies to tributary economies of rationalized global financialization) is leading to consequences seemingly as predictable as electronic databasing can make them: impatient philanthropy caught in organizational priorities rather than continuing hands-on engagements that would allow nonhierarchical understanding to develop; intervention into cultural systems in the mere name of "woman." The United Nations in its contemporary formation operates as and gives shelter to the International Civil Society—the forum of NGOs. (2003b, p. 31)

This throws light onto the ways in which resistance is planned and articulated in ways that are legitimate and legible to the state and neoliberal and corporatized agendas. Gender and development (GAD) in the Global South have assumed a largely bureaucratic and institutional form, following its Eurocentric predecessors, as a result of which pluralities and everyday modes of resistance practiced by women are minoritized based on social class, caste, ethnicity, religion, language, geography, and age. This is not only a denying of such practices among such women, but also of the Global South as a space of enunciation.

Sri Lanka had vibrant women's movements in the nineteenth and twentieth centuries. Circa the 1890s, more education opportunities became available to the liberal middle class. In 1932, women obtained the right to vote. But from the 1920s to the 1990s, mostly middle-class women's movements became prominent. Commenting on this context, Kumari Jayawardene notes that "all women do not as a whole belong to the separate homogenous class" (Giles, 2002, n.p.). Its impact has been mostly an urban-centric one, while the role of women was still conceived as an embodiment of cultural, and thereby national, interests. As a result , the "[n]ormative (middle-class) femininity came to stand in for the nation with specific consequences for 'real' women who had to negotiate this symbolic burden within and outside the home" (Roy, 2012, n.p.).

In the context of Sri Lanka, the NGO-ization of dominant feminist discourse and mainstream forms of resistance has shed light on the ways in which the #MeToo movement has been appropriated and responded to. As Narayanswamy (2016) contemplates, what is being solidified through such interventions is "southern elite feminist priorities" and "the disciplining effects of neoliberal frameworks" (p. 2156) that cater to what Spivak calls "epistemic violence"—erasure or denying of the knowledge ecologies of the margins geopolitically, historically, and economically. Given the central role played by NGOs empirically and ideologically, everyday forms of resistance that women practice when they travel by public transport have been pushed back under the totalizing, monolithic screen of professionalized and legible forms of resistance performed by professional, middle/upper-middle-class, urban, English-speaking women. As mentioned above, not disclosing the perpetrators has been informed by the fear of losing one's independence or losing the privilege to wear trousers. As Malathi de Alwis (2009) cites, "The compulsions of taking up and 'successfully' completing specific projects has meant that that there is hardly any fresh thinking on what constitutes "feminism." . . . It is as if we know what 'feminism' is, and only need to apply it unproblematically to specific instances" (Menon, 2004, p. 220) (p. 86).

## Intersectional and Decolonial Paradigms: Global South as a Space of Enunciation

Under the universalizing impact of the #MeToo movement in the Global South, particularly in Sri Lanka, it has become paramount to reclaim the Global South as a space of enunciation rather than one that is enunciated—the "geo-political and body-political location of the subject that speaks" (Grosfoguel, 2007, p. 213). The purpose is to challenge dominant, Eurocentric, and Western articulation of the "Third World" subject and, by extension, those of the urban middle/upper-middle-class feminist rhetoric that render women on the margins invisible. Against such singular and teleological conceptions of feminism, I argue for women's activism at the bottom—of women at the margins of the history: the subaltern. Going by Spivak's spirit, the task is to create infrastructure so that their everyday modes of resistance can be heard. It is, therefore, important, to reimagine movements like #MeToo at the intersections of postcolonial, decolonial, and intersectional imaginaries. Lukose observes, "It is important to remember that feminist interventions within the terrain of knowledge have always had a decolonizing imperative. As feminism critiqued the universalizing assumptions of the category of 'man' within a variety of disciplines, including anthropology, it sought to challenge hegemonic assumptions about subjectivity, corporeality, humanity, reason, culture, society, and the like (2018, p. 36). Sarah Gorman, Geraldine Harris, and Jen Harvie, in a recent issue of *Feminisms Now*, note the "inadequacy of the term 'feminist' for non-white artists and scholars" (2018, p. 280). To this effect, I invoke the feminist scholarship of Rajeswari Sunder Rajan to seek possibilities of exploring this space of enunciation on the margins.

"Theory is normally produced in the metropole and exported to the periphery, while the periphery normally produces data and exports this raw material to the metropole. All academic disciplines show these patterns; viewed as a whole, feminist, women's and gender studies are no exception," state Roberts and Connell (2016, pp. 135–136). This shows how urban middle/upper-middle-class knowledge economies occupy and organize narratives of resistance in the public sphere. As scholars of feminism, I concur it is incumbent on us to work on a "radical refiguring of the political," as stated by Malathi de Alwis (2009, p. 82). Said differently, how the political is articulated and appropriated by urban middle/upper-middle-class feminist circles as the right to occupy public space unencumbered by the male gaze not only undermines the everyday practices of resistance of lower/working-class and subaltern groups but also denies their agency. A further point of contention is disinvesting from the radical imperative that a feminist critique/movement fosters—acknowledging that the different axes of identity intersect with each other, creating a subject with complex subjectivities.

Rajeswari Sunder Rajan's conceptualization of resistance that "there is a politics that surrounds the concept of resistance, not only a resistance politics" (2000, p. 154) is a useful point of departure when envisioning a feminist politic crisscrossing post- and decolonial paradigms, social class, and other axes of identity. According to her:

> Women's quietism, passivity, their consent and acquiescence to, and even complicity with, patriarchy are no longer understood simply as signs of abject powerlessness or of false consciousness. These are instead recognised as real alternatives to "resistance" available to women in negotiating a better deal for themselves in an objectively real situation of disempowerment. (2000, p. 158)

Such day-to-day modes of resistance, that have been rendered absent by the mainstream feminist discourse, reinforced by highly striated movements like the #MeToo movement in Sri Lanka and backed by professionalized gender mainstreaming agendas of NGOs, are considered impervious to initiatives such as "speaking out," "breaking the silence" and "creating a scene." What Sunder Rajan advocates for is

> . . . installing in the space vacated at the centre (of history, society, politics) a resisting subject—one who will be capable of the agency and enabling selfhood of the "active" earlier subject, while at the same time acknowledging the politics of difference. The cleared site of the subject must provide the grounds of (new) gendered subjectivities that will enact more contingent, varied and flexible modes of resistance. (2000, p. 11)

Thus, what is required of a feminist praxis that acknowledges and provides infrastructure for diverse acts of resistance to be heard is deviating from "a tenuous individualism [that] shapes the female subject's resistance" (2000, p. 71) as that which is discussed above. Such praxis should also take into consideration the current postcolonial/decolonial moments—the most ethical and productive axes of those, rather than subscribing to an authoritative, masochistic erasure of certain subject positions.

The Sri Lankan response to the global #MeToo movement is geared toward establishing the imperatives of the neoliberal socioeconomic paradigm, with strong emphasis on individual accountability, social consciousness, and civic surveillance. The two projects; "16 Days, 16 Stories" and #CreateAScene, therefore, are working their way toward establishing a particular response as the "norm" or "standard," whereas it should have been an acknowledgment of the diversity of responses generated at the intersections of different axes of identity. It is clear that such interventions that use and appropriate "feminism" as a mere provocative dressing are an act of producing knowledge on how women "should" respond to harassment in the public transport system. As mentioned from time to time, attempting to popularize a singular response is a gesture or a politic that justifies who deserves to stand up against their perpetrators and who does not, and whose act of resistance is counted acceptable and/or recognized.

## Conclusion

This chapter argues for acknowledging and creating infrastructure for feminist resistance at the margins to be acknowledged. Sri Lankan response to the global #MeToo movement, monopolized by a universalized, singular, and individualist narrativization of feminist resistance by professionalized NGO bodies, has excluded and rendered absent the everyday modes of resistance employed by women marginalized by social, economic, and cultural franchise of the state (and shadow states). By default, such initiatives have laid the cornerstone to define, produce, and disseminate knowledge economies that are based on urban middle/upper-middle-class politics and ethos. This chapter draws on Rajeswari Sunder Rajan's call for acknowledging feminist resistance that is more "contingent, varied and flexible" (2000, p. 11).

## Note

1. Here, the Global North and South are not considered abstract categories, nor are they thought of as monolithic and homogeneous (see Sparke, 2007; Ballestrin, 2020).

## Works Cited

"Amethystinia Is a Pottymouthed Old Internet Auntie." 2019. *I believe you*, March 7 [Twitter]. https://twitter.com/Amethystinia/status/1103625968378273792.

Ballestrin, Luciana. 2020. "The Global South as a Political Project." *E International Relations*, July 3. https://www.e-ir.info/2020/07/03/the-global-south-as-a-political-project/.

Basu, Srimati. 2000. "The Bleeding Edge: Resistance as Strength and Paralysis." *Indian Journal of Gender Studies* 7, no. 2: 185–202.

Boyle, Karen. 2019. "#MeToo, Weinstein and Feminism." In *#MeToo, Weinstein and Feminism*, pp. 1–20. London: Palgrave.

Chandra, Giti., and Irma Erlingsdóttir, eds. 2020. *The Routledge Handbook of the Politics of the #MeToo Movement*. New York: Routledge.

Create A Scene. 2018. Facebook. https://www.facebook.com/createascenelk.

De Alwis, Malathi. 2009. "Interrogating the 'Political': Feminist Peace Activism in Sri Lanka." *Feminist Review* 91: 81–93.

Don't Look Away: 16 Stories. (n.d.). UNFPA. https://www.unfpa.org/16-stories.

Fairbairn, Jordan. 2020. "Before# MeToo: Violence against Women Social Media Work, Bystander Intervention, and Social Change." *Societies* 10, no. 3: n.p.

Fileborn, Bianca, and Rachel Loney-Howes, eds. 2019. *#MeToo and the Politics of Social Change*. New York: Springer Nature.

Sarah Gorman, Geraldine Harris, and Jen Harvie. 2018. "Feminisms Now." *Contemporary Theatre Review* 28, no. 3: 278–284. doi: 10.1080/10486801.2018.1487192.

Giles, Wenona. 2002. "The Women's Movement in Sri Lanka: An Interview with Kumari Jayawardena." May 6. https://btlbooks.com/chapters/feminists_underfire/xhtml/c15.html.

Grosfoguel, Ramon. 2007. "The Epistemic Decolonial Turn: Beyond Political-Economy Paradigms." *Cultural Studies* 21, no. 2–3: 211–223.

Hanoun, Marianne. 2019. "How Eliza Hatch and UNFPA Created a Social Campaign to Tackle Sexual Harassment in Sri Lanka." *Creative Lives in Progress*, January 16. https://www.creativelivesinprogress.com/article/how-eliza-hatch-and-unfpa-created-a-social-campaign-to-tackle-sexual-harassment-in-sri-lanka.

Hensman, Rohini. 1996. "A Feminist Movement in Sri Lanka: The Potential and the Necessity." *Contemporary South Asia* 5, no. 1: 67–74. doi: 10.1080/09584939608719779.

Higgins, A. Lynn, and R. Brenda Silver, eds. 1991. *Rape and Representation*. New York: Columbia University Press.

Jayawardena, Kumari. 2016. *Feminism and Nationalism in the Third World*. New York: Verso Books.

Jayawardena, Kumari, and Govind Kelkar. 1989. "The Left and Feminism." *Economic and Political Weekly* 24, no. 38: 2123–2126.

Lukose, Ritty. 2018. "Decolonizing Feminism in the# MeToo Era." *The Cambridge Journal of Anthropology* 36, no. 2: 34–52.

Marcuse, Herbert. 1964. *One Dimensional Man; Studies in the Ideology of Advanced Industrial Society*. Boston: Beacon Press.

Murdock, Donna F. 2008. *When Women Have Wings: Feminism and Development in Medellín, Colombia*. Ann Arbor: University of Michigan Press.

Nair, Sharada. 2020. "Metropolitan Feminisms of Middle-Class India: Multiple Sites, Conflicted Voices." *Indian Journal of Gender Studies* 27, no. 1: 127–140. doi: 10.1177/0971521519891483.

Narayanaswamy, Lata. 2016. "Whose Feminism Counts? Gender(ed) Knowledge and Professionalisation in Development." *Third World Quarterly* 37, no. 12: 2156–2175.

Niyanthini. 2019. நீங்கள் ஒரு பெண்ணாக, March 7 [Twitter]. https://twitter.com/EnHui/status/1103645263221145605.

Parvez Butt, Anam, and Sharanya Sekaram. 2019. "Smashing Spatial Patriarchy: Shifting Gender Norms Driving Sexual and Gender-Based Violence on Public Transport in Sri Lanka." OXFAM. https://oxfamilibrary.openrepository.com/handle/10546/620845.

Rajan, Rajesweri S. 2000. "Introduction: Feminism and the Politics of Resistance." *Bulletin (Centre for Women's Development Studies)* 7, no. 2: 153–165. doi: 10.1177/097152150000700201.

Rajan, Rajesweri Sunder. 2003. *Real and Imagined Women: Gender, Culture and Postcolonialism*. New York: Routledge.

Rentschler, Carrie. 2017. "Bystander Intervention, Feminist Hashtag Activism, and the Anti-carceral Politics of Care." *Feminist Media Studies* 17, no. 4: 565–584. doi: 10.1080/14680777.2017.1326556.

Roberts, Celia, and Raewyn Connell. 2016. "Feminist Theory and the Global South." *Feminist Theory* 17, no. 2: 135–140. doi: 10.1177/1464700116645874.

Roy, Srila. 2011. "Politics, Passion and Professionalization in Contemporary Indian Feminism." *Sociology* 45, no. 4: 587–602.

Roy, Srila. 2012. "Introduction: Paradoxes and Possibilities." In *New South Asian Feminisms: Paradoxes and Possibilities*, edited by Srila Roy, pp. 1–26. London: Zed Books.

Roy, Srila. 2015. "The Indian Women's Movement." *Journal of South Asian Development* 10, no. 1: 96–117. doi: 10.1177/0973174114567368.

Serisier, Tanya. 2018. *Speaking Out: Feminism, Rape and Narrative Politics.* New York: Springer.

Shepela, T. Sharon, et al. 1999. "Courageous Resistance: A Special Case of Altruism." *Theory & Psychology* 9, no. 6: 787–805.

Sparke, Matthew. 2007. "Everywhere but Always Somewhere: Critical Geographies of the Global South." *The Global South* 1, no. 1: 117–126.

Spivak, C. Gayatri. 1978. "Feminism and Critical Theory." *Women's Studies International Quarterly* 1, no. 3: 241–246.

Spivak, C. Gayatri. 2002. "Feminism and Deconstruction, Again: Negotiating with Unacknowledged Masculinism." In *Between Feminism and Psychoanalysis*, edited by Teresa Brennan, pp. 214–232. New York: Routledge.

Spivak, C. Gayatri. 2003a. "Can the Subaltern Speak?" *Die Philosophin* 14, no. 27: 42–58.

Spivak, C. Gayatri. 2003b. *Death of a Discipline.* New York: Columbia University Press.

Transformeurope. 2020. *The Left Reflects on the Global Pandemic: Gayatri C. Spivak.* May 15. https://www.youtube.com/watch?v=EseEPBQoVLE.

The GEST Podcast. 2020. #MeToo Special: Kinita Shenoy (Sri Lanka) [Audio Podcast]. December. https://soundcloud.com/gestpodcast/metoo-special-kinita-shenoy-sri-lanka.

Thiruchandran, Selvy. 2012. *Women's Movement in Sri Lanka: History, Trends and Trajectories.* Colombo: Social Scientists Association.

Tirkey, Joy, 2018. "#MeToo: Arjuna Ranatunga among Sri Lankan Cricketers Accused of Sexual Harassment." *NDTV Sports*, October 11. https://sports.ndtv.com/cricket/metoo-arjuna-ranatunga-among-sri-lankan-cricketers-accused-of-sexual-harassment-1930596.

Wickrematunge, Raisa, 2017. "#MeToo—Analysing the Conversation." *Groundviews*, October 26. https://groundviews.org/2017/10/26/metoo-examining-the-conversation/.

# 11
# The Precarity of #MeToo in Pakistan

*Afiya Shehrbano Zia*

## Timeline

- 1947: Several women of the All India Muslim League participated in the movement for the independence of Pakistan from British colonial rule and in the partition from India, including Fatima Jinnah, Rana Liaqat Ali, Begum Abdullah Haroon, Begum Ghulam Hidayatullah, Jehan Ara Shahnawaz, Viqar un nisa Noon, and Begum Tassaduq Hussain.
- 1948: The first legislature of Pakistan had two women representatives, Jahanara Shahnawaz and Shaista Ikramullah; Begum Rana Liaqat Ali Khan, freedom fighter and wife to Pakistan's first prime minister, started the Women's Voluntary Service (WVS), dedicated to rescue and rehabilitation services; the Democratic Women's Association was established along Marxist principles.
- 1949: The Women's National Guard and Pakistan Women's Naval Reserve formed in response to the war with India. Rana Liaqat Ali Khan founded the All-Pakistan Women's Association (APWA) which made invaluable contributions to welfare, legal reform, and advocating reserved seats in Parliament.
- 1951: The Muslim Personal Law of Shariat became effective, recognizing Muslim women's right to inherit, including agricultural land.
- 1954: The Karachi Business and Professional Women's Club was established.
- 1961: Recommended by APWA and members of the women's committee, the Muslim Family Law Ordinance extended some of the most progressive rights to women across the Muslim world with regard to marriage, the custody of children, divorce, and registration of marriages and divorces.
- 1965: Fatima Jinnah, sister of the founder of Pakistan, stood in the elections against General Ayub Khan.
- 1973: A new Constitution gave more rights to women than in the past. Article 25 of rights declared that every citizen was equal before the law, and Article 25 (2) stated there would be no discrimination based on sex alone. Article 27 of fundamental rights stated that there would be no

Afiya Shehrbano Zia, *The Precarity of #MeToo in Pakistan* In: *The Other #MeToos.* Edited by: Iqra Shagufta Cheema, Oxford University Press. © Oxford University Press 2023. DOI: 10.1093/oso/9780197619872.003.0011 discrimination based on race, religion, caste, or sex for appointment in the service of Pakistan.

- 1975: Pakistan was represented at the International Women's Year (IWY) by Prime Minister Z. A. Bhutto's wife, Nusrat Bhutto, who signed the Mexico Declaration.
- 1979: President General Zia ul Haq promulgated the Hudood Ordinances as part of a series of Islamic laws, which include the Zina laws that criminalized all extramarital sex and compounded rape (amended in 2006).
- 1970s: Women's organizations, such as Shirkat Gah, the Aurat Foundation, and the Women's Front, were formed to work on rights-based development and political mobilization. Sindhiani Tehreek (the women's wing of the Awami Tehreek, a Marxist party) mobilized a peasant women's movement in the province of Sindh and launched a grassroots feminist struggle for women's rights, national democracy and provincial autonomy, secular opposition to religious orthodoxy, and for class equality.
- 1981: The Fehmida and Allah Bux case, filed under the Zina Ordinance, motivated women to form the Women's Action Forum (WAF) in Karachi, and in 1983, they led a street protest in Lahore against the proposed discriminatory Law of Evidence where they were baton-charged, tear-gassed, and some were arrested. The law was diluted down in response to the pressure of the protest. Asma Jahangir and Hina Jilani fought legal cases for women and minorities, along with other members of their all-women founded legal firm, AGHS.
- 1983: The Ansari Report of the Council of Islamic Ideology recommended that women's participation in politics should be limited to nominated women over the age of fifty.
- 1985: The Shariat Bill (9th Amendment) threatened to abolish the Family Law Ordinance of 1961.
- 1988: Benazir Bhutto was elected as prime minister—the first woman leader in the Muslim world. She launched a mass-scale pre- and post-natal outreach service led by women, called the Lady Health Workers Program.
- 1995: Women-led nongovernmental organizations (NGOs) prepared thematic policies and participated in the Fourth World Conference on Women, and Prime Minister Benazir Bhutto signed the Convention on the Elimination of Discrimination Against Women (CEDAW), despite opposition from the religious party of the Jamaat e Islami.
- 1997: The first women's cricket team was formed and was permitted to play at international levels after an informal ban on women's participation in sports.

- 2000: WAF expanded with a new chapter in Hyderabad and mobilized women to participate in mass campaigns in rural areas, while taking up dozens of cases of violence against women and honor crimes.
- 2002: President General Pervez Musharraf introduced an unprecedented high number of quotas for women in all tiers of government.
- 2002: Peasant women of Okara joined male protestors against tenancy contracts with the military administration of several farms in Punjab.
- 2002–2008: The religious alliance of the Mutahida Majlis e Aml governed in Khyber Pakhtunkhwa and women of right-wing parties colluded to institute several anti-women policies through provincial and national assemblies.
- 2003: The National Commission on the Status of Women, constituted as a statutory body in July 2000, recommended the repeal of the Zina Ordinance, which was amended in 2006 with the passing of the Women's Protection Act (declared contrary to Islamic injunctions by the Federal Shariat Court in 2010).
- 2004: A weak honor crime law was passed (strengthened via an amendment in 2015–2016).
- 2005: Gang rape survivor Mukhtara Mai's case made international headlines when General Musharraf dismissed it as a ploy that women use to gain asylum to Canada.
- 2007: The women of the Jamia Hafsa madrassa in the capital, Islamabad, launched vigilante campaigns preaching hardline Islam and kidnapped a woman suspected of running a brothel. In 2014, they pledged allegiance to ISIS.
- 2007: Benazir Bhutto was assassinated shortly after her return from exile.
- 2007–2009: The Lawyers' Movement rose against General Musharraf, demanding the restoration of democracy and rule of law nationwide, in which women's organizations participated fully.
- 2008: The Benazir Income Support Program was launched as one of the largest cash-handout programs for women in the world.
- 2011: A series of pro-women laws were passed by the Pakistan People's Party, including the Protection Against Sexual Harassment at the Workplace (2010) and the Domestic Violence Act (2012).
- 2012: Sharmeen Obaid Chinoy won the Oscar Award for her documentary film on the practice of throwing acid to deface women.
- 2012: Student and education advocate Malala Yousufzai survived an assassination attempt by the Taliban. She went on to win the Nobel Prize for Peace in 2014.
- 2014: Over 140 students and faculty members of the Army Public School in Peshawar were mass murdered by the Taliban. "Mothers of APS Martyrs" continue to fight for justice for their slain children.

- 2016: Social media celebrity Fozia Azeem (Qandeel Baloch) was killed on the pretext of honor for her risqué posts, inspiring an amendment to the "forgiveness" clause for such crimes.
- 2018: A series of women's marches—Aurat Marches—were held across cities, protesting sexual harassment and demanding sexual autonomy. They generated controversy for their core slogan—*mera jism meri marzi* (my body, my choice).
- 2018: Hazara women protested the ethno-sectarian killing of their community; activist Jalila Haider vowed to fast to death unless the Chief of the Army visited the widows—which he then did.
- 2018: WAF filed a judicial reference against the excesses of a populist Chief Justice, Saqib Nisar—pending with the Judicial Council.

## Introduction

Pakistan was the first South Asian country to pass a law for the Protection Against Sexual Harassment at the Workplace (hereafter, PaSH) in 2010.[1] This is significant because the country ranks at the bottom of global gender indices, and as a postcolonial Islamic Republic it carries the legacy of discriminatory colonial personal laws. The steady theocratization of the juridical system has added to the layers of gender discriminatory laws and policies.[2] The Citizenship Act is unequal for women; they hold lesser status as legal witnesses and qualify for lesser inheritance under sharia law—all of which render Pakistan noncompliant in its commitment to the UN Convention for the Elimination of Discrimination Against Women (CEDAW).[3] Pro-women legislation is consistently challenged by the religious orthodoxy, right-wing political parties, and conservatives within the state offices, including the male-dominant Council of Islamic Ideology, which advises on the conformity of laws with Islam.

The PaSH legislation was an even more admirable achievement considering that it was passed in a political landscape dominated by the global "War on Terror" (WoT) that affected Pakistan directly in the decade of 2004–2014. Casualties amounted to hundreds of thousands of soldiers and citizens, while Islamic and pietist narratives dominated all spheres of life. Organized religious lobbies undermined women's rights directly by opposing any pro-women laws and inciting gender-based vigilantism (Brohi, 2006; Shehrbano Zia, 2018).

In the post-conflict period, democratic governments passed a series of progressive landmark laws for women's rights, and PaSH was conceived with a supportive apparatus involving workplace committees and special ombudspersons. It was not until 2017, however, that the #MeToo campaign trickled into Pakistan and eventually converged into its most visible representation by way of a series of Aurat Marches (women's marches) – street protests that were initiated in 2018. These protests became annual events held on International Women's Day in different cities across the country.

Historically, the role of individual women of courage has been crucial in Pakistan, as they repeatedly found themselves up against state patriarchy that relied on the collusion of men, *maulvis* (clerics), and the military (Shehrbano Zia, 2018). In response, feminist collectives and women's nongovernmental organizations (NGOs) were committed to a holistic treatment of sex crimes and directed their advocacy with the larger goal of secularizing the legal regime and democratizing and feminizing the state. In the new millennium, the neoliberal climate in which the #MeToo movement erupted, with social media as its main tool of activism, has influenced a departure from these prior methods and has realigned the vision and strategic outcomes of the women's movements in Pakistan with mixed results.

This chapter traces the pathway of the shifts in activism related to the #MeToo movement in Pakistan. It discusses its successes, along with some core tensions, departures, and disconnects within this movement, which confirm many similar findings documented in the growing body of international feminist analyses on #MeToo movements. It will reference select cases related to #MeToo in Pakistan to illustrate the importance of predisposition and historical context—political, legal, and religious—that affect the reception of global movements and trends, and which demonstrate how ideological theories and projections tend to fragment unpredictably when they hit against the specificities of local contexts. It outlines some of the principal sites and conflicts that challenge the #MeToo movement in Pakistan, which include the role of celebrities and the entertainment industry; legal preconditions; the neoliberal tool of social media; performativity and concern over propriety and generational divisions; class dynamics and grassroots activism; and the perilous politics of gendered piety. The chapter argues that Pakistan's religious and legal ecosystems temper the more optimistic expectations of the liberatory politics championed by the #MeToo movement in the West. In light of this, in order to sustain the cause, women's groups will need to recalibrate their legal, media, and communications strategies and reconsider how to engage with the state and political parties, and deal with religious backlash. Most of all, new methods will need to be devised to guide survivors and sustain personal and financial support for those who suffer the consequences of call-outs and who pursue legal recourse for harassment/sex offenses.

The sources used in this analysis include participatory observation, a case study, news reports, interviews with lawyers and activists who deal with sexual harassment cases and organize resistance movements—including a feminist scholar and mobilizer who works with rural women's movements in Sindh,

Pakistan. My findings also stem from personal involvement in some of the cases and from meetings with several survivors or their family members.

## Celebrity Feminism

The origins of the #MeToo movement in 2006 by Black American feminist Tarana Burke, and its subsequent rekindling by Hollywood actress Alyssa Milano, who exposed the influential film producer Harvey Weinstein in 2017, have been detailed elsewhere in this volume. It cannot be coincidence that the role of celebrities (in the arts, politics, or academia), or the entertainment industry itself, are common sites that feature in #MeToo movements across the world. Pakistan is no exception.

On October 23, 2017, Pakistan's controversial Oscar Award–winning filmmaker Sharmeen Obaid-Chinoy posted a tweet objecting to a doctor's Facebook request sent to her sister after he had earlier treated her at a hospital emergency unit. Chinoy's tweet also expressed her resolve to report him for the intrusive behavior, adding that "Harassment has to stop!" (*Dawn*, 2017). The Aga Khan University hospital released a statement refraining from confirming or denying the rumor, but social media speculated that the concerned doctor had been suspended/dismissed. What followed was a litany of outrage on social media directed at Chinoy, particularly from conservative commentators and nationalists who were already provoked by her films that exposed the dark side of Pakistan's misogynistic practices of acid-throwing, honor crimes, and of women's resistance and resilience against such criminal behavior (Okeowo, 2018).

The case was discussed within activists' groups, but most feminists remained cautiously silent. They refrained from a public debate on the issue, partially due to their social relationships with Chinoy. There is discomfiture over debating the veracity of a call-out by a member from a small pool of liberal progressive activists working on women's causes, especially since as a class, they are already commonly perceived as elite, Westernized, and anti-men. A few weeks after the incident, I wrote a newspaper column on Chinoy's method of calling out the doctor and argued that a Facebook request by doctor to a patient may be unethical, but did not amount to sexual harassment, even by a broad definition of the law. The article cautioned against the slip toward liberal conservatism in the context of Pakistan in suggesting that: "Women must beware of surrendering their own agency. They should be able to reject an online request without depending on some paternalistic law. There are guidelines that flag the tipping point of sexual harassment. We need to follow these rather than succumb to a moral panic such that a rights-based law begins to be interpreted as a patriarchal one" (Shehrbano Zia, 2017).

The article suggested that "fairness demands that activists abstain from social media mob lynching," and concluded with the observation that, "[d]espite Chinoy's bungling activism, the abuse and vitriolic hate directed at her on social media reveals a perverse kind of male bonding and threatened male privilege and entitlement" (Shehrbano Zia, 2017). The caution was based on a historical and contextual consideration of the prevailing legal and religious restrictions on Pakistani women, which already impose limitations on their sexual autonomies, physical and social mobility, and decision-making. These in turn weaken them into targets of violence, punitive behavior, and even death for women's sexual transgressions on the pretext of male dishonor.

The commentary around Chinoy's tweet and responses to my article signaled some early cleavages within feminist positionality on the issue of call-outs. One comment posted below my article retorted, "Writing three tweets and not naming the doctor hardly amounts to social media 'mob lynching.' If anything the barrage of violent, sexist responses [Chinoy] received in response would be much more akin to this. Such exaggeration is only feeding into the rhetoric of misogynists."[4] This form of abstract virtue gesturing and self-rightousness has come to define many online debates in Pakistan, particularly on the topics of gender and religion. The broader point in the article about responsible use of social media by activists was twisted and redirected to Chinoy's tweets. Despite Chinoy's posted warning that the doctor had "messed with the wrong family,"[5] the defensive comment to the article contended that a mere three tweets calling-out the doctor were not a purposeful act but an innocuous gesture. In fact, any feminist would be aware that it was Chinoy's class power, status, and fame that drew far more traction and immediate response and action by the hospital, which then dismissed the doctor. No ordinary woman citizen's call-out could possibly have such an impact or consequence. This certainly does not exonerate the deluge of violent abusive reactions that Chinoy received, as the article pointedly states, but the decontextualized flippancy represented in the comment dismissed the overall caution that call-outs were not neutral tools.

Subsequently, as events have unfolded around sexual harassment cases, it has become clear that dismissing such warnings as "exaggeration" has been incredibly myopic. Call-outs against sexual harassment have become traps that have ensnared women survivors *of all classes* into harrowing litigious and lonely battles with devastating professional, personal, financial, and health-related consequences for the survivor and, sometimes, for those who support the call-out. The online community of the outraged rarely turn up in real life to support the survivor in the aftermath of the call-out, raising the connected dilemma about the limitation of social media trials and virtual moral support for survivors of sexual offenses.

Globally, celebrities speaking out about their experiences have inspired other survivors, but the energies of activists and followers on social media have also tended to become polarized opinion-based verdicts that circulate in the virtual public after any call-out. Selectivity in call-out politics, split loyalties, activism fatigue, uncertainty about the place of LGBTQ rights, the dubious role of "male allies," and the rocky interface with patriarchal formal legal regimes have been key features in call-out cases in Pakistan. Many of these applied to the case of the celebrity singer/model/actress Meesha Shafi and her alleged harassment by male performing star Ali Zafar.

## Legal Preconditions 1: Name and Shame

On April 19, 2018, Meesha Shafi released a statement, using the hashtag #MeToo on Twitter, alleging that her fellow male celebrity singer, Ali Zafar, had on "more than one occasion, [subjected her] to sexual harassment of a physical nature" (BBC, 2018). No details were revealed, but a few hours later, Ali Zafar responded on Twitter, denying Shafi's claims and his intent to pursue legal action. This triggered a series of solidarity statements by various celebrities, who were divided in their support for either the alleged victim or the accused. Two days later, Meesha offered some details in an interview with a newspaper magazine: "I'm finding it hard on my conscious [*sic*] to stay silent any longer than this because I'm seeing such brave girls and women speaking up—not just around the world—but here as well" (Sabeeh, 2018, n.p.).

Soon after, Ali Zafar's counsel sent a legal notice to Meesha for the sexual harassment allegations, demanding that she delete the tweets and issue an apology on Twitter, failing which he intended to file a defamation suit to sue her for Rs100 crore (approximately US$6 million). Meanwhile, Meesha filed a complaint before the ombudsperson under the Protection against Sexual Harassment law (PaSH) on April 30, 2018, which was rejected on May 3, 2018, on the basis that the ombudsperson lacked jurisdiction in the matter since she did not fall under the definition of an "employee." Meesha then filed a statutory appeal/representation before the governor on May 23, 2018, which was also rejected on July 11, 2018, on the same grounds—that the ombudsperson did not have jurisdiction to hear the case. Her legal team then filed a constitutional petition in the High Court against the order of the governor, which remained unheard for over a year. Finally, it was heard and dismissed by the Lahore High Court (LHC) on October 2, 2019.

In November 2019, Meesha then petitioned the Supreme Court against the Lahore High Court judgment, which remained unheard for over a year, as two judges recused themselves. (It is worth noting here that Ali Zafar's father-in-law is a well-established lawyer and runs one of the most influential law firms in the country.) In her filing, Meesha asked the apex court to set aside the LHC decision in which the court took a narrow view of the PaSH and held that since Meesha was not an "employee" under the law, she could not avail any remedy before the special forum of ombudsperson created to hear allegations of sexual harassment. One of Meesha's lawyers, Saqib Jillani, stresses that "[t]hese proceedings were not about the merits of the case, simply that the question of jurisdiction must first be answered" (personal correspondence, July 2021). After countless applications for an early hearing, Meesha's petition was finally heard on January 11, 2021, and the Supreme Court granted her leave to appeal. This meant that the points raised by Meesha deserved to be heard before the court on the matter of jurisdiction and to determine if she qualified for protection under the PaSH law. The important point at which this case now hinges is that the Supreme Court will decide a point of law, i.e., whether the ombudsperson has jurisdiction to look into Meesha's allegations, but in the meantime, the case has sprung new legal tentacles.

## Legal Preconditions 2: Fame and Defame

In June 2018, Zafar had filed a defamation lawsuit against Meesha,[6] seeking a billion rupees in damages. The court admitted the lawsuit for hearing and placed a gag order on Meesha, preventing her from discussing the allegations in public. She challenged the order but the LHC has not decided the matter in over two years. Meesha Shafi had also filed a Rs. 2 billion lawsuit against Ali Zafar in 2019, for defaming her on national media and hurting her sentiments and reputation. In contrast to Zafar's injunctions against Meesha, her civil defamation case against him remains stayed, which enables him to publicize claims to innocence or to continue leveling allegations against Meesha. He appears regularly on national television, where he has cried in appeal for public sympathy. His lawyer also claims Ali's innocence or implies that he has been cleared of all charges. These perceptions are false and are manufactured to ensure impunity for Zafar and create bias in public perception.

As the case developed, several women and some men gathered the courage to come out in support of Meesha on social media, including some who alleged assault by Zafar, too. Among them was Leena Ghani, who took to Twitter to accuse Zafar of "inappropriate contact, groping, sexual comments" (Dawn, 2020a). By July 2019, dozens of people, mainly women, who had written social media posts either making allegations about Zafar or expressing support for Shafi, began to receive notices to appear before the Federal Investigation Authority (FIA) for questioning. The FIA invoked jurisdiction under Section 20 of the controversial new law, "Prevention of Electronic Crimes Act (PECA) 2016," based on a complaint filed by Zafar against Meesha and others who had spoken in her favor, claiming that his reputation has been harmed on an online forum.

On September 29, 2019, the FIA registered a case against singer Meesha Shafi for harassment, and eight others who echoed the allegations were also booked for the supposed vilification of Ali Zafar (Dawn, 2020a). The "suspects" named in Zafar's application were summoned on several occasions by the cybercrime wing but could not afford to fly to different cities to attend. The FIA then decided to proceed with criminal charges against the nine accused for defamation and social media "character assassination" of Zafar (September 2020). These charges carry a three-year jail sentence. The original list had twenty-five names identified, but it became obvious that several had retracted their call-out and had settled the case by apologizing to Zafar. As the number dwindles down to those who refuse to apologize and remain committed to bearing legal witness rather than just social media solidarity, such resiling strengthens Zafar's case, who takes pride in tweeting these apologies. Meanwhile, eight of the nine remaining supporters/witnesses are women, and they are compelled to appear before a criminal court in Lahore. Apart from legal implications, they face a barrage of online rape and death threats, harassment, and vilification, even in mainstream media.

On December 15, 2020, the FIA presented evidence that Meesha and others in the case were "guilty" of defamation and asked for court proceedings against them to begin. Meesha's lawyers say she was not given the opportunity to present witnesses in her defense. Zafar's lawyer maintains that her client is an "innocent man [who] was made a target of a criminally motivated malicious campaign by a group of closely related women" (Ellis-Peterson, 2021, n.p.). The eight women facing defamation charges deny any previous relationship or participation in any campaign and say they intend to fight the case in court and push for the cyber defamation law to be repealed. Ghani has argued: "People keep saying #MeToo is dying in Pakistan, which is so terrible because it's not like women are not getting harassed and assaulted and raped, but we are being silenced. We all realise that Pakistan's #MeToo movement hinges on this case.... The whole system is against us; Ali Zafar is a powerful man, and going to court is hard—but what can be harder than lying and living with that lie," she adds. "I would rather go to jail" (Ellis-Peterson, 2021, n.p.).[7]

The reprisal tool of legal defamation is not limited to Pakistan or even South Asia (Malkani, 2019; Nagarai, 2021). According to research by the feminist legal aid organization, Yuanzhong Gender Development Center (YGDC), among the tens of millions of lawsuits in China during the years 2010–2017, only 34 cases were related to sexual harassment, and 55.9% of those 34 cases were defamation suits or illegal discharge suits lodged by offenders as the plaintiff, and where the victims were plaintiffs in only two cases (Jun, 2021, p. 348). A mere 32.4% of sexual harassment complaints were confirmed by the court; in the seven cases where the victims had turned to the police, effective investigations were rarely conducted, and only in one case did the police confirm that sexual harassment had occurred (Jun, 2021, p. 348). Pakistan's leading feminist pressure group, the Women's Action Forum (WAF), has demanded that the criminal defamation law be amended because, in effect, it voids the PaSH law (Geo News, 2019).

The feminist dependency on and the limits of prevailing patriarchal political systems, law, and the justice system, including concepts of due process and bureaucratic hindrances such as habeus corpus, are seen by many younger feminists as part of an entire apparatus that favors perpetrators (see Khan and Aziz, 2022). They are drawn to the processes of punitive and restorative justice, but their lack of experience or encounters with the state (which feminists of the 1990s who fought against discriminatory laws were all too familiar with) created a strategic impasse by the time that the Meesha case unfolded. The divided opinions also presented a schism in the historically intersectional feminist approaches adopted by the earlier women's movements which centered the state and religio-military establishments in their analysis and whose critiques aimed for transformative politics but did not focus on sexual politics or intimate partner relations, which were overwhelmingly steered by state policies (Shehrbano Zia, 2019a).

For the women who pledged solidarity by joining Meesha's social media call-out, the irony lies in the fact that PECA was passed in 2016 under the paternalistic justification of protecting women from online harassment, but the wing of the FIA tasked with prosecuting these cases regularly maneuvers the process for the benefit of the accused (Aziz, 2018). This points to the predicament of injecting pro-women laws in a masculinist postcolonial legal regime layered with religio-conservative judicial institutions and where the virtual lever of social media often turns out to be a double-edged tool in real-life battles.

## Anti-social Media

Meesha Shafi's case is in its third year, and Zafar's financial, social, and political resources sustain his career, earning him social goodwill and even civil rewards. His legal team is led by a woman who defends him against criticism from feminists, often by misleading legal claims. His career has thrived as corporations extend him credibility (including those led by empowered women leaders and entrepreneurs who claim feminist solidarity) by repeatedly inviting him, and not Meesha, to perform and host events from their platforms. In the midst of the case in 2020, the president of Pakistan awarded Zafar the Pride of Pakistan award—one of the country's highest honors (Dawn, 2020b).

The case has exposed wider unresolved relationships between the state, sex, and social media. In the twenty-first century, the Pakistani state's fraught relationship with freedoms of media and its historic investment in censorship and crushing of dissent were originally fueled by anxieties over religious content (particularly, what is considered blasphemy) and obscenity (Shehrbano Zia, 2014). This has now extended to curbing sexual harassment cases as a threat to the socio-sexual order and is wielded as a counter-strategy defense of men's "honor."

The transnational spread of the #MeToo movement in different countries gestures to a democratic amplification of voice. It provides a platform for the shamed and stigmatized to access and participate in a liberatory politics or appeal for social justice, or at the very least, to connect with a network of survivors or sympathizers. Several younger Pakistani feminists have argued that digital tools have played an important role in developing feminist consciousness and providing confessionary spaces (Dad, 2016). Acknowledging the accompanying hostility, harassment, and misogyny unleashed online, they consider these to be spillovers of the overall patriarchal social structures and behavior that prevail in Pakistan. However, several researchers who have studied the role of social media (particularly, Twitter) for call-outs of sexual harassment cases, have observed the individualistic and neoliberal climate that has enabled the turn of activism on sex crimes toward digitally mediated hashtag activism (David, 2021). They note that trial by social media may be a new form of bearing witness and has introduced new vocabularies and expressions and slogans, but there are many fault lines and limitations to this mode of redressal.

In cases such as Meesha Shafi's, there is an additional challenge about how the "workplace" does not include many (neoliberal) sites of contractual work or recording studios. The law then does not apply to non-employees (for example, students in universities) and the survivor's recourse falls in a legal limbo. Under such circumstances, despite the risks of defamation, or from lack of knowledge of the consequences of naming and shaming, women continue to resort to social media for some kind of alter-parity justice.

Hashtag activism has signaled intergenerational differences in several contexts where an older generation of feminists holds reservations about the mode of social media as a neoliberal tool that channels individual redress. An older generation of feminists is concerned that due process is not observed in social media call-outs, but feminists are equally aware and critical of the biases in law enforcement and the judiciary, the lack of expertise on the law, forensics, and the non-supportive social context. They are mindful of the persistent social pressure to settle cases, which results in impunity for the accused. With reference to the #MeToo movement in India, feminist scholar Nivedita Menon (2019, n.p.) observes how the "old tradition in Indian democratic politics [was] to conduct debates publicly through statements," but she notes the shift in a feminist politics that used to be "about collective functioning, collective credit and collective blame taking," to the current culture of call-outs that appears to be far more about demanding individual credit. Menon argues that the focus on individualized occurrence of sexual harassment prevents it from being tackled collectively as a structural problem.

A second problematic with call-outs that do not specify the offensive behavior is that these cannot then be assessed or targeted for protest and transformation and amount to an abdication of responsibility. Several Pakistani feminists belonging to older collectives tend to share these concerns on both counts. Additionally, they question feminist responsibility beyond the courageous act of calling-out, and urge #MeToo activists to commit equal energies to issues related to the economy, democracy, and development. They also caution that social media is the preferred tool of contemporary populist governments and the religious right-wing and conservative rear-guard, globally.[8] All this points to the manner in which many issues get reduced to a battle of online narratives where considerable energies are focused but quickly forgotten as the next case breaks into the rapid news cycle. Often, these even get drowned out by the online rear-guard community which effectively discredits feminists and their causes.

The logical arc of a social media call-out of sexual harassment or abuse would be legal recourse which requires interface with the state's law enforcement agencies and justice system. The implications are not just the tiresome long trials and wading through sexist biases, but the added risk is that law enforcement and the state often treat survivors as inconvenient troublemakers. This risk and duality are a global pattern—Romanian feminist organizers cooperate with the local police and legislators, whereas in China (and Kashmir), feminist organizations have been tracked through social media and censored while feminist activists have been imprisoned, harassed, and displaced (Chandra and Erlingsdóttir, 2021, p. 8). At any given time, feminists in Pakistan have also experienced these contradictory responses simultaneously from the Pakistani state.

Two other points of overestimation regarding digital feminist activism: first, the disconnect between the global #MeToo movement and local grassroots ones; and second, the growing imbalance in protest methodologies, which leaves just a handful to pursue, advocate, or support survivors in sustained legal proceedings or lobbying for political accountability for sex offenses. The limits of digital activity on these counts are important in the context of Pakistan and are discussed below, but first, some background to the success and potential of this mode of activism, as best demonstrated in the emergence of the Aurat March events.

## Aurat March: Performativity, Rage, and Radical Rudeness

Inspired by the global #MeToo movement, a younger generation of women in Pakistan's urban centers who had already been connecting and politicking online for a few years, converged their anger and creative energies on March 8 (International Women's Day) in 2018. They decided to reclaim the streets to march against patriarchy. The climate in which the global #MeToo gained momentum was one in which women's movements were agitating against populist sexist male leaders or right-wing governments. It was no coincidence that in 2018, Pakistan was on the threshold of electing a new government, led by the popular celebrity cricketer and socialite turned politician, Imran Khan. The bold and provocative slogans and banners carried in the different cities by the Marchers were met with predictable backlash from religio-cultural conservatives (Raza, 2019), but what took a younger generation of feminists by surprise was the disapproval expressed by other women's rights groups and some older feminists (Zahra-Malik, 2019). Both reactions were indicators of differences and contradictions that simmered under the surface of the new activism.[9]

The hostility over the politics and posters that defined the Aurat Marchers' protest in 2018 from conservative critics was predictable. The explicit language used to protest male norms of propriety was unfiltered, as it mocked the various culturally specific modes of sexual harassment practices in Pakistan. Such agitprop ranged from "*Apna moza khud dhoondo*" (Look for your own sock); "*Apni roti khud banao*" (Make your own roti); "*Dick pics apnay paas rakho*" (Keep your dick pics to yourself); but the most provocative one simply stated, "*Mera Jism Meri Marzi*" ("My Body, My Choice/Consent"). There were posters of women flipping the finger at patriarchy and another that drew a woman sitting akimbo scoffing, "There, Now I'm Sitting Correctly." The messages were sardonic, humorous, and subversive, but also sexually overt. In Karachi and Lahore, some even carried refrains of lesbian, gay, bisexual, trans, queer, and intersex politics. The condemnations were swift, alleging that the Aurat March event was a violation of "our culture" and "Islamic teachings" (Shehzad, 2019), while neoconservatives, who make a career of denouncing feminism as "liberal–secular–Islamophobic," led an almost Freudian choir on national television (Jan, 2019). The provincial legislature of Khyber Pakhtunkhwa even passed a resolution demanding an inquiry into the "foreign hands" behind the Aurat March as a plot to undermine Pakistan's social norms (Hayat and Akbar, 2019).

The conservatives were not the only ones outraged; several feminists of the older generation objected to the impropriety of language, which they considered a trivializing of feminist causes to just sex. These feminists' confrontational and radical struggles against the state from the 1990s have laid the most significant feminist footprint across Pakistan, as they have challenged state powers and religious actors through acts of individual and collective courage and defiance. Theirs has also been the most intersectional and interdisciplinary movement. Some from this collective saw the political methods of the Aurat March as an invitation for women to behave and emulate men and their masculinist language.

Feminists from literary circles were critical, too, in particular poet and activist Kishwar Naheed, who advised the Aurat March participants to locate their freedom in the law, not in "bodies and tongues," and remarked, "we want independence but such things will distract us in the same way as jihadist [*sic*] went intractable having the believe [*sic*] that with the killing of 70,000 people they will fly off to heaven" (Dawn, 2019, n.p.). In defense, several supporters of the March reacted on social media by shaming Naheed (Dawn, 2019, n.p.). This signaled not just a generational difference, but a competitive elbowing for feminist spaces by social media shaming, rather than dialogue, debate, or collectivism. While Naheed's choice of words discredited the feminist aims of the event, the reaction was not a considered critique but a knee-jerk shaming—a favored practice of those who use social media platforms as a predominant form of their feminist activism.

## Generational Divides

One of the most contentious debates in feminist politics that emerged during the War on Terror (WoT) decade in Pakistan (2004–2014) was the scholarly objection to the pretext of "rescuing Muslim women" from their men as a moral justification for the invasion of Afghanistan by NATO-allied countries. This rhetorical cudgel that argued that "Muslim women did not need to be rescued" (Abu Lughod, 2002), although a timely caution, complicated the prevailing suspicion in Muslim-majority contexts that viewed women's rights campaigns, movements, and NGOs as inspired by "Western feminism" and for promoting "foreign," "anti-Muslim" agendas. Nearly twenty years later, the hashtag #MeToo, which originated in the United States as a transnational signifier and brand, is facing similar distrust. The supporters of the #MeToo movement are regularly accused of attempting to import Western feminism in order to defame Muslim men, subvert Muslim culture, and pollute Muslim women's pious aspirations by luring them toward sexual autonomy and immodesty. The unresolved place of sexual freedoms is the legacy of the earlier waves of feminist movements that did not prioritize this, and an ascetic state that has been invested in virtue policing.

In the 1990s, an older generation of feminists struggled against the military dictatorship and discriminatory Islamic laws passed by General Zia ul Haq's regime (1977–1988) and pitched their demands for secular state laws and policies. They maintained a stable ideological vision that was committed to changing institutions and in strategic engagement with democratic political parties. These activists fought for women accused of *zina* (adultery) and survivors of rape (*zina bil jabr*) who could become culpable for illicit fornication if they could not prove their lack of consent—but the defense would always be framed in terms of the woman's innocence, since consent was irrelevant in illegal non-marital relations (Khan 2006). In this climate, where the state was criminalizing sexual relations and colluding in social vigilantism of gender relations, sexual rights and sex positivity carried limited currency—instead, activists prioritized economic, social, and democratic crises as their ideological frames. But this generation still supports the Aurat March and has been urging the organizers to connect protest marches on sexual freedoms and violence with women's bodily, health, and labor rights. Many remained uncomfortable with public discussions around sexual pleasures or desire and the politics of sexually explicit language, which they consider sensationalist and even violent, and a patriarchal tool.

The various poststructuralist theories that influence the politics of a younger generation of activists and the alternative spaces of social media as a political forum have enabled wider spread, creativity, and impressive mobilization tactics, but this has also made collectivism more diffused. This is especially challenging since ideological differences are widening and more "male allies" are jumping directly into feminist causes—the goals get more blurred and buried under a competitive race for and disagreements over representation on panels, platforms, and performances on progressive causes. Underlying all this, there is a millennial distrust and distancing from the state that rides on the back of a post–9/11 ambiguity which is convinced that secular political confrontation to Islamic politics is always "Western" and colonial. Many younger feminist scholars or activists are convinced that some unspecified hybrid and fluid combination of politics can overcome false discursive binaries and rescue Islam simultaneously from Islamophobia and Islamic extremism, all the while observing liberal and secular lifestyles and sexual freedoms themselves.

While social media has changed activism and potentially democratized communication, it has also amplified cynicism, disinformation, and hate. Most of all, it has encouraged tribalism even among feminists in Pakistan. Competitive online promotions and "cancel" politics have become a strategic focus of younger feminists. This emulates a masculinist corporatized exercise that only serves to exclude and is counterproductive to the whole principle of a non-hierarchical, leaderless feminism. The role of "male allies" who join some feminists to broadcast online opinions about other Pakistani feminists is a form of politics that has no codes or parameters and is a growing source of concern over such individualism. So, the tool of social media afforded the #MeToo movement to go "viral" and gathered some critical mass of courageous voices who exercised their agency by revealing their experiences of sexual offenses. But after the very first wave of backlash, it was clear that internal contradictions and unpreparedness for entering "the field" could not withstand the offline encounter with the state, legal, and social conservatism or pietist politics.

A "middling" generation in Karachi attempted to bridge this political distance observed in the first March, by encouraging the older feminists to recognize the importance of challenging the sexual order, on the one hand, and to encourage the Aurat March organizers to connect their performative activism with legal cases and state policies. Most of all, they urged the need to develop an ideological strategic framework for the rights that Aurat Marchers were demanding. This was critical, since the wide-ranging backlash to the Aurat March was because its tone and messaging clearly transgressed and contradicted the Islamic gendered and sexual orders as defined in the Islamic Republic. Initially, the younger feminists did not take the critique or warnings well. Several reacted to these as rebuffs and turned to social media to express their resentment against such cautioning, with support from the growing phenomenon of online "male allies." Three years later, the organizers of the Marches found themselves facing very serious legal charges following the Aurat March of 2021. The implications of these are discussed below, but prior to that is the critical issue of the class dimensions of the #MeToo movement in Pakistan.

## Social Class, Cultural Politics

Amar Sindhu is a professor, poet, and one of the women's rights activists who founded the Hyderabad city chapter of the Women's Action Forum (WAF)—the national lobby and pressure group formed in 1981 to organize resistance against the military dictatorship of General Zia ul Haq (1977–1988). Since 2000, the Hyderabad branch of WAF has worked closely with women in rural districts across the province of Sindh, and their mobilization at grassroots levels makes for an impressive feminist record. Their experiences testify to the femicidal level of violence that motivates women's resistance to patriarchal landlordism and oppressive practices for women agricultural workers, as well as the routine sexism among the urban middle classes, which include "progressive" men in Bar associations, literary circles, NGO sectors, and in academia.

In an interview with me in June 2021, Amar explains the mixed methods employed by her sister activists to gain political credibility in a climate where they were initially discredited as separatists, for departing from the larger Marxist or other sub-nationalist groups that they were affiliated with, when they pursued their feminist cause as WAF. She recalls the shift in attitudes when WAF became successful at pursuing cases of violence against women (especially, those involving powerful men committing acts of violence against lower-class women) and gained the trust of communities. She observes that there are now growing expectations of voters from politicians to resolve such cases, and having gained credibility, WAF Hyderabad now gets unreserved cooperation and responsiveness from political representatives across the province in assisting in cases of violence against women.

It is this milieu that makes the Hyderabad chapter's experience with the #MeToo movement particularly relevant with reference to class dynamics. After the initial success of the debut Aurat March held in Karachi in 2018, the Hyderabad-based activists decided to organize the 2019 event locally. Amar reports some key findings: first, the realization that due to the specificity of their location and reliance on a standpoint feminist perspective, they knew their March had to be intersectional—it could not pivot around the single issue of sexual freedoms. Second, the mobilizers have always received overwhelming response to their calls for protest from rural women who face direct and unfiltered oppression, in contrast to the reservations of urban middle-class women who, according to Amar, remain immobilized due to a certain false consciousness and "internalized patriarchy," and their economic and social dependency on men. She offers a comparison when she points out that in the rural districts it is not institutional sexual harassment but domestic violence that is an imminent life-threatening concern. So, while the issue of sexual harassment does not resonate as directly, any cause related to violence motivates rural women to grasp the connectivity and join protest campaigns.

Specifically, with regard to organizing the #MeToo Aurat March in 2019, the Hyderabad chapter named their event "Aurat Azaadi March" (Women's Freedom March) to sharpen its purpose for the larger cause of gender equality. This irked some progressive men and allies who preferred the more fluid overarching title, "Women's March." Amar confirms that they wanted to maintain an ideological commitment to class and gender equalities and consciously did not adopt the controversial slogans around sexual rights that were raised in the metropolises in 2018. Their organizing committee maintained caution about the protest slogans and banners. She explains that protest performance has to be carefully curated—that even though women activists do not subscribe to conventional dress or appearance, they purposefully never wear "fashionable clothes or sunglasses" at such events to avoid allegations of elitism. She compares the example of "perfect victims" who qualify for men's sympathy with that of women activists and observes how "men in Sindh celebrate women leaders but just do not want to invest in or support the actual making of one."

Amar acknowledges the complication of sexual harassment call-outs in professional institutions. She maintains that taking cases to court or appealing to formal laws is often a long-winded and futile exercise for survivors, who are often intimidated and whose experiences are discredited. Amar also notes the trend where women build the courage and sound the call-out against their harassers, but their families and parents insist on retracting the allegations and reaching a compromise to avoid the disapproving gossip that lingers around such cases. The focus is less on justice and more about sexual morality. She does concede that some women resort to false allegations, but she attributes this to a frustration with a patriarchal system where women are repeatedly denied advancement and subjected to systemic sexism. At the same time, in genuine cases the sexual harassment committees in institutions rarely dispense any resolution, let alone just ones, and the legalities are no threats to male impunity.

Perhaps, the most crucial observation by Amar is her sense of how the Aurat March has yielded unintended consequences as a Trojan horse. She notes that precisely because of the controversies that the event has generated by publicizing harassment and demanding sexual autonomy in such graphic and explicit manner, it has inadvertently given legitimacy to cases of extreme violence as comparatively "legitimate" violations against women. She notes how the Hyderabad Aurat March events are perceived by law enforcement as a reasonable, unprovocative, middle-path protest that offers a secular push-back in support of poor disenfranchised brutalized women from what the people of Sindh consider to be the overall nuisance of the religious right and their regressive anti-women politics.

In Amar's assessment, however, the backlash of the religious right in the 2021 Aurat March in the country's capital signals the precarity of pegging the event to a single focus without recognizing its consequences for future events, or the implications for those who hold these events at grassroots levels. She argues that such misguided decisions and performative single-day events can result in discrediting their political activism in the constituencies where they have mobilized feminist consciousness for decades. Her advice is to plan, strategize holistically, and to be open to negotiations with the state and with the expectation that pietist and religious organizations will always oppose women's rights movements. She argues that "they are more powerful—there's no shame in conceding that but just don't organize naively thinking faith-based politics is benign or that their women are docile."

The Aurat March organizing committees in Hyderabad and across Sindh adhere very clearly to the vision of a secular Marxist feminism and have dealt with religious backlash deftly, defiantly, and sometimes, strategically nonconfrontationally. But in other cities, internal differences within the collectives who organize and lead the Aurat Marches had increased, and there was seemingly little consensus on the place of religion or on how to strategically relate to the state, political parties, and the legal-judicial system.

## Piety Turns Political

Women's pietist organizations had been gaining strength over decades in Pakistan but escalated in the post–9/11 period and even competed with male pietist politics. These movements have been the subject of interest of several Pakistani post-secular scholars inspired by Saba Mahmood's (2005) influential thesis that advocates how Muslim women's pietist politics must not be assessed according to the goals of Western feminism or liberal emancipatory ideals, but instead should be measured on their own terms by way of their docile agency and virtuous goals. Other post–9/11 scholars have argued for gender empowerment within the Islamic ethos (see Shehrbano Zia, 2018). These proposals were well received, celebrated, and well circulated, but the political reality in Pakistan did not align quite so conveniently (Brohi, 2006; Shehrbano Zia, 2018).

In 2018, the pious women's not-so-docile response to the first Aurat March was to reclaim the public from the "vulgar" and anti-Islamic invitation represented in the March events, which took some younger supporters by surprise (Saigol and Chaudhry, 2020). The following year, in 2019, these pious women led oppositional marches to the Aurat March with a purposeful rebuttal banner claiming, *Mera jisam Allah ki Marzi* (My Body, Allah's Choice) as opposed to Aurat March's banner, *Mera jism, Meri Marzi* (My Body, My Choice/Consent). Following the event, online obscenities targeted women participants and distorted and photoshopped images from the Aurat March events were circulated on social media. In 2019, based on meetings, dialogue, and reflection on the process, my observation was that:

> As the Aurat Marches graduate to courtrooms, legislatures, public offices, corporations, and union councils—and they must—then more backlash in the name of culture and religion can be expected. In an Islamic Republic, sexual transgressions interrupt the Islamic gendered order—there's no denying this. Supporters of feminist movements will have to be prepared for the abuse and even photo-shopped counterattacks by insecure men who cannot bear that their privilege is being challenged by mere words on a poster. (Shehrbano Zia, 2019c)

In 2020, this caution was repeated, since it seemed that the coming-of-age activists were unwilling to confront the contradictions between religious/pietist politics and their own aspiring feminism. It was not just religion, but class and gender identities that were clashing too, in sexual harassment politics in Pakistan. For the Aurat March organizers to challenge these boundaries would mean taking on fundamental differences of views on the place of sexual rights and even legal reasonings of Islamic laws. It would have required that those who lectured other feminists on the need to understand and "engage" with the supposedly benign politics of pietist or Islamist women, to ensure that these pious women were not offended or excluded by the Aurat March campaigns. Otherwise, these feminists invite criticism of doublespeak because they had accused other secular feminists of being guilty of Orientalism and other generic grandstanding allegations. In 2020, I had suggested that unless such caution was heeded, the defenders of gendered piety politics "should be prepared to swim in the pool of accusatory arsenal that casts casual accusations of Islamophobia and to which they have contributed themselves" (Shehrbano Zia, 2020, p. 55). The following year testified to this warning.

In 2021, several conservative critics of the Aurat March actively filed legal cases in courts in an attempt to thwart the annual events. Their preemptory criticism was amplified by popular script-writers and actors. The serving Prime Minister Imran Khan weighed in his disapproval and preached for the need to "weed out foreign cultural influences such as those observed in the Aurat March" (Dawn, 2020c). These conservative men and pious women reinforce the a priori categorization of sexual violence as a *social phenomenon* and the stress on *ikhlaaqiyut* (moral conduct), which shifts the burden of prevention onto women's and other vulnerable bodies' dress, pious conduct, and location, rather than on gendered social relations or the perpetrator's exercise of power.

Still, in the difficult pandemic year, the Aurat March organizers showed admirable commitment in their decision to hold their annual March events, but without any reflection on the above prevailing challenges. The event was undoubtedly watered down; the manifesto focused on noncontroversial health and pandemic-related demands (Ahmed, 2021). Prior slogans on sexual autonomies were either diluted or refuted, while the challenge to piety politics was deflected. But the appeasement did not deter the right wing—the slogans and multimedia displays were manipulated into pornographic renderings, but this time with a vicious turn, where falsified blasphemous content was planted to discredit the March. Blasphemy is an offense that carries the death penalty in Pakistan and has incited routine vigilante attacks and murders in the past, including that of the late governor of Punjab, Salmaan Taseer, and several scholars and students (HRW, 2019). A doctored audio that faked a blasphemous voice-over of the original slogans was broadcast by some mainstream media channels without verification, which led to threats of charges of blasphemy against the organizers of Aurat March—some of these were quashed, but others are being legally pursued (Farmer, 2021).

The irony in all of this punitive pietist politics is that this fetishization of female sexuality, production of erotica, prevalence of male obscenities, and distortions that lead to blasphemy accusation were the exact premise of the feminist protests. The Aurat March participants were understandably nervous—some deleted their social media accounts and erased their timelines. Others reportedly considered leaving the country. The attack was blatantly mala fide but revealed what activists have been saying for years—that Pakistan's blasphemy laws are not only weaponized for settling personal or political vendettas through false allegations, but they are tools for those faithful who claim genuine religious injury and offense. Any perceived secular demand can qualify as blasphemy.

The three antidotes to the patriarchal trinity of military-mullah-men are quite obvious—complete civilian supremacy, institutional and societal secular options, and sexual autonomies for all genders equally. Curative treatment of just one symptom simply activates collaborating patriarchal structures into rescue mode. Organizationally, the Aurat March members of each city follow their own direction, but organically, it is neither a political movement, nor a purely celebratory event or performative protest. The manifesto still does not specify an ideological framing for its demands—are these to be within Islamic reasonings and limits, or aligned with secular, universal human rights? Are they addressing the state directly or lobbying the political parties to fulfill the demands? What makes them radical, or even different from other more experienced pressure groups, such as the Women's Action Forum or the Lady Health Workers, or Home-Based Workers or labor rights groups?

The potential of the Aurat March was in moving the narrative on sexual and gendered relations in the Islamic Republic outside of the religious framing that criminalizes non-marital sex as illicit and immoral, and where any challenge to the family unit is seen as a subversion of religious commandments. The Aurat March's original agenda was to empower women to exercise sexual agency safely instead of covertly—to expose the secrecy, silence, and stigma that extend impunity for male violence practiced in these relationships. The logical progress for Aurat March politics would have been to promote the empowerment of women and the sexually marginalized to say "no"—to not just marriage, but also to sex or force within non-marital relationships, on their own terms but without taking away their sexual agency and right to engage in such relations. Kamayani Sharma (2020, n.p.) points out that sex-positivity is not about saying "yes," but that "women all through childhood and adolescence into adulthood, are never actually empowered to say 'no' on their own terms." This requires direct challenge to religious laws and strategizing for the expectant social and political backlash.

The Aurat March may host members from the sexually marginalized communities, but the platform has lost its radical edge and is unlikely to be able to foreground the theme of sexual autonomies meaningfully in the future. In wake of the former prime minister, Imran Khan's damaging comments associating women's dress with sexual violence when in office (Tariq, 2021), and the gruesome spree of murders and sexual violence in Pakistan, the Aurat March has retreated visibly and politically, and some chapters have pointedly avoided participation in subsequent protest events held in 2022. The religio-legal predilections related to Pakistan's #MeToo movement (blasphemy charges and defamation cases) have had a chilling effect on the movement.

## Conclusion

Complicated as the #MeToo movement and associated politics may be in Pakistan, it is indisputable that the movement was inspired by an international wave and empowered by a preexisting law that had broken some of the stigma and succeeded in gaining state recognition for the offense of sexual harassment. Adapted as the Aurat March events in Pakistan, the global calls for accountability on male violence and privilege were merged with prior local resistance movements. As the Indian journalist Rana Ayyub (2018) observes, "What started as a foreign import has become a moment of reckoning at home."

The Aurat March movement has uncloseted sexual harassment and other offenses on the spectrum of sexual violence against women by the medium of personal narrative and public performance. It has provided ventilation for survivors to speak out in an environment that was stifling at state and societal levels. It has cracked the taboo that sex is an illicit topic of discussion and has opened up conversations about the meaning, purpose, and methods of justice for women and sexually marginalized groups. However, it has done so without grappling with some of the preconditions listed in this chapter and probably more. Until these contradictions are addressed, the movement will likely continue to be questioned for not being inclusive or politically consistent enough. It will remain a target for the reactionary rear-guard and will be suspected by the state. The potential strength of the movement is that it focuses on social systems and gender relations, but in Pakistan this cannot be done at the expense of individual legal cases, or state and religious context, structures, and politics.

This chapter has discussed some of the characteristics and preconditions that challenge the #MeToo movement and its potential in Pakistan, including the role of celebrities and the entertainment industry; legal preconditions; the neoliberal tool of social media; performativity and concern over propriety and generational divisions; class dynamics and grassroots activism; and the perilous politics of gendered piety. It finds that the attention absorbed by cases involving celebrities and the selectivity observed by activists regarding "controversial cases" tend to divide the energies of activists and render social shaming a limited leverage in a context where legal and religious impunity shields male privilege. Given that the legal preconditions only boost this privilege—especially, by way of the criminal defamation laws and judicial biases about sex crimes—it seems that a blend of formal and informal strategies is the only strategic route to prosecute sex offenses while attending to the flaws that emerge in the testing of both mechanisms.

An added challenge is that precisely because this law is well designed[10] with implementation codes, guidelines, and training, in many cases, the sexual harassment law gets brandished as a substitute to overall gender policy and has become a single lens for all-pervasive patriarchy. Many organizations are finding it convenient to flash their compliance with this law as a badge of merit at the expense of their other discriminatory practices, including unequal pay, unfair hiring policies, maternity rights, quotas for minorities, and violations of other labor rights for men and women. The harassment law changes only one aspect of work culture, but not all the other hierarchies and unfair practices, and tends to serve as a fig leaf for other unequal workplace practices.

On the issue of legal recourse, Nivedita Menon (2019, n.p.) has accurately clarified that "due process" has never meant law alone; "A feminist practice of justice has been ready to play off eclectically, various systems of regulation against one another depending on the situation—laws against rules, rules against laws, judicial orders against government—and, when necessary, as a community, making public the violation with responsibility. All of this within the context of live feminist movements, demonstrations, protests, media campaigns—*due process* is all of this."

Regarding class dynamics associated with the #MeToo movement, Anna Sedysheva (cited by Chandra and Erlingsdóttir, 2021, p. 6), with reference to Russia, argues that complex interconnections between local, vernacular, and grassroots struggles and English-based movements operating from anglophone cultures are often tagged as "Western" and seen as a conspiracy against the local culture. In light of this, she finds the #MeToo movement has done as much harm as good. This applies to the experience of grassroots activists in Pakistan, too. The Hyderabad chapter of WAF has found that many top-down feminist initiatives carry precarious implications for local movements, which may just reproduce the generational and ideological divisions prevalent in national politics at local levels. When the Aurat March stressed sexual autonomy, feminist politics became repurposed as sexual subversion and elitist. In reaction, patriarchal structures (including "the family") are presented as a defense of religio-nationalist pride and cultural/pietist indigeneity.

The chapter concludes with the observation that the #MeToo movement would need to recalibrate its interpretive frame of reference with regard to Islamic laws and ethos in relation to their demands for sexual autonomy. Otherwise, the issue will remain stuck in the language and frame of religious morality, *ikhlaqiyaat*, socialization, and individual responsibility, rather than in the language of control, hegemony of male homosocial public space, and domination in power relations—gendered, sexual, and material. The route of feminist Quranic exegesis and reinterpreting Islamic traditions is a tried strategy that has not yielded any substantive or legal rewards in Pakistan, and the narrative benefits are dubious and easily co-opted by the right wing to empower patriarchal privilege and its anti-women agenda (Shehrbano Zia, 2018). Pious women in their individual, political, and organizational capacities are committed in their opposition to the Aurat March, and this feeds into hegemonic masculinity's fantasy playbook of women fighting other women. Despite a valiant effort, for now, the victory belongs to the anti–Aurat March agitators and leaves the #MeToo movement in Pakistan in a very precarious position.

## Notes

1. This Act of Parliament was published in the Gazette of Pakistan (Extraordinary), Pt. I, on March 11, 2010 (pp. 63–74). Originally a Federal law, the subject was devolved to the provinces by virtue of 18th Amendment in the Constitution in 2011, after which it has been adapted, with amendments, by each of the four provinces of Pakistan. A gazette copy can be found here: https://ndu.edu.pk/temp/PROTECTION_AGAINST_HARASSMENT_OF_WOMEN_ACT_2010.pdf. Workplace committees and special ombudspersons have been mandated through the Act for hearing complaints.
2. One of these was the disputed Zina Law under the Hudood Ordinances (1979), which criminalized adultery and sex outside of marriage and conflated it with rape, before its procedural applications were amended in 2006 under the Women's Protection Act. See Khan (2006) cited below.
3. European Parliamentary Questions, February 28, 2019, https://www.europarl.europa.eu/doceo/document/E-8-2019-001104_EN.html.
4. *Dawn* (2017), November 1, https://www.dawn.com/news/1367504/can-of-worms#comments.
5. Chinoy later explained her tweet but stood by it; see *Dawn* (2018), "My Tweet Wasn't Meant to Suggest Privilege: Sharmeen Obaid Breaks Silence on Harassment Claim," December 13, https://images.dawn.com/news/1178725.
6. Pakistan Penal Code (Act XLV of 1860) Act XLV of 1860, http://www.pakistani.org/pakistan/legislation/1860/actXLVof1860.html. This was amended in 2020 to include defamation of the Armed Forces of Pakistan, http://www.na.gov.pk/uploads/documents/1600179373_877.pdf.
7. Meesha and others have challenged the criminal charge against them before the Lahore High Court for its quashment on the ground that invoking criminal defamation under section 20 of PECA is a blatant attempt to silence a victim of sexual harassment. Hina Jilani, a leading human rights lawyer, is representing them with a legal team. They have also sought to declare Section 20 of PECA as unconstitutional and in violation of the fundamental right of free speech, and which has been weaponized by the government against journalists, activists, and other critical voices.
8. Even the military establishment of Pakistan maintains social media accounts for public relations purposes and for pushing state narratives—one army officer who handled the Twitter account of the armed forces would regularly spar with journalists, feminists, and human rights activists who challenged hyper-nationalism or were critical of the state, for which he gained the status of a social media celebrity (Hussain 2020).

9. This generational difference has been observed by several commentators across the world. Jun (2021) summarizes the commonalities in her assessment on how "Chinese feminists can be divided into two generations—the first emerging in the 1990s and the second around 2010—based on their relationship with the State, status, resources, and mobilisation paradigms. The older generation relies on the status of experts and interpersonal networks within the system, embedding issues related to gender equality and women's rights into the government's agenda. By contrast, younger feminists tend to turn to commercial mass media and adopt diverse channels such as drama, art exhibitions, and the internet to promote feminist agendas to the public" (p. 344). Chandra and Erlingsdóttir (2021) discuss the divisions between older generation feminists and younger women who dispute "the desirability of the strategies of triage or guerrilla warfare resorted to by the vulnerable who felt disenfranchised by the systems of due process already in place" (p. 4) and cite Moira Donegan's classification of this rift as one between social and individualist feminists and system and individual reform.
10. Legal experts have been critical of the law for its omissions, but it has been designed with implementation in mind, and so it is packaged with guidelines which make it easy to adapt in institutions.

## Works Cited

Abu-Lughod, Lila. 2002. "Do Muslim Women Really Need Saving? Anthropological Reflections on Cultural Relativism and Its Others." *American Anthropologist New Series* 104, no. 3: 783–790.

Ahmed, Umaima R. 2021. "'Aurat March' 2021 Presents Feminist Healthcare Manifesto in Pakistan." *Global Voices*, March 14. https://globalvoices.org/2021/03/14/aurat-march-2021-presents-feminist-healthcare-manifesto-in-pakistan/.

Ayyub, Rana. 2018. "In India, Women Are No Longer Prepared to Stay Silent." *The Guardian*, October 21. www.theguardian.com/commentisfree/2018/oct/21/india-women-silent-metoo-movement-battle.

Aziz, Farieha. 2018. "Pakistan's Cybercrime Law: Boon or Bane?" *Heinrich Boll Stiftung*, February 14. https://www.boell.de/en/2018/02/07/pakistans-cybercrime-law-boon-or-bane.

*BBC News*. 2018. "Meesha Shafi: Pakistan Actress Says Pop Star Ali Zafar Harassed Her." April 20. https://www.bbc.com/news/world-asia-43836364.

Brohi, Nazish. 2006. "The MMA Offensive: Three Years in Power 2003–05." Monograph. Islamabad: Action Aid International.

Chandra, Giti, and Irma Erlingsdóttir, eds. 2021. *The Routledge Handbook of the Politics of the #MeToo Movement*. New York: Routledge.

Dad, Nighat. 2016. "Online Harassment in Pakistan—and How Women Are Fighting Back." *Amnesty International*, January 11. https://www.amnesty.org/en/latest/campaigns/2016/01/online-harassment-in-pakistan-and-how-women-are-fighting-back/.

David, Mirela Violeta. 2021. "#MeToo in Post-Socialist Countries: A Comparative Analysis of Romanian and Chinese Feminist Activism against Sexual Violence." In *The*

*Routledge Handbook of the Politics of the #MeToo Movement*, edited by Giti Chandra and Irma Erlingsdóttir, pp. 343–359. New York: Routledge.

*Dawn*. 2017. "My Tweet Wasn't Meant to Suggest Privilege: Sharmeen Obaid Breaks Silence on Harassment Claims." December 13.

*Dawn*. 2019. "Poet Kishwar Naheed Slammed the Aurat March, and Then Twitter Slammed Her." March 13. https://images.dawn.com/news/1182047.

*Dawn*. 2020a. "Meesha, Eight Others Booked over Vilification of Ali Zafar." September 29. https://www.dawn.com/news/1582156.

*Dawn*. 2020b. "Women's Rights Activists Urge Govt to Rethink Ali Zafar's Pride of Performance Award." August 20. https://www.dawn.com/news/1575475.

*Dawn*. 2020c. "PM Imran Khan Says Aurat March Is a Result of Cultural Differences like It's a Bad Thing." March 14. https://images.dawn.com/news/1184828.

Ellis-Peterson, Hannah. 2021. "Pakistan's #MeToo Movement Hangs in the Balance over Celebrity Case." *The Guardian*, January 1. https://www.theguardian.com/global-development/2021/jan/01/pakistans-metoo-movement-hangs-in-the-balance-over-celebrity-case.

Farmer, Ben. 2021. "Online Blasphemy Smear Campaign Threatens Pakistan's Women's Day Marchers." *The Telegraph*, March 12. https://www.telegraph.co.uk/global-health/women-and-girls/online-blasphemy-smear-campaign-threatens-pakistans-womens-day/.

*Geo News*. 2019. "Women's Action Forum Calls for Decriminalising Defamation, Says Law Used as 'Silencing Tool.'" https://www.geo.tv/latest/245870-pakistan-womens-group-says-defamation-being-used-to-silence-survivors-metoo-cases.

Hayat, Arif, and Ali Akbar. 2019. "KP Assembly Unanimously Passes Resolution against Aurat March, Terming It 'Shameful.'" *Dawn*, March 20. https://www.dawn.com/news/1470834.

Hussain, Abid. 2020. "Pakistan Two-Star General: Farewell to a Social Media Celebrity." *BBC News*, January 18. https://www.bbc.com/news/world-asia-51148762.

Jan, Orya Maqbool. 2019. "Women What Do You Want: Sigmund Freud." *YouTube*, March 11. https://www.youtube.com/watch?v=3Oto9joC-sM&t=24s.

Jun, Li. 2021. "In the Name of #RiceBunny; Legacy, Strategy, and Efficacy of the Chinese #MeToo Movement." In *The Routledge Handbook of the Politics of the #MeToo Movement*, edited by Giti Chandra and Irma Erlingsdóttir, pp. 343–359. New York: Routledge.

Khan, Maryam S., and Farieha Aziz. 2022. The "Defamation Backlash": Law and the Feminist Movement in Pakistan. In *Handbook on Law & Social Movements*, edited by Steven Boutcher, Corey Shdaimah, Michael Yarbrough. Forthcoming. https://ssrn.com/abstract=4258714 or http://dx.doi.org/10.2139/ssrn.4258714.

Khan, Shahnaz. 2006. *Zina, Transformational Feminism and the Moral Regulation of Pakistani Women*. Islamabad: Oxford University Press.

Mahmood, Saba. 2005. *Politics of Piety: The Islamic Revival and the Feminist Subject*. Princeton, NJ: Princeton University Press.

Malkani, Sara. 2019. "Criminal Defamation," *Dawn*, September 21. https://www.dawn.com/news/1506467.

Menon, Nivedita. 2019. "How the Feminist Conversation Around Sexual Harassment Has Evolved." *The Wire*, February 28. https://thewire.in/women/how-the-feminist-conversation-around-sexual-harassment-has-evolved.

Nagarai, Anuradha. 2021. "Lawsuits Seen Having "Chilling Effect" on #MeToo Movements in South Asia." *Thomson Reuters Foundation News*, February 19. https://news.trust.org/item/20210219131935-xns59/.

Okeowo, Alexis. 2018. "An Activist Filmmaker Tackles Patriarchy in Pakistan." *The New Yorker*, April 2. https://www.newyorker.com/magazine/2018/04/09/an-activist-filmmaker-tackles-patriarchy-in-pakistan.

"Pakistan: End Ordeal for 'Blasphemy' Defendants." 2019. *Human Rights Watch*, October 6. https://www.hrw.org/news/2019/10/06/pakistan-end-ordeal-blasphemy-defendants.

Raza, Talal. 2019. "Understanding Hatred against #Aurat March in Pakistan." *Digital Rights Monitor*, March 19. https://digitalrightsmonitor.pk/understanding-hatred-agai nst-auratmarch-inpakistan/.

Sabeeh, Maheen. 2018. "I've Done the Thing I Feared and I've Taken the Leap of Faith: Meesha Shafi." *Instep Today, The News*, April 21. https://www.then ews.com.pk/magazine/instep-today/307339-ive-done-the-thing-i-fea red-and-ive-taken-the-leap-of-faith.

Saigol, Rubina, and Nida Usman Chaudhry. 2020. *Contradictions and Ambiguities of Feminism in Pakistan: Exploring the Fourth Wave*. Monograph. Islamabad: Friedrich Ebert Stiftung. http://library.fes.de/pdf-files/bueros/pakistan/17334.pdf.

Sharma, Kamayani. 2020. "#MeToo: Understanding Consent and Sex-Positivity in a Patriarchal Society." *Firstpost*, November 12. www.firstpost.com/long-reads/metoo-understanding-consent-and-sex-positivity-in-a-patriarchal-society-5535191.html.

Shehrbano Zia, Afiya. 2014. "Freedoms and Bans in the Politics of Contemporary Pakistan," *Economic and Political Weekly* XLIX, no. 34 (August 23). https://subscript ion.epw.in/journal/2014/34/commentary/freedoms-and-bans-politics-contempor ary-pakistan.html.

Shehrbano Zia, Afiya. 2017. "Can of Worms." *Dawn*, November 1. https://www.dawn. com/news/1367504/can-of-worms.

Shehrbano Zia, Afiya. 2018. *Faith and Feminism in Pakistan; Religious Agency or Secular Autonomy?* Brighton, UK: Sussex Academic Press.

Shehrbano Zia, Afiya. 2019a. "Sex and Secularism as Resistance Politics." In *Rethinking Pakistan: A 21st Century Perspective*, edited by Bilal Zahoor and Raza Rumi, pp. 197–208. Lahore: Folio Books.

Shehrbano Zia, Afiya. 2019b. "Defiance not Convenience." In *Gender, Governance and Islam*, edited by Deniz Kandiyoti, Nadje Al-Ali, and Kathryn Spellman Poots, pp. 165–185. Edinburg: Edinburgh University Press.

Shehrbano Zia, Afiya. 2019c. "Propriety and Protest." *The News on Sunday*, March 17. https://www.thenews.com.pk/tns/detail/567418-propriety-protest.

Shehrbano Zia, Afiya. 2020. "Who's Afraid of Pakistan's Aurat March?" *Economic and Political Weekly* 55, no. 8 (February 22). https://www.epw.in/journal/2020/8/special-articles/who-afraid-pakistans-aurat-march.html.

Shehzad, Seerat. 2019. "Little, Insecure People." *Daily Times*, March 12. https://dailytimes. com.pk/364279/littleinsecure-people/.

Tariq, Soofia. 2021. "Outrage after Pakistan PM Imran Khan Blames Rape Crisis on Women." *The Guardian*, June 25. https://www.theguardian.com/world/2021/jun/25/ outrage-after-pakistan-pm-imran-khan-blames-crisis-on-women.

Zahra-Malik, Mehreen. 2019. "Pakistan Torn as Women's Day March Sparks Wave of 'Masculine Anxiety.'" *The Guardian*, March 15. https://www.theguardian.com/world/ 2019/mar/15/pakistan-torn-as-womens-day-march-sparkswave-of-masculine-anxiety.

# 12

# #MosqueMeToo and Muslim Cultures

*Ayesha Murtza and Atiya Murtaza*

## Timeline

- Nineteenth century: modern Islamic feminism started as a movement.
- 1899: Qasim Amin published *Women's Liberation*, an influential book for women's movements in the Arab world.
- 1993: Leila Ahmed critiqued Amin's book for being androcentric.
- 1994: Amina Wadud delivered a Friday *khutbah* (or, according to some, a pre-*khutbah* sermon) in Cape Town, South Africa—a task that women were not allowed to perform.
- 2005: Amina Wadud led a Friday prayer for a mixed-gender congregation in the United States, much to the dislike of most Muslim leaders.
- Twenty-first century: Amina Wadud categorized Islamic feminist scholars into three generations: first-generation scholars: Riffat Hassan, Fatema Mernissi, Aisha Abd al-Rehman, Leila Ahmed; second-generation scholars: Kecia Ali, Sa'diyya Shaykh, Asmaa Barlas; a new generation: Jerusha Lamptey and Aishah Hidayyatullah.
- 2018: #MosqueMeToo began.

## Introduction

In 2018, Sabika Khan, a Pakistani woman, shared via a Facebook post that she was sexually assaulted several times during Hajj,[1] which is one of the five pillars of Islam, in Mecca, the holiest place for Muslims. She prefaced her post with "I was afraid to share this because it might hurt your religious sentiments." Soon after, she deleted her post for unknown reasons. Her post read:

> While performing my *tawaaf* around the Kaaba after *isha* prayer, something really weird happened. It was my 3rd *tawaaf*,[2] and I felt a hand on my waist. I thought it was just an innocent mistake. I completely ignored. Then . . . I felt it again. It made me feel very uncomfortable. . . . During my 6th *tawaf* I suddenly

Ayesha Murtza and Atiya Murtaza, *#MosqueMeToo and Muslim Cultures* In: *The Other #MeToos*. Edited by: Iqra Shagufta Cheema, Oxford University Press. © Oxford University Press 2023. DOI: 10.1093/oso/9780197619872.003.0012

> felt something aggressively poking my butt, I froze, unsure of whether it was intentional. I ignored and just kept moving slowly because the crowd was huge. I even tried to turn around but woefully couldn't. When I reached the Yemeni corner, someone tried to grab and pinch my butt. I decided to stop there. Grabbed his hand and threw it off me *couldn't move or turn around*. I was literally petrified. Couldn't even escape, so I stood, and turned around as much as I could, to see what's happening, I turned around but . . . couldn't see who it was. I felt so violated. I felt unable to speak out. Stayed quiet because I knew no one would trust me, or nobody would take it seriously, except my mum. So, I told her everything when I returned to the hotel room. She was incredibly confused and devastated. After this incident, she never allowed me to go there again alone. It's sad to say that you are not even safe at holy places. I've been harassed, not once, not twice, but thrice. My entire experience at the holy city is overshadowed by this horrible incident. I believe *it's totally okay and important to be open about harassment* [emphasis added]. Don't know how many of you had a similar experience there but this incident has unfortunately left me feeling upset.[3]

Unsurprisingly, Muslims were upset about Khan's post: some because Muslim men desecrated the Ka'aba by assaulting Muslim women while the women believers were performing the mandatory pilgrimage, and some because they believed that Khan maligned and disparaged Islam and Muslim men in the non-Muslim communities by sharing her experience of sexual abuse at the Ka'aba. These remain the two big camps when it comes to conversations about sexual violence in Muslim religious communities. Muslim women with similar experiences of abuse condemned these incidents, and most Muslim men refused to believe Khan's experience or bashed her for publicizing it. But despite negative community responses, more women started sharing their experiences of sexual abuse at holy places. Later in 2018, an Egyptian-American feminist, Mona Eltahawy, learned of Khan's post, which led Eltahawy to share her own experience of sexual abuse at the Ka'aba. Using the hashtag #MosqueMeToo, she shared that she too was sexually assaulted during Hajj in 1982, when she was only fifteen years old.

After Eltahawy's tweet about her experience, #MosqueMeToo soon started trending and became transnational, with more than 2,000 people sharing her tweet in 24 hours. Multiple Muslim women across the Muslim world started using #MosqueMeToo to share their experiences of assault, most of which had occurred during *tawaf* and in the queue leading to the *Black Stone*. Other twitter users shared: ". . . I had virtually the same experience during Hajj in 2010"; "I had the same encounter when I was trying to touch the Holy walls of Kaaba, a man groped me. Later, I was verbally tortured by another Muslim man there. . . .

Envision, being sexually assaulted in front of Allah's house . . . "; "it was someone else's hands, which nudged me when I was trying to touch the Holy black stone"; "one of my friends had a similar experience . . . you would expect this to happen anywhere but in Mecca. I've never been able to make sense of it, people are meant to be in their purest form during Hajj." Dr. Lina Abirafeh, director of Women's Studies in the Arab World, pointed out that the hashtag #MosqueMeToo has spread in Saudi Arabia, and women are coming out and talking about their issues of sexual violence and abuse in religious spaces, but it still related to a specific class of women because of societal pressure.[4] #MosqueMeToo was shared in Arabic, Spanish, Urdu, Turkish, Hindi, Persian, French, and other languages. Muslim men, and some women, were enraged at the women sharing these experiences despite their personal testimonies. They refuted the tweets shared under the hashtag #MosqueMeToo, accusing these women of serving as tools for Islamophobia and Western propaganda to further defame Muslim men and Islam.

Analyzing the hashtag #MosqueMeToo and its relationship with the #MeToo movement, this chapter argues that #MosqueMeToo shows that Muslim women's religious practices or beliefs are separate from their experiences of being women in Muslim communities. The chapter further unveils imprecise arguments that women are sexually abused and violated because of their physical appearance, their detachment from Islam, their immodest behaviors—arguments that are unequivocally used by a large majority of Muslim men, women, and legislative/governmental bodies to shame, blame, or disbelieve victims of sexual violence. For this argument, I employ feminist scholarship and feminist exegesis of the Quran by Amina Wadud and Lila Abu-Lughod, along with the tweets shared under #MosqueMeToo on Twitter. This chapter locates #MosqueMeToo in the global #MeToo conversations to examine the relationship between gender, religion, culture, and the politics of these in complex religious Muslim patriarchies.

## #MosqueMeToo and Muslim Cultures

Before tweeting about her experience at Ka'aba, Eltahawy had described her experience in her book, *Headscarves and Hymens: Why the Middle East Needs a Sexual Revolution* (2015). She wrote:

> I could not understand how, at this holiest of holy places, the place we all turned to when we prayed, someone could think to stick his hand on my ass and to keep it there until I managed to squirm away. He was persistent. Whenever I broke free, he persisted in groping my ass. I burst into tears because that's all

I could do. I did not have it in me to tell my parents the truth, so I told them the crowds were getting to me. (p. 50)

The experiences also show that sexual abuse at the Ka'aba has been going on for a long time and probably has only worsened because women never spoke about it or reported it. Those who did choose to report would have to report the abuse to the same men who assaulted them or who were guilty of committing similar acts of abuse. Besides her first experience, Eltahawy shared that she was assaulted a second time during the same Hajj by a Saudi police officer, when she and her mother were kissing the Black Stone:[5]

A Saudi policeman who was standing there signaled to the men to wait while we kissed the stone. As I bent toward the stone, the same policeman surreptitiously groped my breast. Surreptitiously: I came to learn during my years in Saudi Arabia and then in Egypt that this was how most men did it. That's how they got at your body—so surreptitiously that you ended up questioning your own sense of having been violated; your disgust at what happened. . . .

While Muslim communities are not monolithic, their patterns of sexual and gender-based violence in religious patriarchies remain similar, as the discussions in some other chapters in this volume evidence. According to a United Nations Women's report (2020) on the Arab States, the rate of sexual and gender-based violence in some countries is as high as 70%, with some forms of violence like street harassment being even higher. According to the same report, 6 out of 10 survivors of sexual and gender-based violence choose to remain silent rather than reporting the violence. A study conducted in 2013 in Egypt by the United Nations showed that of all the cases of violence, 99% were reported by women and girls, with more than 83% saying they feel insecure when out of their houses. Overall, only 6.5% out of 99% of women felt comfortable reporting their cases of sexual abuse to the police amidst of shame and fear (Schultz, 2014). Rothna Begum, a women's right researcher in North Africa and the Middle East for the *Human Rights Watch Wing*, confirms that "given the taboo nature of sexual harassment, women are probably not reporting this" ( Gharib, 2018, n.p.). Even Eltahawy shared the utter hopelessness of reporting sexual violence:

If a policeman standing next to the Ka'aba in Mecca gropes my breast, what chance do I stand of complaining and getting anything done about it?. . . If a policeman who tells the men to stand aside so that women can kiss the Blackstone unhindered gropes my breast there, right next to the holiest site for Muslims, what chance do I or other women stand of fighting violations of our bodies? (2015, p. 51)

In this deplorable condition of reports of sexual and gender violence, social media platforms like Twitter and Facebook become virtual platforms of solidarity. Additionally, they also serve as spaces for women to support each other and openly talk about stigma around reporting violence (Manikonda et al., 2018). A study at the Qatar Computing Research Institute found that countries where women face a high rate of gender violation and hegemonic masculine attitudes in their offline life have a significant presence on social media platforms. For instance, in Pakistan, women on average have more followers on Twitter (600 versus 222) and on Google+ (25 versus 16) in comparison with their male counterparts (Weber, 2014, n.p.). This is despite gender disparity in internet access. For example, 56% of women in Arab States had access to the internet, as opposed to 68% of the male population,[6] while this ratio was 24% to 35% in Africa.[7] This already debilitating disparity in internet access poses a challenge to women using social media, along with the fact that the higher number of women's followers is in itself an indication of the objectification and sexualization of women. Women have to exercise more caution when sharing/reporting these experiences on social media. When women do report these cases to law enforcement agencies or via social media, legislative bodies, as well as other citizens across the Muslim world, resort to victim blaming or perceiving the victim as sexually perverted. These factors point toward the need for an intersectional approach since the issue has been spread across multiple Muslim countries that each have their own widely different historical, cultural, social, and religious histories.

A transnational and intersectional feminist approach provides a better understanding of sexual and gender violence highlighted via #MosqueMeToo, as women are "constituted as women" through various intersecting components like class, caste, ethnicity, race, education, religion, religious sects (Robin, 1984; Wadud, 1999; Mohanty, 2002; Herr, 2014). Even though various transnational and third world feminists call for attention to the role of the nation-state in women's oppression, #MosqueMeToo serves as a unifying platform for solidarity to all victims of gender and sexual violence in which religion plays a role. Muslim feminist scholars play a key role in these conversations about women, gender roles, and Islam. These writers accentuate the various intersectional aspects of this problem and explore its place in feminist movements and its role for feminist causes in the Muslim world to, eventually, enable people to understand the magnitude of the issue (Rodino-Colocino, 2018). But this magnitude does not mean a solution to the problem since these feminist scholars themselves are usually criticized and called imperial feminists, religious dictators, Islamophobes, traitors, and native informants by Muslim men.

Muslim women then must choose between loyalty to Islam and their nation (which really only translates into unconditional protection of men) or their safety and humanity. Despite an increase in these conversations, most men fail to recognize the wave of #MuslimMeToo as a call for self-reflection and behavioral rectification. Eltahawy also tweeted in light of Tariq Ramadan rape accusations,[8] "Muslim women are caught between a rock and a hard place: between Islamophobes & racists who want to demonize all Muslim men and a community that wants to defend all Muslim men. Most of the time women are worried about speaking out as it will give a chance to the general public to further blame Muslims."[9] A man tweeted in response to these conversations to say that due to the rise in such cases of assault, it is time to realize why Islam has put distance between men and women and that the main cause behind such incidents is the so-called modernism in which its nearly impossible to draw a line between the issue of harassment and flirting.[10] These responses further highlight the impossibility of any positive change at the institutional or state level anytime soon. In *Women, Islam and the State* (1991), Deniz Kandiyoti notes that "the plight of fallen Muslim women is admittedly, an extreme illustration of the constraining influence of social values on the state action. Social conditioning and no state initiative were the more pronounced factors shaping attitude towards women" (p. 88).[11] In 2012, only one case of sexual harassment was registered in Pakistan, which rose up to 25–38 the next year, and in 2016, around 134 cases were filed. In the following six years, a sudden 197 percent rise in cases was witnessed.[12] Thus the implications of proper legal actions and awareness about such cases is the dire need of the time.

On the other hand, along with improper legal actions, the other main cause behind such criticism toward women's sexual experiences is the abuse and interpretation of Islamic laws and practices. According to them, by following Islamic rituals, sharia, and values, women can save themselves from sexual harassment. Najeed Sayed (2018, n.p.) says: "using religion to induce a secondary harm is a form of dehumanization that creates permanent outsidership. There is no welcoming community after this."[13] Fatima Mernissi, in her book *The Veil and The Male Elite: A Feminists Interpretation of Women Right's in Islam* (1992),[14] also talks about Islamic laws which are misused by Muslim men when it comes to conversations about the relationship between Muslim women and men and women's rights in Muslim society. She rhetorically asks, "how did the tradition succeed in transforming the Muslim woman into that submissive, marginal creature who buries herself and only goes out into the world timidly and huddled in her veils? Why do the Muslim men need such a mutilated companion?" (p. 194). This far, Muslim feminist scholars have highlighted the urgency of this issue by talking about the impetus behind sexual violence against women. As feminism became more mainstream, a debate ensued regarding the role of Islamic values, Quranic verses, and Hadith in women's rights in the past few years in Muslim heteropatriarchies.

Culturally, Muslim women are not only expected to perform religious rituals more than Muslim men, but selected readings of these religious texts are also frequently invoked to increase Muslim heteropatriarchies. These rituals range from covering one's head to submitting to the will of men in the household. If women are not fully covered, that implies that they are irreligious and are not following the *true* teachings of Islam—hence they are termed immoral. Men believe that women demean themselves by not following the Islamic dictates and turning themselves into the objects of male sexual desire. Many men read an uncovered head or revealing clothes of a woman as her consent for a sexual encounter, thereby discarding respect and consent. Ironically, men refuse to consider their own divergence from Islamic dictates when they look at a woman, assault her, or make unwanted advances toward her. In Ka'aba, all women are covered from head to toe and no part of their body is visible. Neither do women try to seduce men in the house of Allah. But they still get attacked, not only by ordinary Muslims but also by Saudi policemen. Eltahawy was in hijab when she was assaulted. Thereby, she affirms that her dress did not have anything to do with sexual assault. She further shares: "I wore hijab for 9 years and I lost count of how many times I was sexually assaulted, while dressed that way. Men are responsible for sexual assault, not the wardrobe."[15]

University of Michigan's Institute for Social Research conducted a survey regarding women's dress code in the seven most populated Muslim countries: Iraq, Saudi Arabia, Tunisia, Turkey, Pakistan, Egypt, and Lebanon. A card, showing six dress codes for women, was showed to men to ask about their preferences regarding women's clothing. Dresses on the card included options from a burqa-clad woman with a veil on her face to a woman with her head uncovered. The results showed that men prefer women to dress conservatively. Muslim men in most of these countries preferred women to cover themselves completely from head to toe, with only their face visible (Poushter, 2014). In Lebanon and Turkey, men expressed they were okay with women not covering their heads in public. Besides that, Asia-Pacific nations had the second most countries with incidents where women are harassed for violating the dress codes. Even academic institutions, where usually men hold administrative positions of power, prescribe specific dress codes for women.[16] This demonstrates the underlying perceptions that becomes the reasons for sexual and gender violence in Muslim countries. In this situation, many women choose to cover themselves not for religious reasons, but for sociocultural attitudes where they feel the need to perform an outwardly pious subjectivity.

The downside of these conversations about women's clothing is that women's humanity gets erased, and the focus affectively shifts to the cultural structures and men. Lila Abu-Lughod, in *Do Muslim Women Need Saving?*, notes that international societies attempt to save the female Muslim bodies because they assume Muslim women to be oppressed (2013). Chandra Mohanty, in *Feminism Without Borders*, also challenges the monolithic assumption of Western women writers about third world women, saying "neither Western feminist discourse nor Western feminist political practice is singular or homogenous in its goals, interest, or analyses" (2003, p. 17). She further points to the ethnocentric attitude that leads to monolithic interpretation of hijab in Muslim societies. Though it is legally mandated in Afghanistan, Saudi Arabia, and Iran, it remains a voluntary action in most other Muslim countries.

Besides Lila Abu-Lughod and Chandra Mohanty, multiple other Muslim scholars have also pointed to the various ways in which Muslim women's bodies are represented in political discourse and media (Ziaba Mir-Hosseini, Leila Ahmed, and Deniz Kandiyoti). Mostly, Muslim women are regarded as a political tool between two different political parties, neither of which have much concern for women's agency. Muslim women are then "only acknowledged to the extent that they can be used as a rhetorical tool. Islamophobia and misogyny are carried out on the back of Muslim survivors of sexual violence without any regard for their actual well-being, mental health and safety. Their experience and stories get lost, swallowed up by political noise" (Grabill and Minister, 2019, p. 81). #MosqueMeToo, then, gave Muslim women the chance and voice to take control of their own narratives and share their experiences.

## Conclusion

#MosqueMeToo helped highlight the pervasiveness of sexual harassment during Hajj, which came as a shock to many but also made them realize the gravity of the issues of gender and sexual violence. Saba Ghori, the president of the *Peaceful Families Project*, considers the #MosqueMeToo movement as an awakening message for women who are afraid of talking openly about their issues. She shares that they are working specifically toward ending gender-based harassment or violence specifically in Muslim families through various academic programs and workshops. Furthermore, they seek help from Muslim men and imams to help women to speak out and ask for justice.[17]As Eltahawy herself observes, "Saudi Arabia should give the authority to the Imam of the Mecca to give sermons to the whole Muslim ummah about this heinous crime and warn them that it's an act of brutality to harass a woman and everyone must restrain from it." She further proposes that "Saudi police should also help women in this regard and must handle their complaints properly without assaulting them," as the second time she herself was assaulted by a policeman in Mecca (Gharib, 2018, n.p.). In this situation, it is compulsory to also mobilize the revisionists readings of the Quran to popularize more nuanced, alternative exegesis and interpretations of Quranic texts so the more egalitarian and equitable teachings of Islam may be highlighted.

For example, Amina Wadud's *Quran and Women: Reading the Sacred Text from a Woman's Perspective* (1999) offers such an alternative reading of the Quran that challenges the patriarchal interpretation of Quranic texts. Wadud highlights the problems with insistence upon a singular interpretation of the Quran to advocate for room for multiple interpretation according to the varying Muslim cultural contexts to accommodate diversity. It is vital for people to invoke and popularize these readings to promote gender parity. #MosqueMeToo, then, proved vital in creating awareness around these problems. Often when confronted by the rise in gender and sexual violence, many practicing Muslims shift the blame on abandonment of religious practices by Muslim communities in Muslim states. These proclamations are particularly ineffective in the case of #MosqueMeToo because both the victims and perpetrators were present at the Ka'aba especially for performance of a mandated religious duty.

#MosqueMeToo, by becoming a platform for Muslim women transnationally, highlights the extent of sexual violence and its relationship with Islamic teachings. By doing so, it emphasizes the need for legislative changes as well as behavioral transformation both toward women and Islam in Muslim communities. This is a call for Muslim communities to reconsider the connections between Islam, modesty, women's practice of their Islam, and gender and sexual violence in heteropatriarchal Muslim communities. It is about time that people acknowledge each other as human beings who are equally worthy of respect and dignity, and change their belief that physical appearance, detachment from Islam, unvirtuousness, and neglecting religious values have anything to do with the victims of sexual abuse. #MosqueMeToo, then, helps undo the mistaken assumption that sexual and gender violence is caused by not adhering to Islamic teachings. Muslim scholars and Muslim leaders play the most important role in further destabilizing these wrong perceptions and offering alternative, corrective interpretation of the Quran. Reworking and reinterpreting the Quran and other Muslim texts for more egalitarian and more equitable readings of gender to promote human agency and consent are vital for rectifying the issues of gender and sexual violence in Muslim communities.

## Notes

1. Hajj is a five-day pilgrimage undertaken by about 2.5 million Muslims each year. It is one of the five pillars of Islam and a mandatory religious duty for every Muslim who can afford it. The Quran says: "And Hajj (pilgrimage to Mecca) to the House (Ka'aba) is a duty that mankind owes to Allah, those who can afford the expenses

(for conveyance, provision, and residence); and whoever disbelieves (i.e., denies Hajj, then he is a disbeliever of Allah), then Allah stands not in need of any of the worlds" (Qur'an 3:97). For further reading: S. A. Nigosian, *Islam: Its History, Teaching, and Practices* (Bloomington, Indiana: Indiana University Press, 2004).

2. Walking contraclockwise around the Ka'aba seven times, each circle starts with touching, kissing, or pointing toward the Black Stone.
3. Taslima Nasreen, "Women Reveal the Sexual Harassment They Face Even on Haj," March 20, 2018, https://theprint.in/opinion/women-reveal-sexual-harassment-face-even-haj/43222/, viewed September 14, 2021.
4. Masood Hina, "A #MeToo-Like Wave Is Taking the Middle East by Storm. Here's Why it Matters," *Statecraft*, September 2020, https://www.statecraft.co.in/article/a-metoo-like-wave-is-taking-the-middle-east-by-storm-here-s-why-it-matters.
5. The Black Stone has been a revered piece since before Islam. After the conquest of Mecca in 630, Prophet Muhammad (PBUH) is said to have ridden round the Ka'aba seven times on his camel, touching the Black Stone as a gesture of reverence. Muslims touch or kiss the stone emulating the tradition set by the prophet, while chanting "God is the greatest."
6. https://www.statista.com/statistics/491387/gender-distribution-of-internet-users-region/.
7. https://www.statista.com/statistics/491387/gender-distribution-of-internet-users-region/.
8. A Muslim Swiss nationalist, a writer, scholar, and professor of contemporary Islamic Studies at St Antony College, Oxford, in February 2018 he was accused of raping two disabled women.
9. @monaeltahawy, May 28, 2020, "Muslim women are caught between a rock & . . . ," https://twitter.com/monaeltahawy/status/1266083219922968576?s=20.
10. Further reading: *Rape Culture and Religious Studies* (2019) by Rhiannon Graybill, Meredith and Beatrice (Lexington Books, 2019).
11. See Kandiyoti (1991), *Women, Islam and the State*, chapter 4, Ayesha Jalal, "The Convivence of Subservience: Women and the State of Pakistan."
12. See "Sexual Harassment: Pakistan's Tipping Point?" Nazish Brohi, May 6, 2018, https://www.dawn.com/news/1405703.
13. "Muslim #MeToo Isn't Just a Man Problem. It's Also a Male-Led Theology Problem," October 2018, https://religionnews.com/2018/10/26/muslim-metoo-doesnt-have-a-man-problem-it-has-a-male-theology-problem/.
14. For further reading, see Mernissi (1992), *The Veil and The Male Elite: A Feminist Interpretation of Women's Rights in Islam*.
15. @monaeltahawy, "And also: I was in hijab. The way you dress . . . ," *Twitter*, February 2018, https://twitter.com/monaeltahawy/status/960654844066516992?s=20.
16. "Women in Many Countries Face Harassment for Clothing Deemed Too Religious—or Too Secular," December 2016, https://www.pewresearch.org/fact-tank/2020/12/16/women-in-many-countries-face-harassment-for-clothing-deemed-too-religi ous-or-too-secular/.
17. Malaka Gharib, "#MosqueMeToo Gives Muslim Women a Voice about Sexual Misconduct at Mecca," *NPR*, February 2018, https://www.npr.org/sections/goatsands

oda/2018/02/26/588855132/-mosquemetoo-gives-muslim-women-a-voice-about-sexual-misconduct-at-mecca.

## Works Cited

@monaeltahawy (Mona Eltahawy). 2018. "It's imperative to emphasize that I was sexually assaulted during . . . ," Twitter, January 5, 5:10 p.m. https://twitter.com/monaeltahawy/status/960651936352686083?s=20.

@monaeltahawy (Mona Eltahawy). 2021. "It's imperative to emphasize . . . ," February 5, 2018. Mona Eltahawy. Twitter. https://twitter.com/monaeltahawy/status/960651936352686083.

Abu-Lughod, Lila. 2013. *Do Muslim Women Need Saving?* Cambridge, MA: Harvard University Press.

Eltahawy, Mona. 2015. *Headscarves and Hymens: Why the Middle East Needs a Sexual Revolution*. New York: Farrar, Straus and Giroux.

Eltahawy, Mona. 2018. "#MosqueMeToo: What Happened When I Was Sexually Assaulted during the Hajj." *Washington Post*, February 15. https://www.washingtonpost.com/news/global-opinions/wp/2018/02/15/mosquemetoo-what-happened-when-i-was-sexually-assaulted-during-the-hajj/.

Gharib, Malaka. 2018. "#MosqueMeToo Gives Muslim Women a Voice about Sexual Misconduct at Mecca." *NPR*. https://www.npr.org/sections/goatsandsoda/2018/02/26/588855132/-mosquemetoo-gives-muslim-women-a-voice-about-sexual-misconduct-at-mecca.

Grabill, Rhiannnon, and Meredith Minister. 2019. *Rape Culture and Religious Studies: Critical and Pedagogical Engagements*. Lanham, MD: Rowman & Littlefield.

Herr, Ranjoo Seodu. 2014. "Reclaiming Third World Feminisms: Or Why Transnational Feminism Needs Third World Feminism." *Meridians: Feminism, Race, Transnationalism* 12, no. 1: 1–30.

Kandiyoti, Deniz. 1991. *Women, Islam and the State*. Philadelphia: Temple University Press.

Kunst, Jonas R., et al. 2018. "Sexism, Rape Myths and Feminism Identification Explain Gender Differences in Attitude towards the #MeToo Social Media Campaign in Two Countries." *Media Psychology* 22, no. 5: 1–26.

Manikonda, Lydia, Ghazaleh Beigi, Huan Liu, and Subbarao Kambhapati. 2018. "Twitter for Sparking a Movement, Reddit for Sharing the Moment: #MeToo through the Lens of Social Media." *Arxiv*. https://arxiv.org/abs/1803.08022. Accessed December 6, 2022.

Mernissi, Fatima. 1975. *Beyond the Veil: Male-Female Dynamics in Modem Society*. Bloomington: Indiana University Press.

Mernissi, Fatima. 1992. *The Veil and the Male Elite: A Feminist Interpretation of Women's Rghts in Islam*, translated by Mary Jo Lakeland, New York: Basic Books.

Mohanty, Chandra. 2002. "Under Western Eyes' Revised: Feminist Solidarity through Anti-Capitalist Struggles." *Signs* 23, no. 2: 499–535.

Mohanty, Chandra. 2003. *Feminism without Borders: Decolonizing Theory, Practicing Solidarity*. Durham: Duke University Press.

Morgan, Robin, ed. 1984. *Sisterhood Is Global*. New York: Doubleday Anchor.

Nasreen, Tasleema. 2018. "Women Reveal the Sexual Harassment They Face Even on Haj. *The Print*. March 20. https://theprint.in/opinion/women-reveal-sexual-harassment-face-even-haj/43222/. Accessed December 6, 2022.

Poushter, Jacob. 2014. "How People in Muslim Countries Prefer Women to Dress in Public." *Pew Research Center*. January 8. https://www.pewresearch.org/fact-tank/2014/01/08/what-is-appropriate-attire-for-women-in-muslim-countries. Accessed December 6, 2022.

Powell, Catherine. 2018. "How Social Media Has Reshaped Feminism." 18 June 2018. *Council on Foreign Relations*, June 18. https://www.cfr.org/blog/how-social-media-has-reshaped-feminism. Accessed January 13, 2021.

Rodino, Michelle. 2018. "Me too #MeToo: Countering Cruelty with Empathy." *Communication and Critical/Cultural Studies* 15, no. 1: 96–100. https://doi.org/10.1080/14791420.2018.1435083.

Saadawi, Nawal El. 1997. *The Hidden Face of Eve: Women in the Arab World*. London: Zed Books.

Sadruddin, Munir Moosa. 2013. "Sexual Harassment at Workplace in Pakistan: Issues and Remedies about the Global Issue at Managerial Sector."

Schultz, Colin. 2014. "In Egypt, 99 Percent of Women Have Been Sexually Harassed." *Smithsonian Magazine*. https://www.smithsonianmag.com/smart-news/egypt-99-women-have-been-sexually-harassed-180951726/#:~:text=According%20to%20a%202013%20United,report%20having%20been%20sexually%20harassed. Accessed December 6, 2022.

Weber, Ingmar. "What Does the Gender Gap in Online Social Networks Looks Like?," *Aljazeera*. https://www.aljazeera.com/opinions/2014/9/5/what-does-the-gender-gap-in-online-social-networks-looks-like.

Wadud, Amina. 1999. *Qur'an and Woman: Rereading the Sacred Text from a Woman's Perspective*. Oxford: Oxford University Press.

White, Rebecca. 2018. "Title VII and the #MeToo Movement." *Emory Law Journal Online* 68: 1014–1033.

# 13

# "You Are Not Alone"

## #EnaZeda and #Masaktach as Voices against Violence

*Antonella Cariello*

### Timeline

#### Morocco

- 1956: Moroccan gained independence from France.
- 1963: Moroccan women gained the right to vote.
- 2004: Reforms of the family code, called *Moudawana*, introduced stricter measures for men wanting to marry additional wives, greater leniency for a divorce initiated by the wife, more equitable inheritance rights for women, and an increase in the legal age of marriage for women.
- 2011: Arab Spring demonstrations took place and a new Moroccan Constitution was adopted. The new constitution offers broader protection of individual rights and recognizes women's rights.
- 2011: Law No. 59-11 created a quota system that allocates one-third of the seats in the Lower House of Parliament to women.
- 2014: The "marry-your-rapist" law (Article 475 of the Penal Code) was repealed.

#### Tunisia

- 1956: The Code of Personal Status was enacted. It abolished polygamy and repudiation, enabled women to ask for divorce, enacted a minimum age for marriage, and ordered the consent of both spouses before marriage.
- 1957: Tunisian women gained the right to vote.
- 1965: Abortion was legalized.
- 1975: Tunisia ratified the Convention on the Elimination of All Forms of Discrimination Against Women (CEDAW).
- 2011: Arab Spring demonstrations took place and a new Constitution was adopted.

Antonella Cariello, *"You Are Not Alone"* In: *The Other #MeToos.* Edited by: Iqra Shagufta Cheema, Oxford University Press.
 DOI: 10.1093/oso/9780197619872.003.0013

- 2017: The "marry-your-rapist" law was repealed.
- 2017: Law 58 was enacted to eliminate violence against women. It amends certain discriminatory provisions of the penal code and requires state institutions to develop a coordinated approach to prevention as well as assistance and support for victims of violence.

## Introduction

> What would happen if a woman told the truth about her life?
> The world would split open.
>
> —Muriel Rukeyser[1]

The #MeToo Rising Database shows the movement's increasing significance internationally. The reasons behind this evolution are manifold. On the one hand, the #MeToo movement deals with topic like sexual harassment, gender-based violence, and violence against women that unfortunately are an international constant; on the other hand, this premise can explain only the initial spread of the movement, but it does not justify its impact and worldwide growth. Because, even if patriarchy and violence seem to be the "golden rule" of virtually every society, the paradigms and the power relationships of this violence respond to culturally specific reasons. In her analysis, Dubravka Zarkov (2018) highlights that not only the context of the #MeToo movement matters, but also "within the context, the question has to be asked about the social locations of the perpetrators and victims" (p. 4).

To understand the social locations of the perpetrators and the victims means to understand which unequal power relationships between genders reiterate this violence in every different social and legal context. This is the first step to understand how the #MeToo movement has been able to evolve and find new roots and shapes in Tunisia and Morocco. This is a crucial point because the fact that the #MeToo movement started in a Western context (i.e., with the first Hollywood cases) is often used as an argument against the possibility of the #MeToo movement of reaching and adapting to different cultures and contexts. However, a study by Roee Levy and Martin Mattsson (2020) demonstrates that the impact of the movement goes far beyond Hollywood. Indeed, they studied the #MeToo movement across twenty-four countries and established that the movement inspired many women internationally, by resulting in an increase in the number of women reporting abuses to the police. But, most importantly, the researchers did not find any significant variation based on race or socioeconomic status, meaning that the #MeToo movement has been able to reach women across races and classes internationally.

But if we consider Figure 13.1, during the period of the boom of #MeToo hashtag, countries like Morocco and Tunisia were mostly untouched. This does not mean that the movement has not reached those countries, but it means that, before taking roots in the cultural and social structure of the two countries, it had first to find its new shape. This is what the chapter adds to the conversation about the other #MeToos: I want to show how the #MeToo movement has the intrinsic power of adapting and changing itself according to the specific context, because despite the common objective of speaking up against sexual and gender-based violence, the ways to reach that goal can differ based on the context, and women all over the world have taken different actions to take their power back.

Indeed, any conversation about the ability to stand for oneself, claim one's rights, and act against violence is a conversation about power and agency. The #MeToo movement is intrinsically linked to power and sex and gender, and how they unequally intersect: to have power means to have the authority of saying "yes" or "no," and therefore it is strictly linked with the idea of consent (Gill and Orgad, 2018). Sex is political (Rubin, 1999); therefore, sexual violence against women must be understood not only for what it is, namely a crime against the freedom of another member of society, but also for what it means in terms of power relations. Those who possess power are usually stronger and think they

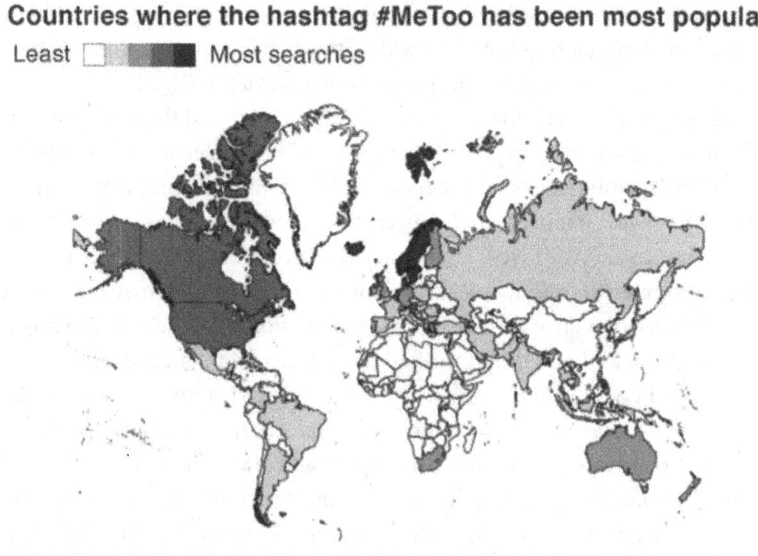


**Figure 13.1.** Countries where the hashtag #MeToo has been most popular.
Source: Google Trends, data from May 2017–2018. BBC News (2018); https://www.bbc.com/news/world-44045291.

have the right to decide over the life of those who, instead, are powerless. The relation that is therefore structured is:

Power = I/YOU can = Subject
Powerless = I/YOU can't = Object

To use violence, and specifically sexual violence, against women implies that women are not subjects but objects, because violence entails a nullification and a disempowerment of their will. The #MeToo movement, therefore, starts as an empowerment movement where women take back their power of denunciation, saying that gender-based violence (GBV) is not an inescapable or imperative part of being a woman. Regardless of cultural and contextual specificities, the #MeToo movement aims at redistributing power and affirming women's agency of women as subjects.

Before understanding how the #MeToo movement encouraged women in Tunisia and Morocco to come together and speak up, it is first important to highlight which systems were put in place to silence women and disempower them. For this purpose, the first section of this chapter explicates the legal context of GBV and the cultural meaning of violence against women (VAW) in Morocco and Tunisia. This will clarify the pitfalls and boundaries that the #MeToo movement has to face in Tunisia and Morocco. Additionally, it shows "how the intersection of power, privilege, and context can enhance the power of the aggressor while crushing the voice of the victim" (Rachidi, 2018, n.p.). The second section investigates the recent #EnaZeda and #Masaktach actions and compares those movements with the U.S. #MeToo movement to explore their similarities and dissimilarities. Before moving forward, I would like to clarify that this chapter does not aim to compare Tunisia and Morocco. My decision to focus on these two countries stems from both my personal experience and interest. Most importantly, I chose these two countries to explore the potential of #MeToo movement for international change and its ability to lend itself to diverse cultural contexts, even in the same North Africa region. This chapter reinforces that #MeToo movement(s), and the idea behind it, are universal. The #MeToo movement has the power and ability to develop, change, and grow in different contexts with specific and unique local actions, which are different but respond to the shared international aim of giving back power and agency to women and assuring them that they are not alone.

## Legal and Social Structures and Gender-Based Violence in Morocco and Tunisia

Until 2017, in both Morocco and Tunisia, the law allowed perpetrators accused of rape to escape legal prosecution by marrying the victim. This law considered rape as an issue of honor and reputation and offered marriage to re-establish the honor of the victim, and consequently, re-establish the social order. Therefore, this law did not focus on the criminalization of the perpetrator but, through the marriage, offered a solution to re-establish the honor and the social position of the victim, damaged by the rape. This legal system, along with sociocultural conditions, disempowered women and failed to address the causes of GBV, leaving GBV survivors without any legal or social support (EuroMed, 2018a, 2018b).

Even though this law has been repealed in both countries,[2] the social heritage of this law is still present and affects women's lives (Amnesty, 2017, 2020). According to the national survey conducted during the first trimester of 2019 by the Ministry of Family, Solidarity, Equality and Social Development (2020) in Morocco, 54.4% of women have been victims of violence, with a higher rate of 55.6% in urban settings as compared to 51.6% in rural areas. Furthermore, the Social Institutions and Gender Index (SIGI, 2019) also reports a 51% level of discrimination and inequality in the country. The Index shows that the highest values of inequality can be found in the legal structure of the country. For instance, women face 75% inequality in laws, 100% in inheritance laws, and 75% in divorce laws. In her study of sexual and gender violence in Morocco, Habiba Chafai (2020) identifies three larger issues: normalizing harassment, self-objectification of women, and blaming the harassed versus excusing the harasser. In her interviews with women, they shared street harassment as "a minor routine for negotiating power relations in public space" (Chafai, 2020, p. 9). Street harassment is "culturally acceptable" because women are "socialised to be responsible for their attitudes" while men are "encouraged to experience their virility and manhood" and are likely to be "excused for their (mis)deeds" (Chafai, 2020, p. 13). Furthermore, women also tend to blame the victim in cases of sexual violence.

In 2016, the Tunisian Center for Research, Studies, Documentation, and Information on Women (CREDIF), with the support of the United Nations Entity for Gender Equality and the Empowerment of Women (UN Women), has conducted a national study on GBV in public spaces in Tunisia. The study is significant because after the Arab Spring events in 2011, women's participation in different spheres of public space was steadily increasing . However, women experience different forms of violence in the public sphere. According to the study, 78.1% of women reported having experienced psychological violence, 41.2% physical violence, and 75.4% sexual violence (Chafai, 2020, p. 13). The study also reveals the sociocultural beliefs that cause sexual and gender violence: the idea that women should stay home, and that they should behave properly so as not to attract attention when outside of the home, remains one of the major causes of violence against women. This view is shared by both men and women. According to the CREDIF's study, women choose silence, which "acts as a shared social code, a method to avoid the worst" (Chafai, 2020, p. 37).

Even though Tunisia has gone through substantial changes, the position and participation of women in public life seem to still suffer from the cultural stigma and political legacy that relegates women only to the private, family life. Petkanas (2013) highlights the difficulty for women to be visible and accepted in the public sphere in what she terms Tunisia's gendered democracy paradox. She takes the example of elections and compares the experiences of male and female candidates to highlight that:

> [v]erbal, online, and even physical harassment was a huge problem for many female candidates during the campaign, even in places that are not designated male spaces, real or virtual. Although both men and women faced difficulties during the campaign, women faced some uniquely gendered ones. Whereas men often received questions about their platforms and ideas, women were judged, challenged, and often harassed about their personal appearance, their morality, their marital status, and personal life. (Petkanas, 2013, p. 13)

This representation is powerful, and this example points out the core problem: in theory, women are granted a space and a recognition in the public sphere; in practice, those spaces are not safe for them. This problem is simultaneously the cause and the effect of the high level of violence and harassment against women.

This framework highlights the revolutionary value of the #MeToo movement in these countries. Through the #MeToo Movement and its respective versions in Morocco and Tunisia, women have overcome their loneliness as victims and survivors to demand justice and accountability for the crimes committed against them. These hashtags not only have made women more aware of their rights, but also have made them realize that they are not alone. The feeling of belonging to a social movement, like in the cases I will present later, have encouraged women in Tunisia and Morocco to claim their agency and rights, becoming the protagonists of the #MeToo movement. Women and activists in North Africa have used the momentum and power of the #MeToo movement to strengthen the social media movements that were already in place to raise awareness and advocate against violence against women (Bash-Harod, 2019). Indeed, social media had already played an essential role in supporting the revolution and mobilizing people during the Arab Spring, both in Morocco and in Tunisia (Khondker, 2011; Breuer and Groshek, 2014; Zaid, 2016). Moreover, in 2013 in Morocco, the #RIPAmina[3] campaign went viral on Twitter and Facebook. This campaign eventually led to the repeal of Article 475 of the Penal Code, which previously allowed a rapist to marry his victim and avoid persecution (Bash-Harod, 2019). Therefore, the #MeToo movement has reinvigorated the common fight that was already started by many Tunisian and Moroccan activists and feminists, but that with the #Mazactach and #EnaZeda movements has evolved and has found a way to reach even more women and girls to let them know that they are not alone (Abdulaal, 2019).

## Place for Denunciation: #Masaktach and #EnaZeda and Their Intersections with the #MeToo Movement

### #Masaktach

Morocco has a consolidated civil society which includes both feminist and queer associations that in the last years have constantly challenged the culture of gender-based and sexual violence. In this social and cultural framework, the Masaktach movement (translated as "I will not keep silent" (Collet, 2020) started as an answer to the street harassment after the case of the young girl Khadija.[4] To respond and express their anger at the violence enacted upon this young girl, a group of young women ran a protest with whistles, to symbolize that women will not be silent anymore and will fight for safety in the streets. "With the whistles, we wanted to challenge this lack of space, take back public space and make sure men understand that we all belong here, that their attempts to intimidate us won't hold us back," said a #Masaktach activist (*The Guardian*, 2018, n.p.). This action was highly symbolic because the protest with the whistle showed not only the need for women to be safe in public space, but also their readiness to denounce violence.

Like the #MeToo movement, #Masaktach did not start as an organized movement but was first an urgent action to respond to an episode of violence against women. This is a shared aspect of many #MeToo movements in different countries: a reaction to an incident of violence. In this way, the #MeToo movement initiated a new way of looking at the victim of violence, subverting the victim blaming, offering support, and giving back agency and power to the victim. This solidarity in Tunisian and Moroccan contexts and its unity with the international #MeToo movement are what differentiates the #MeToo movement from previous movements. #MeToo amplifies the action started by a small group of women on social media. These smaller movements gain more participants via a snow-balling effect and turn into a more structured movement. #EnaZada and #Masaktach started from one incident and voice, to later become thousands of voices who had similar experiences. #Masaktach, "I will not keep silent," highlights the agency of the "I," assigning a voice to the victim of violence.

In Morocco, women were already organizing protests against gender-based and sexual violence via the effective use of social media, which made #MeToo more successful. Aida Kheireddine, a Moroccan feminist activist, shared that in the past years feminists and activists have mobilized many times to support victims and survivors of violence. While #Masaktach started in the same way as a spontaneous and angry reaction to a terrible case of violence, its strength and power relies both on this group of women and on the possibility of using the social network and #MeToo to connect with larger communities of women victims and survivors.

If the original objective of the #Masaktach movement was to support Khadija and her family, today the movement aims at creating awareness and sensitizing all people. The movement aims at twofold action: first, lobby for women's protection and safety and make GBV a priority political agenda; second, the movement wants to talk directly to people. Laila Slassi, cofounder of Masaktach, explains in an interview (Eyala, 2019, n.p.):

> We are not going to keep begging the governments to take these issues seriously. If politicians do not care, too bad; we will talk to people directly on social networks. We will make them understand the importance of this fight. That way, even if politicians do nothing, at least the citizens can do their part.[5]

The main channel of communication of Masaktach is its Facebook page, followed by more than 7,100 followers. The contents of the posts on the page show that the collective is working to sensitize public opinion regarding GBV. The movement supports three agendas on its social channels: (i) providing women a safe space to share their experiences; (ii) deconstructing "myths" or stereotypes about violence and rape; (iii) campaigning against increased violence during the Covid-19 pandemic. Below I discuss Masaktach's three agendas separately.

## Creating a Safe Space to Share Experiences

#Masaktach's objective is to create a community where victims and survivors of violence can emerge from their isolation and can feel free and safe to share their experience and denounce their aggressors. This replies to the needs of raising awareness about violence against women, as well as giving visibility to victims and survivors and offering them a place where they can feel supported and heard. The first call for testimony was launched in February 2020 for all women who did not want to publicly denounce their aggressors. This call came after the confirmation hearings of Brett Kavanaugh in the United States, where there had been a similar call for testimonies. In the Moroccan movement, the call for testimony was launched through a post on the movement's Facebook page (#Masaktach, Facebook, February 9, 2020):

> Because the word of survivors must be freed, because fear must change sides, because evidence of rape and assault is often difficult, we make our platform available to your testimonies, while maintaining your anonymity. Our Facebook and Twitter messages are open to you, we will publish the testimonials you send there. Denounce these predators who act with impunity, comforted by your silence. We also call on men who have witnessed aggression or attempted aggression to report it. Only the initials of the attackers will be published. If several people report the same attacker, and with their agreement, we will put those women in contact. We hope that these testimonies will facilitate the judicial work to fight against violence against women: rapes are crimes that are only prescribed after 20 years. Sexual assaults are offenses that are only prescribed after 5 years. In any case, the testimonies of one can help the other. You are not alone.

These testimonies, which were then posted on #Masaktach's official page, show two recurrent effects of violence. First, sexual violence dramatically changed these women's lives forever and it changed and reshaped their identity. One woman describes the memory of the violence she suffered like having "a clandestine passenger in [her] heart, in [her] soul" (#Masaktach Facebook, February 11, 2020). Second is the difficulty of sharing their experience with their family and asking for help and support. Many victims have not reported the violence to the police, or even shared It with their families because of the fear of their reactions. In many instances, the violence happened when the victims were children inside the family house, by perpetrators who are family members or friends. Because of the sociocultural perceptions, some victims shared that they felt guilty and responsible for the violence that was committed against them.

The idea of creating an online space to share testimonies and offer support is similar between Masaktach and #MeToo. Indeed, in both cases, women are not only sharing their personal experience, but also regaining their agency by raising awareness and finding the courage to speak up. In both cases, the courage to speak, which sometimes means also to recall a violence that had happened many years before, is rooted in the certitude of being heard by the #MeToo or #Masaktach community, and women decide to speak up in these because they know they are no longer alone.

The initiative was highly appreciated by the #Masaktach community: in the comments of the post with those testimonials, many women express their support and understanding. #Masaktach later launched another call for testimonials, this time to women during the lockdown period of COVID-19 (#Masaktach, Facebook, April 17, 2020):

> With the constant aim of amplifying the voice of women in Morocco, whose responsibilities, mental load, and suffering have been increased, we would like to inform you that our platform is always at your disposal to send your testimonies there. Our mailbox is open to you, we will continue to publish the testimonials that you will send there anonymously. You can also directly post your testimonies through the use of the hashtag #3yalat_El7ajr_Si77i, which we will re-post on our digital platforms.
>
> We hope that these testimonies will support the inclusion of the fight against violence against women in crisis management and in the implementation of a coordinated response to this health emergency.
>
> In any case, the testimony of one woman may help many other women.
>
> You are not alone."

### Deconstructing "Myths" about Violence and Rape

Masaktach aims to educate people about sexual and gender violence. The first prerequisite is that people unlearn sociocultural stereotypes, or what Masaktach calls "myths" about violence. For this purpose, Masaktach posts "myth" note cards on their Facebook page to deconstruct these myths that come from inadequate media coverage and persistent social and cultural norms. These myths include the following: if a woman is unable to stop the rapist or attacker, she wanted it; sexual and gender violence is committed by strangers and could be avoided if women avoided desolated streets or interaction with strangers. But Masaktach's myth cards explain that sometimes psychological shock, the aggressor's physical power, or the fear of stronger violence can bar a victim from resisting the violence too long. Masaktach also demonstrates via victim testimonies that often the aggressor is someone whom the victims knows and trusts, such as a friend, partner, colleague, neighbor, or family member. While these concepts are known in academic circles, the average person needs more awareness about these, and Masaktach is creating that awareness.

### Campaigning against Violence during the Covid-19 Pandemic

During the first wave of the pandemic, specifically during the lockdown, domestic violence against women increased alarmingly (EuroMed, 2020). For this reason, in April 2020, Masaktach shared a new call for testimonies from women who experienced increased violence during the Covid-19 lockdown. In June, the movement started a survey to understand the extent of the effect that the pandemic had on women's safety. The results of this survey will be soon published. All of these activities help educate people and create public awareness regarding gender-based and sexual violence. This also educates women on ways to fight gender violence, as well providing a place for support and solidarity.

## #EnaZeda

EnaZeda is a young movement in Tunisia that gained prominence in October 2019. The hashtag #EnaZeda, which means #MeToo, was first used to support a young girl who denounced a member of Parliament who was masturbating outside her school in his car in a bid to harass her. #EnaZeda was created in 2017 following the #MeToo movement, but it only became viral because of its support for this case (Ben Salah, 2020). The action of #EnaZeda is mainly built on Facebook. The movement has two pages: one public page with more than 40,000 followers, and a private group with more than 39,000 members. The aim of the private community is to "put together resources, information and citizen and individual initiatives that aim to counter all forms of sexual violence" (Ena Zeda Facebook page). The group is open to both women and men because, through the witnesses of GBV survivors, #EnaZeda wants to sensitize all genders.

The work of #EnaZeda relies upon the support of various feminist organizations, and particularly upon the help of the nongovernmental organization Aswat Nissa (translated as Women's Voices). The organization administers the private #EnaZeda group. Aswat Nissa also carries out different campaigns of sensitization. For instance, in March 2020, the organization launched a campaign based on the witnesses received through the #EnaZeda group to educate young people about legislation regarding gender-based and sexual violence. The target audience of the campaign was university students. According to Aswat Nissa: "What was at the beginning only a hashtag on social networks, became, within a few months, an unprecedented social movement in Tunisia. #EnaZeda has instilled courage in several victims to come break their silence and file a complaint against their attacker" (Aswat Nissa, 2020).

Moreover, to increase the outreach of the movement, Aswat Nissa also created a campaign requesting that several Tunisian actors and actresses read some of the testimonies the organization receives on a daily basis. This resulted in a short video where four actors read the touching and shocking stories of those who were abused by family members or strangers and who received no support. The video raised awareness about the everyday occurrences of violence against women. Ultimately, the video became a strong call for action that reiterated that "sexual harassment comes in two forms: the harasser and whoever keeps quiet" (Aswat Nissa, 2020, n.p.). This became another shared connection between the

#MeToo and #EnaZeda because influential, famous women played a key role in making gender-based and sexual violence more visible.

The widespread impact of #EnaZeda encouraged many women to speak up. This was also the case, for instance, of Saida Ounissi, a former minister from the Ennahda party. In October 2019, she posted on her Facebook account that she was raped when she was only 12 years old. In this post, she accused "pseudo-intellectuals" of condemning the publication of photos and witnesses of abuse and sexual harassment rather than the crime and the criminals. In her strong denunciation, she wrote:

> It is them. It is this public opinion itself that promotes impunity and sets it up as rule. They are also responsible for empowering those who attack our daughters. They, too, who push the victims to hide in silence. They, too, are responsible for the suicide of a young man from Beja who was the victim of repeated rapes during his childhood by an animator and who could no longer bear the feeling of guilt. They allowed generations of children in Sfax[6] to be abused when the cycle of abuse could have been stopped with courage and denunciation. (Saida Ouinissi, Facebook post, October 11, 2019)[7]

Her witness invokes the core question of the #EnaZeda movement in Tunisia. It is not just about saying #MeToo, but it is also about saying #TheyToo. This is another significant tool from the #MeToo movement: for every woman who speaks out as a victim-survivor of GBV, there is a perpetrator of this violence who should be named and shamed. The #MeToo and #EnaZeda movements share the objective of disempowering the aggressors and re-establishing justice for the crime that has been committed. Najma Kousri, one of the managers of the #EnaZeda page, said in an interview with an Egyptian journal:

> The testimonials aim to give more visibility to women victims of sexual harassment, but we also aim to make authorities more aware of the extent of violence suffered by women in everyday life. They are called to effectively enforce Law 58 (the Organic Law Related to the Elimination of Violence against Women) so that it does not just remain as ink on paper but put[s] a stop to the impunity of sexual predators. (Abulaal, 2019, n.p.)

This is an important aspect of the #MeToo movements worldwide that is sometimes underestimated, but that in #EnaZeda show its force: the potential to influence the law, ask for improvements, and seek its implementation, so that more women can denounce their aggressor, without the fear of not being heard or believed.

## #UsToo: The Strength of the Community

The analysis of the main objectives of the EnaZeda and Masaktach movements in Tunisia and Morocco highlights that these movements would not have had their impact without being connected to the international #MeToo movements. If in the United States, the movement was popularized by an actress denouncing powerful men in the workplace, in Morocco and Tunisia the movement was born from ordinary people with their experiences of gender-based and sexual violence. Khadija's story in Morocco and the young girl's story in Tunisia were the spark for the explosion of the movements in both countries, though the Tunisian #EnaZeda is more similar to the U.S. movement since its first denunciation was against a well-known politician. In both cases, the perpetrators had more economic and social power than the survivors. In both cases, the fight was first linked with the abuse of power by powerful men. Moreover, as I mentioned above, the movement included the touching testimony of a Tunisian member of Parliament, who, like Alyssa Milano, used her name and her following to offer support to other women.

Overall, the #MeToo, #Masaktach, and #EnaZed movements have demonstrated the power of communal support and solidarity despite their differing sociopolitical contexts. They have given the victims and survivors a space to denounce the perpetrators of violence and to start conversations on difficult topics like sexual abuse, harassment, and violence in the workplace, in the streets, and in the family. Because of #MeToo, women know they are not alone and that they can find support and solidarity via this hashtag that connects them with millions of others across the globe. #MeToo then creates a room for understanding and for validation of one's experiences. This solidarity and support connect different movements like #Masaktach and #EnaZeda to the international #MeToo movement. This chapter demonstrates that the #MeToo movement has influenced and furthered the feminist agendas in Tunisia and Morocco. #MeToo inspired local adaptations in the form of #EnaZeda and #Masaktach that are linked to the international experience via #MeToo but also consider and cater to local sociocultural needs. Both movements have helped shift the cultural discourse from victim blaming to shaming of the perpetrator and accountability.

Additionally, both #EnaZeda and #Masaktach offer women a safe space to share their stories and seek support, creating a virtual online community that has a profound impact in these women's lives. This enables a slow but persistent change, one person at time, one law at time, one tradition at time. These continuous, sustained movements are inevitably reshaping Moroccan and Tunisian society, with the aim of creating a safe community not only in the virtual spaces of social networks, but also in the public and private spaces. When women find a community, they learn that it is not just "me" fighting against an unfair system, but it is "us" together, fighting for a fair and more equal society.

## Notes

1. See: https://metoorising.withgoogle.com/.
2. In Tunisia the "marry-your-rapist" law was repealed in September 2017, while in Morocco it was repealed in 2014.
3. In 2012, the sixteen-year-old Amina Filali was kidnapped, raped, and forced to marry her rapist. This decision forced the girl to marry this man and tragically ended with the decision of the young girl to commit suicide to escape the abusive relationship. Read more: https://www.amnesty.ca/blog/sexual-and-reproductive-rights/remembering-amina-forced-to-marry-the-man-that-raped-her/.
4. The story of Khadija shocked Morocco in 2018. This girl was only seventeen years old when she was captured, raped, and tortured for months by a gang (Inside Arabia, 2019).
5. Original in French, translation by the author.
6. City in Tunisia.
7. https://www.facebook.com/saida.ounissi.org/posts/10157797366557425.

## Works Cited


Abdulaal, Mirna. 2019. "In Tunisia, '#EnaZeda' Is Encouraging Women to Speak Up about Sexual Harassment." *Egyptian Street*, November 22. https://egyptianstreets.com/2019/11/22/in-tunisia-enazeda-is-encouraging-women-to-speak-up-about-sexual-harassment/. Accessed August 2, 2020.

Amnesty International. 2017. *Morocco: Amnesty International Submission for the UN Universal Periodic Review 27th Session of the UPR Working Group, April/May 2017*. https://www.refworld.org/pdfid/590c86804.pdf.

Amnesty International. 2020. *Tunisia's Victim-Blaming Laws Are Punishing Survivors of Sexual Abuse*. https://www.amnesty.org.uk/tunisia-women-violence-sexual-abuse-laws. Accessed July 25, 2020.

Aswat Nissa. 2022. Website. https://www.aswatnissa.org/en/home/.

Bash-Harod, Heidi. 2019. "#MeToo and the History of "Hashtag Feminism" in the MENA region." Mediterrannean Yearbook 2019. https://www.iemed.org/publication/metoo-and-the-history-of-hashtag-feminism-in-the-mena-region/.

Ben Salah, Fairouz. 2020. "#EnaZeda: Tunisian 'Me Too' Movement Met with Both Support and Smear Tactics." *Middle East Eye*. https://www.middleeasteye.net/news/enazeda-tunisian-me-toomovement-support-smear-campaigns.

Breuer, Anita, and Groshek Jacob. 2014. "Online Media and Offline Empowerment in Post-Rebellion Tunisia: An Analysis of Internet Use during Democratic Transition." *Journal of Information Technology Politics* 11, no. 1. https://www.tandfonline.com/doi/abs/10.1080/19331681.2013.850464.

Chafai, Habiba. 2020. "Everyday Gendered Violence: Women's Experiences of and Discourses on Street Sexual Harassment in Morocco." *The Journal of North African*

*Studies*: 1–20. https://www.tandfonline.com/doi/full/10.1080/13629387.2020.1743184?scroll=top&needAccess=true.

Collet, Déborah. 2020. "#Masaktach, le movement #MeToo au Maroc."*Le Petit Journal*, February 27. https://lepetitjournal.com/casablanca/masaktach-le-mouvement-metoo-au-maroc-274929.

CREDIF. 2016. *Gender-Based Violence in Public Space in Tunisia*. Republic of Tunisia Ministry of Women Affairs, Center for Researchs, studies, Documentation and Information on Women. https://morocco.unwomen.org/sites/default/files/Field%20Office%20Morocco/Documents/Publications/2016/12/The%20Gender%20Based%20Violence%20in%20Public%20Spaces%20in%20Tunisia.pdf.

EuroMed. 2018a. *Morocco: Situation Report on Violence against Women*. https://euromedrights.org/wp-content/uploads/2018/03/Factsheet-VAW-Morocco-EN-Mar-2018.pdf.

EuroMed. 2018b. *Tunisia: Situation Report on Violence against Women*. https://www.euromedwomen.foundation/pg/en/documents/view/7820/situation-report-on-violenceagainst-women-in-tunisia.

EuroMed. 2020. *Covid-19 and the Increase in Domestic Violence against Women*. https://euromedrights.org/wp-content/uploads/2020/07/Domestic-violence-amid-COVID19-EuroMed-Rights.pdf.

Eyala. 2019. *"L'activisme, c'est dans notre ADN"—Laila Slassi, co-fondatrice de Masaktach*. https://eyala.blog/entretiens/masaktach-maroc-laila-slassi-activisme. Accessed July 9, 2020.

Gill, Rosalind, and Orgad Shani. 2018. "The Shifting Terrain of Sex and Power: From the 'Sexualization of Culture' to #MeToo." *Sexualities* 21, no. 8: 1313–1324.

Inside Arabia. 2019. "#Masaktach: A Movement against Sexual Harassment in Morocco." *Inside Arabia*. August 18. https://insidearabia.com/masaktach-a-movement-against-sexual-harassment-in-morocco/. Accessed July 12, 2020.

Khondker, Habibul Haque. 2011. "Role of the New Media in the Arab Spring." *Globalizations* 8, no. 5: 675–679. doi: 10.1080/ 14747731.2011.621287.

Levy, Roee, and Mattsson, Martin. 2020. "The Effects of Social Movements: Evidence from #MeToo." SSRN. https://papers.ssrn.com/sol3/papers.cfm?abstract_id=3496903.

Petkanas, Zoe. 2013. *From Visible to Invisible: Tunisia's Gendered Democracy Paradox*. CGHR Working Paper 3. Cambridge: University of Cambridge Centre of Governance and Human Rights.

Rachidi, Soukaina. 2018. "#MeToo Movement Clashes with Arab Patriarchy." *Inside Arabia*. September 19. https://insidearabia.com/metoo-movement-clashes-arab-patriarchy/. Accessed June 17, 2020.

Rubin, Gayle. 1999. "Thinking Sex: Notes for a Radical Theory of the Politics of Sexuality." In *Culture, Society and Sexuality*, edited by Richard Guy Parker and Peter Aggleton, pp. 143–178. London: University College London Press.

The Guardian. 2018. "'I Will Not Keep Silent': Khadija Rape Case Spurs Women into Action in Morocco." *The Guardian*, November 23. https://www.theguardian.com/global-development/video/2018/nov/23/i-will-not-keep-silent-khadija-case-sparks-backlash-in-morocco-video. Accessed July 12, 2020.

Tunisian Penal Code. 2017. https://www.jurisitetunisie.com/tunisie/codes/cp/cp1200.htm#:~:text=Article%20227%20(Nouveau).&text=L'article%20modifi%C3%A9%20depuis%2C%20a,en%20dehors%20des%20cas%20pr%C 3%A9c%C3%A9dents.

UN Women. 2017. *Tunisia Passes Historic Law to End Violence against Women and Girls.* https://www.unwomen.org/en/news/stories/2017/8/news-tunisia-law-on-ending-violence-against-women.

Zaid, Bouziane. 2016. "Internet and Democracy in Morocco: A Force for Change and an Instrument for Repression." *Global Media and Communication* 12, no. 1: 49–66. doi: 10.1177/1742766515626826.

Zarkov, Dubravka. 2018. "Ambiguities and Dilemmas around #MeToo: #ForHow Long and #WhereTo?" *European Journal of Women's Studies* 25, no. 1: 3–9.

# 14

# #MeToo in the Post–Arab Spring Era

## A Strategy of Resistance

*Jihan Zakarriya*

### Timeline of Arab Feminisms

#### 1912–1950s under Colonialism

- 1923: Egyptian Feminist Union was founded by Huda Shaarawi.
- 1933: Al-Hadaya al-Khalifiya School for Girls was founded in Bahrain.
- 1943: The Union of Algerian Women was established.
- 1957: Algerian feminist and nationalist Djamila Bouhired was arrested by colonizing French authorities.

#### 1952–1979 after Independence

- 1952: The Lebanese Council of Women was founded.
- 1956: Egyptian women were given the right to vote.
- 1957: A historic victory of Tunisian feminists resulted in the Personal Status law that raised the age of marriage for girls to seventeen, banned polygamy, and gave women the right to divorce and to child custody.
- 1960: Saudi Arabia acknowledged girls' right to education.
- 1965: Islamist feminist Zeinab al-Ghazali was imprisoned for political activism.
- 1972: Nawal Saadawi's *Women and Sex*, which criticized sexual and gender-based violence against Arab women, was published.
- 1975: Fatima Mernissi's *Beyond the Veil*, against the use of sharia and Islam to oppress and sexualize women, was published.
- 1979: The Personal Status Law was modified in Egypt to grant women more rights.

Jihan Zakarriya, *#MeToo in the Post–Arab Spring Era* In: *The Other #MeToos.* Edited by: Iqra Shagufta Cheema, Oxford University Press. © Oxford University Press 2023. DOI: 10.1093/oso/9780197619872.003.0014

## 1980s–2010s

- 1980: A huge demonstration was organized on the occasion of the International Women's Day in Algeria, demanding that the decree which hampered women's freedom of movement be revoked.
- 1981: Nawal El-Saadawi's feminist organization *Arab Women Solidarity Association* (AWSA) was banned in Egypt.
- 1985: The Democratic Association of Moroccan Women was founded.
- 1989: Zeinab al-Ghazali's memoir *Days from my Life* allegedly revealed her experiences with sexual violence and abuse in prisons in Egypt.
- 1993: Article 218 of the Tunisian Penal Code introduced punishments for perpetrators of family violence. The first female member of Parliament was elected in Morocco.
- 1990s: Bahraini women joined the Shi'ite opposition movement for equality and freedom. Some feminists were arrested and tortured in detention camps. One of them was killed; others were exiled.
- 1997: Female genital mutilation was banned in Egypt.
- 2000: Khullaw in Egypt gave women the right to divorce.
- 2001: Saudi Arabian women were given the right to their own identity card as citizens.
- 2002: Women were allowed to participate in politics and vote in Bahrain.
- 2005: Kuwaiti women were given full political rights, including electoral rights.

## Post-2010

- 2010: The famous Facebook page "We are all Khaled Said" was created, led by feminist and political activist Asmaa Mahfouz, against police violence in Egypt. This page mobilized for the 2011 revolution in Egypt. #HarassMap and @SalwaendSH, online campaigns against sexual harassment and violence in public and domestic spaces, started in Egypt and Lebanon.
- 2011: The Coalition of Egyptian Feminist Organizations called for an end to sexual violence against protesters. The Libyan Women's Platform for Peace was founded.
- 2014: Article 46 of the Tunisian Constitution, "The State shall take the necessary measures to eliminate violence against women," was enacted. Article 227 of the Penal Code criminalizes sexual crimes, including rape, and Article 226 of the Code prohibits sexual harassment.
- 2016: Male guardianship system was criticized and put for reform in Saudi Arabia.

- 2017: Saudi Arabian women were allowed to drive.
- 2020: The Saudi Arabian male guardianship law was reformed. New laws against sexual and domestic violence were passed in Egypt.

## Introduction

This chapter examines the Arab #MeToo movements and hashtags, accessible to locals in their own languages, as acts of what Maria Lugones calls "infra-politics" that show "the power of communities of the oppressed in constituting resistant meaning and each other against the constitution of meaning and social organization by power" (2010, p. 746). Before discussing the #MeToos, I will provide a brief review of the gender-based violence in various Arab countries. Then, I discuss #MeToos in the Arab world as a resistance strategy against different forms of vulnerability. Arab #MeToo hashtags endorse resistance to oppression, and sexual and gender-based violence in the Arab world through solidarity, collective action, and steady change in gendered preconceptions. Sexual and gender-based violence in the Arab world has been described as "an epidemic" and a "dire" phenomenon that includes domestic violence, harassment, trafficking, honor crimes, harmful traditional practices, such as female genital mutilation and early marriages, and other forms of violence against women's bodies and minds (Status, 2017; Sexual Harassment, 2012). Arab countries with the highest sexual harassment rates are Egypt (99%) and Sudan (90%). But only 6.6% of the Egyptian victims of sexual violence feel comfortable to report the harassment to the police (Masood, 2020; Duvvury et al., 2015, p. 11). The situation is pretty much the same across the region.

Rates of sexual harassment in other Arab countries, such as Libya, Tunisia, Lebanon, Morocco, Iraq, and Palestine, range from 35% to 45% (Bouhlila, 2019, p. 8; Sexual Harassment, 2012, p. 7; Survivors, 2013). In 2018, Tunisia's family planning office announced that 47% of women aged 18–64 have experienced violence of some kind, especially domestic (Moghadam, 2018, p. 8). Likewise, the Lebanese research organization KAFA (translated as "Enough") states that more than 2,600 calls of domestic abuse are received by its helpline each year (*KAFA: Violence & Exploitation*, 2014, p. 5). Thirty-five percent of women in Lebanon were found to be exposed to violence (Usta, Feder, and Antoun, 2015). Out of a population of 9.5 million Moroccan women aged 18–64, nearly 6 million, or 62.8%, were subjected to some form of violence, with 23% of women, or 2.1 million, having experienced sexual violence at some point in their lives (#Masaktach, 2018). Women in many Arab countries, including Lebanon, Oman, and Bahrain, are not allowed to transit their nationality to their children when they marry foreign men (*Background Note*, 2021, p. 7). Official unwillingness to either issue or implement legislation and other "cultural and legal barriers" often discourage women from "speaking out in the Middle East and North Africa" (Friedson and Altmann, 2018, p. 1), which results in safety for aggressors.

In addition to prevalent acts of domestic violence and public sexual harassment, Arab women have been exposed to systematic, politically oriented sexual violence in protest spaces. Kathrine Van Den Bogert explains how sexual abuse became a tool of visible, public oppression during the 2011 Egyptian revolution: "the violence was often gendered and sexualized: baltagiya (thugs) got orders from the police to sexually harass and touch female protestors, arrested female revolutionists were subjected to virginity tests by SCAF, and men got electroshocks on their genitals" (2019, p. 64). Likewise, during the 2011 revolution in Libya, Gaddafi's militias raped women in numerous cities and towns to dishonor the tribes or the villages, to scare people into fleeing, and to assert their power by announcing: "we have raped your women" (Engel, 2014, p. 7). In the final days of Ben Ali's regime in Tunisia, women became victims of sexual violence at the hands of the security forces. The target for the gendered violence was mostly oppressed, powerless women in poorer areas, but it can be inferred that the regime was trying to send a clear, systematic message of dissuasion to the emphasized woman lest they are next in line for such acts (Johansson-Nogués, 2013, pp. 399–400). In war-zone areas such as in Sudan, Yemen, Iraq, Libya, and Syria, women face systematic sexual violence at the hands of militarized and armed groups (*Survivors Speak Out*, 2013, p. 1). Women's bodies are thus used not only to humiliate their families and communities and to stop revolutionary and political change, but also to relegate women to the traditional social roles as passive agents in society. Moreover, such cases of organized sexual violations against male and female protesters in detention and in protest spaces are forms of silencing, animalizing, and othering the protesters. They are subordinated to superior politicians, powerful entities, and security apparatuses.

Since the independence of Arab countries in the 1950s to the present time, women's causes have been subalternized and relegated to a secondary position to globalized processes of nationalist challenges, capitalism, terrorism, and neocolonialism (Zakarriya, 2019, p. 2). Nonetheless, after the Arab Spring, Arab women's relentless activism and utilization of digital and social media document and publicize different cases of public, political, and domestic violence. By doing so, they raise awareness and consciousness about women's legal and human rights and form a collective pressure on authorities in their countries to act against gender-based violence. Moreover, Arab women's activism and resistance acknowledge the diversity of violence and political motives in different Arab contexts. For example, women in Egypt, Morocco, Lebanon, and Tunisia prioritize issues of gender-based and sexual violence, while women in Saudi Arabia have succeeded in reforming legal and social forms of gender oppression such as the concepts of male guardianship and women's seclusion.[1]

In this sense, the Arab #MeToo hashtags continue these struggles. These hashtags inspire, encourage and support women throughout the Arab world to fight different forms of sexual and gender violence and discriminations. Arab versions of #MeToo, such as #@KAFA أنا ايضا in Lebanon, #Ena Zeda أنا زادة in Tunisia, #MeToo انا كمان in Egypt, #TaAna حتى أنا in Morocco, and other local #MeToo movements in the Arab world resist gender and sexual violence both on personal and political levels: they challenge various forms of violent sexual, physical, and psychological practices against women. Moreover, they fight legal, cultural, and political forms of discrimination. For example, #@KAFA أنا ايضا in Lebanon includes stories of sexual abuse of female domestic workers, of Syrian and Palestinian refugees, and of LGBTQ+ people in Lebanon. Similarly, #Ena Zeda أنا زادة in Tunisia encourages women and LGBTQ+ communities to tell their experiences of sexual violence. #TaAna حتى أنا in Morocco criticizes discriminatory articles of the Moroccan Penal Code, particularly Article 475[2] that allows the rapist to marry his victim and thus escape legal punishment.

These hashtags also mark a turning point in the advocacy, activism, and initiatives for gender equity and freedom through balancing between local collective actions because Arab women can all access these local hashtags in their languages, come together, and situate themselves in international conversations on gender and sexual violence as well. For instance, the long- running campaigns #IAmMyOwn Guardian أنا ولية أمري, and #WomenToDriveMovement قيادة المرأة في السعودية in Saudi Arabia, utilize the #MeToo hashtag to promote their activism for the legal and social liberation of Saudi women. The internationalization of Saudi women's activism generated international support and put pressure on Saudi Prince Mohammad bin Salman to adopt a more progressive agenda toward women citizens and activists, especially after the atrocious assassination of Saudi journalist and thinker Jamal Khashoggi.[3]

In the following analysis, I explain how, through #MeToo hashtags, Arab women achieved a high degree of inner awareness and critical self-realization that enabled them to change the constructions of gender, sexuality, and culture. Then, these individuals united to effect social and political change, realizing collective resistance. The private and public spaces interchangeably shaped the local #MeToo hashtags in the Arab world. I specifically regard local #MeToo hashtags in the Arab world as anti-vulnerability activities. They aim at deconstructing deep-rooted stereotypes and preconceptions that established women and their bodies as helpless and inferior sexual objects.

## Arab #MeToo: Diversity of Resistance to Vulnerability Post–Arab Spring

> There is the fact that women and minorities, including sexual minorities, are, as a community, subjected to violence, exposed to its possibility, if not its realization. This means that each of us constituted politically in part by virtue of the social vulnerability of our bodies—as a site of desire and physical vulnerability, as a site of a publicity at once assertive and exposed and seem to follow from our being socially constituted bodies, attached to others, at risk of losing those attachments, exposed to others, at risk of violence by virtue of that exposure.
>
> (Butler, 2004, p. 20)

In this quotation from *Precarious Life: The Powers of Mourning and Violence* (2004), Judith Butler discusses the concepts of vulnerability and violence as sociopolitical constructs aimed at dividing and separating people into unequal and hierarchical categories of betters and lessers, powerful and weaker, adherents and dissenters, normal and deviant, and safe people and the punishable. For Butler, violence and vulnerability are tools of disciplining and silencing difference and revolt. Since women, minorities, and LGBTIQ+ are often identified as lessers, weaker, dissenters, and deviants, these positions subsume their need for equality and highlight their obligation to conform to established categories, and often to hide their differences. If women, minorities, and LGBTIQ+ speak or challenge their vulnerability, they are punished. Thus, they are responsible for their personal security in cases of dissent, and the oppressors, particularly within patriarchal and authoritarian regimes, escape any accountability and responsibility. As described in the first section of this chapter, women in the Arab world are often seen as vulnerable, and hence punishable and subjected to violence if they resist. Nonetheless, in the period following the 2011 Arab Spring revolutions, patriarchal and hierarchical power and social structures collapse, and vulnerable women gain voice, effect, and power while the oppressors themselves become vulnerable to both political and historical change. Many Arab women have taken Arab Spring as an opportunity to rethink, criticize, and re-evaluate their social positions and vulnerability to violence. In the following analysis, I trace how local #MeToo hashtags have strengthened post–Arab Spring activism in the Arab world to oppose various forms of vulnerability and violence.

Egypt's #MeToo offers an inspiring and hopeful form of resistance and resilience to violence and vulnerability. Since the 2011 revolution to the present, Egyptian women have led protests and have been at the forefront of public opposition and political conflict with patriarchal and corrupt authorities in Egypt. Yet, since El- Sisi's rule in 2014, civil and women protest spaces have been remilitarized. Utilizing regional and global conditions of wars in Libya and Syria and the rise of the authoritarian rule of Trump in the United States, El- Sisi tightly controls public places and media so that "media is censored by the military- backed regime that has banned all forms of protest and just about every form of dissent you can imagine" (Ashendouek, 2020, par. 11). Despite repressive conditions, Egypt's #MeToo انا كمان has become a strong platform for women to share and document their experiences with sexual harassment and to embrace and/ or negotiate with authority. #MeToo انا كمان, in partnership with #assaultpolice, documents and shares a flood of stories about all types of sexual and gendered violence (Saleh, 2020). Below, I focus specifically on four recent cases discussed on Egypt #MeToo انا كمان and explain their significance.

From April to July 2020, #MeToo in Egypt led online campaigns that mark a great boost for feminist and women's legal, sociocultural, and political resistance against gendered and sexualized abuse and violence in Egypt. The first is Farshout's girl, or Farha's case. Farha was a nineteen-year-old lower-class girl who lived in Upper Egypt, Qena Governorate. In 2018, Farha was kidnapped by three young men who raped her ("Farshout's Girl," 2020). Although the rapists planned to kill Farha after raping her, she escaped and reported the rape to the police. Farha lived with her divorced mother, who worked as a cleaner in a school to support herself and her daughter. The rapists came from affluent families so they were not persecuted. Rather, Farha's mother was fired, and they had to leave their village after receiving threats and humiliating treatment from the rapists, their families, and the community ("Farshout's Girl," 2020; Zaki 2021). Despite their poverty, fear, and loneliness, Farha and her mother did not drop the case. They sought help from feminist and women's organizations, who introduced her case to print and electronic media and highlighted it on social media using #MeToo. As Farha's case drew public attention and sympathy, the rapists offered her money and even marriage to concede the case. But Farha refused. In 2020, the rapists were sentenced to death ("Three Men Who Kidnapped," 2020).

The second and third cases are quite similar to the first. Ahmed Bassam Zaki, an affluent student at the American University in Cairo, was accused by his colleague, on their Facebook page, of sexually harassing her and two of her friends. After that, more women and girls shared their own similar experiences with Zaki (Tarek, 2020; Saleh, 2020). Zaki threatened these women after these allegations; later, he left for Barcelona to join a business school. However, an Instagram account, @assaultpolice, with the support of Egypt's #MeToo participants, collected and reported more than 100 anonymous testimonies from women who had been assaulted or harassed by Zaki, including a fourteen-year-old girl (Tarek, 2020;

Saleh, 2020). It turned out that Zaki had been coercively assaulting, harassing, and threatening women and girls for years. Zaki was arrested and is under trial now. The third case is known as Fairmont Crime. The crime happened in 2014 when a group of up to six men from wealthy families drugged, raped, and video recorded a woman after a tea party at Cairo's five-star Fairmont Nile City Hotel. The rapists blackmailed and threatened the victim, who remained silent for six years after the incident. However, the growing impact of #MeToo in Egypt and in the world encouraged the Fairmont Crime victim to share her experience with rape and blackmail (Egypt #MeToo, 2020). Six other women, three of whom were also video recorded, were also gang-raped by the same men. The viral hashtag put pressure on the authorities to act. Prosecutors in Egypt ordered the arrests of the men involved in the gang rape (Younes, 2021).

Unlike Farha's case, Zaki's and Fairmont's victims came from educated, affluent families. Yet, even those victims remained silent out of fear of social stigma, shame, and blame that are directed at victims of sexual violence. Nonetheless, Egypt's #MeToo and @assaultpolice mobilized women's organizations and pressured legal institutions against the rapists and the harassers. Though these incidents show that sexual violence occurs irrespective of the victims' socioeconomic class, Farha and her poor mother's case was successful because of the public attention it gained after #MeToo.

For the first time, the public focused on the crimes, instead of the blaming the victim. What is also important about these three cases of sexual harassment and rape is the fact that the assaulters and rapists come from powerful families who feel empowered and advantaged under El-Sisi's rule. Nevertheless, the success of #MeToo and @assaultpolice in mobilizing and supporting victims to defend their rights is impressive. The support and solidarity via these hashtags online are not limited only to women. Two heterosexual male actors, Tameem Youness and Abbas Abu al-Hassan, issued sexual harassment and molestation complaints against a famous Egyptian dentist, Bassam Samir ("For Thirty Years," 2021). Other celebrities and common men also accused Samir of sexual harassment. In July 2021, Samir was sentenced to sixteen years in prison for his sexual violations (Makary, 2021). It is because of #MeToo that celebrities and men publicly speak about their sexual abuse. Youness and Abu al-Hassan share that they were inspired and encouraged by Egyptian women and #MeToo and @ assaultpolice. While Abu Al-Hassan praised women for fighting "ambivalence and shameful silence in the society" ("Long Live a Sex," 2020, par. 3), Youness expressed "his empathy towards every woman who had to go through such a situation and stressed the fact that it's never the victim's fault; on the contrary, it causes a never-ending trauma" to the victim (Henein, 2020, video ). Youness's and Abu Al-Hassan's sexual abuse helped them understand the sufferings and trauma of abused women. This understanding motivates them to act individually and collectively. Their gender and sexual differences are not an obstacle to their empathic engagement with women.

Like in Egypt, Moroccan #TaAna حتى أنا focuses on incidents of sexual violence. Moroccan #TaAna حتى أنا emerged in 2018 when a twenty-two-year-old woman revealed that for years she was raped by her brother, to the indifference of her parents (#TaAnaMeToo, 2021; "Moroccan #MeToo Comics," 2021). In August 2018, women started sharing their experiences of sexual violence under another Moroccan version of #MeToo, #Masaktach ماسكتش. #Masaktach started when seventeen-year-old Khadija explained that she was kidnapped, raped, and tortured for two months by men from her village (Al Saadi, 2018). Khadija also showed scars, cigarette burns, and markings on her body, which she said were given to her by her captors (Al Saadi, 2018). #TaAna حتى أنا and #Masaktach ماسكتش led a media campaign to help Khadija, who, like Egyptian Farha, appeared on Moroccan station Chouf TV (#Masaktach, 2019). Due to such huge media pressure, Khadija's rapists were caught and are under trial (Al Saadi, 2018).

#TaAna حتى أنا and #Masaktach ماسكتش also engaged with the major rape case of Moroccan star Saad Lamjarred, who was prosecuted in France in a rape case for the fourth time. Via the two hashtags, hundreds of tweets have called Moroccan radio stations, the leading radio station, to stop broadcasting the songs of Lamjarred as an example of punishing rapists and harassers (Koundonno, 2018). Unlike in Egypt ,where victims of sexual abuse revealed their identity while sharing their experiences, the majority of Moroccan victims remained anonymous because, as feminist and artist Zainab Fasiki explains, they are afraid to testify openly out of fear of reprisals and because the female body is taboo (Bouknight, 2018). Because more Moroccan women highlighted their experiences of sexual and gender violence, a new law that criminalizes violence against women was passed in 2018 (*Morocco-Western Sahara*, 2020). The new law refers to certain acts considered as forms of harassment, aggression, sexual exploitation, or ill-treatment, though it does not include marital rape (#Masaktach, 2019; #TaAnaMeToo, 2021; "Moroccan #MeToo Comics," 2021).

Unlike more conservative Egypt and Morocco, Tunisia is seen as the most progressive Arab country regarding women's rights (#Masaktach, 2019). In 1957, Tunisia banned polygamy and gave Tunisian women the right to vote, marry, divorce, and gain custody of their children (Tanner, 2020; Moghadam, 2005). In 1993, Article 218 of the Penal Code introduced punishments for perpetrators of family violence, and in 2018, Organic Law No. 58,[4] a comprehensive law that protects against all types of gender-based violence, including political violence and marital rape, was passed (Yerkes and Youssef, 2020). In 2020, Tunisian women had equal inheritance laws (Tanner, 2020). Although Tunisian women have many important laws and legislations that protect their rights, Sarah Yerkes and Maro Youssef explain, "such legislations and laws exist on paper, with significant work remaining to implement the laws" (2020, par. 5). Yerkes and Youssef argue that it is becoming increasingly "difficult for [Tunisian] victims to find justice" because "for example, between 2016 and 2018, marital rape increased from 7,869 cases to 40,000 cases annually. Between March and May 2020, government GBV hotlines received over 7,000 complaints" (2020, par. 9). Observing this, the local #MeToo, Ena Zeda أنا زادة in Tunisia adopted a progressive agenda in its fight against Tunisian women's vulnerability to sexual and gender-based violence and for the effective implementations of laws.

Tunisia's Ena Zeda أنا زادة is an anti– sexual harassment movement that started in 2020 when a nineteen-year-old student shared pictures of member of Parliament Zouheir Makhlouf allegedly masturbating in his car outside her high school in a bid to harass her (Ben Saleh, 2020; Abduaal, 2019). The hashtag gained immediate traction as 32,648 women tweeted their experiences with sexual harassment, and added forty new stories to the hashtag (Ben Saleh, 2020). Though at the time the student did not know the identity of the harasser, who then turned to be a powerful politician, she used the virtual space to name the aggressor and assert her rights to a safe, respectful environment. Another female student at Rue de Russie high school in the center of Tunis accused a teacher of sexual harassment; the teacher was detained after the complaint. Saida Ounissi, a former minister, also supported the hashtag #EnaZeda أنا زادة, and shared her experience with sexual harassment as a child. So far, #EnaZeda أنا زادة receives about forty new stories of sexual violence daily and has almost 21,600 members on twitter (Ben Saleh, 2020). According to Tunisia's Ena Zeda أنا زادة, "most of the testimonies they received were about street harassment. They postulate that this is due to sociocultural structures that restrict and limit women's access to public spaces" (Ghzaye 2020, p. 2). Still, the absence of the implementation of sexual harassment laws such as Law 58 and political corruption are hindrances in the face of justice. So, the case against MP Makhlouf has been brought to a complete standstill because of his political immunity and power as a member of Parliament (Ghzaye, 2020; Foroudi, 2019; Abduaal, 2019).

Like Tunisia, Lebanon is also relatively liberal in the Arab world. Yet, Lebanese women, unlike Tunisian women, have been suffering from the lack of laws concerning sexual and gender violence and discriminations. Statistics revealed that 75% of Lebanese women have experienced domestic violence at some point in their lives (Antelava, 2009; *Lebanon: Domestic Violence*, 2011). Lebanese activists and feminists started their online activism against sexual violence in Lebanon in 2005 with KAFA, a research organization publishing and documenting cases of gender-based and sexual violence in Lebanon to break the silence around systemic gendered and sexual violence and called for anti–sexual violence laws in Lebanon (*KAFA: Our Aims*, 2005). In 2010, the online campaign Salwa's Adventure, @SalwaendSH, emerged. Salwa's Adventure posted stories, videos, and information on how Lebanese women can defend themselves and act against increasing rates of gender-based and sexual violence in private and public spaces (Elle, 2011; Tazi and Oumlil, 2020; Khamis 2011). For years, Lebanese women did not report sexual and gendered violence, which is a social taboo in Lebanon and the security apparatuses deny it (Farah, 2013, pp. 12–13). Girls and women use the @SalwaendSH website, Twitter account, and Facebook page to share their stories of sexual violence. Kimi Elle, a Lebanese student, described that she has been harassed by university security guards on a daily basis (Elle, 2011; Sara, 2015). Moreover, @SalwaendSH was the first Arab feminist campaign to expose cases of sexual harassment in workplaces (Elle, 2011; Sara, 2015). Because of the pressure of feminists and civil society, along with the Arab Spring protests in Lebanon, the Lebanese Parliament issued domestic violence Law No. 293/2014 to "penalize economic and psychological violence, but it did not specifically criminalize marital rape" (Abumaria, 2020, par. 15).

Like in Egypt, Morocco, and Tunisia, sexual and gender violence laws such as Law No. 293/2014 are not adequately implemented in Lebanon. Consequently, in 2017, #MeshBasita مش بسيطه(translated as "it is not OK") emerged as an online movement raising awareness and calling for legislation to fight sexual violence in Lebanon (McKernan, 2017). #MeshBasita مش بسيطه was founded by the research project Knowledge Is Power (KIP) at the American University of Beirut (AUB) and the Minister of State for Women's Affairs. A greatly effective online anti–sexual violence campaign called #@KAFA أنا ايضا emerged in 2019 and was a combination of #MeToo and the Lebanese feminist group KAFA. In 2019, #@KAFA أنا ايضا published the story of an eighteen-year-old Lebanese girl who accused the thirty-two-year-old Lebanese volleyball player Marwan Habib of raping her (Hajj, 2019). Around fifty women, including American University of Beirut and Lebanese American University female students, also came forward with their stories of sexual assault by Habib. Now, Marwan Habib faces a lawsuit, accused of sexually harassing and raping (Hajj, 2019; Moussa, 2020). The pressure of women's organizations and #@KAFA أنا ايضا forced the Lebanese authorities to arrest Habib at the airport as he attempted to escape Lebanon (Moussa, 2020). Zahraa Mahfoodh was another Lebanese student who shared her experience of being sexually harassed by the owner of the bar Karma, who harassed and followed her on Instagram and texted her every weekend to come to Karma and bring her friends over. Other female students also shared similar incidents regarding the owner of Karma (Moussa, 2020). Lebanon hosts almost 1.5 million Syrian refugees, 80% of whom are women and children. Because of poverty and exile, many Syrian women and girls are more vulnerable to sexual exploitation in public spaces and workplaces in Lebanon (Munshey, 2020; Zapater, 2018; Italia, 2014). Habib and the bar owner felt powerful over women because in the highly sectarian and gendered Lebanon, women are silenced by violent, patriarchal, and politicized mentalities, structures, and laws. Providing Lebanese women with a safe and supportive platform to share their experiences of sexual and gendered violence, #@KAFA Lebanon أنا ايضا encourages women to speak against violence. In 2020, the Parliament issued the "first law in Lebanon to penalize perpetrators of sexual harassment and abuse" (Azhar, 2020, par. 10). In addition to this, @SalwaendSH, #MeshBasita مش بسيطه, and #@KAFA Lebanon أنا ايضا gave refugee women a space to reveal their experiences of sexual violence and rape in Lebanon (Zapater, 2018; Italia, 2014).

A distinctive characteristic shared by Tunisian #EnaZeda أنا زادة and Lebanese @KAFA # أنا ايضا is that LGBTQI+ in the two countries use these hashtags to reveal their experiences with sexual and gender- based violence, and about human rights violations of LGBTQI+ people. Homosexuality is illegal in Tunisia and Lebanon, and LGBTQI+ people in the two countries have been vulnerable and silenced victims of harassment and discrimination for social and religious reasons ("The LGBTQI+ Community in Lebanon," 2021, p. 8; Fitzsimons, 2018). Yet, Arab Spring protests encouraged various oppressed groups to talk about and defend their rights. For instance, Rania Said, a cofounder of Tunisian Ena Zeda #أنا زادة, told that most men shared their experience with sexual and gender violence "anonymously. A couple of Tunisian gay men shared their stories about being sexually abused as children. . . . One man posted several stories about rapes that he had witnessed happening regularly in prisons, mostly in the Mornaguia prison" (Odone and Zrig, 2019, para. 14-15). Likewise, LGBTQI+ people have been integral to the #MeToo nationwide protests that began on October 17, 2019, to denounce sexual violence in Lebanon. Young gay and queer people openly participate in protests, using #@KAFA أنا ايضا to fight sectarianism and homophobia in Lebanon (Harb, 2019; "Lebanese LGBT People," 2020). Hosam and Farah, two LGBTQI+ protestors, faced rejection and social and sexual violence; they admitted that combating anti-LGBT sentiment in Lebanon is not easy, but they are optimistic (Harb, 2019; "Lebanese LGBT People," 2020). Due to the persistent activism of LGBTQI+ communities and Ena Zeda أنا زادة, the Tunisian president, Beji Caid Essebsi, called for "the de-criminalization of homosexuality in Tunisia" (Fitzsimons, 2018, par. 2).

In this way, #MeToo and Arab Spring revolutions empowered women to speak and to explore new media, such as social media, to affect decision-making processes. Ena Zeda أنا زادة, @KAFA Lebanon #أنا ايضا, Egypt's #MeToo انا كمان and #TaAna حتى أنا then became the localized iterations of global #MeToo. Their locality and credibility convince their supporters and solidify their resistance. These localized iterations of #MeToo, then, represent Arab women's daily experiences and are also more accessible in their own languages. In this respect, the Saudi Arabian #MeToo hashtag signifies a different form of Saudi women's daily activism against oppressive experiences. In collaboration with the long-running campaigns, #IAmMyOwnGuardian أنا ولية أمري and #Women2Drive قيادة المرأة في السعودية , Saudi feminists utilize the hashtag #MeToo to continue their efforts against the male guardianship system described as "the most significant impediment to realizing women's rights in the country" (Mallott, 2020, par. 10). As Saudi women are dehumanized and disempowered, they face different forms of psychological, physical, and domestic violence. In 2015, the Saudi Ministry of Labor and Social Development reported 8,016 cases of physical and psychological and physical abuse (Mallott, 2020). Although Saudi Arabia criminalized domestic violence in 2013, the implementation of laws is lacking. Some young girls, such as Rahaf Mohammed, managed to successfully flee her allegedly abusive family and to talk publicly about her experience (*Women and Saudi Arabia's Male Guardianship*, 2016). Yet, other Saudi Arabian girls, such as Mariam al-Otaibi and Dina Ali Lasloom, failed to escape and were forced to stay with their allegedly abusive families (*Women and Saudi Arabia's Male Guardianship*, 2016; "Saudi Arabia: 10 Reasons Why Women Flee," 2019).

Fighting deep- seated repressive and conservative religious- political systems, Saudi Arabian feminists and activists have met with imprisonment, detention, and exile for their progressive calls for the social and sexual liberation of Saudi women ("Prominent Saudi Women Activists Arrested," 2018; al-Qadi, 2020). For example, activists Samar Badawi, Nassima al-Sadah, Amal al-Harbi, Loujain al-Hathloul, Aziza al-Yousef, Eman al-Nafjan, Nouf Abdelaziz, Mayaa al-Zahrani, Hatoon al-Fassi, and others were arrested, and some activists such as Loujain al-Hathloul were exposed to sexual violation in detention ("Prominent Saudi Women Activists Arrested," 2018; al- Qadi, 2020). Nevertheless, post-2011 Arab women, including Saudi Arabian women, show historic resilience and persistence to defend their rights and to challenge fear. Despite the unprecedented violence against Saudi feminists and activists, #Women2Drive قيادة المرأة في السعودية succeeded and Saudi women were given the right to drive in 2017. Moreover, almost 15,000 women joined the #IAmMyOwnGuardian أنا ولية أمري hashtag. Eventually, Saudi Prince Mohammad Bin Salman issued a royal decree in 2020 to reform the male guardian system so that women over the age of twenty-one can obtain passports and travel abroad without requiring a close male relative's permission. Saudi women can now register births, marriages, or divorces (Mallott, 2020; Hincks, 2019). I argue that Saudi women's persistence and their openness to international anti–gender violence activism, such as #MeToo, are the main reasons behind Bin Salman's progressive attitudes toward women's rights. As news and information about coercive detention and abuse of female prisoners and activists spread worldwide, along with the assassination of Jamal Khashoggi, Saudi authorities became vulnerable to international criticism and condemnation and decided to concede to women activists' demands (Ensor, 2018; Mallott, 2020).

A final, inclusive, radical Arab version of #MeToo is #MosqueMeToo, which is discussed elsewhere in this volume (see Chapter 12). #MosqueMeToo is the most controversial anti–sexual harassment movement in the Arab world. Since it criticizes and breaks silence about religious and moral hypocrisy, patriarchy, and masculinity in all Arab and Islamic countries, #MosqueMeToo has been accused of "enabling Islamophobia or reinforcing racist perceptions of Muslim men" (Stahl, 2018, par. 8). Nonetheless, the unprecedented responses to #MosqueMeToo highlight that women are ready to come together and challenge deep-seated patriarchal and hypocritical attitudes that cause sexual and gender violence.

## Conclusion

In this chapter, I have discussed the localized iterations of the global hashtag #MeToo in the Arab world as campaigns against female vulnerability. Arabic versions of #MeToo, such as #@KAFA أنا ايضا in Lebanon, #Ena Zeda أنا زادة in Tunisia, #MeToo انا كمان in Egypt, #TaAna حتى أنا in Morocco, #IAmMyOwnGuardian أنا ولية أمري and #Women2Drive قيادة المرأة في السعودية in Saudi Arabia, and #MosqueMeToo raise awareness and fight against gender and sexual violence in the Arab world. These hashtags have furthered and strengthened the post–Arab Spring changes in historic legal and cultural progress toward women's sexual and gender rights. Yet, all local #MeToo hashtags in the Arab world share a concern with the lack or the reluctant implementation of sexual and gender-based violence laws. These hashtags are critical in raising awareness and starting conversations that will eventually change the attitudes toward sexual and gender violence and increase implementation of the laws.

## Notes

1. According to the male guardianship system, a Saudi woman's father, brother, husband, or son has the authority to make critical decisions on her behalf. Saudi women cannot travel, work, marry, get a divorce, access healthcare, or enroll in schools or universities without the permission of a male guardian (Mallott, 2020).
2. In 2012, sixteen-year-old Amina Filali killed herself after being forced to marry her rapist. After pressure by #TaAna حتى أنا, Article 475 was amended in 2021 (Morocco, 2020; Johnson, 2021).

3. Jamal Khashoggi was a Saudi Arabian journalist, dissident, author, and columnist for *The Washington Post*. He was assassinated at the Saudi consulate in Istanbul on October 2, 2018, by agents of the Saudi police, allegedly sent by the Crown Prince Mohammed bin Salman (Kirchgaessner, 2021).
4. Law 58 was passed in 2018 for the elimination of violence against women in Tunisia. The law provides victims of sexual violence with necessary legal, medical, and mental health support and services.

## Works Cited

Abduaal, Mirna. 2019. "In Tunisia, '#EnaZeda' Is Encouraging Women to Speak Up about Sexual Harassment." *Egyptianstreets*, November 22. https://egyptianstreets.com/2019/11/22/in-tunisia-enazeda-is-encouraging-women-to-speak-up-about-sexual-harassment/. Accessed July 14, 2021.

Abumaria, Dima. 2020. "Lebanon Finally Criminalizes Sexual Harassment." *The Medialine*, December 22. Lebanon Finally Criminalizes Sexual Harassment - The Media Line. Accessed July 14, 2021.

Al-Qadi, Fadi. 2020. "Do Not Forget the Jailed Saudi Women's Rights Activists." *Aljazeera*, March 8. Do not forget the jailed Saudi women's rights activists | Women | Al Jazeera. Accessed July 14, 2021.

Al Saadi, Abdul Wahid. 2018. "Morocco: Arrests Made in Khadija Rape and Torture Case." *BBC*, August 28. https://www.bbc.co.uk/news/world-africa-45337930. Accessed July 14, 2021.

Antelava, Natalia. 2009. "Lebanon's Hidden Problem of Domestic Abuse." *BBC*, December 3. BBC News - Lebanon's hidden problem of domestic abuse. Accessed July 14, 2021.

Ashendouek, Jenna. 2020. "Finally, the Feminist Revolution Has Begun: Egypt's #MeToo Moment." *MS Magazine*, February 8. https://msmagazine.com/2020/08/02/finally-the-feminist-revolution-has-begun-egypts-metoo-moment/. Accessed July 14, 2021.

Azhar, Timour. 2020. "Lebanon Passes Landmark Sexual Harassment Law." *Aljazeera*, December 21. Lebanon passes landmark sexual harassment law | Sexual Assault News | Al Jazeera. Accessed July 14, 2021.

*Background Note on Gender Equality, Nationality, Laws and Statelessness*. 2021. UNHCR. Available from: 604257d34.pdf (refworld.org). Accessed July 14, 2021.

Barron, Laignee. 2018. "With #MosqueMeToo, Muslim Women Are Speaking Out about Abuse." *The Time*, February 16. https://time.com/5159888/mosquemetoo-muslim-women-speaking-out-about-abuse/. Accessed July 14, 2021.

Ben Salah, Fairouz. 2020. "#Ena Zeda: Tunisian "Me Too" Movement Met with Both Support and Smear Tactics." #EnaZeda: Tunisian 'Me Too' movement met with both support and smear tactics | Middle East Eye. *Middle East Eye*. February 22. Accessed July 14, 2021.

Bogert, Kathrine Van Den. 2019. "Blood, Bodies, and Violence: Gender and Women's Embodied Agency in the Egyptian Uprisings." *Frontiers: A Journal of Women Studies* 40: 62–92.

Bouhlila, Donia Smaali. 2019. *Sexual Harassment and Domestic Violence in the Middle East and North Africa*. University of Tunis el Manar, Arab Barometer. https://www.

makers.com/blog/alyssa-milano-and-tarana-burke-reflect-on-year-after-me-too. Accessed July 14, 2021.

Bouknight, Sebastian. 2018. "Illustrator Zainab Fasiki Takes on Taboos and Patriarchy with Art." *Inside Arabia*, September 22. Illustrator Zainab Fasiki Takes on Taboos and Patriarchy with Art - Inside Arabia. Accessed July 14, 2021.

Butler, Judith. 2004. *Precarious Life: The Powers of Mourning and Violence*. New York: Verso.

Duvvury, Nata and et al. 2015. *The Egypt Economic Cost of Gender-Based Violence Survey (ECGBVS)*. United Nations Population Fund. https://egypt.unfpa.org/sites/default/files/pubpdf/Costs%20of%20the%20impact%20of%20Gender%20Based%20Violence%20%28GBV%29%20WEB.pdf. Accessed July 14, 2021.

"Egypt #MeToo: Arrests over Alleged Gang Rape after Instagram Campaign." 2020. *BBC*, August 25. https://www.bbc.com/news/world-middle-east-53903966. Accessed July 14, 2021.

Elle, Kimi. 2011. "Harassed Daily by the Guards at Lebanese University." *Qawemeharassment*, January 23. Harassed daily by the guards at Lebanese University | Resist Harassment Lebanon / قاومي التحرش - لبنان (wordpress.com). Accessed July 14, 2021.

Engel, Andrew. 2014. *Libya as a Failed State: Causes, Consequences, Options*. Washington, DC: Washington Institute for Near East Policy.

Ensor, Josie. 2018. "Saudi Arabia Accused of Torturing Women's Right-to-Drive Activists in Prison. *The Telegraph*. November 21. Saudi Arabia accused of torturing women's right-to-drive activists in prison (telegraph.co.uk). Accessed July 14, 2021.

Farah, Lydia, and Kiwan Dina. 2013. *Domestic Violence in Lebanon*. Beirut: Issam Fares Institute for Public Policy.

"Farshout's Girl after Submitting the Defendants' Papers to the Mufti: She Was Subjected to Death Threats and His Death at the Oath." 2020. *EG24 News*, July 22. https://www.eg24.news/2020/07/farshouts-girl-after-submitting-the-defendants-papers-to-the-mufti-she-was-subjected-to-death-threats-and-his-death-at-the-oath.html. Accessed July 14, 2021.

Fitzsimons, Tim. 2018. "Tunisian Presidential Committee Recommends Decriminalizing Homosexuality." *NBC News*, June 16. https://www.nbcnews.com/feature/nbc-out/tunisian-presidential-committee-recommends-decriminalizing-homosexuality-n883726. Accessed July 14, 2021.

"Celebrities' Dentist Faces Accusations of Molesting Male Patients in Egypt." 2021. *Albawaba*, February 1. Celebrities' Dentist Faces Accusations of Molesting Male Patients in Egypt | Al Bawaba. Accessed July 14, 2021.

Foroudi, Layli. 2019. "Setback for Tunisia's #MeToo Movement as New MP Gets Immunity." *Reuters*, November 13. Setback for Tunisia's #MeToo movement as new MP gets immunity | Reuters. Accessed July 14, 2021.

Friedson, Felice, and Altmann, Julia. 2018. "#MeToo Movement Struggles to Resonate in Arab Countries." *The Medialine*, February 17. '#MeToo' Movement Struggles To Resonate In Arab Countries - The Media Line. Accessed July 14, 2021.

Ghzaye, Hanen Ben. 2020. "EnaZeda: A Tunisian Movement against Sexual Harassment." *IVI* (January 22): 1–12. https://www.ivint.org/enazeda-a-tunisian-movement-against-sexual-harassment/. Accessed July 14, 2021.

Hajj, Lama. 2019. "Lawsuit Filed against Marwan Habib for Sexual Harassment." *Beirut*, December 5. Update: Lawsuit Filed Against Marwan Habib For Sexual Harassment :: Beirut.com :: Beirut City Guide. Accessed July 14, 2021.

Harb, Ali. 2019. "This Revolution Has Raised the Bar: How Lebanon's Protests Have Created a Surprising Space for LGBT Rights." *Time*, November 13. https://time.com/5726465/lgbt-issues-lebanon-protests/. Accessed July 14, 2021.

Henein, Baher. 2020. "Tameem Youness Declares He Is One of Bassem Samir's Victims." *CTownchatter*, C-Town Chatter Magazine på Instagram: "Tameem Youness Declares He Is One of Bassem Samir's Victims. Head over to www.ctownchatter.com for more information or visit our stories . . . ". Accessed November 18, 2021.

Hincks, Joseph. 2019. "Saudi Arabia Is Introducing Landmark Reforms for Women. But the Activists Who Pushed for Them Remain in Prison." *The Times*, August 5. https://time.com/5644080/saudi-arabia-guardianship-women/. Accessed July 14, 2021.

Human Rights Watch. 2019. *Saudi Arabia: 10 Reasons Why Women Flee: Rampant Discrimination, Abuse*. https://www.hrw.org/news/2019/01/30/saudi-arabia-10-reasons-why-women-flee. Accessed July 14, 2021.

Italia, Redazione. 2014. "*Syrian Refugee Women Tell Stories about Sexual Exploitation in Lebanon*." Pressenza International Press Agency, August 13. Syrian Refugee Women Tell Stories about Sexual Exploitation in Lebanon (pressenza.com). Accessed July 14, 2021.

Johansson-Nogués, Elisabeth. 2013. "Gendering the Arab Spring? Rights and (In)security of Tunisian, Egyptian and Libyan Women." *Security Dialogue* 44: 393–409.

Johnson, Sarah. 2021. "Marry Your Rapist" Laws in 20 Countries Still Allow Perpetrators to Escape Justice." *The Guardian*, April 14. 'Marry your rapist' laws in 20 countries still allow perpetrators to escape justice | Women's rights and gender equality | The Guardian. Accessed July 14, 2021.

*KAFA: Our Aims*. 2005. About KAFA | كفى. Accessed July 14, 2021.

*KAFA: Violence & Exploitation*. 2014. Beirut, KAFA. Available from: PRpdf-82-635689245975040950.pdf (kafa.org.lb). Accessed July 14, 2021.

Khalife, Leyal. 2019. "Women in Tunisia Launch Arabic #MeToo Campaign Following MP Scandal." *Stepfeed*, October 16. Step Feed. Accessed July 14, 2021.

Khamis, Sahar. 2011. The ARAB 'Feminist' Spring? *Feminist Studies*, Vol. 37, No. 3: 692–695.

Kirchgaessner, Stephanie. 2021. "Top Saudi Official Issued Death Threat against UN's Khashoggi Investigator." *The Guardian*, March 23. Top Saudi official issued death threat against UN's Khashoggi investigator | Jamal Khashoggi | The Guardian. Accessed July 14, 2021.

Koundonno, Tamba Francois. 2018. "To Boycott or Not to Boycott: How Saad Lamjarred Is Dividing Moroccans." *Morocco World News*, October 2. To Boycott or Not to Boycott: How Saad Lamjarred Is Dividing Moroccans (moroccoworldnews.com). Accessed July 14, 2021.

*Lebanon: Domestic Violence, Including Legislation, State Protection, and Services Available to Victims*. 2011. https://www.refworld.org/docid/507550cf2.html .Accessed July 14, 2021.

"*Lebanon's LGBT People Reclaim Their Power*." 2020. *Human Rights Watch*, May 7. https://www.hrw.org/news/2020/05/07/lebanons-lgbt-people-reclaim-their-power. Accessed July 14, 2021.

"Long Live a Sex Criminal among Us: The Full Story of the Incident of a Dentist Molesting Men." 2020. *Newsbeezer*, September 2. https://newsbeezer.com/egypteng/long-live-a-sex-criminal-among-us-the-full-story-of-the-incident-of-a-dentist-molesting-men/ Accessed July 14, 2021.

Lugones, Maria. 2010. "Toward a Decolonial Feminism." *Hypatia 25*, no. 4: 742–759.

McKernan, B. 2017. "Lebanese Women Fight Back against Sexual Harassment with New Campaign." *The Independent*, August 16. Lebanese women fight back against sexual harassment with new campaign | The Independent | The Independent. Accessed July 14, 2021.

Makary, Marina. 2021. "Egyptian Dentist Bassem Samir Sentenced to 16 Years in Prison for Sexually Assaulting Men." *Egyptian Street*, July 17. Egyptian Dentist Bassem Samir Sentenced to 16 Years in Prison for Sexually Assaulting Men | Egyptian Streets. Accessed July 14, 2021.

Mallott, Paula. 2020. "Saudi #MeToo: International Models and Pressure for the Kingdom." *Modern Diplomacy*, March 12. Saudi #MeToo: International Models and Pressure for the Kingdom - Modern Diplomacy. Accessed July 14, 2021.

"#Masaktach: How the Moroccan #MeToo Began." 2018. *Euronews*, October 17. #Masaktach, how the Moroccan #MeToo began | Euronews. Accessed July 14, 2021.

"#Masaktach: A Movement against Sexual Harassment in Morocco." 2019. *Inside Arabia*, August 18. #Masaktach: A Movement Against Sexual Harassment in Morocco (insidearabia.com). Accessed July 14, 2021.

Masood, Hana. 2020. "A #MeToo-Like Wave Is Taking the Middle East by Storm. Here's Why It Matters." *Statecraft*, September 11. Statecraft | A #MeToo-Like Wave is Taking the Middle East by Storm. Here's Why it Matters. Accessed July 14, 2021.

Moghadam, Valentine. 2005. *Freedom House, Women's Rights in the Middle East and North Africa—Tunisia. Refworld*, October 14. https://www.refworld.org/docid/47387b702f.html. Accessed July 14, 2021.

Moghadam, Valentine. 2018. *The State and Women's Movement in Tunisia*. Northeastern University: The James A. Baker III Institute for Public Policy of Rice University. The State and the Women's Movement in Tunisia: Mobilization, Institutionalization, and Inclusion (bakerinstitute.org). Accessed July 14, 2021.

"Moroccan #MeToo Comics." 2021. *Global Times*, April 1. Moroccan #MeToo comics - Global Times. Accessed July 14, 2021.

"Morocco-Western Sahara." 2020. *Human Rights Watch*. World Report 2022: Morocco and Western Sahara | Human Rights Watch (hrw.org). Accessed July 14, 2021.

Moussa, Lynn Sheikh. 2020. "Women on Twitter Speak up about Harassment and Rape in Lebanon." *Beirut Today*, February 18. Women on Twitter speak up about harassment and rape in Lebanon - Beirut Today (beirut-today.com). Accessed July 14, 2021.

Munshey, Menaal. 2020. "Collective Silence and Accountability for Sexual Harassment in Lebanon." *IDS Bulletin* 51. Collective Silence and Accountability for Sexual Harassment in Lebanon | IDS Bulletin. Accessed July 14, 2021.

"Prominent Saudi Women Activists Arrested." 2018. *Human Rights Watch*, August 1. Prominent Saudi Women Activists Arrested | Human Rights Watch (hrw.org). Accessed July 14, 2021.

Odone Maisie and Zrig, Hanen. 2019. "Thousands of Sexual Violence Victims Share Their Stories. *Meshkal*, November 5. Thousands of Sexual Violence Victims Share Their Stories - Meshkal. Accessed July 14, 2021.

Saleh, Heba. 2020. "Egypt #MeToo Moment: Laws Themselves Are Not Enough." *Financial Times*, July 24. Egypt's #MeToo moment: 'Laws themselves are not enough' | Financial Times (ft.com). Accessed July 14, 2021.

*Sexual Harassment in the Arab Region: Cultural Challenges and Legal Gaps*. 2012. Egyptian Center for Women's Rights. Cairo: Egyptian Center for Women's Rights. Available from: https://arabstates.unfpa.org/sites/default/files/pub-pdf/2010-ICPD%4015RegionalReport-EN_0.pdf (accessed 14 July 2021)

"Saudi Arabia: 10 Reasons Why Women Flee." 2019. *Human Rights Watch*, January 30. Saudi Arabia: 10 Reasons Why Women Flee | Human Rights Watch (hrw.org). Accessed July 14, 2021.

Stahl, Aviva. 2018. "Controversy over #MosqueMeToo Sheds Light on Sexualized Violence and Xenophobia." *Women's Media Center*, February 19. https://www.womensmediacenter.com/news-features/mosquemetoo. Accessed July 14, 2021.

*Status of Arab Women: Violence against Women*. 2017. *United Nations: ESCWA*. Beirut: Lebanese American University.

*Survivors Speak Out: Sexual Violence in Sudan*. 2013. *Ottawa: Nobel Women's Initiative.*

"#TaAnaMeToo, So That No Raped Woman Is Silent" (video). 2021. *Twitter*, March 9. #TaAnaMeToo - Twitter Search / Twitter. Accessed July 14, 2021.

Tanner, Victor. 2020. "Strengthening Women's Control over Land: Inheritance Reform in Tunisia." *DAI*, February 20. Strengthening Women's Control Over Land: Inheritance Reform in Tunisia · DAI Publications (dai-global-developments.com). Accessed July 14, 2021.

Tarek, Mohamed. 2020. "Ahmed Bassam Zaki's charges highlight flaws in penal code." *Madamasr*, July 12. https://www.madamasr.com/en/2020/07/12/feature/politics/ahmed-bassam-zakis-charges-highlight-flaws-in-penal-code/. Accessed July 14, 2021.

Tazi, Maha and Kenza Oumlil. 2020. The Rise of Fourth-Wave Feminism in the Arab region? Cyber feminism and Women's Activism at the Crossroads of the Arab Spring. *Cyber Orient*, Vol. 14, Iss.1, pp. 44-71.

"Three Men Who Kidnapped, Raped Farshout Girl in 2018 Charged with Death Sentence Two Years Later." 2020. *CairoScene*, July 21. Three Men Who Kidnapped, Raped 'Farshout Girl' in 2018 Charged with Death (cairoscene.com). Accessed July 14, 2021.

Usta, Jinan, Gene Feder, and Jumana Antoun. 2015. "Attitudes towards Domestic Violence in Lebanon: A Qualitative Study of Primary Care Practitioners." *The British Journal of General Practice*, 623: 313–320.

"*Women and Saudi Arabia's Male Guardianship System*." 2016. *Human Rights Watch*. https://www.hrw.org/sites/default/files/report_pdf/saudiarabia0716web.pdf. Accessed July 14, 2021.

Yerkes, Sarah, and Maro Youssef. 2020. "Coronavirus Reveals Tunisia's Revolutionary Gains for Women Only Exist on Paper." *Carnegie Endowment for International Peace*, June 22. Coronavirus Reveals Tunisia's Revolutionary Gains for Women Only Exist on Paper - Carnegie Endowment for International Peace. Accessed July 14, 2021.

Younes, Rasha. 2021. "Justice Stalled in Egypt's Fairmont Rape Case." *Human Rights Watch*, February 8. Justice Stalled in Egypt's 'Fairmont' Rape Case | Human Rights Watch (hrw.org). Accessed July 14, 2021.

Zakarriya, Jihan. 2019. "Vulnerability, Resistance and Sexuality in Revolutionary Egypt." *Women's Studies international Forum* 77: 1–8.

Zaki, Hind Ahmed. 2021. "How Egyptian Women Have Broken the Stigma around Sexual Violence." *The Wire*, March 10. How Egyptian women have broken the stigma around sexual violence | Progressive International. Accessed July 14, 2021.

Zapater, Josep. 2018. "*#MeToo and Syrian Refugee Women in the Bekaa.*" September 11. #MeToo and Syrian refugee women in the Bekaa - Josep Zapater. Accessed July 14, 2021.

# 15

# The Iranian #MeToo Movement

*Farinaz Basmechi*

## Timeline

- 1910: The Iranian Constitutional Revolution took place and the women's rights movement emerged in Iran.
- 1932: The Second Congress of Women of the East was organized in Tehran, Iran.
- 1936–1941: The mandatory unveiling of women (Kashf-e-Hijab) was instituted by Reza Shah Pahlavi.
- 1955: The Women's League of Supporters of the Declaration of Human Rights was founded.
- 1959: The High Council of Women's Organizations was established in Iran.
- 1963: The right to vote was granted to women as part of the White revolution, a reformation plan implemented in the second Pahlavi era.
- 1975: Family protection law was passed by Iran's Senate. According to this law, abortion became legalized and women and men had equal rights in marriage and divorce.
- 1979: Islamic revolution took place, and mandatory hijab laws were passed.
- 1990: The women's cultural center was established.
- 1992: *Zanan* magazine (women's magazine) was founded.
- 2006: One million signatures were collected for the family protection law and the campaign against stoning.
- 2014: "My Stealthy Freedom" movement began.

## Introduction

"The disaster of countless sexual assaults on Western women—including incidents leading to #Metoo campaign—and Islam's proposal to resolve it: By introducing the hijab, Islam has shut the door on a path that would pull women towards such deviation. . . . Islam does not allow this through the hijab" (Khamenei, 2018, n.p.). This is a claim of the leader of Islamic Republic of Iran,

Farinaz Basmechi, *The Iranian #MeToo Movement* In: *The Other #MeToos*. Edited by: Iqra Shagufta Cheema, Oxford University Press. © Oxford University Press 2023. DOI: 10.1093/oso/9780197619872.003.0015

Ali Khamenei, shared on his website and his Twitter account, responding to the #MeToo movement in 2018. He had previously blamed Western societies, arguing that they did not advocate freedom, but turned women into tools for men's pleasure using media (Khamenei, 2012). He contended that wearing the Islamic hijab accelerated women's partaking in social and political activities (Khamenei, 2012). Since Khamenei is currently the most powerful political figure in Iran, I start this chapter with his point of view and his solution to the problems posed by the #MeToo movement.

Khamenei employs this argument to implement mandatory hijab in Iran.[1] Despite Khamenei's belief in the positive influence of hijab on Iranian women's lives, #MyStealthyFreedom, an online movement against mandatory hijab laws, went viral in Iran concurrently with #MeToo. The movement demanded for the annulment of laws that required all women to wear a hijab in public (read more: Stewart and Schultze, 2019). When #MeToo movement became globally viral in 2017, at the same time, Iranian women started #MyStealthyFreedom,[2] #WhiteWednesdays,[3] and other related hashtags protesting mandatory hijab laws and demanding a cultural and legal change in compulsory hijab laws. In September 16, 2022, following the death of Mahsa-Zhina Amini while in custody of the morality police, a new wave of protests against mandatory hijab laws and the Islamic Republic government have started in Iran which centered around the main slogan of "Women, Life, Liberty," demanding fundamental change in the political and legal systems of Iran.

The feminist movement has a long history in Iran and was not just focused on the issue of hijab. For the first time, Iranian women's right movement emerged after the Iranian constitutional revolution in 1910. Victories such as the right for women to vote in 1963 (Shaditalab, 2005), taking part in public offices, the family protection law, divorce, and custody rights also were parts of the achievements of the movement before the Islamic revolution. But following the revolution in 1979, several laws were established that mandated wearing hijab while in public. Despite the growing restrictions regarding women's rights in Iran after 1979, the movement continued its activities. The "one million signatures" campaign was one of the popular campaigns aiming to repeal discriminatory laws, promote equal rights in marriage and inheritance for women, and end polygamy, honor killing, and other forms of violence against women in Iran (Sameh, 2010). The #MyStealthyFreedom movement, as mentioned earlier, aims to produce solidarity through social media activism and demand women's right to choose their form of dress (Stewart and Schultze, 2019). Addressing women's issues and sensitive subjects of sexual violence could be challenging in a context where the laws aim to control women's bodies and when the most prominent political figure blames the victims of assault and rape. Despite legal, cultural, and social barriers, the #MeToo movement found its way to Iran through social media. Analyzing the #MeToo movement in the Iranian sociopolitical context is necessary because the movement was reframed and redefined to suit different women's rights condition. For this analysis, the chapter looks at Iranian laws and the tweets under the Iranian #MeToo movement shared on Twitter from August 6, 2020, to September 15, 2020, to find the shared themes of the movement, as well as the ways that Iranian women adapted #MeToo to their own needs and to continue their fight against gender and sexual violence.

But it is important to assess the prevalence of the problem of sexual harassment or sexual assault in Iran. In 2007, the Iranian police said sexual attacks were a prioritized issue (ISNA, 2007). However, in 2008, the number of reported rape cases increased. According to the *Shargh* daily newspaper, the largest number of reported rapes in Iran in 2020 was for the largest city in Iran, Tehran, which had 1,650 reported cases (Sharghdaily, 2020). However, only 20% of women report rape since there is not much legal support for victims. Regarding sexual harassment, a study on 350 women living in Sari, Iran, shows that almost 90% of women have experienced nonverbal assault and 95% of them have experienced some form of sexual harassment (Kurdi and Hosseininozari, 2015). Globally, many of the experiences of sexual harassment or assault take place in the workplace or in confrontation with people in higher hierarchal positions, and the victims would rather ignore their experience due to their job security (Smartt, 2017), and this is the case for Iranian women as well. According to the *Etemad* newspaper, 90% of female Iranian journalists experienced sexual harassment, but 60% of them ignored it. Also, 36% of women experienced such harassment from a manager in government or private sector (EtemadOnline, 2019). In order to have a better grasp of the issue of sexual harassment, it is necessary to know the laws related to rape and sexual harassment. After the 1979 revolution in Iran,[4] the new legal system was based on Islamic criminal code (sharia) and religious authority found its ways in both private and public policy (Aghtaie, 2011).

Islamic criminal code criminalized sexuality in a way that considers any sexual contact outside a legal marriage a crime. The main category of such crime is *Zena*,[5] which is defined as any act of illicit sexual intercourse between a woman and a man. The punishment of Zena—100 lashes for the unmarried and death by stoning for the married (Mir-Hosseini, 2011; Qur'an Sura An-Nur)—is also gender based.[6] The punishment is less severe for men, as they are "only" buried to the waist. Also, the Islamic criminal code has severe punishment regarding rape. If someone has sexual intercourse with a woman without her consent or when she is unconscious, he is convicted of adultery and sentenced to the death penalty (Nayyeri, 2012). Despite the laws against rape, there are other forms of legal rape, for example child marriage and marital rape. This line of thinking not only gives sexual agency completely to men, but also defines sex as a quid pro quo exchange.

Unfortunately, the term "sexual assault" does not specifically exist in the Islamic Penal Laws in Iran. Since the term does not exist, most kinds of sexual assaults also do not get reported because there is a lower chance of punishment to the aggressor. Adultery and physical assault are the two closest terms to sexual assault. Article 223, paragraph 61, of the Constitution states: "(Women) have the right to have protection and immunity against verbal abuse by others and duty toward members of the society to refrain from verbal abuse." While Islamic criminal code in Iran implicitly refers to verbal sexual harassment (Tavasolian, 2016), it does not identify non-consensual touching or groping as forms of sexual assault (Torabi, 2018). This lack of accurate legal definitions of such crimes increases the chance of biased court decisions in the cases of sexual assault. Additionally, such ambiguous laws put men at an advantage in the marriage contract or its negotiations. However, the #MeToo movement in Iran helped feminists introduce more vocabularies to the public regarding sexual and gender-based violence and increase their understanding of these problems.

#MeToo and other related hashtags have encouraged conversations regarding the issues of sexual and gender-based violence. Not only does the media try to eschew reporting cases of sexual violence because of censorship laws (Torabi, 2018), people also avoid reporting such incidents to the police to protect the family honor. Additionally, being harassed and sexually assaulted could be interpreted in a way that could determine women's own behavior, their irreligious and cultural practices, and immodest behavior as the reasons for sexual assault.[7] Rape victims, particularly, are blamed for provoking the violence on their bodies (Aghtaie, 2011). The victim of rape is blamed for behaving immodestly or not wearing a proper hijab, since according to the beliefs of the Islamic state of Iran and Iranian leaders, "modesty in dress, especially women's hijab, secures society against chaos and individuals against self-incurred harmful thoughts and deeds" (Shahidian, 2002, p. 212). A study showed that different dress codes experience various levels of sexual harassment, but none can protect women from sexual violence (Seraj Zadeh et al., 2015). Furthermore, according to the Islamic point of view, addressing sexual acts shall not be shared in public discourse to keep public morality untouched (Aghtaie, 2011). All of these elements together not only target and blame the victims of sexual harassment, but also make the ways to take legal actions against the harassers more challenging.

## The Iranian #MeToo Movement

The #MeToo movement in Iran started on August 6, 2020, when a Twitter account "Emanel" shared sexist advice for men about "how to connect and have sexual intercourse with girls" (Blue Seat Studios, 2015; Mirza, 2020). Some women revealed the fact that Emanel is not just a random Twitter troll, but that the account holder had raped some women. Emanel deleted his Twitter account later, but it did not silence the wave that started against sexual assault and rape (Mirza, 2020). Many women, including some journalists, shared their experiences with sexual violence. They revealed the names of the persons who had raped or sexually assaulted them. These names included some famous figures, like the Iranian painter Aydin Aghdashloo, and the Iranian singer and musician Mohsen Namjoo. Sara Ommatali, an Iranian journalist, revealed that Aydin Aghdashloo sexually harassed her during one of their interviews. Ommatali shared her experience on Twitter and later with different media and took her case to court. She claimed that Aghdashloo tried to kiss her when they had arranged a meeting in his office and planned to visit a museum to conduct an interview. This resulted in #Rape and #SexualHarassment campaigns, along with #MeToo. Using these hashtags, Iranian women of various backgrounds shared their own #MeToo moments, posting their experiences with rape, sexual assault, and sexual harassment. Although some of victims of such incidents, like Ommatali, took their cases to court, some only shared their experiences publicly to create awareness about sexual violence and to offer social and legal support to other victims.

In addition to #Rape and #SexualHarassment hashtags, #NoMeansNo became viral as well, and more than thousand people of all genders tweeted and retweeted these hashtags and shared their stories of sexual violence in Iran. These hashtags attracted a wide range of participants and generated discussions about consent and Iranian laws, as well as sociocultural attitudes toward sexual and gender-based violence. In 2016, the Tea Consent[8] (Blue Seat Studios, 2015) metaphor video became viral, comparing sex with having a cup of tea with someone. In August 2020, the tea metaphor video became viral in Iranian communities on Twitter under the hashtag #NoMeansNo. Among women who revealed their stories were groups of journalists who had been assaulted by one of their colleagues and influential men whom they had interviewed. Also, many anonymous accounts on Twitter shared their experiences of rape and sexual harassment, mostly by men in a position of power, using #Rape and #SexualHarassment hashtags.

In some cases, multiple women mentioned the names or used the initials of the attackers, and hundreds more asked for their prosecution. For the first time, Iranian women in large numbers raised their voices in social media and shared their stories of rape and sexual harassment. As a result of the power of Iranian women's united voice, many of these harassers lost their social positions, went to court, and were tried by a jury. Below, I analyze the top tweets from August 2020 to September 2020 that used any of the three viral hashtags (#Rape, #SexualHarassment, and #NoMeansNo). These tweets not only highlight the problems about sexual violence, but also show that Iranian laypersons have a reductive understanding of sexual violence. Thus the conversations sparked because of #MeToo become all the more important in Iranian context.

## #MeToo Tweets: Revealing Stories

Hashtags like #Rape, #SexualHarassment, and #NoMeansNo that started after #MeToo became a space for victims to share their experiences with violence. Twitter, then, became a space for the kinds of conversations that would not happen elsewhere in Iran with such public engagement. For instance, @miss_james_69 lauded those sharing their experiences:

> آفرین به جراتت، اگه در مقابل تجاوز همگی برخورد میکردن و داد میزدن و متجاوز رسوا میکردن، قطعا انقدر تجاوز در خفا وجود نداشت .. #نه_یعنی_نه (Bravo, if everyone reveals their experiences and ashamed rapists, there would not be this much of concealed rape happening in the society, #NoMeansNo).[9] (August 7. 2020)

While these tweets received support, some people also question the veracity of claims in these tweets. @aliizadi83 tweeted:

> فضای مجازی دادگاه نیست!
> اگه بهت #تجاوز شده برو شکایت کن و تا زمان اثبات جرم باید سکوت کنی!
> مفهومه؟! (Social media is not a court. If you got #Raped, take your complaint to the court. You should remain silent till the affirmation of your case, is it clear?). (August 30, 2020)

In this tweet, it has been asked not to judge and make a decision about people who are accused of rape or sexual assault, based on the information people got from different accounts on social media. It is worth mentioning that taking these issues to court and establishing the truth of these cases usually take years after they took place. People also blamed the victims for their choice of clothing and for trusting men that they did not know well. All of these comments in one way or the other shift the blame of violence to the victim. These comments usually invite critique from feminists and lead to more victims of rape revealing the identity of their rapists on social media.

Many other tweets encouraged people to believe the victim/survivor. The only thing that public opinion needs to provide is sympathy, acceptance, and support to those who had to face sexual violence. For example, one tweet read: حرف قربانی تجاوز را باید باور کرد بی چون و چرا و همانجا باید متجاوز را اعدام کرد و اجازه حرف زدن هم به او نداد#نه_یعنی_نه (@Maghsoodi20, August 30, 2020). ("We should accept the words of victims of rape without any doubt and the rapist should be executed . . . #NoMeansNo"). Another tweet read: حداقل مسئولیت ما در برابر راویان آسیب دیده #تجاوز و #آزار_جنسی این است که بگوییم #من_باور_میکنم #من_هم #MeTooIran ("Our least responsibility facing the victims of #Rape is saying #IBelieveYou. #MeToo") (@BorideNafas, September 9, 2020). Another supporter tweeted: "اگر تجربه ی به اشتراک گذاشته یک قربانی #تجاوز را باور نمیکنید خود، متجاوزید!" ("If you do not believe in the shared experiences of victims of rape, you, yourself are a rapist") (@yarayii, September 6, 2020). While many of these tweets do not address the complexity of sexual violence, related laws, and its reportage, even starting these conversations and thinking through these problems on a public forum where stakeholders are a part of the conversation is a step in the right direction. Despite some backlash, the collective agreement was on the importance of support for victims of sexual violence like rape. It frames a new supportive perspective toward the victims of rape in Iran since, as I discussed earlier, this point of view was not common before the #MeToo movement. One can hope that these Twitter conversations result in better understanding of these issues and the problems of seeking justice in an already biased legal and administrative structures.

Besides, some interrogate #NoMeansNo and mention a standup comedy presented by Bill Burr, saying that "no" does not always means "no," but most of the time women are willing to be in such a situation and they do not really mean "no." However, such a point of view was challenged. One Twitter user tweeted: نه یعنی نه من یک #زن هستم. من #انسان هستم، برده تو نیستم ابزار و اشیاء خانه تو نیستم، حق تجاوز به من را نداری من صاحب جسم خودم هستم. علیه تجاوز به زنان! #نه_یعنی_نه #تجاوز #انقلاب_زنانه (@ranarahimpour, September 11, 2020). ("#NoAlwaysMeansNo, I am a woman. I am human, not your slave, not your house's object, you do not have the right to rape me. I am the owner of my own body. Against women's rape! #NoMeansNo, #Rape, #Women'sRevolution . . .").

## Awareness

Because of the simplistic arguments of those who questioned the participants of Iranian #MeToo, some Twitter users also used their space to increase awareness about Iranian #MeToo. Twitter users explained different aspects and forms of sexual and gender-based violence to make the cases clearer. By sharing links that talk about each of these terminologies, Twitter activists distinguished between various forms of violence against women to prepare and empower them to fight these issues in the future. These links and Twitter threads also helped women identify the sexual violence that they had gone through and grasp the complexity of it. Distinguishing between various forms of sexual violence helps women to share their stories more accurately and use the proper hashtag to make their participation in the Iranian #MeToo more visible and make the movement more effective.

These campaigns also focused on teaching the next generation and providing safe spaces for children to share their experiences. For example, @FallenleafRed shared that “لطفا یک نسل از پدران و مادران در بچه ها ایمنی ایجاد کنید که بتوانند حرف بزنند. دختر و پسر فرقی ندارد. اولین قدم برای پیشگیری از شنیدن های شما شروع می شود. اولین اصل درمان پناهگاه امن برای درددل است.” (“Parents should provide a safety net for children, boys or girls to talk. The family should be their shelter. Listening to their experiences prevents further sexual violence”) (September 7, 2020), and that, ما باید به نسل آینده آموزش بدهیم که #نه-یعنی-نه. این بهشون کمک میکنه که زندگی بهتری از ما داشته باشن اگه مورد تجاوز قرار گرفتن ساکت نمونن . . . نباید خجالت بکشن. #بدن-من-تصمیم-من (“we have to teach our next generation that #NoMeansNo. It helps them to live a better life than us. They should not remain silent in case of harassment. They should not be ashamed, #My-Body-My-Decision”) (@StoryTellerFati, August 23, 2020).

Many tweets use various videos and contents to teach about sexual violence and consent. One of the most retweeted videos was the Tea Consent metaphor (Blue Seat Studios, 2015) that explains the idea of consent in a sexual relationship as an offer for tea. This video and its content were accessible by most people who were using Twitter and hence was very fruitful in promoting awareness regarding consent and the ways to navigate a sexual relationship respectfully and consensually.

## Blaming Political and Cultural Context

Many tweets also argued that the political and educational system influenced understanding of rape and sexual violence in Iran. Many rape victims do not report the crime to the police because sexual intercourse outside of marriage is not legal in Iran. But Twitter users tried to convince people to report the incidents of sexual violence: نکته مهم اینه در صورتی که مورد تجاوز قرار گرفتید حتما به پلیس مراجعه کنید و شکایت کنید این فرهنگ لاپوشونی و نگفتن اسم متجاوز به نظرم به بقیه افراد هم ضربه میزنه متجاوزی که احساس امنیت کنه از این فرد آسیب دیده کاری بهش نداره به تجاوز ادامه میده #نه_یعنی_نه (“You need to go to the police and file your complaint. This is not a good way to be afraid of revealing such stories since concealing such stories gives the feeling of immunity to rapists. While you can stop them. #NoMeansNo”) (@SaghiLagha, August 7, 2020). But reporting in such cases can harm the victim, instead of helping them.

Those who blamed formal and informal education systems argued that children do not learn about healthy sexual relationships in their schools or at homes.

For example, one tweet shared: اگه از اول دبستان تفکیک جنسیتی نمیشدیم و اگه بجای آخوند، یک آدم مطلع توی مدرسه برامون از سکس حرف میزد که مجبور نشیم اطلاعاتمون رو از پورنهای فیک بدست بیاریم، اونوقت یه عده میفهمیدن اونی که میاد خونه باهات گل بکشه شاید فقط اومده گل بکشه، نه اینکه بهش #تجاوز بشه. #نه_یعنی_نه ("If there was no gender segregation in school, and if we had a sex education class rather than a cleric talking about religion in our schools . . . , then some people would understand if someone comes to your house to smoke, she just came to smoke, not to be #Raped. #NoMeansNo.") (@nazkm, August 8, 2020). The cultural and educational setup that indoctrinates young minds with the prejudiced gendered role of a good daughter, wife, or mother also leads to gender and sexual violence. Some Twitter users connect sexual violence with the mandatory hijab laws in Iran and argued that hijab laws aim to own women's bodies in public. Ultimately, these laws give the state control over the female body and lead to more cases of moral judgment and sexual violence. According to Khomeini's point of view, women are the source of temptation, and they should be modest and cover their body and head to keep Islamic society away from sin (Hoffman-Ladd, 1987). These factors turn women into objects to be used by men, take away women's agency, and give the state control over female bodies.

These factors further aggravate the gender imbalance and power relations. Many tweets mentioned a rape story revealed by a woman named Zahra Navidpour, who accused Salman Khodadadi, one of the members of Iran's Parliament, of rape. Zahra released videos and audio clips about her experience. She died suspiciously and was secretly buried without an autopsy in 2019 (Iran-Hrm, 2019). Many #MeToo activists remembered this horrible story, arguing that آزار جنسی در خلأ اتفاق نمیافته بلکه شرط تحقق اون یک مناسبات قدرت خاصه ("rape and sexual harassment are not happening in a vacuum . . . it needs specific power relations") (@Safoor1372, September 20, 2020). Activists also attempted to raise awareness about the abuse of these power relations in the absence an effective and equitable legal system that supports victims. While appeals for executing the rapists started trending after #MeToo, a conversation regarding its effectiveness also started. As mentioned earlier, the penalty of rape is execution of the rapist, according to Islamic laws in Iran. Many activists also argued that if the stakes are life and death of the rapist, victims will be hesitant to take their cases to court.[10]

All of the above are taboo subjects for the public in Iran, but the Iranian #MeToo movement vocalizes these voices and these issues with public engagement. The movement also found its way into the official newspapers published in Iran that would usually shy away from publishing content about sexual violence.

Following the start of the Iranian #MeToo movement, many newspapers and websites began to cover different topics related to sexual harassment and rape in Farsi or English, such as defining terminology of sexual violence and harassment

(KeyhanLondon, 2020); informing Iranian citizens about the existing laws and punishment regarding sexual harassment and rape and elaborating the legal punishment for sexual violence (HamshahriOnline, 2020; AsrIran, 2020); recognizing sexual harassment as a crime (Ansari, 2020); the rate of women and children's rape and sexual harassment in Iran (AsrIran, 2020); naming the documents the victim needs to bring to court (IranWire, 2020); difficulties victims face by revealing their experiences of rape (Darvishpour, 2020); social, cultural, political, and psychological aspects of rape (Naghibi, 2020; Sharghdaily, 2020); the ways to support rape victims (Harass Watch, 2020); and covering the latest news about the movement (Alinejad and Hakakian, 2020). Along with local news channels, news channels like BBC Persian, Iran International, France 24, and Wionews also covered news related to the Iranian #MeToo movement and its related Twitter trends. These reports also increased the conversations around these taboo subjects and increased public understanding of sexual violence in Iran.

Along with the understanding and awareness, it also led to some accountability of the perpetrators of sexual violence. Following the stories shared via #MeToo and #NoMeansNo, one of the people who was accused of serial rape was arrested. Additionally, Digikala, known as "Iranian Amazon," responded to some of the complaints about sexual harassment that one of their former managers committed, apologized, and claimed that they will be more cautious and sensitive about these issues from then on (Mirza, 2020). The Iranian Sociological Association also canceled the membership of one of its researchers who had been accused of sexual harassment in different narratives to show the importance of such a sensitive subject and the necessity of guarding morality in the scientific and civil associations (BBC News, 2020).

In 2008, a police officer reported an increase in the number of reported cases of rape and sexual harassment during an interview with the Iranian Students News Agency (ISNA). In this interview, the police officer partly blamed the victims of rape, claiming: "The main targets of perpetrators are young girls and women. They are the ones who take the first steps and fall into men's traps" (Aghtaie, 2011, p. 123). After #MeToo in Iran, such perspectives, that held victims of harassment or rape accountable about enabling the perpetrators of sexual violence, are being challenged on social media forums. The #MeToo movement changed and encouraged women's rights activists to empower women to tell their stories and to not be afraid of sharing their experiences with others. Although there have been ongoing discussions about sexual harassment in Iran (Ahmadi, 2006; Ahmadi et al., 2016; Najjar Nahvandi and Ahangar Salabati, 2010; Nazari, 2018) it seems one of the preconditions for the formation of social and cultural change is the engagement of a large number of people who experience the problem and are willing to make things better collectively.

The Iranian #MeToo movement helped clarify some of the misunderstandings regarding what counts as gender-related and sexual abuse and violence (Torabi, 2018). It educated both men and women regarding consent and sexual violence. Using the hashtag #NoMeansNo, elaborating on its meaning, and discussing the opinions of both genders teach men to not perceive sex as their right. Also, it teaches everyone that women are the owners of their bodies. Hanging out with someone, going to someone's place, wearing revealing dresses, etc., are not necessarily indicators of their agreement to have a sexual relationship.

Though limited criminal justice arrangements can be found in many different countries regarding street harassment (Fileborn and Vera-Gray, 2017), the Islamic Penal Law in Iran does not even provide specific protections for the victims of sexual assault, and this paradoxical approach to sexual harassment and assault has resulted in repetition and hence normalization of this form of violence (Torabi, 2018). Also, having rape as a subdivision to Zena leaves victims of rape in a vulnerable situation, where women have to be co-defendants as well as complainants in rape cases (Aghtaie, 2011). However, the Iranian #MeToo movement is making women claimants of social and legal change more and more, highlighting the flaws in existing laws, and looking for a change. The Iranian #MeToo movement has also been pivotal in refocusing the conversation in public space to protection against gender-based and sexual violence.

Reading the Twitter posts makes many feel that society is more ready to listen to the narrative of those who have experienced sexual abuse and to press for accountability and change (Sepehrifar, 2020). Similar to the global trend of cultural transformation following the #MeToo movement (Crocker and Sibley, 2020; Gordon and Silva, 2015), the culture regarding rape and sexual harassment in Iran also has experienced change in which more people in society feel supported to disclose or report, more bystanders feel responsible to intervene in the incidents, and more supportive legislations are passed to strengthen the support. In addition to the changes mentioned above, the definition of sexual and gender harassment and violence has also evolved through such movements and discussions. These current events have shown that more women are aiming to defy traditional, ideological, and political norms to speak out against sexual assault and rape, naming their attackers and demanding accountability. Social media are changing public discourse about sexual violence (Mendes et al., 2018). Twitter hashtags have indisputably been a great connector and amplifier, letting Iranian women read one another's stories and the experiences of women in other countries.

Although it is a hard process to put oneself out "in the line of fire" through participating in online feminist activism, Iranian women took the responsibility and engaged in this movement. Using social media as the main platform for this movement enables feminist activists to have the opportunity to vocalize their voices on a global scale, rapidly and immediately. It also allows them to connect and create a dialogue toward reaching, as Mendes et al. mentioned, a shared understanding (Mendes et al., 2018). The formation of various hashtags based on the experience of Iranian women helped them to find and narrate their own specific stories based on their unique social, cultural, and legal context. Additionally, the Iranian #MeToo movement is taking advantage of its peers, the other #MeToo movements that have been formed all over the world. Using the content that has been already made for other #MeToos helps this movement to move forward even more effectively since such a problem is not limited to one geographical or cultural location.

However, engaging in digital feminist activism definitely "depend[s] on the context" (Mendes et al., 2018: p. 244; Starkey et al., 2019). The Iranian #MeToo movement has formed in a political context in Iran that is demanding that all women wear the hijab modestly to keep the society away from sin; the educational system is not teaching children about sexual harassment and rape and their rights about their bodies; the legal system defines any sexual relationship outside marriage as illegal; being a victim of rape culturally and historically was taboo in Iran; a rapist's punishment is execution; and marital rape is legal. Analysis of the main themes in the dialogues that formed in the movement on Twitter shows these specific concerns regarding the unique context of Iran. This unique context is demanding a unique, context-specific approach to address sexual violence. Though the #MeToo movement framed in Iran took some components of the global #MeToo, it modified some other components based on the cultural and contextual needs of Iranian society. For instance, following the start point of the #MeToo movement in Iran, two Instagram pages, @harasswatch, @me_too_movement_iran, started their activities in order to empower women, share their stories, and increase public awareness regarding sexual assault and sexual violence. These pages on Instagram play an important role because at the time of conducting this study Instagram was the most popular social media in Iran that everyone can have access without using a proxy, while access to Twitter was not as convenient since users need to have some proxies active on their phones. These Instagram pages also provide platforms for Iranian society to remain involved in the ongoing Iranian #MeToo movement and to make a persistent effort to stop sexual violence against women in Iran.

Despite the progress and increased accountability of perpetrators after #MeToo, much still needs to be done regarding judicial processes and the ways that they deal with other more powerful accused sexual predators, as one of the biggest concerns of #MeToo is focused on the intersection of sex and power (Gill and Orgad, 2018). Policymakers also ought to maintain the high-quality provision of advocacy and counseling and commit themselves to bringing forth the policies that advance gender equality and address shortfalls in the criminal justice system. The law has to not only sanction discrimination based on gender, but also defend women instead of accusing them (Torabi, 2018). They must attempt to draft a rigorous law that clearly defines what counts as sexual assault.

In addition to the concerns mentioned above, there are many reasons to be pessimistic about how far requests for accountability could go under the current Iranian civil society's repression and legal restrictions. Some critics point to the fact that the Iranian #MeToo movement is not inclusive until women from lower economic strata as well as women of other ethnicities speak out and share their experiences (Rahmani, 2020). Also, Iranian #MeToo remains lacking regarding violence happening inside families, as well as speaking out about sexual violence against men and sexual minorities.

Women sharing their experiences under #MeToo and related hashtags show that they are not waiting for authorities to give them their rights, but they continue to push forward for change in various ways, regardless of the existing limitations. Feminist activists are using social media and innovative hashtags to educate new generations about body ownership and sexual harassment. The role of female journalists in formation and promotion of feminist movements in Iran is impressive and worth mentioning since two of the influential movements in Iran in the twenty-first century, including the #MeToo Movement and the #MyStealthyFreedom movement (see Basmechi et al., 2022) have been started and framed by Iranian female journalists. However, lobbying with legislators to demand that more accurate legal terms be established and implemented seems a necessary step to secure the society from sexual harassment; the strength of the online hashtags also pressures legislators to respond to the demands for change.

In the second wave of Iranian #MeToo movement which started in April 2022, female Iranian actresses joined the movement and tried to vocalize their experiences of sexual assault and sexual violence in their workspace throughout the years in the film industry in Iran and demanded their rights. They urged industry figures to mobilize through institutions such as the Iranian Alliance of Motion Picture Guilds to form a female majority committee to securely receive and review the cases of sexual assault and aggression (Motamedi, 2022). The Iranian #MeToo movement and feminist activists inspired common Iranian women to fight for their rights and be a part of the movement. I can say confidently that these are only the first few steps in the formation and growth of the Iranian #MeToo movement and a new era of feminism.

## Notes

1. There is a long history of contention around hijab after the 1979 revolution in Iran. The leader of the 1979 revolution in Iran, Khomeini, called for the wearing of hijab while in public for all women. Though many women protested (Basu, 2016; Shojaee, 2009), wearing hijab in public became a legal mandate in 1983. In response to women's resistance to the law, Article 139 in the Islamic Criminal Code was added in 1995 to mandate 10 to 60 days of imprisonment for anyone who publicly resisted the hijab (Sedghi, 2007). Also, in 2005, the government authorized a new branch of the police known as the morality police to impose Islamic dress code and compulsory hijab in public (BBC, 2010).
2. Asking women to share unveiled pictures of themselves on Instagram or Facebook protesting mandatory hijab laws through online platforms.
3. Inviting women to wear white scarf on Wednesdays while in public and share their videos and pictures on social media to show their disagreement with mandatory hijab laws online and offline.
4. The 1979 Islamic revolution in Iran (January 7, 1978–February 11, 1979) was a series of events which culminated in the overthrown of the dynasty and replacement of the Pahlavi government with an Islamic Republic government (see Behrooz, 2012; Daneshvar, 2016).
5. Qur'an claims related to Zena are as follows: "Nor come nigh to fornication/adultery: for it is a shameful (deed) and an evil, opening the road (to other evils)" (Sura 17 (Al-Isra), ayat 32); "The woman and the man guilty of zinā' (for fornication or adultery), flog each of them with a hundred stripes: Let not compassion move you in their case, in a matter prescribed by Allah, if ye believe in Allah and the Last Day: and let a party of the Believers witness their punishment" (Sura 24 (An-Nur), ayat 2); "And those who accuse chaste women then do not bring four witnesses, flog them, (giving) eighty stripes, and do not admit any evidence from them ever; and these it is that are the transgressors. Except those who repent after this and act aright, for surely Allah is Forgiving, Merciful" (Sura 24 (An-Nur), ayat 4–5).
6. Although this law is not implemented in Iran due to a campaign against stoning. Feminist activists started a campaign against stoning in 2006 named "The Stop Stoning Forever Campaign" in order to show the world that stoning was still happening in Iran, although the government denied this (Kar, 2007; Terman, 2007). The activists started with raising public awareness on both local and international levels about the reality of stoning in Iran. They also put pressure on decision-makers in Iran and encouraged international pressure on the decision-makers in Iran. Finally, they tried to advocate for the reform of Islamic laws and started the argument that stoning is not Islamic. Religious reform was a helpful strategy to show that stoning is un-Islamic using different Islamic sources and clerical fatwa. In May 2009, a new draft was passed to Iran's parliament which eliminated stoning. Finally, in 2012, stoning was removed from Iran's Islamic Punishment Law and was legally abolished as a punishment for adultery and was replaced by the unspecified death penalty.

7. The culture expected women to behave modestly, which means women need to wear modest clothing, behave modestly in public and not attract the attention of others, not laugh or speak loudly in public, etc.
8. In this video, having sex is metaphorically compared with having a cup of tea, and it claims if someone does not want to have tea with you, you do not pour tea into their mouth by force!
9. All tweets are translated by the author from Persian.
10. One of the viral cases of #MeToo was the case of Keyvan Emamverdi, who was accused of drug-raping dozens of women. He was sentenced to death on July 9, 2022 (Iranwire, 2022).

## Works Cited

Aghtaie, N. 2011. "Breaking the Silence: Rape Law in Iran and Controlling Women's Sexuality." In *International Approaches to Rape*, edited by N. Westmarland and G. Gangoli, pp. 121–145. Bristol: Bristol University Press.

Ahmadi, F. 2006. "Islamic Feminism in Iran: Feminism in a New Islamic Context." *Journal of Feminist Studies in Religion* 22, no. 2: 33–53.

Ahmadi, Y., A. Bokharayi, and S. Bivarani. 2016. "A Sociological Analysis of Street Sexual Harassment from the Perpetrator perspective." *Iran's Social Problems* 10, no. 2: 5–27.

Alinejad, M., and R. Hakakian. 2020. "Opinion: Iranian women Are Staging an Offensive against Sexual Abuse. It's Long Overdue." *Washington Post.* https://www.washingtonpost.com/opinions/2020/08/26/iranian-women-are-staging-an-offensive-against-sexual-abuse-its-long-overdue/. Accessed November 22, 2022.

Ansari, N. 2020. "Sexual Harassment Is a Crime." https://www.tribunezamaneh.com/archives/239846. Accessed November 21, 2022.

AsrIran, 2020. "Statistics Regarding Women and Children's Sexual Harassment in Iran." https://www.asriran.com/fa/news/742607. Accessed September 25, 2020.

Basmechi, F., D. Barnes, and M. Heydari. 2022. "Hashtag Activism: Tactical Maneuvering in an Online Anti-Mandatory Hijab Movement." *Sociological Spectrum* 42, no. 1: 18–39.

Basu, A. ed. 2010. "Introduction." In *Women's Movements in the Global Era: The Power of Local Feminisms*, edited by Amrita Basu. Boulder, CO: Westview Press.

BBC News. 2020. "Iranian Sociological Association Renounced Kamil Ahmadi Membership Following his Accusation of Sexual Harassment." BBC News Farsi. https://www.bbc.com/persian/iran-54123786. Accessed September 25, 2020.

Behrooz, M., 2012. "Iran after Revolution (1979–2009)." In *Oxford Handbook of Iranian History*, edited by T. Daryaee, pp. 365–390. Oxford: Oxford University Press.

Blue Seat Studios. 2015. "Tea Consent (Clean)." https://www.youtube.com/watch?v=pZwvrxVavnQ 10/17/2020.

Crocker, Diane, and Marcus A. Sibley. 2020. "Transforming Campus Rape Culture." In *Collaborating for Change: Transforming Cultures to End Gender-Based Violence in Higher Education*, edited by S. Marine and R. Lewis, pp. 23–46. Oxford: Oxford University Press.

Daneshvar, P. 2016. *Revolution in Iran*. New York: Springer.

Darvishpour, M. 2020. "Challenges on the Way of Revealing Sexual Harassment and Violence." *Shahrvand*. https://shahrvand.com/archives/115461. Accessed September 25, 2020.

EtemadOnline. 2019. "How Many Female Iranian Journalists Have Experienced Sexual Harassment?" https://www.etemadonline.com. Accessed September 9, 2020.

Fileborn, B., and F. Vera-Gray. 2017. "'I Want to Be Able to Walk the Street Without Fear': Transforming Justice for Street Harassment." *Feminist Legal Studies* 25: 203–227. https://doi.org/10.1007/s10691-017-9350-3.

Gill, R., and S. Orgad. 2018. "The Shifting Terrain of Sex and Power: From the 'Sexualization of Culture' to# MeToo." *Sexualities* 21: 1313–1324.

Gordon, L. E., and T. J. Silva. 2015. "Inhabiting the Sexual Landscape: Toward an Interpretive Theory of the Development of Sexual Orientation and Identity." *Journal of Homosexuality* 62: 495–530.

Hamshahrionline. 2020. "What Is the Penalty of Women's Sexual Harassment? When Does the Perpetrator Be Executed?" *HamshahriOnline*. https:// www.hams hahr ionl ine.ir/ news/ 545 527/مجا زات-جرم-آزار-و-اذیت-زنان-چیست-در-چه-موا قعی-آزا رگر-جنسی. Accessed September 25, 2020.

Harass Watch. 2020. "Ways to Support Survivors of Rape." https://harasswatch.com/news/1548. Accessed November 21, 2022.

Hoffman-Ladd, V. J. 1987. "Polemics on the modesty and segregation of women in contemporary Egypt." *International Journal of Middle East Studies* 19, no. 1: 23–50.

Iran-hrm. 2019. "Rape Victim Who Died Suspiciously Was Secretly Buried without Autopsy." https://iran-hrm.com/2019/01/13/rape-victim-zahra-navidpour-suspiciously-died-buried-without-autopsy/. Accessed November 21, 2022.

IranWire. 2020. "What Kinds of Evidence Do We Need to Make a Complaint Regarding Sexual Harassment and Rape?" *Iran Wire*. https://iranwire.com/fa/practical-resources/40565. Accessed September 25, 2020.

IranWire. 2022. "As a Serial Rapist is Sentenced to Death, Victims Slam Lack of Justice." https://iranwire.com/en/women/105617-as-serial-rapist-is-sentenced-to-death-victims-slam-lack-of-justice/. Accessed September 6, 2022.

Islamic Criminal Code. 2020. "The Parliament Institute of Research." *Majlis*. https://rc.majlis.ir/fa/law/show/845048. Accessed October 17, 2021.

ISNA. 2007. "International Day for the Elimination of Gender Based Violence against Women, the Most Prevalent Violation to the Human Rights in Today's World." https://www.isna.ir/news/8609-01930. Accessed October 17, 2021.

Kar, M. 2007. "A Brief History of Grassroots Struggles to End Stoning." http://www.meydaan.com/english/showarticle.aspx?arid=320. Accessed September 8, 2021.

KeyhanLondon. 2020. "What Is Sexual Harassment? What Are Sexual Abuse and Rape?" https://kayhan.london/fa/1399/06/12. Accessed October 17, 2021.

Khamenei, A. 2012. "Leader's Speech to Panegyrists" [online], http://english.khamenei.ir/news/1642/Leader-s-Speech-to-Panegyrists. Accessed October 17, 2021.

Khamenei, A. 2018. "Can Hijab Save Western Women?" [online], http://english.khamenei.ir/news/5986/10-facts-by-Ayatollah-Khamenei-Can-hijab-save-Western-women. Accessed September 9, 2020.

Kurdi, M., and A. S. Hosseininozari. 2015. "Women's Experiences of Sexual Harassment Types." *Social Welfare* 15, no. 57: 7–30. http://refahj.uswr.ac.ir/article-1-2161-fa.html.

Mendes, K., J. Ringrose, and J. Keller. 2018. "#MeToo and the Promise and Pitfalls of Challenging Rape Culture through Digital Feminist Activism." *European Journal of Womens Studies* 25: 236–246. https://doi.org/10.1177/1350506818765318.

Mir-Hosseini, Z. 2011. "Criminalizing Sexuality: Zina Laws as Violence against Women in Muslim Contexts." *International Journal Human Rights* 15: 7–34.

Mirza, M. 2020. "Once Rape Victims Seek Refuge in Twitter." DW.COM. https://www.dw.com/fa-ir/a-54732971. Accessed September 9, 2020.

Motamedi, M. 2022. "Iranian Women Denounce Violence in Film Industry." *Aljazeera*, April 3. https://www.aljazeera.com/news/2022/4/3/iranian-women-call-for-accountability-in-film-industry. Accessed September 6, 2022.

Naghibi, N. 2007. *Rethinking Global Sisterhood: Western Feminism and Iran*. Minneapolis: University of Minnesota Press.

Najjar Nahvandi, M., and A. Ahangar Salabati. 2010. "A Sociological Analysis of Women's Feeling of Sexual Security." *Iran's Social Problems Review* 1, no. 1: 167–177.

Nayyeri, M. H. 2012. "New Islamic Penal Code of the Islamic Republic of Iran: An Overview." *Research Paper Series*: 1–25.

Nazari, T. 2018. "Analysis of the Factors Influencing on Women's Sexual Harassment in Khorram Abbad." *Crime Prevention Approach* 1, no. 4: 51–72.

Radiozamaneh. 2016. "Sexual Harassment in Islamic Penal Code." *Radio Zamaneh*. https://www.radiozamaneh.com/261562. Accessed September 14, 2020.

Rahmani, M., 2020. "Which Women Are Vocalizing about Which Men Harassment? Do Everyone's Voices Been Heard?" *Akhbar Rooz*. https:// www.akh bar- rooz.com/-کدام-زنان-از-آزار-کدام-مردان-می-گوی/. Accessed September 26, 2020.

Sameh, C. 2010. "Discourses of Equality, Rights and Islam in the One Million Signatures Campaign in Iran." *International Feminist Journal of Politics* 12: 444–463.

Sedghi, H. 2007. *Women and Politics in Iran: Veiling, Unveiling, and Reveiling*. Cambridge: Cambridge University Press.

Sepehrifar, T. 2020. "Iran and the #MeToo Moment." https://www.hrw.org/fa/news/2020/09/09/376370. Accessed November 21, 2022.

Serajzadeh, S., F. Javaheri, and A. Rahmati. 2015. "Women's Ways of Dressing and Feeling of Security in Public Spheres." *Social Sciences Studies Journal* 9: 135–159.

Shaditalab, J. 2005. "Iranian Women: Rising Expectations." *Critique: Critical Middle Eastern Studies* 14: 35–55.

Shahidian, H. 2002. *Women in Iran: Gender Politics in the Islamic Republic*. Westport: Greenwood.

Sharghdaily. 2020. "Saeed Madani Narrative about Silent Assaults." *Shargh Daily*. http://sharghdaily.com/fa/main/detail/269252. Accessed September 9, 2020.

Shojaee, M. 2009. "The History of International Women's Day in Iran." *Feminist School*. http://www.feministschool.com/english/spip.php?page=print&id_article=253. Accessed February 8, 2021.

Smartt, N. 2017. "Sexual Harassment in the Workplace in a #MeToo World." *Forbes*. https://www.forbes.com/sites/forbeshumanresourcescouncil/2017/12/20/sexualharassment-in-the-workplace-in-a-metoo-world/#3bcfa9c85a42. Accessed November 22, 2022.

Starkey, J. C., A. Koerber, M. Sternadori, and B. Pitchford. 2019. "#MeToo Goes Global: Media Framing of Silence Breakers in Four National Settings." *Journal of Communication Inquiry* 43: 437–461. https://doi.org/10.1177/0196859919865254.

Stewart, M., and U. Schultze. 2019. “Producing Solidarity in Social Media Activism: The Case of My Stealthy Freedom.” *Information and Organization* 29: 1–23. https://doi.org/10.1016/j.infoandorg.2019.04.003.

Surah An-Nur—1–64, n.d. [online], https://quran.com/an-nur?locale=en&font=v1&reading=false&translations=131%2C20. Accessed October 17, 2021.

Tavassolian, N. 2016. “Sexual Harassment in Islamic Penal Code.” https://www.radiozamaneh.com/261562/. Accessed November 21, 2022.

Terman, R. 2007. “The Stop Stoning Forever Campaign: A Report. Women Living under Muslim Laws.” http://www.meydaan.com/english/default. Accessed September 15, 2021.

Torabi, A. 2018. “The Hidden Reality of Sexual Assault in Iran” [online], https://www.google.com/search?q=Torabi+2018%2C+the+hidden+reality+of+sexual+assault+in+Iran&rlz=1C1GCEV_en&oq=Torabi+2018%2C+the+hidden+reality+of+sexual+assault+in+Iran&aqs=chrome..69i57j69i60.708j0j7&sourceid=chrome&ie=UTF-8. Accessed September 14, 2020.

# 16
# #MeToo and the Need for Vegetarian-Feminist Approaches in the Czech Republic

*Denisa Kraśna*

## Timeline

- 1843: The feminist Božena Němcová became the first professional Czech female writer.
- 1860s: The first emancipation endeavors sought economic independence.
- 1865: The first women's association, "Americký klub dam," was founded by Vojta Náprstek.
- 1890: The first girls grammar school was founded by Eliška Krásnohorská.
- 1897: Women first entered universities.
- Late nineteenth century: Marie Riegrová-Palacká and Alice Masaryková established social work as a profession.
- 1903: Tomáš Garrigue Masaryk published his famous lecture, "Woman and Politics."
- 1905: Political meetings and demonstrations by women for the right to vote took place in Prague.
- 1920: Women won the right to vote.
- 1920–World War II: The first wave of feminism; many feminist associations were formed.
- 1918–1935: T. G. Masaryk became the first president of Czechoslovakia (vegetarian feminist abstinent).
- 1948: The Constitution established that men and women are equal.
- 1948–1989: During the Communist totalitarian regime, men and women worked as allies.
- 1989: The Velvet Revolution ended forty years of Communism; Czech women rejected Western feminism.
- 1990s–present: Some women's organizations were established; gender studies programs opened at some universities.

Denisa Kraśna, *#MeToo and the Need for Vegetarian-Feminist Approaches in the Czech Republic* In: *The Other #MeToos*. Edited by: Iqra Shagufta Cheema, Oxford University Press. © Oxford University Press 2023. DOI: 10.1093/oso/9780197619872.003.0016

## Introduction

Recent research indicates that 58% of Czech people blame the rape victims for their rape, that is why women remain reluctant to report sexual crimes despite rampant sexual violence in the Czech Republic ("Stop tabu," 2018).[1] In 2020, Deník N, an independent digital media outlet, published testimonies of thirty-five women of diverse backgrounds, ages, and professions who shared their experiences with sexual harassment and violence. The article was published with the hashtag *#PromluvilyJsme* (#We[Women]Spoke)[2] in July 2020, more than two years after #MeToo conversations in Czech media and in the public. The authors neither claimed nor disclaimed the article's connection to #MeToo. In 2018, Jana Zbořilová started an initiative, *#Stoptabu* (#StopTaboo), that aimed at helping survivors of sexual abuse. Jana herself was raped when she was ten years old and then again at age nineteen. *#Stoptabu* uses hashtags *#nerikamsioto* (#I'mNotAskingForIt) and *#pribehypomahaji* (#StoriesHelp) that capture the spirit of the initiative. Jana first shared her story in a YouTube video and then created a website and a YouTube channel to encourage others to talk about their experiences ("Stop tabu," 2018). Over the last two years, Jana has received more than 800 stories from both women and men survivors of sexual abuse and violence (Skřivánková, 2020).

While these are noteworthy initiatives, they remain rather marginal and not widely known. The absence of a wider feminist movement such as #MeToo in the Czech Republic reflects not only the tendencies of large sections of Czech society, but also the negative perception of the #MeToo campaign and feminism. This is surprising, considering that a century ago, Czech women had more power than women in most other European countries (Lauder, 2008; Šiklová, 1997, pp.264–265). But the Communist era meant that the second and third waves of feminism never reached Czech society. After the Velvet Revolution of 1989, which marked the end of forty years of Communist rule, Czechs adopted the distorted and generalized image of Western feminism as an aggressive ideology directed against all men and advocating for the supremacy of women rather than equality of men and women (Lauder, 2008).

The absence of a strong feminist movement in the post-Communist Czech Republic[3] resulted in more sexism and gender and species inequity. First, this chapter employs Carol J. Adams's feminist-vegetarian[4] critical theory that connects misogyny with meat-eating to show the many ways in which the Czech cultural traditions and consumption patterns, which are built on what I call the sexism-meat-alcohol triad, perpetuate power hierarchies that cause both gender and species inequality. Using Adams's theory, the chapter then analyzes Czech reactions to the #MeToo movement to demonstrate how the meat and alcohol tropes have been used by powerful men to degrade and downplay #MeToo.

Finally, the chapter argues for a joined movement of feminists and vegetarians that would oppose violence against women and other animals, and by advocating for equality between all genders and species, it would concurrently disrupt the current speciesist and sexist discourse that permeates the Czech society. Czech responses to #MeToo underscore the importance of a separate, context-specific movement, adapted to the Czech environment. Both feminism and vegetarianism in the Czech Republic have similar historical roots, and many of their pioneers advocated for the concurrent focus on the emancipation of both women and other animals by following a just, empathetic, alcohol-free, vegetarian lifestyle.

In order to highlight this connection, the first part of this chapter traces the simultaneous roots of both feminist and vegetarian movements in Czech Republic from the nineteenth to the twentieth century that was marked by two world wars and a long Communist totalitarian regime (1948–1989). It explains the reasons for the rejection of Western feminism in the post-Communist Czech Republic and highlights how the same patterns have been used to dismiss vegetarianism. It also shows how Czech cultural traditions that are built on misogyny and violence provide further justification for speciesism. The second part of this chapter analyzes the reactions of prominent Czech figures to the #MeToo movement and identifies the commonalities in these responses to determine the main factors that negatively influence Czechs' perception of feminism and their approaches to gender violence. This part also employs Adams's feminist-vegetarian critical theory as an analytical framework to underscore how the critics of #MeToo often rely on speciesist discourses that frame both women and other animals as consumable and treat them as *pieces of meat*.

## Feminism in Post-Communist Czech Society

In her article "Feminism and the Roots of Apathy in the Czech Republic" (1997), Jiřina Šiklová, a sociologist and dissident feminist, argues that the totalitarian regimes—be it the Habsburg monarchy, the fascists during World War II, or the Communist Party—created an environment in which Czech men and women conceived their struggle as interconnected and thus worked as allies to fight the enemy, i.e., those in power (Šiklová, 1997, p. 264). She draws attention to the fact that the first prominent public figure who advocated for women's rights was in fact a man. Tomáš Garrigue Masaryk, the first president of Czechoslovakia, wrote and lectured about the importance of gender equality (Šiklová, 1997, p. 264). He was also a prominent advocate of alcohol abstinence and a vegetarian diet.

Masaryk's supporters embraced his ideas and gradually implemented them in both public and domestic spheres. The long era of fascist and Communist rule further solidified what Šiklová (1997) calls "a specific cohesion between men and women as allies against the state" (p. 263). Several women, including Milada Horáková and Olga Hrubá, were well-known figures in the dissident movement. Šiklová, whose study largely informs this section of the chapter, was also a dissident who was imprisoned for her activities (Heitlinger, 1996, p. 79). But women never broke away from totalitarian-era union with men to fight for their own issues (Šiklová, 1997, p. 265). There is a heightened interest in research about the participation and role of women in resistance initiatives, such as Charter 77,[5] among the younger Czech generations.

Šiklová (1997) also highlights that the politics of women's right to work was different in the West as compared with post-Communist countries. While Western women fought for their right to work outside their home, the latter were forced to work for the totalitarian regimes, first in World War II and later in the 1950s when they were forced to "build socialism" (Šiklová, 1997, p. 265). Stalinism encouraged female labor and glorified the "heroic woman worker" (Heitlinger, 1996, p. 83). Home, as a private sphere outside of the state's direct control, thus became the longed-for sanctuary for both women and men, where most of them could retreat and express themselves freely (Šiklová, 1997, p. 269). Alena Heitlinger (1996) also contends that home was "a woman's domain" where she felt empowered and motivated to embrace "the cult of motherhood" that was liberating rather than restricting (p. 85). Western feminism's emphasis on women's participation in the job market was therefore unappealing to Czech women who, after the Velvet Revolution of 1989, celebrated their freedom by becoming housewives and stay-at-home mothers.

Lastly, Czech women rejected Western feminism because of its ideological framing. Czech women's objections to Western feminism also included "the leftist language of feminism," "the excessive rhetoric of Western feminists, their craving for a global solution, [and] their teleological character and feminist eschatology" (Šiklová, 1997, p. 274). Czechs were wary of ideologies as they highlight "common experiences" and build "collective identity," expressions reminiscent of the Communist Party's political program (Heitlinger, 1996, p. 82). All of these traits of Western feminism were evocative of the Communist Party's propaganda; hence they incited an instant distrust. The system of quotas and affirmative action were also renounced by Czech female politicians for their leftist undertones (Šiklová, 1997, p. 273). Overall, women's participation in politics lowered after the Velvet Revolution. This is also due to the Marxist-Leninist portrayal of a strong woman as a passionate, politically active defender of the Communist ideals (Heitlinger, 1996, p. 83). Retreating from politics was therefore another form of protest and emancipation from the fallen regime (Heitlinger, 1996, p. 84).

Additionally, Western feminists' criticism of capitalism has been undesirable in the Czech Republic, a country that had long craved to be part of the capitalist system which it idealized and (wrongly) associated with unrestricted liberty (Šiklová, 1997, p. 275). Czech's abrupt economic transition to capitalism was not an easy task, and men and women, yet again, approached this challenge as allies rather than two divergent groups (Heitlinger, 1996, p. 86). Tereza Kynčlová (2011) rightfully marvels at "the failure of the Czech public and its political elites to recognize capitalism itself as a sort of ideology" (p. 25). The Communist regime perpetuated homogeneity, simplification, and binary thinking, all of which Czechs wanted to avoid in their newly formed post-revolutionary society (Šiklová, 1997, p. 261). However, the way Czechs embraced capitalism, with blind faith in its potential, and categorically rejected Western feminism without any prior scrutiny is reminiscent of the binary mindset of the loathed Communist regime. The context of post-Communist society enabled the rejection of Western feminism and all its values and facilitated the transition to a male-dominated capitalist economy in which women's rights continued to be disregarded and feminism remained a marginal concept.

Czech women's dismissive attitude toward Western feminism, however, was also influenced by their instilled confidence in their societal position. Ferber and Raabe (2003) assert that Czech women "reject any implication that women are inferior; in fact, they rather take for granted that they are not inferior and feel no need to prove it" (p. 423). Not doubting her equality, an average Czech woman is also more tolerant of sexist jokes and stereotypes that she does not perceive as a threat to her societal position. The Czech feminist Helena Skálová affirms, a Czech woman does not "see what consequence tolerating [them] might have. She does not admit to or see the limits it poses in other areas of life, such as equal conditions in the workplace" (quoted in Pilat, 2018, n.p.). In the labor market, women receive substantially lower wages, with the gender pay gap in the Czech Republic being among the highest in Europe (Du Parc, 2020; Lazarová, 2020).[6] At home, women "do the lion's share of homemaking while most of them are also employed full-time" (Ferber and Raabe, 2003, p. 409). Most Czech women have experienced sexual harassment at least once in their lifetime (Deník N, 2020). Here, the lack of Western feminism's influence is evident and the effects are felt. Statistics and hard data show that gender equality in the Czech Republic is an imagined illusion.

## The Sexism-Meat-Alcohol Triad: Vegetarianism in the Czech Republic

The general acceptance of gender roles and the perception of "gender differences as embedded in nature" (Ferber and Raabe, 2003, p. 409) hinder the re-evaluation of harmful sexist traditions that glorify violence by presenting male virility as connected to the killing of other animals, meat consumption, and heavy drinking. Women play the supporting role of enabler in these traditions, which further bolsters gender roles and stereotypes and creates an environment where sexism and misogyny thrive. Disrupting the sexism-meat-alcohol triad and shifting attention to the intersections of different forms of violence are necessary in order to reject toxic masculinity as the country's defining characteristic. Carol J. Adams, in her intersectional feminist-vegetarian critical theory,[7] connects the oppression of women with the exploitation of other animals to show that meat-eating culture enables gender disparities and feeds an environment that perpetuates harmful gender-related oppression. Adams's theory can be enhanced by including the excessive and eulogized alcohol consumption that is an important ingredient that solidifies men's dominant position in Czech society and that was therefore abstained from in the early Czech vegetarian movement.

In her seminal work *The Sexual Politics of Meat: A Feminist-Vegetarian Critical Theory* (1990), Adams argues that carnism[8] is a patriarchal construct and serves as a symbol of virility. Adams breaks down common interactions between men and women over meat, as well as popular culture's representation of meat and animals, to unmask parallels between patriarchal behaviors and the consumption of animal protein. She terms this connection "the sexual politics of meat" that, she maintains, is characterized by the myth that male strength and virility comes from meat eating and by male dominance in the house where men traditionally dictate "the contents of the dinner plate." (Adams, 2010, p. 22). Jacques Derrida (1991) also affirms that "carnophallogocentrism," a worldview that places the carnivorous male at the center, is embedded in European and Western cultures. The practice of vegetarianism is therefore a feminist act that challenges these widespread carnophallogocentric behaviors dictated by the hyper-masculine rhetoric. In the Czech Republic, early vegetarians in the first half of the twentieth century were already ascribing gender, racial, and class inequality in society to human treatment of other animals, calling for a change in behavior that includes empathy as consideration of other animals as living beings worthy of compassion, which can lead to empathetic, fair, and just people. Hence, the Czech vegetarian movement has been intersectional from its beginnings.

In the nineteenth century a few predominantly alternative healers propagated a meat-free diet for its health benefits. In 1884, the versatile intellectual Emanuel Mírohorský published his book *O vegetarismu* (*About Vegetarianism*), in which he argues for just treatment of animals and a vegetarian diet. While he also focuses on the health benefits of the meat-free diet and opposes smoking and alcohol consumption, he considers ethics as the strongest argument for the adoption of a vegetarian diet. Mírohorský blamed a blind adherence to traditions for the unchanged consumption patterns in our society. Similarly, in 1920, the journalist Gustav Jaroš (using the pen name Gamma), published an article "Vánoce zvířat" ("Animals' Christmas") in which he criticizes traditional Christmas consumption customs for providing people with an excuse for inconsiderate behavior stripped of any ethical awareness. Jaroš was among the first Czech vegetarians who exposed the intersecting nature of gendered and speciesist oppression, arguing for a concurrent focus on the liberation of laborers, people of color, women, and especially other animals: "the solution must start with animals, not with humans" (Jaroš, 1920, p. 40). The roots of the feminist-vegetarian critical theory in the Czech Republic can thus be traced to a pre–First World War I period.

Vegetarian feminists nowadays continue to emphasize the violent foundations of many cultural traditions that perpetuate both speciesism and sexism as they are fueled by *toxic masculinity, meat, and alcohol.* In the Czech Republic, this is evident in many rituals and popular folk entertainments, often presented as "traditions.". *Zabijačka*, a ceremonial and brutal killing of a pig by a male, is still practiced in rural areas. This ritual act reinforces the connection between masculinity and violence. Women, silent observers of the murder, then prepare and cook the meat—thus showing that they have to clear and support the male violence even when they do not take part in it. *Slivovice*, a homemade liquor with high alcohol volume, is also served throughout the day, together with other alcoholic drinks. Another similar "tradition" is *myslivecké hody*, i.e., a hunters' feast. Hunters' wives prepare meals from hunted-down animals while the hunters/men get drunk. Adams's assertion that "the more important meat is in their life, the greater relative dominance will the men command" is exemplified here (Adams, 2010, p. 58). Sexual harassment is common during these feasts, but is tolerated and goes largely unacknowledged.

The combination of sexism, carnophallogocentrism, and alcohol is striking during Czech Easter, that mixes pagan and religious traditions. On Easter Monday, boys and men visit their relatives, neighbors, and acquaintances using *pomlázka*, a braided whip made from pussy willow twigs, decorated with colorful ribbons, to whip women and girls in each household while reciting a chant that requests a reward for this "service"—usually in the form of decorated eggs (for boys) or liquor (for adults). According to the old pagan tradition, women are said to stay fertile, healthy, and beautiful if they receive an Easter whipping. The symbolism behind the tradition reinforces male dominance and traditional gender roles where women are expected to serve meat and liquor; it also normalizes male violence against women as something that is expected and acceptable as part of the cultural traditions. It is not unusual for the whipping to become more aggressive later in the day when men are intoxicated (Prucha, 2009). Like the other aforementioned Czech traditions, Easter customs encourage hypermasculine and aggressive behavior towards women where sexism, meat, and alcohol render sexual and gendered violence normal.

But traditions are not the only place where carnophalogocentric attitudes manifest. Often, home is where men safeguard their dominance via dietary habits. Three of my female friends practiced a vegetarian lifestyle for several years, but they eventually returned to meat-eating to accommodate their diets to their partners' habits to avoid conflict (Adams, 2010, p. 22). "Placing the partner's needs first" (Adams, 2010, p. 22), they conceded to cook meat for their carnivorous partners and gave up their lifestyle and philosophy. Refusal to cook would translate as an act of resistance, and the nonconforming woman would be likely shamed as a "failing" wife/partner (Adams, 2010, p. 23). While during the Communist era, the home served as a sanctuary where women could express themselves freely (Šiklová, 1997, p. 269) and where they felt empowered and liberated (Heitlinger, 1996, p. 85), the context changed in the capitalist modern-day society where media frames both women and other animals as consumable in advertising and in popular culture. In an analysis of hidden meanings in such representations, Adams concludes that "viewing other beings as consumable is a central aspect of our culture" (*The Pornography of Meat*, 2015, p. 12). Giving up meat means giving up these behavioral practices that view women and animals as flesh and something to be consumed for pleasure.

This idea of consumability was touched upon in the Czech context in 1928 by Ctibor Bezděk, who identifies the gradual gaining of pleasure from meat-eating as a major problem of the carnivorous diet. He believed that indulgence in carnism leads to other forms of consumption habits that give gratification, such as alcohol and, nicotine, but also unhealthy sexual habits. Bezděk was among the first ones who identified and articulated the sexual politics of meat in the Czech Republic. He also wrote about the colonial politics of meat, comparing the peaceful Indian nation with the imperial Britain that uses violence to conquer the whole world. Adams explains that this idea was formed by the nineteenth-century Romantic writers who connected the notion of the British "beefeater" with tendencies to dominate, colonize, and conquer other peoples (Adams, 2010, pp. 54, 231). Bezděk (1928) also laid the foundations of Czech ecocriticism, rejecting the anthropocentric attitude that leads to environmental destruction, and instead arguing for an approach that views humans as interconnected with other living entities.

But Czech women were also active advocates of the vegetarian lifestyle. The first three Czech vegetarian cookbooks were written by women who included both vegetarian and vegan recipes in their books. Ludmila Barthová published the first vegetarian cookbook in 1909, Marie Úlehlová-Tilschová followed her suit in 1930, and Anuše Kejřová in 1933. Úlehlová-Tilschová enriched her cookbook with a list of moral, environmental, economic, and social reasons to become a vegetarian, again emphasizing the interconnected nature of oppression and proposing vegetarianism as a possible solution. Barthová defined the vegetarian lifestyle as an abstinence from all animal products as well as tobacco and alcohol. The exclusion of alcohol seemed to be a common practice for Czech vegetarians in the late nineteenth and early twentieth centuries. The aforementioned first Czechoslovak president Tomáš Garrigue Masaryk, who fought for women's emancipation, was also an advocate of an alcohol-free vegetarian diet. In his essay "On Ethics and Alcoholism,", Masaryk writes that "the future belongs to the sober, that is, to those who have opted for a higher, more moral worldview and way of life" (Masaryk, 1912, p. 29). It was during Masaryk's time that the Czech society was heading towards a more just, emancipated, and equal society for all.

The era of the First Republic, with Masaryk and other intellectuals forming the new society, was rich in liberation ideas and movements. The two World Wars suspended these endeavors, and the Communist era halted them completely. Vegetarianism as a political movement, like feminism, was forbidden in the Communist Czechoslovakia, and vegetarian societies were forced to stop their activities. Those who continued to gather unofficially were often under surveillance and were persecuted for their dissident activities. This further shows that vegetarianism in the Czech Republic was interlinked with other liberation movements aiming for freedom and equality in the pre-Communist era and therefore considered a potential risk for the new totalitarian regime. The result was a gradual disappearance of vegetarian ideas from the public discourse as vegetarianism was suppressed, similarly to feminism.

Hence, throughout the 1990s, only a handful of people recognized the word "vegetarian," and the only ones who knew the meaning of the word were usually the practitioners of this alternative and, in fact, "underground" lifestyles. Vegetarianism, as a diet and a lifestyle, was embraced by those who were already on the margins of mainstream society, especially artists and musicians who were influenced by the hippie counterculture of the 1960s that adopted vegetarianism for ethical and political reasons, opposing the cruelty linked to animal agriculture. My father and uncles also became vegetarians at a young age for moral reasons. The day my father, who was an athlete, gave up meat in 1980s, he symbolically completed a long-distance run. With his physical strength and athletic body, my father broke stereotypes about the link between male virility and meat-eating. In time, my father and my uncles also strictly limited alcohol consumption, which estranged them from the society even more. During my adolescence, I witnessed a gradual shift in Czech society's attitudes toward vegetarian, alcohol-free, and feminist discourse. While I was still being mocked for my nonviolent lifestyle during my high school years, today, both vegetarian and feminist ideas penetrate the Czech society and are gaining traction among young people.

## Czech #MeToo: Thirty Years After the Velvet Revolution

In the contemporary Czech Republic, both vegetarianism and feminism are moving out of the margins of the public consciousness. Three decades after the Velvet Revolution, Czechs were once again confronted with Western feminism when the #MeToo campaign spread across the world and turned into a modern women's movement of unprecedented proportions. But, instead of seizing this opportunity to re-evaluate and improve their social standing, Czech women, once again, tended to reject Western feminism. But their rejection of #MeToo was largely influenced by an aggressive male reaction to the #MeToo campaign. Like before, men in power played a principal role in shaping the public opinion by ridiculing, downplaying, and firmly renouncing the movement and its goals. In the 1990s, Šiklová (1997) explained this widespread behavior of men as a natural reaction of their defense mechanisms: "a man in danger of systemic anomie tries . . . to quickly restore his world and structure it in such a way as to be able to orient himself in it" (Šiklová 1997, p. 261). #MeToo was evaluated by the majority of Czechs as a potentially dangerous movement that could disrupt the current capitalist patriarchal order, and as such it needed to be curbed. Hence, under this imagined new feminist "threat," both conservative and liberal men in power joined forces to oppose #MeToo and framed it as a fabrication of bored American women (CTK, 2016; Hrdličková, 2019; Pilat, 2018). By using sexist and speciesist discourse, they solidified the hierarchical structure from which the oppression of both women and other animals derives (Adams, 2010, p. 220).

It was during the Czech presidential elections in 2017–2018 when the #MeToo movement was gaining momentum. Despite their otherwise opposite views on most issues, all presidential candidates held similar opinion about #MeToo. Jiří Drahoš, who lost to Miloš Zeman by a narrow margin, is a liberal politician who is also a scientist. Unlike Zeman, Drahoš holds progressive views on most issues, including climate change and immigrants (Drahoš, 2018). Still, when asked about #MeToo, Drahoš said he was somewhat "disconcerted" by the campaign and was following it "from a distance" (ČTK, abe, 2017). Marek Hilšer, the youngest and the most progressive candidate, took a similar stance, sharing that now "one can simply be accused of anything" (ČTK, abe, 2017). He made a joke that "maybe it's a shame" that he had never been sexually abused by anyone (ČTK, abe, 2017). Hilšer's disrespectful "joke" was echoed by Michal Horáček, a left-wing/centrist candidate. Horáček stated that he liked the general message of #MeToo as most cases of gender violence go unreported, but he downplayed sexual abuse by expressing his "deep regret" that beautiful women had never tried to sexually harass him (ČTK, abe, 2017). Endorsing sexual violence as something to be desired creates a culture where consent is taken lightly and unwanted sexual advances are rampant and tolerated. The idea that people "want" to be sexually assaulted, even humorously, feeds into the diminishing of heinous acts and reinforces the dangerous narrative that no means yes. Another candidate Vratislav Kulhánek exaggerated #MeToo: "I admit that during my long life, I opened the doors for ladies many times, or I helped them put on their cloaks. And now I fear for the day when one shows up, claiming that it left her with sexual trauma" (ČTK, abe, 2017, n.p.). Similarly, Petr Hannig warned that #MeToo could lead to "a loss of contact between the two genders" as "young men will be afraid to reach out to a beautiful girl" (ČTK, abe, 2017, n.p.). These statements build a cultural environment where certain acts are diminished, that fails to understand the lived experience of women, and therefore it re-highlights the privileged and patriarchal views of these politicians, even ostensibly progressive ones. This shared stance highlights how powerful men come together to fight feminism. But it also shows the threat that #MeToo poses to sexism and gender discrimination. The Czech public embraced a similar stance.

The topic of sexual harassment is downplayed in the Czech Republic, and very soon after its launch the #MeToo campaign was considered as an untrustworthy and offensive movement that demonizes men. Moreover, #MeToo was misunderstood in the Czech Republic and the debate revolved around topics such as whether a man can open a door for a woman and invite her for a drink without being accused of sexual harassment. This narrative is reinforced by public figures and politicians, as is demonstrated in the above preceding paragraph. Czech society is generally convinced that sexual harassment, like sexual violence, does not affect our society and culture. The problem is not accepted as ubiquitous and is therefore downplayed and ridiculed. This predominantly negative response from both common people and public figures has stopped serious debates about sexual violence and the spontaneous sharing of stories of personal experiences with sexual harassment. According to the sociologist Iva Šmídová, polarized political culture and its atmosphere in recent years is also to blame for the moderate response to #MeToo in the Czech Republic. Topics related to inclusion, diversity, or emancipation are perceived negatively, and Czech society is not yet ready to acknowledge the widespread gender-based violence. Šmídová was among the first Czech women who participated in the hashtag #MeToo on social media networks. Predominantly, it was academics and students from gender studies departments who used the hashtag in the Czech Republic and motivated other people to join them (Daňková, 2018). Even though this initial positive response to #MeToo was soon sidelined, there are still Czechs who keep the conversation alive, especially in academic circles. Gradually, they try to dispel the misunderstanding that sexual harassment is not motivated by "natural" sexual impulses, but represents a structural problem made possible by the cultural environment. Effective resistance must therefore be pursued, especially at the cultural and societal level.

Nothing evidences the endorsement of sexism and misogyny in Czech society more than the re-election of Miloš Zeman for the second Presidential term. His frequent public drunkenness and audacious statements draw the attention of international media, but they rarely cause any controversy in the Czech Republic. For example, in 2015, Zeman was in the spotlight for his openly sexist and racist statements. First, he reinforced the idea that travelling and exploration is not the right lifestyle choice for women when he condemned two Czech tourists who were kidnapped and held captive by terrorists in Pakistan for two years. By framing the women's behavior as irresponsible, he employed the classic blaming-the-victim rhetoric. On another occasion, Zeman commented on the refugee crisis in a butcher shop, saying that "we will be deprived of the women's beauty since they will be shrouded in burkas from head to toe, including the face. . . . Well, I can imagine women for whom it would mean an improvement, but there are few of them and I cannot see any such here" (CTK, 2016, n.p.). Zeman reduces women to mere objects of male desire to be given a value based on the current beauty standards. Instead of protecting and defending discriminated and marginalized people, the Czech president insults them openly, perpetuating Islamophobia and misogyny as a result. This blatantly racist and sexist statement, reminiscent of those made by Donald Trump, got almost no reactions from the Czechs and went largely unnoticed by the media.

Besides being anti-feminist and anti-#MeToo, Zeman also stands against the Czech vegetarian movement. His statement "death to abstainers and vegetarians" that he pronounced as a toast raised genuine concerns among vegetarians and teetotalers (Tait, 2016; Day, 2015). But Zeman's daring declaration was condemned more abroad than in the Czech Republic, where it gained him even more popularity among his supporters (Tait, 2016). Zeman is an embodiment of a general tendency that dismisses both feminist and vegetarian endeavors; the endorsement and popularity of his behavior demonstrates the need for an intersectional feminist-vegetarian approach to fight the culture of sexual, gender, and species violence.

Powerful men often join forces to oppose vegetarian and feminist ideas. One of Zeman's most fervent critics and the Czech popular talk show host, Jan Kraus, shares Zeman's anti-feminist and anti-vegetarian views, despite their otherwise opposing political beliefs. When #MeToo gained momentum, Kraus became the movement's zealous opponent and aggressively forced his (women) guests to dismiss it. In a radio program, "Kraus and the Blonde," he declared #MeToo "a movement for the eradication of sex from human life" ("Kraus a blondýna," 2018, n.p.). He then ironically listed all the things that could be dangerous for their association with sex, such as skirts and make-up that he sarcastically termed "*prasečinka*,"[9]", i.e., something filthy or vulgar ("Kraus a blondýna," 2018). In his words, "we must also consider women, so that they do not provide a pretext, so as not to give the impression at all that sex exists" ("Kraus a blondýna," 2018, n.p.). This victim-blaming rhetoric is insulting and dangerous, as it is often used as an excuse for sexual abuse and even femicides (Messmer, 2012).[10] The popular female stand-up comedian Adéla Elbel pointed out that "Jan Kraus does not even have one episode of his show in which he would not ridicule the [#MeToo] campaign" (Maca, 2018, n.p.). Elbel views the widespread trivialization of #MeToo among Czechs, especially by influential people such as Kraus, as highly problematic.

Elbel provides an important counter-narrative to Kraus's anti-#MeToo show. She strikes back by using humour to spark discussions about sexual harassment and gender inequality and to point out the dangerous trivialization of gender violence. She stands in sharp contrast to Kraus also in her approach to meat-eating and environmental issues, effectively demonstrating the link between vegetarianism and feminism. In his offensive satire, Kraus evoked the sexism-meat-alcohol triad by painting a picture of the future in which "we will abandon sex and will all drink water and feed on organic food" ("Kraus a blondýna," 2018, n.p.), simultaneously ridiculing both #MeToo and healthy, non-violent lifestyles. In comparison, in one of her stand-up segments titled "Animals, Kids, and Plastic," Elbel mentions she does not eat meat because it "grosses her out" and uses humor to draw attention to global problems such as plastic pollution in oceans: "you go buy fish which is gross and slimy not to mention filled with plastic; a stuffing, right. You ask for a bag to put it [the fish] in and they tell you the bag is already inside" ("Na Stojáka," 2020, n.p.). Apart from being a successful comedian, Elbel translated a children's book from Dutch that sparked negative reactions in the Czech Republic because of its homosexual themes. Elbel became a target of aggressive homophobic comments that shamed her as a lesbian who should be burned. In reaction to #MeToo, Elbel criticized Czech sexism and misogyny, underscoring that she does not know many women who have never been sexually harassed (Maca, 2018). Elbel represents the younger generation of Czechs who may just be ready to abandon or redefine the old misogynist traditions and meat-eating habits.

Still, the mainstream media's influence is powerful and dictates the general opinion of the majority, providing influential men with a platform to downplay #MeToo. The political commentator Anne Applebaum (2018) explains that in the Czech Republic "the independent media is extremely weak . . . . . . and public debate is dominated by conspiratorial websites and cheap tabloids" (Applebaum

2018, n.p. ). One such debate was started when a major Czech brewery, Bernard, released a sexist image on social media mocking the #MeToo movement. In defense of the posting, the brewery-owner Stanislav Bernard expanded his criticism of what he calls a "pathological campaign" (Pilat, 2018, n.p.). By attributing an ideological character to #MeToo, he applied the same rhetoric as critics of feminism three decades ago and compared its strategy to the persecutions of innocent people during the Communist era: " ' "Innocent until proven guilty' " is ignored" (Pilat, 2018, n.p.). Such a parallel is highly disrespectful to the victims of both the Communist regime and sexual abuse. But Bernard's defense motivated an overwhelmingly sympathetic reaction from the Czech public, whose perception of #MeToo had already been heavily distorted. Rather than a movement against gender violence, Czechs view it as an attack on gender differences and traditional gender roles that most of the Czech population wants to see preserved. Bernard summed up what many Czechs fear might be the outcome of the #MeToo campaign: "we may find ourselves in a situation where a guy will be scared to ask a girl out for a coffee and tell her that she looks beautiful." (Pilat, 2018, n.p.). These unfounded exaggerations have proven to be a highly effective tools, uniformly employed by influential men in their joined effort to prevent #MeToo in Czech society.

Another persuasive strategy to downplay the #MeToo movement has been to frame it as an exaggerated campaign by using humor, as I already showed above in the example of Jan Kraus. The journalist Martin Miko published a satirical piece, co-created by experts from various fields, to highlight the sexism-meat-alcohol triad. In this piece, Miko makes fun of the #MeToo and ridicules feminist-vegetarians. He invents the hashtag #Meatoo that refers to a "daring campaign that tries to draw attention to people who, in the past, have had their meat eaten by someone else" (Miko, 2018, n.p.). The language used throughout the piece echoes the language in the #MeToo and hence emphasizes the #MeToo movement's ideological character. The author encourages people to join the #Meatoo campaign and adds that "unsolicited tasting or explicit hints and sweet looks are also wrong" (Miko, 2018, n.p.). Like Kraus, Miko (2018) insinuates that women who dress provocatively are complicit in sexual harassment: "you have [no] right to speak publicly and inappropriately about your subordinate's appetizer or dessert at work. And it does not matter how provocative the food looks on a plate!" (n.p.). Comparing the gravity of gender violence to the act of taking meat from men's plates effectively highlights the connection between toxic masculinity and meat consumption in the Czech Republic. Like women who dress "provocatively" and are viewed as *pieces of meat*, the tasty-looking meat is treated as a consumable absent referent that is objectified and not seen as being (or having been) some*one* before it became some*thing*, an object of male desire (Adams, 2010, p. 13).

Although rare, #MeToo also received some positive reactions among influential Czech women. Apart from Adéla Elbel, the acclaimed writer Radka Denemarková also speaks out about misogyny and sexism in Czech society. She wrote a novel titled *A Contribution to the History of Joy* (2014) about gender violence after hearing a man use the adjective "only" when describing rape. The historical novel now enjoys great acclaim in Germany ("Buranství Zemana," 2019). According to Denemarková, #MeToo has not changed the way Czechs look at gender violence, partially because of the influence of powerful men like Zeman whose vulgarity and rude manners contribute to the victims' humiliation ("Buranství Zemana," 2019). Still, as popular and influential women, both Elbel and Denemarková hope that the situation in the Czech Republic might be changing for the better as their words resonate with their fans and will hopefully alter their followers' perspectives on sexual violence, feminism, and vegetarianism. Furthermore, media outlets such as Respekt and Deník N have been publishing feminist-oriented articles and critiques that present a counter-narrative to the widespread anti-feminism rhetoric in Czech society. Even though they represent the views of a minority of urban, progressive, educated, young people, their presence points towards a slow and steady shift among a portion of the next generations.

## Conclusion

Due to historical circumstances, Czech women never went through the second and third waves of feminism like their counterparts in the West and thus never really solidified a joined identity as women (Lauder, 2008). The #MeToo campaign sparked a much-needed discussion about sexual harassment and gender inequality and revealed deep-rooted sexism and misogyny that permeates all spheres of Czech society. Politicians, popular celebrities, and mainstream media largely downplayed #MeToo as an invention of, in the words of the former Czech senator Jaroslav Kubera, "ultrafeminists" (quoted. in Hrdličková, 2019, n.p.). Powerful men of all backgrounds and political views unanimously opposed #MeToo by framing men as victims of #MeToo and by employing rhetorical tools like misogynistic humour to influence the public opinion. Analysis of the reactions to #MeToo in the Czech Republic also shows the strong connection between meat, alcohol consumption, and misogyny. Carol J. Adams's critical feminist-vegetarian theory not only proves useful as an analytical tool in the Czech context, but it could also serve as a practical guide for change in the Czech Republic.

Adams's work reveals that feminists and vegetarians have more in common than any other liberation groups, and her assertion is also relevant in the Czech

Republic, where both movements, feminism and vegetarianism, emerged around the same time and often intersected. With the increasing popularity of vegetarian and vegan lifestyles in the Czech Republic, people's perspectives on racism and gender violence are also shifting. Behavioral changes that include empathy and consideration of other living beings can create an empathic, equal, and just society. Lauder explains that "the persisting aversion to feminism does not automatically mean that the aversion to feminist topics also persists," and hopes that Czechs are slowly becoming more receptive to gender and sexual violence (Lauder, 2008, n.p.). Young celebrities also bring positive influence by discussing feminist and vegetarian topics, with Adéla Elbel (stand-up comedian), Tomáš and Tamara Klus (musicians), Ben Cristovao (musician, actor, athlete), and Tereza Mašková (singer) being just a few prominent examples. Czech responses to #MeToo highlight the link between sexual violence and meat consumption, which is crucial for the understanding of the links between sexism and misogyny permeating the Czech society. Giving up meat requires giving up the behavioral practices that view women and animals as flesh and something to be consumed for pleasure. After all, Miko's #Meatoo could be re-appropriated and re-defined by vegetarian-feminists to underline the intersecting nature of carnism and sexism. As both vegetarianism and feminism are slowly gaining momentum in the Czech Republic, uniting the two movements could just be the key factor in ridding the Czech society of its toxic masculinity and escaping cyclical gender and sexual violence.

## Notes

1. This chapter is written from the perspective of a Czech woman who self-identifies as a feminist, vegan, and teetotaller.
2. Czech language is heavily gendered and the final letter "y" in the word *"promluvily"* (spoke) indicates that the speakers are women.
3. In the 1860s, the first emancipation endeavors seeking economic independence emerged in Czech lands. First women's associations were formed, often initiated or co-led by men who advocated for women's emancipation. Before World War II, Czech feminism was on the rise, but all endeavors were halted in 1948 with the start of the forty-year-long Communist totalitarian regime during which men and women worked as allies. The second and third waves of feminism never reached Czechoslovakia. After the Velvet Revolution of 1989, Czech women rejected Western feminism as an ideological and radical movement, as it was described by dissidents (men) returning from abroad. Today, "feminism" still carries mostly negative connotations.
4. This chapter uses the term "vegetarian" to refer to both vegetarian and vegan diets and lifestyles. While the newer term "vegan" would be more suitable as a description of what is generally meant here, i.e., abstaining from using all animal products, the

term "vegetarian" is used as this chapter employs historical sources written before the word "vegan" was coined. Similarly, Carol J. Adams also uses the term "vegetarian" to refer to what is now known as "vegan."

5. A powerful dissent movement called after the political manifesto Charter 77, written in 1976 and signed by many prominent public figures, including the future Czech president Václav Havel.
6. In 2019, the average hourly pay was *21.6% lower for women than for men (*Du Parc, 2020).
7. Tereza Kynčlová (2011) proposes intersectional theory that addresses the gender, race, and class inequality as a potentially useful theoretical and practical approach for the future of the Czech feminist movement. However, as Kynčlová herself notes, any discourse that revolves around class issues is bound to still be treated with suspicion and, despite having a fairly large population of Roma people, Czech remains very homogeneous and discussions about race are rare (p. 25). While Kynčlová's intersectional theory could be applied to the analysis of the lamentable situation of Roma women (and such analysis is long overdue), it does not offer any viable tools for a larger Czech feminist movement.
8. Melanie Joy's term referring to the invisible "belief system in which eating certain animals is considered ethical and appropriate." (2010, p. 30).
9. It is also worth noting that the word *prasečínka* has a root in the word *prase*, i.e., "pig." As such it falls into the category of speciesist slurs that reinforce human supremacy and perpetuate oppression (see Dunayer, 2001).
10. Femicide is defined as "the killing of a woman or girl, in particular by a man and on account of her gender" ("Femicide," n.d., n.p.).

## Works Cited

Adams, Carol J. 2010. *The Sexual Politics of Meat: A Feminist-Vegetarian Critical Theory*, 20th ed. New York: Continuum.

Adams, Carol J. 2015. *The Pornography of Meat*. New York: Lantern Books.

Applebaum, Anne. 2018. "The Czech Election Says More about the State of Western Democracy than We'd Like to Admit." *Washington Post*, January 29. www.washingtonpost.com/news/global-opinions/wp/2018/01/29/the-czech-election-says-more-about-the-state-of-western-democracy-than-wed-like-to-admit.

Barthová, Ludmila, and Jaroslav Barth. 1909. *První česká vegetářská kuchařka: sbírka vyzkoušených předpisů k přípravě chutných a zdravých pokrmů bez masa (The First Czech Vegetarian Cookbook: A Collection of Tested Recipes for Preparing Tasty and Healthy Dishes without Meat)*. Praha: Nová kultura.

Bezděk, Ctibor, and Přemysl Pitter. 1928. *Vegetarism pro a proti (Vegetarianism For and Against)*. Praha: Hnutí pro křesťanský komunismus v Československu.

"'Buranství Zemana': Kampaň #MeToo v Česku nic nezměnila, zoufá si spisovatelka" ('Zeman's Obcenity': The #MeToo Campaign Has Not Changed Anything in the Czech Republic, Despairs the Writer)." 2019. *Eurozpravy*, March 24. eurozpravy.cz/kultura/literatura/252696-buranstvi-zemana-kampan-metoo-v-cesku-nic-nezmenila-zoufa-si-spisovatelka.

CTK. 2016. "Zeman 'Aawarded' for His Sexist Statements." *Prague Daily Monitor*, March 9. www.praguemonitor.com/2016/03/09/zeman-awarded-his-sexist-statements.

ČTK, abe. 2017. "Prezidentští kandidáti se ke kampani #MeToo staví odtažitě. Míří prý pouze na bohaté muže (Presidential Candidates Are Taking a Stand on the #MeToo Campaign. They Say It Targets Only Rich Men)." *INFO.cz*, December 20. www.info.cz/volby/prezidentske-volby-2018/prezidentsti-kandidati-se-ke-kampani-metoo-stavi-odtazite-miri-pry-pouze-na-bohate-muze.

Daňková, Magdaléna. 2018. "#MeToo v Česku? Sexuální násilí zlehčujeme, děláme, že se nás netýká, říká socioložka (#MeToo in the Czech Republic? We Trivialize Sexual Violence, Pretend It Doesn't Concern Us, Says the Sociologist)." *Aktuálně.cz*, October 16. magazin.aktualne.cz/lide-kteri-se-prihlasi-k-metoo-jsou-hrdinove-rika-sociolozka/r~f521ece6cfbf11e8b295ac1f6b220ee8/.

Day, Matthew. 2015. "Death to Vegetarians and Teetotallers, Says Czech President." *The Telegraph*, March 2. www.telegraph.co.uk/news/worldnews/europe/czechrepublic/11444544/Death-to-vegetarians-and-teetotallers-says-Czech-president.html.

Deník N. 2020. "Promluvily jsme: Pětatřicet žen popisuje svou zkušenost se sexuálním obtěžováním (We Spoke: Thirty-five Women Describe Their Experience with Sexual Harassment)." *Deník N*, June 17. denikn.cz/399571/promluvily-jsme-petatricet-zen-popisuje-svou-zkusenost-se-sexualnim-obtezovanim.

Derrida, Jacques. 1991. "'Eating Well,' or the Calculation of the Subject: An Interview with Jacques Derrida." In *Who Comes after the Subject?*, edited by E. Cadava, P. Connor, and J.-L. Nancy, pp. 255–274. New York and London: Routledge.

Drahoš, Jiří. *Jiří Drahoš*. Whenever, s.r.o. www.jiridrahos.cz. Accessed July 4, 2018.

Dunayer, Joan. 2001. *Animal Equality: Language and Liberation*. New York: Lantern Books.

Du Parc, Charles. 2020. "Czech Gender Pay Gap Still One of the Worst in Europe." *JobSpin*, June 25. www.jobspin.cz/2020/06/czech-gender-pay-gap-still-one-of-the-worst-in-europe.

"Femicide." n.d. Noun. *Oxford Learner's Dictionaries*. Oxford: Oxford University Press. https://www.oxfordlearnersdictionaries.com/definition/english/femicide. Accessed March 28, 2018.

Ferber, Marianne A., and Phyllis Hutton Raabe. 2003. "Women in the Czech Republic: Feminism, Czech Style." *International Journal of Politics, Culture, and Society* 16, no. 3 (Spring): 407–430. www.jstor.org/stable/20020174.

Heitlinger, Alena. 1996. "Framing Feminism in Post-Communist Czech Republic." *Communist and Post-Communist Studies* 29, no. 1 (1996): 17–93.

Hrdličková, Lucie. 2019. "V Česku se sexuální obtěžování bagatelizuje víc než jinde. Politici ho neberou vážně, říká novinářka Lauder (In the Czech Republic, Sexual Harassment Is Trivialized More than Elsewhere. Politicians Don't Take It Seriously, Says Journalist Lauder)." *Seznam Zprávy*, January 20. www.seznamzpravy.cz/clanek/v-cesku-se-sexualni-obtezovani-bagatelizuje-vic-nez-jinde-politici-ho-neberou-vazne-rika-novinarka-lauder-64625.

Jaroš, Gustav. 1920. *Vánoce I (Christmas I)*. Praha: B. Kočí.

Joy, Melanie. 2010. *Why We Love Dogs, Eat Pigs, and Wear Cows: An Introduction to Carnism*. San Francisco: Conari.

Kejřová, Anuše, and Vilém Emil Kejř. 1933. *Česká vegetariánská kuchařka Anuše Kejřové (Anus Kejrova's Czech Vegetarian Cookbook)*. Hradec Králové: St. Kuchař.

"Kraus a blondýna: MeToo je hnutí za vymýcení sexu z lidského života (Kraus and the Blonde: MeToo Is a Movement to Eradicate Sex from Human Life)." 2018. *Frekvence*

*1*, February 8. www.frekvence1.cz/audio-video?porad=kraus-a-blondyna&clanek=kraus-a-blondyna-metoo-je-hnuti-za-vymyceni-sexu-z-lidskeho-zivota.

Kynčlová, Tereza. 2011. "Prospects of Anzaldúan Thought for a Czech Future." *Signs* 37, no. 1 (September): 23–29. doi: 10.1086/660172.

Lauder, Silvie. 2008. "Nová Vlna Feminismu (New Wave of Feminism)." *Respekt*, August 12. www.respekt.cz/tydenik/2008/29/nova-vlna-feminismu.

Lazarová, Daniela. 2020. "Gender Pay Gap Still a Big Problem in the Czech Republic." *Radio Prague International*, March 14. english.radio.cz/gender-pay-gap-still-a-big-problem-czech-republic-8105610.

Maca, Tomáš. 2018. "Češi jsou experti ve zlehčování #MeToo, Kraus se hnutí vysmívá pořád, říká komička (Czechs Are Experts in Belittling #MeToo, Kraus Mocks the Movement All the Time, Says the Comedian)." *Aktuálně.cz*, October 24. magazin.aktualne.cz/vetsina-zen-se-nerada-ztrapnuje-mne-to-ale-nevadi-rika-komic/r~61306676d20c11e8acf3ac1f6b220ee8/.

Masaryk, Tomáš Garrigue. 1912. "O ethice a alkoholismu (About Ethics and Alcoholism)." Praha: A. Klíčník.

Messmer, Marietta. 2012. "Transfrontera Crimes: Representations of the Juárez Femicides in Recent Fictional and Non-Fictional Accounts." *American Studies Journal* 57: 1–18. doi: 10.18422/57-03.

Miko, Martin. 2018. "Odvážná kampaň #Meatoo upozorňuje na lidi, kterým někdo v minulosti snědl jídlo (The Brave #Meatoo Campaign Draws Attention to People Who Have Had Their Meal Eaten in the Past)." *G.cz*, December 26. g.cz/odvazna-kampan-meatoo-upozornuje-na-lidi-kterym-nekdo-v-minulosti-snedl-jidlo.

Mírohorský, Emanuel. 1884. *O vegetarismu (About Vegetarianism)*. Praha: E. S. Friedberg-Mírohorský.

"Na Stojáka—Adéla Elbel—Zvířata, děti a plasty (Na Stojáka—Adéla Elbel—Animals, Kids, and the Plastics)." 2020 *YouTube*, May 19. www.youtube.com/watch?v=zODou0Az54c.

Pilat, Kasia. 2018. "Czech Brewer Mocks #MeToo, Calling It a 'Pathological Campaign.'" *New York Times*, May 2. www.nytimes.com/2018/05/02/world/europe/czech-sexism-beer-metoo.html.

Prucha, Emily. 2009. "A 'Proper' Czech Easter: What's Easter without a Whipping?" *Prague Monitor*, April 17. praguemonitor.com/2009/04/17/proper-czech-easter.

Šiklová, Jiřina. 1997. "Feminism and the Roots of Apathy in the Czech Republic." *Social Research* 64, no. 2: 258–280. www.jstor.com/stable/40971185.

Skřivánková, Adéla, "2020. "Znásilnění není naše chyba (Rape Isn't Our Fault)." *Žena a život*, no. 14, July 8, pp. 20–24.

"Stop tabu." 2018. *Stop Tabu*. https://www.youtube.com/watch?v=pX_LDGDzpUE&ab_channel=Stoptabu. Accessed July 29, 2021.

Tait, Robert. 2016. "Miloš Zeman: The Hardline Czech Leader Fanning Hostility to Refugees." *The Guardian*, September 14. www.theguardian.com/world/2016/sep/14/milos-zeman-czech-leader-refugees.

Úlehlová-Tilschová, Marie. 1930. *Moderní kuchařka: Systém rationálního vaření (Modern Cookbook: System of Rational Cooking)*. Praha: Československý Kompas.

Tait, Robert, 2016. "Miloš Zeman: The Hardline Czech Leader Fanning Hostility to refugees". *The Guardian*, September 14. www.theguardian.com/world/2016/sep/14/milos-zeman-czech-leader-refugees.

# Index

*For the benefit of digital users, indexed terms that span two pages (e.g., 52–53) may, on occasion, appear on only one of those pages.*